Theories and Methodologies in Postgraduate Feminist Research

Routledge Advances in Feminist Studies and Intersectionality

Routledge Advances in Feminist Studies and Intersectionality is committed to the development of new feminist and profeminist perspectives on changing gender relations, with special attention to:

- Intersections between gender and power differentials based on age, class, dis/abilities, ethnicity, nationality, racialisation, sexuality, violence, and other social divisions.
- Intersections of societal dimensions and processes of continuity and change: culture, economy, generativity, polity, sexuality, science and technology.
- Embodiment: Intersections of discourse and materiality, and of sex and gender.
- Transdisciplinarity: intersections of humanities, social sciences, medical, technical and natural sciences.
- Intersections of different branches of feminist theorizing, including: historical materialist feminisms, postcolonial and anti-racist feminisms, radical feminisms, sexual difference feminisms, queerfeminisms, cyberfeminisms, posthuman feminisms, critical studies on men and masculinities.
- A critical analysis of the travelling of ideas, theories and concepts.
- A politics of location, reflexivity and transnational contextualizing that reflects the basis of the Series framed within European diversity and transnational power relations.

1. Feminist Studies
A Guide to Intersectional Theory,
Methodology and Writing
Nina Lykke

**2. Women, Civil Society and the
Geopolitics of Democratization**
Denise M. Horn

3. Sexuality, Gender and Power
Intersectional and Transnational
Perspectives
Edited by Anna G. Jónasdóttir, Valerie
Bryson and Kathleen B. Jones

**4. The Limits of Gendered
Citizenship**
Contexts and Complexities
Edited by Elżbieta H. Oleksy, Jeff
Hearn and Dorota Golańska

**5. Theories and Methodologies in
Postgraduate Feminist Research**
Researching Differently
Edited by Rosemarie Buikema,
Gabriele Griffin and Nina Lykke

Theories and Methodologies in Postgraduate Feminist Research

Researching Differently

Edited by Rosemarie Buikema, Gabriele Griffin and Nina Lykke

Routledge
Taylor & Francis Group
New York London

First published 2011
by Routledge
711 Third Avenue, New York, NY 10017

Simultaneously published in the UK
by Routledge
2 Park Square, Milton Park, Abingdon, Oxon OX14 4RN

Routledge is an imprint of the Taylor & Francis Group, an informa business

© 2011 Taylor & Francis
First issued in paperback 2013

The right of Rosemarie Buikema, Gabriele Griffin and Nina Lykke to be identified as the authors of the editorial material, and of the authors for their individual chapters, has been asserted in accordance with sections 77 and 78 of the Copyright, Designs and Patents Act 1988.

Typeset in Sabon by IBT Global.

Library of Congress Cataloging-in-Publication Data

Theories and methodologies in postgraduate feminist research : researching differently / edited by Rosemarie Buikema, Gabriele Griffin, Nina Lykke.
    p. cm. — (Routledge advances in feminist studies and intersectionality)
    Includes bibliographical references and index.
    1. Women's studies—Research. 2. Women's studies—Methodology. 3. Feminist theory—Study and teaching (Higher) I. Buikema, Rosemarie. II. Griffin, Gabriele. III. Lykke, Nina.
    HQ1180.T475 2011
    305.4201—dc22
    2010045293

ISBN13: 978-0-415-88881-3 (hbk)
ISBN13: 978-0-415-85163-3 (pbk)

Education and Culture DG

Lifelong Learning Programme

The editing of this volume was kindly supported by a grant from the European Network for Women's/Gender/Feminist Studies, ATHENA III (Advanced Thematic Network in Women's Studies in Europe), Utrecht University, The Netherlands, funded by the Education and Culture DG of the European Commission: Lifelong Learning Programme.

Contents

List of Figures and Tables   xi
Series Editors' Foreword   xiii
Preface: Editors' Note on Naming Practices   xv
Acknowledgments   xvii

Editorial Introduction: Researching Differently   1
ROSEMARIE BUIKEMA, GABRIELE GRIFFIN AND NINA LYKKE

PART I
Feminist Theories

1   Gender Research with 'Waves': On Repositioning a
    Neodisciplinary Apparatus   15
    IRIS VAN DER TUIN

2   Feminist Science and Technology Studies   29
    MAUREEN MCNEIL AND CELIA ROBERTS

PART II
Methodologies

3   Intersectionality: A Theoretical Adjustment   45
    DORTHE STAUNÆS AND DORTE MARIE SØNDERGAARD

4   What to Make of Identity and Experience in Twenty-first-
    century Feminist Research   60
    ALLAINE CERWONKA

5 Histories and Memories in Feminist Research   74
ANDREA PETÖ AND BERTEKE WAALDIJK

PART III
Research Methods

6 Writing about Research Methods in the Arts and Humanities   91
GABRIELE GRIFFIN

7 Feminist Perspectives on Close Reading   105
JASMINA LUKIĆ AND ADELINA SÁNCHEZ ESPINOSA

8 Visual Cultures: Feminist Perspectives   119
ROSEMARIE BUIKEMA AND MARTA ZARZYCKA

PART IV
Multi-, Inter-, Trans- and Postdisciplinarity

9 This Discipline Which Is Not One: Feminist Studies as a
   Postdiscipline   137
NINA LYKKE

10 Why Interdisciplinarity? Interdisciplinarity and Women's/
    Gender Studies in Europe   151
MIA LIINASON

11 Transdisciplinary Gender Studies: Conceptual and
    Institutional Challenges   165
ANTJE LANN HORNSCHEIDT AND SUSANNE BAER

PART V
Professionalisation

12 The Professionalisation of Feminist Researchers:
    The Nordic Case   183
HARRIET SILIUS

13 The Professionalisation of Feminist Researchers:
    The Spanish Case   198
    ISABEL CARRERA SUÁREZ

14 The Professionalisation of Feminist Researchers:
    The German Case   213
    MARIANNE SCHMIDBAUR AND ULLA WISCHERMANN

PART VI
The Choice of Topic and Research Questions: Some Examples

15 My Dissertation Photo Album: Snapshots from a Writing Tour   233
    DORO WIESE

16 Intimate Truths about Subjectivity and Sexuality:
    A Psychoanalytical and a Postcolonial Approach   245
    HENRIETTA L. MOORE AND GLORIA D. WEKKER

PART VII
Coda: The Desires of Writing

17 If Writing Has to do With Desire, What 'Kind' of Desire Is
    That? Between Jacques Lacan and Gilles Deleuze   261
    EDYTA JUST

Contributors   273
Index   281

Figures and Tables

FIGURES

8.1   Katarzyna Kozyra, *Olimpia*, 1996, courtesy of the artist.   121

8.2   Luiz Vasconcelos, Brazil, 2008. ©Luiz Vasconcelos/A
       Critíca/AE/ZUMA   126

14.1   Representation of women in various career stages in
       the German academy in 2008.   215

14.2   Career paths at German universities.   216

14.3   Women's studies graduates' expected and actual
       impact on employment opportunities.   220

TABLES

12.1   Disciplinisation of Women's/Gender Studies in the
       Nordic Countries in 2010   189

12.2   Institutionalisation of Women's/Gender Studies in
       Nordic Universities in 2010   192

12.3   The Degree of Professionalisation of Women's/Gender
       Studies in the Nordic Countries in 2010   194

13.1   Official Postgraduate Programmes in Women's Studies
       at Spanish Universities 2007–8   204

13.2   PhD Programmes in Gender or Women's Studies at
       Spanish Universities Adapted to European Higher
       Education Area (EHEA) 2010   205

13.3   Percentage of Men and Women at Spanish (State)
       Universities   208

Series Editors' Foreword

In this series, *Routledge Advances in Feminist Studies and Intersectionality*, we seek to publish contributions to contemporary feminist studies and analyses conducted in the context and acknowledgement of transnational and intersectional perspectives. In the writing and broader creation of such texts the existence and development of feminist networking and infrastructures are often crucial, sometimes clearly and explicitly, sometimes less so. Many of such forms of organizing are also transnational, doing research and researching *differently*. This has long been a central aspect of feminist theories and practices.

Drawing from these many kinds of networks and actions, feminist theories and practices have shown that gender is a major structuring force and principle in and across societies and cultures, both globally and locally. Gender relations are both subject to change and resistant to change, within what can only be seen as a turbulent historical period. Moreover, at the same time that gender and gender relations have become more fully recognized and analyzed in research, scholarship, intervention, politics and activism, the notion of gender has also become complex and perhaps even less certain.

One major source of these complications is the presence of multiple intersections in and around gender, gender relations and gender powers. These include intersections between gender and power differentials based on age, class, dis/abilities, ethnicity, nationality, racialisation, sexuality, violence, and other social divisions. Further broad intersections continue and change, societally and transsocietally, between culture, economy, generativity, polity, sexuality, science and technology. A third, and crucial, form of intersections is between different branches of feminist theorizing, including: historical materialist feminisms, postcolonial and anti-racist feminisms, radical feminisms, sexual difference feminisms, queerfeminisms, cyberfeminisms, posthuman feminisms, and critical studies on men and masculinities. These themselves present differential understandings of and intersections between discourse, embodiment and materiality, and sex and gender. Together, these various intersections feed into and draw from a fourth set of intersections of the humanities, the social sciences, and the medical, technical and natural sciences. As such, the Series is committed to a process of intense transdisciplinarity.

We see these complex and changing formations as themselves the product of and contributing to the travelling of feminist ideas, theories and concepts, as well as their critical analysis. Thus, the Series is set within a politics of location. More specifically, this reflexivity and transnational contextualizing reflects the basis of the Series framed within European diversity and transnational power relations.

The series, *Routledge Advances in Feminist Studies and Intersectionality*, is committed to the development of new feminist and profeminist perspectives on changing gender relations. More specifically, the Series arises initially from an extensive collaborative network of transnational scholarship and intervention based at and linked to the Centre of Gender Excellence (GEXcel), based at the Universities of Linköping and Örebro, Sweden, but extending to Europe and beyond.

This volume, *Theories and Methodologies in Postgraduate Feminist Research*, is both an example of a volume that derives from transnational feminist networking and infrastructure, and an example of research and analysis done differently. The network and infrastructure in question is ATHENA, the Advanced Thematic Network in European Women's Studies, founded in 1996, funded by the European Commission until 2009, and now metamorphosed into ATGender, the European Association for Gender Research, Education and Documentation. The researching differently involves re-thinking/re-practicing (feminist) theories, methodologies, research methods, academic forms of organizing beyond disciplines, professionalisation, choice of research topics and questions, and the desires of writing, in doing transnational feminist research.

In *Theories and Methodologies in Postgraduate Feminist Research*, the three editors, Rosemarie Buikema, Gabriele Griffin and Nina Lykke, have gathered together excellent scholars from across Europe, who, in different ways, have contributed forcefully to the development of interdisciplinary feminist studies, its theorizing and practice. More specifically, the volume highlights approaches located in the humanities, and textual and visual analysis; approaches located at the borders of humanities and social sciences; and approaches that can be said to be broadly transdisciplinary. In and through this book there is illustrated a set of profound and close connections between feminist organizing structures and feminist knowledge processes. The book is the product of such connections between structures and processes, and is itself a contemporary and ongoing example of the vibrant and developing transnational phenomenon and web of activity that is feminist studies. It is, therefore, with great pleasure that we include this fifth volume in the series; we hope this will inspire new (forms of feminist) theories, methodologies, organizing and knowledge.

Jeff Hearn and Nina Lykke
Managing Series Editors
January 2011

Preface
Editors' Note on Naming Practices

The naming of the field of women's/gender/feminist studies has caused a lot of debate. Is the focus 'women' or 'gender'? Or is it better to take 'feminism' as the starting point? What does it imply to refer to 'feminism'? Does this mean a reference to political activism, and, if yes, which kind? Or does it refer to the field(s) of theory and epistemology which among others through international publishing has made a claim to the name 'feminism'? As there are many branches of feminist theory and epistemology, it is also a question of which one(s) the reference is meant to include? Interrelated with these debates on the meaning of names, the naming issue has also been crucial in the negotiations with various academic authorities on processes of institutionalisation of the area.

Taking the diversity of approaches to the naming issue carefully into account, for many years it has been an established policy of the European curriculum development network ATHENA (which made up the context for the development of this volume; see acknowledgements) to use the inclusive umbrella term women's/gender/feminist studies when referring generally to the field. For the ATHENA collaboration it has, on the one hand, been important to be able to compare notes about institutionalisation and curriculum development processes across borders of different nations, disciplines and university structures. However, on the other hand, it is considered to be just as vital to make ample space for open debates where local differences are reflected in productive transversal dialogues.

In this volume, for similar reasons, we have chosen not to harmonise the naming practices of the different chapters. Instead, the terms 'women's studies,' 'women's and gender studies,' 'gender and women's studies,' 'gender studies' and 'feminist studies' figure in the ways in which they were chosen by the different contributors. Some contributors have argued specifically for their naming practices, and others have used the terms which are standard in their local women's/gender/feminist studies milieu. In this sense, the different naming practices, represented in the chapters of the volume, can be considered to be a reflection of the diversity of local ways to do women's/gender/feminist studies.

Another terminological issue to which we would like, briefly, to draw the readers' attention is the terms 'constructionist/constructivist.' Strictly speaking, the two terms have somewhat different genealogies. Whereas the latter refers specifically to learning theory and among others is attributed to the psychology of Jean Piaget, the term 'social constructionism' is widely adopted by different fields of critical research and has been developed in many directions, among others as part of feminist theorising of sex/gender in their intersections with other power differentials. However, the terms are also often used interchangeably by many feminist researchers, among others. Therefore, we have chosen to let them exist in parallel in this volume as well.

September 15, 2010
The Editorial Team

Acknowledgments

This volume owes its existence to the European Network for women's/ gender/feminist Studies, ATHENA (Advanced Thematic Network in Women's studies in Europe). ATHENA was created in 1996 by the Association of Institutions for Feminist Education and Research in Europe (AOIFE) and was funded by the European Union's Socrates programme from 1998 to 2009. The network was coordinated by Utrecht University (The Netherlands) and gathered more than one hundred women's/gender/feminist studies programmes/units/groups at universities, research institutes and documentation centres from almost all European countries. Over the years, numerous transnational and transdisciplinary panels of experts and working groups were established within the framework of ATHENA. These long-term collaborative links provided crucial inspiration to the curriculum development, institutionalisation, internationalisation and professionalisation of women's/gender/feminist studies in the participating countries and generated a unique, transnational and transdisciplinary feminist milieu for critical transversal dialogues.

Chaired by Rosemarie Buikema and Nina Lykke, one of the many ATHENA working groups made a long-term commitment to the development of curricula for postgraduate training in women's/gender/feminist studies, and the present volume is one of the results of this group's work. Therefore, we want to thank all the members of the ATHENA working group on postgraduate training for their invaluable contributions. Thanks so much to those of you who submitted chapters to this volume and to those of you who participated in the group discussions which led to the volume. We shall also thank the two main coordinators of the ATHENA network, Professor Rosi Braidotti, who chaired the network from the start and Professor Berteke Waaldijk, who took over the position as main coordinator from 2005. A warm thanks also to the shifting ATHENA management teams from Women's and Gender Studies at Utrecht University who together with the main coordinators worked hard to keep together the big and diverse group of enthusiastic, but unruly, women's/gender/feminist studies activists of different generations, nationalities, locations, disciplines, theoretical and political outlooks.

ATHENA has metamorphosed into the professional organisation for European gender research ATGender (The European Association for Gender Research, Education and Documentation), a broad association for academics, practitioners, activists and institutions in the field of women's and gender studies, feminist research, women's rights, gender equality and diversity. ATGender, too, is a context for this volume, and we would like to thank and acknowledge it as such.

As editors of this volume we want to specially thank the ATHENA coordination for giving a grant to support the editing process.

Warm thanks also to postdoctoral scholar Katherine Harrison, The Unit of Gender Studies, Linköping University, Sweden, who assisted us in the editing process and with the language revisions of non-native English speakers' texts. Thank you so much, Katherine, for your thorough, meticulous, patient and altogether great work to transform the contributions into the final manuscript.

Finally, we want to thank the anonymous Routledge reviewers for their valuable comments, and a special thanks also to Routledge Research editor Max Novick for his kind support.

September 15, 2010
Rosemarie Buikema, Gabriele Griffin and Nina Lykke

Editorial Introduction
Researching Differently

Rosemarie Buikema, Gabriele Griffin and Nina Lykke

At the heart of much feminist research is a critical urge to challenge conventional ways of doing scientific and scholarly work. Feminist research is often postconventional and unorthodox. This volume gives an introduction to some of the ways in which feminist researchers do things differently.

The focus of *Theories and Methodologies in Postgraduate Feminist Research: Researching Differently* is theories and methodologies in interdisciplinary feminist research, within a context of increasing globalisation. In particular, the volume addresses postgraduate researchers whose interest is in arts- and humanities-based feminist research. Advanced textbooks in feminist theories and methodologies have had a tendency to focus strongly on research within a social sciences frame, and whilst this volume includes topics, methodologies and theories of interest to social-science-based constituencies, its main emphasis is on arts- and humanities-oriented feminist research within an interdisciplinary, transnational European frame. This approach is a response to clearly articulated needs within the feminist research community.

Importantly, and for the first time, this volume also takes into account the increasing need to engage with the issues of transferable skills and professionalisation in feminist studies.[1] To this end, a section of this volume is devoted to the professionalisation of the field and to the professional opportunities this brings with it, as it is exemplified through selected European case studies.

The volume is the result of a long-term collaboration between major European research training programmes in feminist studies, including a European Union-funded thematic network called ATHENA (Advanced Thematic Network in European Women's Studies)[2] which started in the late 1990s and since then has gathered feminist scholars from over 100 European universities. This network has made it possible for teachers, researchers and students of feminist studies to engage in a long-term commitment to compare notes as far as theories and methodologies are concerned. This has resulted in transversal dialogues across disciplinary, geographic and language borders. The network has opened a unique space for such dialogues, facilitating both in-depth explorations of disciplinary and national differences/similarities and the emergence of new synergies between approaches to feminist research training.

The sharing of ideas and the development of joint curricula are key concerns for the contributors to this volume. However, a central principle is also to pay due respect to differences and to carve out diversity. A one-size-fits-all-approach has never seemed a viable option for the group of authors behind this volume, but methodological nationalism—i.e., that one's own country is taken as the final horizon when thinking about the development of curricula in feminist research training—does not seem very adequate either. Therefore, we pursue notions of feminism that promote a politics of location but have no borders. According to the contributors, new ways of constructing postgraduate research training on gender in its intersections with race, ethnicity, class, sexuality, nationality and so on are best developed in transnational and interdisciplinary dialogues which take into account both common ground and differences, and which pay thorough attention to power differentials.

In the context of existing resources on feminist theories and methodologies, this volume represents a distinctive contribution to the field in terms of its focus, level of study and engagement with European issues. More precisely, its focus on the humanities marks it out as different from the many social-science-oriented textbooks concerning theories and methodologies in feminist research, such as Ramazanoglu and Holland's 2002 volume, *Feminist Methodology: Challenges and Choices*. Furthermore, the humanities profile also makes *Theories and Methodologies in Postgraduate Feminist Research: Researching Differently* different from its sibling *Feminist Studies: A Guide to Intersectional Theory, Methodology and Writing* (Lykke 2010) in the series Routledge Advances in Feminist Studies and Intersectionality, as the latter volume focuses more generally on trans- and postdisciplinary perspectives. With that said, this and the sibling volume will complement each other well as guides to feminist research training programmes and classrooms. *Theories and Methodologies in Postgraduate Feminist Research: Researching Differently* is also different from more basic bachelor- or master-level introductions to the field of feminist studies within the humanities (Buikema and Smelik 1995; Buikema and van der Tuin 2009), addressing itself instead to those engaged in postgraduate research. Finally, *Theories and Methodologies in Postgraduate Feminist Research: Researching Differently* is in dialogue with an earlier volume compiled in the context of the above-mentioned ATHENA collaboration, entitled *Thinking Differently* (Griffin and Braidotti 2002). The purpose of that volume was to introduce European issues in feminist research.

The overall development of the contents as well as the individual contributions to the volume are based on the contributors' long-term commitment to gender research training in different disciplinary and interdisciplinary, national and international contexts. There are six main parts. They cover questions of feminist theory, methodology, research methods, interdisciplinarity and careers in feminist studies, as well as offering a couple examples of what it means to choose a research topic and ask research questions within the field. A coda addresses the writing process. Balancing respect for differences with a search for common ground in gender research training, each section presents key issues with a starting point in different contexts, disciplines and interdisciplines. The volume is necessarily selective, covering cutting-edge gender research issues on the one hand, and seeking to address some of the key methods and methodologies used in arts and humanities based feminist research on the other. The editors have commissioned chapters which give examples of central discussions within each section. Firmly anchored within an interdisciplinary feminist framework, the volume pays special attention to three kinds of approaches:

1) approaches located centrally within the humanities such as textual and visual analysis
2) approaches located at the borders between the humanities and social sciences and based in fields such as cultural studies, anthropology, social psychology and history
3) approaches representing specific discipline-transgressing fields such as feminist technoscience studies.

The theme of Part I is *feminist theories*. Whilst the overall background for this volume is the development of feminist studies at the borders of various disciplinary contexts and spatiotemporal locations, the first part profiles feminist theorising through a cluster of debates about the dynamics of generational and disciplinary locations. More precisely, the contributors to the part discuss which specific knowledges emerge from feminist encounters within the framework of third-wave feminism and technoscience studies.

In chapter 1, 'Gender Research with 'Waves': On Repositioning a Neo-disciplinary Apparatus,' Dutch feminist scholar Iris van der Tuin argues for a revised conceptualisation of 'feminist waves' alongside a third-wave feminist conceptualisation of generationality. The analytical tool of 'feminist waves' is considered to be part of a 'neodisciplinary' apparatus in feminist studies, that is, a scholarly model for understanding the history of feminism, which has been widely used within feminist studies. Van der Tuin argues that the canonising of this 'tool' has resulted in a kind of paralysis experienced by contemporary young feminists. An effect of the modelling via the wave model is that the history of feminism becomes stuck in a dichotomy between a 'second' feminist wave located in the 1970s and a 'postfeminist wave,' implying that feminism is not needed anymore. Interpellating the theoretical framework of feminist scholar Karen Barad (2003), van der Tuin seeks to break the dichotomous logic by rethinking the wave model according to a third-wave feminist economy of dis-identification which acknowledges both kinship *and* a multitude of nonhierarchically organised differences and potentials.

Chapter 2, 'Feminist Science and Technology Studies,' explores another aspect of feminist theorising. UK-based feminist scholars Maureen McNeil and Celia Roberts show how this vigorous and strongly interdisciplinary branch of feminist research is a space for productive encounters between feminism and human- and social-science studies of technoscience. The chapter outlines how feminist science and technology studies is an area of detailed empirical research, lively intellectual and political debate, and cutting-edge conceptual development. It addresses three core questions: What have feminists brought to technoscience studies? What have feminists found to be of most interest in technoscience studies? What have feminists working in other areas borrowed from feminist technoscience studies?

The topic of Part II is feminist debates on *methodologies*. It takes issue with three questions of key concern for many feminist scholars interested in renegotiations of methodological rules and principles for the production of knowledge: How can gender be analysed in intersections with other power differentials and identity markers such as class, race, ethnicity, sexuality, nationality and so forth? What does it mean to revise historical narratives of the past from feminist perspectives? Is the concept of 'experience' useful for, or a barrier to, deessentialising gender analyses, and how can this troubled notion be handled in the wake of the poststructuralist critique of it?

In chapter 3, 'Intersectionality: A Theoretical Adjustment,' Danish social psychologists Dorthe Staunæs and Dorte Marie Søndergaard critically investigate the concept of 'intersectionality' that, in recent years, has given rise to many productive feminist debates. Although gender as an analytical category does useful and important critical work, many feminist scholars today are in agreement that gender analyses should be linked to investigations of other social categorisations and intersections with race, ethnicity, class, sexuality, nationality and so on. According to this view, identities and power differentials are always complex and based on multiple interwoven categorisations. 'Intersectionality' has become the umbrella term which many feminists use when they refer to these complexities, and 'intersectional analysis' is a critical methodological tool for approaching them. In the chapter, Staunæs and Søndergaard provide an overview of recent feminist debates on intersectionality and argue specifically for a poststructuralist approach, paying special attention to the question of whether or not the concept works as a tool for critical feminist analysis of subject formations within social psychology.

The second chapter of this part, chapter 4, 'What to Make of Identity and Experience in Twenty-first Century Feminist Research,' deals with another conceptual tool which has been much discussed by feminist scholars, namely, 'experience.' Hungary-based feminist scholar Allaine Cerwonka discusses an important divide between different kinds of feminist scholars.

On the one hand, feminists anchored in standpoint epistemologies have celebrated methodologies which take as their point of departure explorations of feminist and women's experiences as alternatives to mainstream research. On the other hand, postmodern and poststructuralist feminists have claimed that the subject, and hence experience, are discursively constructed and therefore not to be confused with an 'authentic' inner-core identity. Cerwonka gives an overview of these debates and argues that an unproblematised understanding of experience as 'authentic evidence' may become a trap and reproduce individualist and neoliberal ideologies. Instead, she argues for a relational approach that carefully addresses the all-pervasiveness of power as well as the fluidity of identities and that, in particular, avoids the construction of an innocent 'outside.'

Chapter 5, 'Histories and Memories in Feminist Research,' is written by two feminist historians, Andrea Petö and Berteke Waaldijk, who are located in Hungary and the Netherlands, respectively. It focuses on questions relating to history, memories and historical narratives which—like 'intersectionality' and 'experience'—have attracted much feminist attention. How to subvert the stories of mainstream history, their entanglement in constructions of nation and nationhood and their complicity in processes of marginalisation and exclusion? What does it mean to rewrite history from feminist perspectives? Which methodologies can be mobilised? According to Petö and Waaldijk these questions are crucial not only for feminist historians; to reflect on strategies for approaching history and memories differently can be very useful for feminist scholars from other disciplines and interdisciplines as well. As Petö and Waaldijk argue, important lessons can be learned from the methodologies developed by feminist historians.

Part III is concerned with the *research methods* deployed in feminist research and, in particular, methods originating in the humanities. Gender researchers use many kinds of methods. However, the choice of focus for this section is motivated by the fact that the substantial contributions from the humanities to the toolbox on which many interdisciplinary feminist researchers draw are not as visible as the contributions from the social sciences. Some of the reasons for this are explained in the first chapter of the section, and the remaining two introduce specific methods developed within the framework of the humanities, close reading and visual analysis, which are key to much feminist research.

In chapter 6, 'Writing about Research Methods in the Arts and Humanities,' UK-based feminist scholar Gabriele Griffin argues that many arts and humanities disciplines have tended to remain silent about the research methods they employ as evidenced by the fact that subjects such as literary studies do not at present require PhD theses to contain a methodology section and also by the lack of books on research methods in the arts and humanities compared to similar texts in the social sciences, for example. However, as research-funding bodies as well as interdisciplinary collaborative working increasingly require arts and humanities researchers to be explicit about their research practices, it is necessary for arts and humanities disciplines to develop articulated elucidations of their research methods. This chapter provides a variety of examples of how research methods in the arts and humanities operate and might be articulated.

In chapter 7, 'Feminist Perspectives on Close Reading,' two literary feminist scholars, Jasmina Lukić from Hungary and Adelina Sánchez Espinosa from Spain re/evaluate the importance of close reading while foregrounding gender as a central critical concept. The chapter sets out to show that, far from being neutral as conventionally assumed in literary theory, close reading can be used as a tool to go further when combined with other approaches. The chapter moves on to investigate how the traditional methods of close reading become modified, invigorated and renewed when adapting to the needs and claims of feminist research. It does so, in its second half, through a case study of a number of close readings of the nineteenth-century English novel *Jane Eyre* by Charlotte Brontë (1847)—a text that has received much critical attention from feminist scholars working with different critical positions.

Chapter 8, 'Visual Cultures: Feminist Perspectives,' written by two feminist researchers based in the Netherlands, Rosemarie Buikema and Marta Zarzycka, maps the reception, interpretation and circulation of images within academic research on visual culture, with particular attention paid to gender, ethnicity and the politics of representation. Through a couple of case studies—images from different genres and disciplines, directed to different audiences and yet travelling beyond their original contexts—the authors point out how different methods of visual research can be articulated. This chapter further demonstrates that questions concerning globally available images are not only restricted to academic discourses but are concerned with the larger scope of knowledge, power and their interconnections.

Part IV focuses on the issue of *multi-, inter-, trans- and postdisciplinarity* in feminist studies. It introduces different meanings of disciplinary boundary-crossing, as it is theoretically explored and widely practiced within the field of feminist studies. Many feminists underline the impact of feminist research within the disciplines (understood as human, social, medical, natural and technical science disciplines). At the same time there is also a widespread consensus that transgressions of disciplinary boundaries are crucial when it comes to theorising the complexities of gender/sex and gender relations in their intersections with other power differentials. Against this background, part IV discusses diverse definitions, as well as the overlaps and differences between ways of characterising cross-disciplinary work as multi-, inter-, trans- and postdisciplinary. The contributors analyse the ways in which these different modes of cross-disciplinary work have been very influential in the development of feminist studies.

In chapter 9, 'This Discipline Which Is Not One: Feminist Studies as a Postdiscipline,' Sweden-based feminist scholar Nina Lykke discusses how, on the one hand, feminist theorising leads towards radical multi-, inter-, trans- and postdisciplinarity, while on the other hand, the field of feminist studies is so well developed and established by now that it can pass and claim academic authority as a discipline in itself. Against this background, the author discusses how different feminist epistemological positions may lead to different dilemmas and approaches to the question of disciplining. Drawing on the ontoepistemological framework of feminist scholar Karen Barad and locating herself in a postconstructionist position, Lykke explores the problems and potential of defining the field as a postdisciplinary discipline or postdiscipline.

Chapter 10, 'Why Interdisciplinarity? Interdisciplinarity and Women's/Gender Studies in Europe,' is written by Swedish feminist scholar Mia Liinason. She analyses the interdisciplinary search for knowledge in feminist studies as a twofold strategy. On the one hand, Liinason explores interdisciplinary feminist research as resistant to the knowledge-seeking strategies and inherent power structures of the traditional disciplines. On the other, she interprets the interdisciplinarity of feminist research as a struggle for pluralism in the hope of a democratic and progressive politics of human rights.

In chapter 11, 'Transdisciplinary Gender Studies: Conceptual and Institutional Challenges,' two German scholars, Antje Lann Hornscheidt and Susanne Baer, focus on the interaction between transdisciplinary practices in feminist studies and disciplinary research and underline that gender research—be it disciplinary, interdisciplinary or transdisciplinary—should be understood, first of all, as a transformatory practice. The point is not simply to add to disciplinary canons but also to intervene in them. Illustrating their points with examples from the transdisciplinary gender studies programme at Humboldt University, Berlin, Hornscheidt and Baer point out that it is important to define disciplinarity, inter- and transdisciplinarity in a context-specific way. They analyse disciplinary gender research as an endeavour which aims at the enhancement of disciplines, whereas interdisciplinary gender research combines two or more disciplines in terms of methodological and theoretical approaches with the goal of enhancing the findings. Finally, transdisciplinary gender research is to be understood as an explicitly reflexive mode of research that scrutinises and challenges implicit norms (e.g., in terms of gender blindness, bias and so on) of the disciplines from a critical intersectional gender perspective.

Part V centres on *professionalisation* processes in feminist studies. This is becoming an increasingly important topic in the context of research and transferable skills training where the question of academic career development looms ever larger. The multidimensional institutionalisation and professionalisation of feminist studies which has taken place at many European universities during the last decades has made prominent the question of professional possibilities, developments and destinies. It is important for the students who register for programmes or modules in feminist studies, as well as for the organisers, to know for which kinds of jobs these programmes and modules potentially prepare them. It is also important for employers to know what skills a graduate or PhD with a profile or degree in feminist studies is likely to bring to a position. In addition, the EU's implementation of the so-called Bologna Process on the harmonisation of European teaching systems has forcefully put 'employability' on the agenda of higher education in Europe. The part on the professional outlets for feminist studies is motivated by this backdrop. Its discussion of university structures and career opportunities aims at providing an overview for research students keen to understand higher-education systems in Europe and feminist studies' position within these. As the situation regarding recognition and the conditions for profession-alisation are different in diverse European countries, we have chosen to focus on national/regional examples. As the whole area of professional outlets for feminist studies is very underresearched, the section draws on the only cross-national analysis of the issue to date, a major EU-funded research project titled *Employment and Women's Studies: The Impact of Women's Studies Training on Women's Employment in Europe* (Griffin 2002, 2004 and 2005).

Chapter 12, 'The Professionalisation of Feminist Researchers: The Nordic Case,' is written by Finland-based feminist scholar Harriet Silius. Whereas the field of feminist studies in Europe more broadly seems to have had an uneven institutionalisation, across the Nordic countries it is assumed to look much the same. Not surprisingly, the Nordic countries are frequently believed to be emblematic of feminist studies' smooth and successful professionalisation. Is this really the case? Can one talk about one pan-Nordic development, implying the same patterns in each of the five Nordic countries: Denmark, Iceland, Finland, Norway and Sweden? The chapter explores precisely this question. The theme of professionalisation of feminist studies is analysed from two angles: (1) from the point of view of disciplinisation and (2) from the perspective of institutionalisation. The chapter concludes by assessing the actual degree of professionalisation that has occurred in the various Nordic countries and suggests there are considerable differences between them.

In chapter 13, 'The Professionalisation of Feminist Researchers: The Spanish Case,' Spanish feminist scholar Isabel Carrera Suárez explores the ways in which feminist studies in Spain has rapidly developed since 1975 and has consolidated its position at graduate and postgraduate level, partly through new MA programmes adapted to the European Higher Education Area (EHEA) developed as part of EU integration policies. The transformed structures, together with recent political moves and legislation which explicitly support the creation of courses in the field of feminist studies, should create new opportunities for feminist researchers and experts. However, old obstacles, particularly rigid discipline-based structures and the academic resistance to feminist studies, remain firmly in place. The chapter offers a brief overview of the Spanish higher-education system and the development of feminist studies within it, followed by a discussion of recent developments in academic structures and in legislation, analysing their relationship to professional opportunities for students of feminist studies in Spain, both inside and outside academe.

In chapter 14, 'The Professionalisation of Feminist Researchers: The German Case,' German feminist scholars Marianne Schmidbaur and Ulla Wischermann outline the current conditions and development of feminist studies professionalisation in Germany. This chapter analyses women's participation in academe and the process of feminist studies institutionalisation. Feminist studies graduates' choices of employment and academic career paths are also analysed, and it is above all suggested that gender knowledge and gender competence emerge as key professional and personal qualifications for feminist studies graduates. The chapter makes clear that career planning is becoming increasingly target oriented and is supported by networking and mentoring programmes. It concludes with some best-practice examples and a comment on future trends for feminist studies in view of the Bologna Process.

Part VI, *The Choice of Topic and Research Questions: Some Examples*, exemplifies how the process of choosing a research topic and asking research questions may proceed within feminist studies. It goes without saying that this process can take many different routes, so this part offers a few selected examples. The two chapters each give a glimpse of the process, one from the perspective of a researcher who is at the beginning of her research career and one from the point of view of two professors. Following the attention which this volume gives to the humanities and cultural disciplines within an overall interdisciplinary framework, the examples are drawn from feminist scholars who pursued academic careers in media and cultural studies and in anthropology.

In chapter 15, 'My Dissertation Photo Album: Snapshots from a Writing Tour,' German feminist scholar Doro Wiese retrospectively reflects on the process of choosing a dissertation topic. Dissertation writing is mostly considered a necessary step on the academic career ladder. In this chapter, however, Wiese argues that something else happens when we give in to the experiences offered and mediated through the two key practices of scholarly work—reading and writing—which humanities scholars, in particular, have reflected on as methodologies. Mediating other times, peoples and worlds, reading and writing are precisely those practices that allow us to be othered, to be haunted by difference in and for itself. Wiese offers as an example of this her own experiences of choosing a dissertation topic, which allowed her to engage in the creative act of what cultural theorist Marianne Hirsch has called 'postmemory.' Wiese carves out how a reading of US novelist Jonathan Safran Foer's novel *Everything Is Illuminated* (2002) allowed her to come to terms with a traumatic family history during and after the Nazi regime, in particular, the history of Wiese's grandmother.

Chapter 16, 'Intimate Truths about Subjectivity and Sexuality: A Psychoanalytical and a Postcolonial Approach,' is a conversation between two feminist anthropologists, Henrietta L. Moore from the UK and Gloria D. Wekker based in the Netherlands. Wekker is theoretically located in transnational, intersectional feminist theory, while Moore works within a tradition of psychoanalytical feminist theory. From this dual starting point in intersectional and psychoanalytic feminist theory, Wekker and Moore enter into a dialogue, raising key research questions on the discursive entanglement of gender, sexuality and processes of racialisation. The questions are articulated against the background of a joint rereading of a case story from the historical archives of classic psychoanalysis. While the classic psychoanalytic reading of the case story focuses on gender and sexuality, discussing female masculinity, Wekker and Moore foreground how the discourse on gender and sexuality is intertwined with an underlying racialised discourse which echoes colonial power relations. What does it mean that the Dutch psychoanalyst Van Ophuijsen, who reported on the case (1924), substituted gender for race in his interpretations while he produced a racialised discourse in his paraphrasing of the ways in which the women on whose stories he is reporting talk about their sexual organs? What does this story more generally say about the intersections of gender, sexuality and racialisation, nationalism and colonialism, in the national Dutch cultural imaginary (or cultural archive; Said 1993)?

The *coda* of the book is a chapter on writing, discussed as an inevitable and crucial dimension of all research work that can be both pleasurable and painful. Chapter 17, 'If Writing Has to do with Desire, What 'Kind' of Desire Is It? Between Jacques Lacan and Gilles Deleuze,' is written by Polish feminist scholar Edyta Just and focuses on the role of desires in academic writing processes. Just takes as her starting point the fact that in climbing the stairs to the top of the scholarly world, one must pass through many levels: bachelor, master, doctoral level and so on. She also reminds us that the 'passport' needed to move from one to the other is a degree, and that a written text is a requirement for this. A paper, a thesis, is a *sine qua non* of being finally granted the 'passport.' Referring to philosopher Gilles Deleuze's and psychoanalyst Jacques Lacan's different concepts of desire, Just proposes an approach to the writing process that can make research students more confident and less fearful when it comes to the 'writing exercise' which is supposed to award them 'the passport.'

NOTES

1. We will use the phrase 'feminist studies' throughout this introductory chapter, whilst recognising that both 'women's studies' and 'gender studies' are used by the same constituencies and also by a range of the contributors to this volume. However, since women's/gender studies is not institutionalised in some international sites whilst the concept of feminist research is, we utilise that phrase for our purposes here. For more or less the same reason, we have decided to let the contributors to the volume choose to refer to the subject area in the way each of them have found most appropriate for her

specific purposes and institutional tradition. This means that women's studies, gender studies and feminist studies are used to refer to the subject area in
the volume as a whole.
2. ATHENA Web site, http://www.athena3.org/ (accessed September 9, 2010).

REFERENCES

Barad, K. 2003. Posthumanist Performativity: Toward an Understanding of How
  Matter Comes to Matter. *Signs: Journal of Women in Culture and Society* 28
  (3): 801–31.
Buikema, R., and A. Smelik. 1995. *Women's Studies and Culture: A Feminist
  Introduction to the Humanities.* London: Zed Books.
Buikema, R., and I. van der Tuin. 2009. *Doing Gender in Media, Art and Culture.*
  London: Routledge.
Griffin, G., and R. Braidotti. 2002. *Thinking Differently: A Reader in European
  Women's Studies.* London: Zed Books.
Griffin, G., ed. 2002. *Women's Employment, Women's Studies, and Equal Oppor-
  tunities 1945–2001: Reports from Nine European Countries.* Hull: University
  of Hull Press.
———, ed. 2004. *Employment, Equal Opportunities and Women's Studies:
  Women's Experiences in Seven European Countries.* Königstein: Ulrike Hel-
  mer Verlag.
———, ed. 2005. *Doing Women's Studies: Employment Opportunities, Personal
  Impacts and Social Consequences.* London: Zed Books.
Lykke, N. 2010. *Feminist Studies: A Guide to Intersectional, Theory, Methodol-
  ogy and Writing.* New York: Routledge.
Ophuijsen, J. H. W. van. 1924. Contributions to the Masculinity Complex in
  Women. *International Journal of Psycho-Analysis* 5: 39–49.
Ramazanoglu, C., and J. Holland. 2002. *Feminist Methodology: Challenges and
  Choices.* London: Sage.
Said, E. 1993. *Culture and Imperialism.* New York: Vintage Books.

Part I
Feminist Theories

1 Gender Research with 'Waves'

On Repositioning a Neodisciplinary Apparatus

Iris van der Tuin

Developments in feminism are generally narrated according to a model of two or three waves. The waves function as metaphors for feminist movement in which crests and undercurrents alternate. A 'crest' then refers to heightened or intensified feminist movement. It refers to 'the' feminist movement at a certain time and place. Feminist waves are successive (they presume a progress narrative) and are supposed to respond to one another in a dualist way (they imply a pattern of sequential negation). The first feminist wave crested around 1900 and concerned the struggle for North American and Northern and Western European women's right to vote, for women's access to education, and for changing matrimonial law. The second wave of feminism is generally dated between 1968 and 1980 and again was located in the United States and Northern as well as Western Europe. Second-wave feminists are supposed to have objected to the equality feminism of the first wave; the rights gained had not changed the minds, and practices of men (and women). During the second wave, theories of the body, sexuality, and relationships were revolutionised ('the personal is political'). The third wave is supposed to have started in the US in the 1980s and has a strong relationship to popular culture (e.g., music and on-line fanzines). This last wave is still in the making; despite the fact that an encyclopaedia of third-wave feminism has been published (Heywood 2005), Anglo-US and Western and Northern European feminists under thirty struggle to re/claim the term 'feminism' for their activities. Notwithstanding the overlap between the third- and second-wave feminist agenda (proponents of third wave also politicise the personal), third-wave feminism is often questioned owing to its seemingly individualistic and populist methodologies. If we look at the ways in which the term 'feminist wave' is used nowadays in popular as well as academic discourses, we see that feminist movements seem to be taking place along the 'trans-Atlantic dis-connection' (Stanton 1980). Also, the movement itself is usually narrowed down to second-wave feminism. In other words, when using the wave model, feminism appears spatiotemporally fixed.

Re/describing the history of feminism according to a model of waves, scholars tend to assign individual feminists and feminist groups to certain waves, and vice versa. The waves then become denominators; and despite the continuous movement suggested by the metaphor itself, waves become locatable in time and space. Dutch feminist Anja Meulenbelt for instance has become an archetypical second-wave feminist on the basis of her auto-biographical, self-revealing writings, and as such, is compared to North American Kate Millett. German Verena Stefan is added to this list; all three feminists have engaged with the same writing practice and are from the same age group (the 'baby boomers'). My feminist peers and I are excluded from this writing practice, simply because we are from a different age group ('Generation X'). According to a progressive and dualist spatiotemporal logic, we are differently located from Meulenbelt, Millett, and Stefan; second-wave feminism and its practices are out of reach for us.

Academic feminists of today also question the wave model as a canonised device for feminist theorisation (Aikau 2007). According to these analyses, the waves as descriptive terms are historically inadequate and have become prescriptive. It is sometimes said that doing research with waves has resulted in biased readings as the wave model erases certain (black, lesbian, Southern and Central European) feminists from feminist history. A more personal approach to the normativity of feminist waves results in questions such as, 'Why can't I be a second-wave feminist? I feel closer to Meulenbelt than to the writers of postfeminist chick lit!' Feminist waves are also used normatively to differentiate between feminist theory and feminist practice, between activism and academia. In this case, the second feminist wave is made responsible for the epistemic twist in Western feminism, and its members are blamed for having taken the activism out of feminism as a result of 'the long march through the institutions' (Hemmings 2005). This evaluation can be seen as an equally paralyzing effect of doing research with waves; as feminism gains ground in the academic world, there is supposed to be a loss of activism in the supposedly real world, and second-wave feminists are supposed to comply with the corporate academy. The concept of the feminist wave thus seems to have lost all of its visionary power. Doing research with waves has become in many ways a stifling exercise.

The spatiotemporal fixity becomes fully apparent when we add *post-feminism* to our toolbox. Whereas third-wave feminism has the potential to become many things, postfeminism only repeats the pattern of progress narrative and sequential negation assumed by scholars doing research with feminist waves. Affirming postfeminism alongside second-wave feminism is the most explicit strategy for freezing feminism in the past and for essentialising not only the 1970s, but also the here and now. I would like to suggest naming the postfeminist appeal 'narcissistic' as it is predicated on a celebration of our current times as having reached equality between the sexes (read: as having transcended the need for feminism). This strategy is not necessarily different from a—what I would like to call—'nostalgic' outlook. Nostalgia underlies the reduction of feminism to second-wave feminism. From a nostalgic point of view, a contemporary feminism is not within our reach; rather, it is something that belongs to the past. Researching nostalgically, the 1970s are celebrated as the pro- totypical feminist times: at best, contemporary feminism can be a bad copy of what was done back then. Thus, according to both narcissism and nostalgia, we are cut off from feminism in the here and now. The two ten- dencies are thus 'false opposites' or 'non-exhaustive dichotomies' (Nelson 1993). In both cases, feminism translates into second-wave feminism. In both cases, feminism is no longer in movement; feminism is simply some- thing that has been.

In this chapter I engage with the suspicion that has arisen around research- ing with waves. I approach the feminist wave model as a neodisciplinary apparatus that needs to be repositioned in order for the virtuality of femi- nist movement to make a comeback. I argue that the wave model as well as the disciplinisation of gender research has restrictive rather than enabling effects. This chapter is thus written in what Nina Lykke calls a 'postdis- ciplinary' mode (chapter 9, this volume): I critically engage with ways of organising feminist academic knowledge production. 'Disciplinary appara- tus' is a Foucauldian concept. Karen Barad uses it as a synonym of 'agency of observation,' a concept that she has adapted from Niels Bohr. Adapting it, the concept becomes a tool for understanding (trends in) scholarship in an 'ontoepistemological' manner (Barad 2003, 829; 2007, 409n10), which is to say that not only do we study the epistemological aspect of researching with waves (waves as mapping feminist thought and movement), but also their effect (i.e., the resulting paralysis, whether there actually *is* feminist movement nowadays). In this chapter, I will talk about the wave model as a *neo*-disciplinary apparatus because contemporary gender studies some- times acts as a neodiscipline in Anglo-American and European academia. Gender studies is a relatively young branch of the academic tree that none- theless uses apparatuses such as the wave model for streamlining its debates. Here it should be noted that my use of 'neo-' should not be seen as invoking a progress narrative and a dualism between gender-sensitive and gender- blind academic practices. Both Barad and Elizabeth Grosz, whose work is also important for the argument made in this chapter, do not allow for thinking 'the new' in terms of causal linearity or predictability. They are interested in a continuous rethinking of (feminist) revolutions in thought. Theorising the wave model as an apparatus in gender research, I continue assigning it a central place in feminist theorising. However, I also recognise the importance of studying, not the wave model as such—i.e., if the idea of waves describe or prescribe feminist movement or if it is a metaphor that correctly reflects feminist movement—but rather its ontoepistemic *effects*. In other words, the claim about the nonexistence of feminism in the here and now should be seen as a claim *effected by* the use of a scholarly model of waves, not as one of which the (preferred) truth-value can be verified or falsified. In the next section I will introduce the methodology for studying the effects of scholarly apparatuses.

THEORISING THE DISCIPLINARY APPARATUS

Barad has adapted the work of Michel Foucault and Bohr while inventing the theoretical framework of 'agential realism.' Agential realism addresses the interplay of the material and the discursive/semiotic, the ontological and the epistemological, and the so-called 'end' of (feminist) postmodernism. She aims at overcoming the assumption that once ontological issues are addressed positivist modernism is the only option, whereas for epistemological issues only social constructivist postmodernists are on track. This is her argument:

> [T]here is a tension set up between realism and social constructivism that is an acknowledgment of the dichotomous portrayal of these positionings—a polarization that itself relies upon the ambiguity of both terms. The dichotomized positions of realism and social constructivism—which presume a subject/object dichotomy—can acknowledge the situated/constructed character of only one of the poles of the dualism at a time. Realists do not deny that subjects are materially situated; constructivists insist upon the socially or discursively constructed character of objects. Neither recognizes their mutually constitutive 'intra-action' (Barad 1999, 2).

The fact that two seemingly opposite traditions can understand only one pole at a time and not the ways in which they are actually predicated on (the exclusion of) the other pole is a result of dualism (Van der Tuin, 2011). Barad counteracts this tradition by explaining the assumption of 'representationalism' that is shared by the two poles. Barad argues that traditionally realist approaches to academic work (assuming the mirror of nature in which scientific claims reflect nature 'out there') and social constructivist ones (according to a charged reading, social constructivism assumes the mirror of culture in which scientific claims reflect academic culture and are cut off from what is 'out there') pursue a correspondence theory of truth. She states that the representationalism that is shared construes the opposition between realism and constructivism as a nonexhaustive one (Barad 2003, 802). In other words, Barad develops agential realism by bridging (feminist) positivism's *realist* approaches and (feminist) postmodernism's *constructivist* approaches. Barad's ontoepistemological framework is non-representationalist.

Barad's 'disciplinary apparatus' is developed using agential realism. Agential realism, in turn, is rooted in Barad's study of Bohr's revolutionary insight into physics experimentation. Bohr looked at laboratory instruments as an integral part of both the process of experimentation and its outcomes. He rescued lab instruments from physicists' and philosophers' ignorance and theorised them as influencing what Barad calls, following Donna Haraway, 'world-making practices.' The idea is that instrumentation *does things*; that it *produces* the ontology that we are working with (realism) or cut off from (social constructivism). Barad contends that an interdisciplinary space that is neither pure philosophy nor pure physics enabled Bohr to construct the formula 'measurement = matter + meaning' (1996, 165–66). It is *in* the act of measurement that theory (meaning, epistemology) and practice (matter, ontology) meet. In other words, matter gets meaning just as meaning gets its embodiment/materialisation in measurement. In order to move away from traditional approaches to measurement, Bohr uses the concept 'phenomenon' for instances of measurement. According to Barad, Bohr's view consists of the following:

> [S]ince observations involve an indeterminable discontinuous interaction, *as a matter of principle, there is no unambiguous way to differentiate between the 'object' and the 'agencies of observation'*—no inherent/naturally occurring/fixed/universal/Cartesian cut exists. Hence, *observations do not refer to objects of an independent reality.*
> (Barad 1996, 170; emphasis in original)

Observed objects and the apparatuses or agencies of observation can only be distinguished artificially through a constructed 'cut' (see also Lykke, chapter 9, this volume). Barad adapts Bohr's concept of the apparatus to show that just as the observer is both the scientist and her instrumentation, the thing measured is both the object and the instrumentation (Barad 1996, 172). Hence ontology and epistemology are inseparable. The object and the subject of knowledge, thing and word, nature and culture (ibid., 173, 175; Barad 1999, 2) are material-discursive.

In this chapter I assume that the concept of the disciplinary apparatus can be transposed from the experimental sciences to the interdisciplinary space of women's/gender/feminist studies. This kind of transposition is valid when working in a postdisciplinary mode: as Lykke states, the critical questioning of ways of organising academic knowledge production is accompanied by a creative experimentation with disciplinary boundary crossing and transversal openness (chapter 9, this volume). After all, (academic) feminism is a matter of criticism *and* creativity (Braidotti 1991, 164). Moreover, the transposition can be found in the work of Barad herself.

Let us start by looking at Barad's use of the concept of 'agency,' a concept from the (feminist) human sciences that she applies to the natural sciences. Barad does not assume a world 'out there' that exists prior to language and that comes wholly unmediated to scientists. Nor are we fundamentally cut off from the real. Agential realism relies on Barad's neologism 'intra-action' (1996, 179; see also McNeil and Roberts, chapter 2, this volume). Pairs such as subject/object and thing/word do not exist independent of one another before they are brought into contact (interaction) in measurement; and because subject/object and thing/word intra-act from the start, we cannot think in terms of original and copy or a simple cause and effect relation between the two. What we theorise here is effectuation, or *productivity*, and 'what is produced is constrained by particular material-discursive factors and not arbitrarily construed' (Barad 1999, 2). Barad's definition of 'objectivity' summarises the theorisation of productivity as follows:

> [M]aterial apparatuses produce material phenomena through specific causal intra-actions, where 'material' is always already material-discursive—*that is what it means to matter.* . . . [W]hat is important about causal intra-actions is the fact that marks are left on bodies. Objectivity means being accountable to marks on bodies. (Barad 2003, 824; emphasis in original)

'Marks on bodies' consist of graphs on paper but also include concrete bodies of persons who are literally affected by (sexist, racist, heterosexist, ageist, etc.) theories and other doings. Agency is positioned in scientists' intra-action with the world and in the possibilities of scientists *acting on* the marking process (Barad 2003, 827). Agential realism thus allows for *thinking change*.

Scientists are constantly engaged in world-making practices by enacting (always provisional) cuts (ibid., 817). Barad locates openings for change in the enactment of worlds through the incision of *certain cuts* and *not* others (ibid., 827). Barad thus affirms it is not that we, as scientists or as subjects of knowledge, have the agency for effecting change whereas others (objects, instruments) are inert. Agency means quite simply performing a cut, or a boundary enactment:

> [A]gency is a matter of changes in the apparatuses of bodily production, and such changes take place through various intra-actions, some of which remake the boundaries that delineate the differential constitution of the 'human.' . . . On an agential realist account, agency is cut loose from its traditional humanist orbit. (Barad 2003, 826)

Barad thus accounts for 'posthumanist performativity' (human and nonhuman agency), and for the fact that often the line is drawn (i.e., the cut is enacted) at the human (i.e., closing off agency for nonhumans). The latter she calls a 'Cartesian' rather than 'agential' cut (ibid., 815). Cartesian cuts involve the naturalisation of certain cuts (essentialism). This is a tendency that does not have an eye for change or posthumanist agency. In the context of this chapter it is important to stress that agential realism is a frame within which the restrictive or liberating effects of disciplinary apparatuses, instruments intra-acting with subjects and objects of knowledge, can be studied as well as shifted. Instrumentation has, according to positivist epistemology, been assigned a 'neutral' position in the world-making practices of scholarship. Agential realism assigns it a non-neutral, agential place that also shifts the relativism of postmodernist, constructivist epistemology. Agential realism's ethical layer allows us to shift the outcomes of research.

Using a different terminology, and not referring to Barad or Bohr (but instead to Gilles Deleuze and Luce Irigaray), Grosz implicitly theorises the disciplinary apparatus for the human sciences. However when read in tandem with Barad's work, the work of Grosz makes clear how we can look at the agency of the wave model in feminist scholarship. In *Time Travels: Feminism, Nature, Power*, Grosz engages with what Barad calls an ontoepistemological methodology. Thinking through 'the time of thought' she claims that 'the construction of knowledges and discourses' should be seen as 'labor, production, doing' (Grosz 2005, 158). In other words, one's model of temporality (for instance, the linear model) influences the knowledge one brings forward about time. Grosz makes explicit that this can only be thought when the interplay between epistemology and ontology is taken into account (ibid.). This results in a Baradian reading of the humanities and of the conceptual tools of humanities scholars.

Grosz appears equally critical of representationalism. She says that representationalism characterises the (postmodern) humanities as much as the social and natural sciences:

> Psychoanalysis and deconstruction, today preeminent forms of interpretation and analysis within the humanities, restrict themselves to the inside of representation, which provides its own vested 'reading' of an outside or a real as always already codified, or only accessible through some kind of representational codification. (Grosz 2005, 173)

Here we see that representationalism in the humanities also comes with a certain mode of measuring. Above all, 'representational codification' can be seen as a Baradian measurement. And the measurements of humanities scholars also produce 'matter + meaning.' Although Barad's natural sciences seem to explicitly rely on a 'real' that is 'out there' for scholars to objectify, the humanities imply such an independent real by assuming a binary opposition between a real and representations, and by considering representation to be ontologically primary. Despite the fact that this humanistic practice is predicated on a reading of the linguistic work of Ferdinand de Saussure—a reading that has been dismantled as reductionist (Kirby 1997)—in practice both the natural science and the human sciences assume a schism between the material and the discursive/semiotic; and as such, the scholarly fields are unreal opposites instead of C. P. Snow's 'two cultures.'

Thinking through the disciplinary apparatuses or agencies of observation *of the humanities* consists of leaving behind the representational paradigm assumed by humanists themselves, and moving in the direction of thinking through the *effects* of the representational paradigm (thus thinking through the effects of codifications), with the goal of undoing them (Grosz 2005, 165):

> [It] involves an intimate familiarity with the history of concepts and knowledges, but rather than a reverential relation to history, which keeps us contained within its already existing terms, the history of each discipline can be regarded as the site of unactualized virtualities, of potentialities that never had their time to emerge. (ibid., 168–69)

Here we see that conceptual tools and sedimented knowledges, if used in a representationalist manner, are the disciplinary apparatuses of the humanities. These apparatuses have a constitutive effect: worlds can be opened up by the apparatuses, but it is also possible that worlds do not get actualised and that apparatuses have a paralyzing effect. This further legitimises my claim that the wave model of feminism can be analysed as an apparatus of a neo/disciplinary kind.

THE WAVE MODEL AS A NEODISCIPLINARY APPARATUS

Now that ontoepistemological methodology and the role of the disciplinary apparatus within the human sciences have been clarified, I wish to further specify the effects of researching with waves. I will deal with gender research, i.e., with academic feminism exclusively, and with the ways in which 'waves' feature in this scholarly neodiscipline. This section will further flesh out the argument presented in the introduction to this chapter by focusing on the origin stories that are told about the field. In the introduction I specified that researching with waves has a damaging effect on feminism both in the here and now, and in the future; feminism is relegated to the 1970s, and waves do not allow for current-day feminist activity. *Academic* feminism, which cannot but be said to be thriving nowadays, does not seem to count as *feminist* activity. This has damaging effects, as it upholds a definition of feminism that is reductive (second-wave feminism only) and implements a split between the academic and the activist sphere. In other words, conventional gender research with waves stifles what feminism has wanted to open up. Here I will attempt to reposition the 'wave' in such a way that worlds *do* open up while using this concept and that change *does* become thinkable.

The scholarly field of women's studies dates back to the 1970s, when feminists active in the women's movement in the US, the UK and the Northern and Western parts of Europe brought their academic activities to bear on their activism. Origin stories such as these, Haraway (1991) has argued, are in many ways dangerous stories, owing to the fact that they codify an isolated cause (*this* is *where* academic feminism originated *then*) and a universalised reading (the coming into being of this type of feminism entailed a move from *this* into *that*). Even the codification 'the US, the UK and parts of Europe' homogenises the story as it does not necessarily point out the differences between the regions involved when it comes to the development of the field and its epistemological underpinnings, let alone the differences between the different US regions or European countries with regards to academic feminism. Clare Hemmings (2005) has identified the origin story of women's studies as a Western story that is a dominant narrative with a specific form and function, and clearly delineable effects. When origin stories are represented as True we effectively erase the heterogeneity of academic feminism and homogenise possible narratives. Referring back to Grosz, the history of women's studies is not 'regarded as the site of unactualized virtualities, of potentialities that never had their time to emerge' (2005, 168–69). Waves are apparatuses in these stories (they effectuate a feminism that is spatiotemporally fixed) and, as such, they help effect homogeneity (they only allow for the feminism that had the time to emerge). The wave model is the apparatus that gender scholars use to produce homogenised stories about the origin, the state of affairs, and the (im)possible future of feminism.

One of the ways in which the dominant origin story of the field of women's studies has been retold entails pointing to the fact that the feminist critique of scholarship and the academy did not start in the 1970s, but actually much earlier. This kind of qualification critiques the dominant story *as a dominant story* and diversifies it. By replacing the isolation of a single cause, such alternative stories allow for both historical continuity, and for geo-political singularities. When the research is conducted with waves, however, historical continuity is ruled out by the representational codification of successive, yet dualist waves, and geo-political singularities by assigning a predetermined spatiotemporality to each wave. It is known, for example, that well before the establishment of the neodiscipline of gender studies, (individual) women had characterised the organisation of the academy as gendered (Harding 2006, 69–70). Developing these arguments about academic feminism does not imply refraining from making special mention of the momentousness of the feminist critique voiced in the 1960s and 1970s, a critique backed by an all-pervading social movement, *a cresting feminist wave*. Acknowledging this momentous political consciousness, it is still possible to secure a historical continuity between the exceptional instances of the (late) nineteenth-century critique of the gendered academy and the second-wave feminist critique. Our narrative simply becomes more complex, and we are able to theorise past instances of feminist critique as Grosz's unactualised virtualities: they did not immediately result in a feminist discipline but were definitely feminist, critical, and creative. The neodisciplinary apparatus works with a different notion of feminist critique and creativity. The sequence equality-difference-deconstruction is an integral part of the apparatus and codifies criticality according to a progressive narrative: feminism is becoming theoretically more and more sophisticated, which is accompanied by the so-called loss of feminist activism.[1] In this mode of thinking, equality feminism often signifies feminism in its most rudimentary form. Consequently, exceptional feminist voices from the period between the first and the second feminist wave (e.g., Virginia

Woolf), and of a more distant past (e.g., Christine de Pisan, Mary Woll-stonecraft and the women that in the late nineteenth century critiqued the gendered academy), are often typecast as naïve. These codifications do not to make sense in regards to the work of these thinkers.

When academic feminism came into being in the 1970s, second-wave feminism, in the dominant Anglo-American discourse, began to be con-ceptualised as internally conflicted. Importantly, this self-affirmed conflict dynamics is said to have proven the illusory nature of movement feminism's 'sisterhood' (Hirsch and Keller 1990). Academic feminists in the 1980s began to *negate* the work of 1970s movement feminists. They did not take into account the fact that the membership of these two groups overlapped nor did they keep in mind that academic feminism, as a project (the long march), came out of the second-wave feminist movement. The negation of activist feminism was accompanied by the (implicit) claim that diversified feminist analyses were *better than* the illusion of sisterhood (Stacey 1997, 59). This dualist approach to feminism engendered by the use of a model of waves (what academic feminists can know, epistemology) and the result-ing academic feminism's loss of activism (what feminism can be, ontology) are related (ontoepistemology). Creating a representational split between academic feminism and feminist activism has resulted in the codification of the current era as postfeminist. Our era is considered to be feminist in the sense that gender equality is supposed to exist and that academic feminism is thriving. But simultaneously our era is nonfeminist in the sense that feminist movement has apparently become stuck. Using a wave model that consists of oppositional waves as well as an internally conflicted, yet teleological feminism has resulted in paralysis.

Now that the restrictive effects of the wave model have been discussed, I want to ask: how are we to reposition the wave model for it to be *ben-eficial* for feminism? Here I again connect to Grosz (2005, 168–69) who argued that an 'intimate familiarity' with the concepts and knowledges circulating in a discipline (here the wave model as circulating in gender studies understood as a 'neodiscipline') can help us understand its unac-tualised virtualities. In my reading, the potentialities of researching with waves have remained underutilised in academic feminism. How are we to shift the model of waves in such a way that the 'potentialities that never had their time' due to certain conventional representational codifications and measurement acts *do* emerge?

TOWARDS THIRD-WAVE FEMINISM

Representationally overcodified waves have the ontoepistemic effects of thinking of feminism only as activist second-wave feminism and of revert-ing feminist movement to the past. The paralysis haunting contemporary young feminists, as a result of research with waves, entails a denial of their feminism (i.e., the codification of our times as postfeminist times, and of our academic activities as not activist), and an overcodification of past feminism (when and where the entire battle will have to be fought). How can a third wave of feminism come within our reach? And can third-wave feminism thus produced break through, first, a second-wave feminism owned by/relegated to the generation of baby boomers (whose heyday is assumed to be over, that is, it is assumed that they are no longer active in all possible ways), and second, the current generation of postfeminists? How can we position a third-wave feminism?

Liane Henneron is a French scholar working with a repositioned model of feminist waves. Henneron (2005) cuts across the fixed spatiotemporality of the wave model by reporting on the transmission of second-wave feminist insights and approaches in gender studies classrooms, and by conceptualising this transmission as nonlinear and nonteleological. Henneron's example discusses the theoretical baggage of younger feminists/students who *have absorbed, yet question* the terminologies employed by second-wave feminists/gender studies teachers. Henneron's research material can be understood through the work of Astrid Henry (2004, 7), who in *Not My Mother's Sister: Generational Conflict and Third-Wave Feminism* uses the term 'dis-identification.'[2] Dis-identification *simultaneously* signifies identification against something or somebody and intimate concentration on otherness or the other person. If you wish to identify *against* Simone de Beauvoir, for instance, you will have to know her work *intimately* (thus creating a familiarity with it) before you can discard it. Henry explains that dis-identification does not involve refusal (I refuse to relate to de Beauvoir's work), but rather a resistance to an identification that has already been made (I don't *want* to identify with de Beauvoir because she claims universal rather than specific validity for her statements about women). De Beauvoir's feminism, very much connected to a second-wave feminism, is then acknowledged but not accepted as desirable. The concept of dis-identification allows for thinking through the wave as a notion that involves neither sheer rivalry (dualistically effecting a postfeminism) nor uncritical continuity between generations (building on an archetypical feminism—second-wave feminism—that is to be copied). Dis-identification accounts for both continuity and for specific cases of inequality and difference between feminists (based for instance on geo-political location, generation, 'race'/ethnicity or sexuality). In other words, the ontoepistemic effect of paralysis can be avoided. Thinking continuity *and* change is a movement for which the well-known model of waves does not allow. And this is why I want to argue that dis-identification allows for utilising the full potential of waves. It allows for research with waves without repeating the stale pattern of rivalry between women, or the stereotype of an essentialised 'women's culture.' It qualitatively shifts the terms of academic feminism, finding its fulcrum nowadays in the good-old wave model (a conflict dynamics, a dualism).

Henneron's students can be defined as third-wave feminist subjects whose concepts have a different ontoepistemic effect. They do not reason according to a postfeminism; they want to take up a feminist position, so they effect a present that is not characterised by gender equality. The materials second-wave feminist academics transfer to their students is dis-identified with: it is studied and evaluated for the patriarchal here and now. On the basis of the nonlinearity and nondualism of dis-identification, it should be clear that the 'third' of 'third-wave' does not refer to what comes after second-wave feminism in a progressive manner. I do not deny that what I introduce here is a singular usage of the term third-wave feminism (Van der Tuin 2009). Systematic overviews have brought to the fore that many self-defined third-wave feminists employ, in fact, a postfeminist logic (Gillis 2005): their subject position is produced by the model of waves as we have come to use it in our field, effectuating paralysis. The conceptualisation of the 'wave' I find in the work of Henneron and read with Henry, however, actualises as yet unactualised feminist virtualities. Furthermore, the *partial* definition of third-wave feminism that I employ following Henneron and Henry is one that I consider beneficial for researching feminism and gender in/equality. This definition allows for writing about feminism in the present in a manner that is assertive of the issue: contemporary feminism is not being produced as a bad copy of second-wave feminism, nor is it a postfeminism.

More often than not, feminist academic texts on the issue of third-wave feminism have been dismissive of it. I have argued here that this is because the traditional model of waves was used in which a third wave of feminism is understood necessarily as a postfeminism, dualistically opposing to the second wave that is to be overthrown. Even so, there is a European tradition of texts available that is affirmative of third-wave feminism, but critical of the Anglo-US (unmarked) canon of academic feminist texts on the topic (Bessin and Dorlin 2005; Lamoureux 2006; Fantone 2007, 8, 12–14; Feigenbaum 2008; Grzinic and Reitsamer 2008). I would like to argue that these European texts think third-wave feminism along the shifted model of waves presented above. The way in which third-wave feminism is featured in the texts is not simply descriptive (a third wave of feminists exists out there, a third-wave feminism has been constructed) nor simply prescriptive (a third wave is needed to . . .). The project of the third wave in its European incarnation consists of the *materialisation* instead of representational codification of the third wave. I look forward to its liberating effects.

NOTES

1. Homogeny here does not only refer to the unmarked Anglo-US nature of the narratives (as this is where equality—difference—deconstruction comes from), but also to the ways in which the different feminist subjects (e.g., black and lesbian scholars, but also white/whitened postmodern/poststructuralist theorists) are positioned within the narrative (see Hemmings 2005).

2. The term dis-identification was introduced by Diana Fuss (1995), and apart from research on third-wave feminism, also features in research about "queers of color" (see Esteban Muñoz 1999).

REFERENCES

Aikau, H. K. 2007. Between Wind and Water: Thinking about the Third Wave as Metaphor and Materiality. In *Feminist Waves, Feminist Generations: Life Stories from the Academy*, ed. H. K. Aikau, K. A. Erickson and J. L. Pierce, 232–249. Minneapolis: University of Minnesota Press.

Barad, K. 1996. Meeting the Universe Halfway: Realism and Social Constructivism without Contradiction. In *Feminism, Science, and the Philosophy of Science*, ed. L. H. Nelson and J. Nelson, 161–194. Dordrecht: Kluwer Press.

Barad, K. 2007. *Meeting the Universe Halfway: Quantum Physics and the Entanglement of Matter and Meaning*. Durham, NC: Duke University Press.

Barad, K. 1999. Agential Realism: Feminist Interventions in Understanding Scientific Practices. In *The Science Studies Reader*, ed. M. Biagioli, 1–11. New York: Routledge.

Barad, K. 2003. Posthumanist Performativity: Toward an Understanding of How Matter Comes to Matter. *Signs: Journal of Women in Culture and Society* 28 (3): 801–31.

Bessin, M., and E. Dorlin. 2005. Les renouvellements générationnels du féminisme: mais pour quel sujet politique? *L'homme et la société* 158: 11–25.

Braidotti, R. 1991. *Patterns of Dissonance: A Study of Women in Contemporary Philosophy*. Cambridge: Polity Press.

Esteban Muñoz, J. 1999. *Disidentifications: Queers of Color and the Performance of Politics*. Minneapolis: University of Minnesota Press.

Fantone, L. 2007. Precarious Changes: Gender and Generational Politics in Contemporary Italy. *Feminist Review* 87: 5–20.

Feigenbaum, A. 2008. Review of Different Wavelengths: Studies of the Contemporary Women's Movement by Jo Reger. *Journal of International Women's Studies* 9 (3): 326–29.

Fuss, D. 1995. *Identification Papers*. New York: Routledge.

Gillis, S. 2005. (En)gendering Difference: Postfeminism, Third Wave Feminism and Globalisation. Paper presented at European Gender Chronologies, March 19–20, in Utrecht, the Netherlands.

Grosz, E. 2005. *Time Travels: Feminism, Nature, Power*. Durham, NC: Duke University Press.

Grzinic, M., and R. Reitsamer, eds. 2008. *New Feminism: Worlds of Feminism, Queer and Networking Conditions*. Wien: Löcker.

Haraway, D. J. 1991. *Simians, Cyborgs, and Women: The Reinvention of Nature*. London: Free Association Books.

Harding, S. 2006. *Science and Social Inequality: Feminist and Postcolonial Issues*. Urbana: University of Illinois Press.

Hemmings, C. 2005. Telling Feminist Stories. *Feminist Theory* 6 (2): 115–39.

Henneron, L. 2005. Être jeune féministe aujourd'hui: les rapports de génération dans le mouvement féministe contemporain. *L'homme et la société* 158: 93–109.

Henry, A. 2004. *Not My Mother's Sister: Generational Conflict and Third-Wave Feminism*. Bloomington: Indiana University Press.

Heywood, L. L., ed. 2005. *The Women's Movement Today: An Encyclopedia of Third-Wave Feminism*. 2 vols. Westport, CT: Greenwood Press.

Hirsch, M., and E. F. Keller, eds. 1990. *Conflicts in Feminism*. New York: Routledge.

Kirby, V. 1997. *Telling Flesh: The Substance of the Corporeal*. New York: Routledge.

Lamoureux, D. 2006. Y a-t-il une troisième vague féministe? *Cahiers du Genre* (hors-série 2006): 57–74.

Nelson, L. H. 1993. Epistemological Communities. In *Feminist Epistemologies*, ed. L. Alcoff and E. Potter, 121–59. New York: Routledge.

Stacey, J. 1997. Feminist Theory: Capital F, Capital T. In *Introducing Women's Studies: Feminist Theory and Practice*, ed. V. Robinson and D. Richardson, 54–76. Basingstoke: Macmillan.

Stanton, D. C. 1980. Language and Revolution: The Franco-American Dis-Connection. In *The Future of Difference*, ed. H. Eisenstein and A. Jardine, 75–87. Boston: G.K. Hall.

Tuin, I. van der. 2009. 'Jumping Generations': On Second- and Third-Wave Feminist Epistemology. *Australian Feminist Studies* 24 (59): 17–31.

———. 2011. 'A Different Starting Point, A Different Metaphysics': Reading Bergson and Barad Diffractively. *Hypatia: A Journal of Feminist Philosophy* 26 (1): 22–42.

2 Feminist Science and Technology Studies

Maureen McNeil and Celia Roberts

Feminist science and technology studies (FSTS) is an area of detailed empirical research, lively intellectual and political debate and cutting-edge conceptual development within gender and women's studies, and the social sciences and humanities more broadly. Here, we describe aspects of the complex relationship of feminist researchers to science and technology studies (STS) as a field and suggest what in FSTS might be of interest to feminist academics working in other areas. The chapter addresses three core questions:

1) What have feminists brought to STS?
2) What have feminists found to be of most interest in STS?
3) What have feminists working in other areas borrowed from FSTS?

Although our aim is to provide an overview that acknowledges national and (inter)disciplinary differences, our account is necessarily partial. It reflects our research interests in the areas of reproductive technologies and the new genetics, health and biomedicine, historical and contemporary understandings of biology and cultural studies of science; our national working context (Britain); and our personal histories. Whilst our main focus here is on Europe, we also discuss work produced in the USA, Canada and Australia which informs our perspectives on this field. We are aware that science studies is also flourishing in various other locations, including parts of Asia and some South American countries, with a slowly increasing interchange of workers (students and academics) and work between Asia, Europe, Australia and North and South America.

WHAT HAVE FEMINISTS BROUGHT TO STS?

"Science studies" is the simplest term that designates the research and texts of a broad group of researchers analysing the social and cultural dimensions and making of science and technology. This field may also be referred to as science and technology studies (STS), social studies of science (SSS) or the social study of scientific knowledge (SSK; although some would see this latter term as designating a specific body of STS investigation). As this last comment indicates, some of these terms signify particular intellectual approaches and histories, whilst others are more generic (see Asdal, Brenna and Moser 2007) and there are other, related terms which designate specific orientations and approaches (see Lykke 2008; McNeil 2008). The history and philosophy of science are, arguably, the more traditional 'older sisters' of science studies. In this chapter 'STS' refers to a broad cluster of social science and humanities research. As Kristin Asdal, Brita Brenna and Ingunn Moser recently observed, "feminist issues, tools and texts" are "amongst the most challenging and productive in the field of STS" (2007, 9). Some of the most important figures in the field are feminists, well known not only in science studies but in the social sciences and humanities more broadly. Despite this, it is still common to hear presentations or read texts in STS that make no reference to feminism or relevant feminist research, and which fail to consider issues pertaining to sex/gender and related inequalities. So, STS can be both a place where feminist research is recognised as groundbreaking and significant and somewhere where feminist politics might be troubling. STS, as a complex interdisciplinary field with its own history, has a complicated relation to 'politics' of any sort (e.g., Marxist, feminist, or postcolonial; Asdal, Brenna and Moser 2007; McNeil 2008). There are some who regard any suggestion that there are political dimensions to this field as anathema, old-fashioned, naïve or simply unwelcome.

Feminist researchers have, however, made substantial headway in bringing concerns about sex, gender and inequality to the field. There is much to celebrate and to develop here. One major body of work, for example, focuses on technoscientific and biomedical understandings of sex and gender. These have been of immense interest to feminists for over a century, largely because of their employment in pronouncements about women's lesser abilities and weaker bodies. With contributions from feminist biologists (Haraway 1985/1991; Keller 1985, 1992; Fausto-Sterling 1992; Spanier 1995; Birke 2000), social scientists (Martin 1992; Clarke 1998; Wilson 1998; Balsamo 1996; Hird 2004; Roberts 2006, 2007) and humanities scholars (Jordanova 1989; Russett 1989; Schiebinger 1989, 1999; Terry 1999), this work maps the ways in which technoscientific and biomedical knowledges and practices describe and, indeed, produce material (anatomical, physiological, genetic, hormonal, brain, behavioural, neurological) differences between women and men, girls and boys, female and male foetuses and babies.

Studying particular technoscientific or biomedical fields and examining the details of scientific arguments, experiments and theories, these scholars sometimes criticise the assumptions inherent in the field (evident, for example, in the metaphors used to describe biological processes, the hypotheses developed in empirical studies or the interpretation of results). While these scholars are often critical, in general they are interested in science and medicine as ways of knowing the world, although their work often injects sharp notes of caution in dealing with mainstream technoscientific and bio-medical accounts of sex and gender. Some of these authors (for example, Haraway 1985/1991; Wilson 1998; Hird 2004) also draw attention to the radical potential of some less mainstream scientific knowledges for femi-nist understandings of sex/gender: technoscience can sometimes provide inspiration in rethinking assumptions about how difference works. Such research offers engaged analyses of technoscience and biomedicine that nei-ther deny the value of scientific concepts and thinking nor align themselves uncritically with these. Challenging sexist ideas about women's potentials and 'natures,' such STS are strikingly critical and openly political.

Another significant thread of FSTS has focused on the history of the natural sciences (Easlea 1980; Merchant 1980; Keller 1985, 1992; Schie-binger 1999) and on the institutional and professional structures which have developed in and around them. While tracing how and why modern natural science originated as 'a world without women' (Noble 1992) has been important, feminist historians and biographers have also told stories of 'women worthies' (Harding 1986) whose contributions to various sci-entific fields have been obscured. Feminists have drawn attention to the intensely gendered divisions of labour within the natural sciences. This has sometimes intersected with feminist activism oriented towards improving women's access to science education, technological training and scientific careers (Harding 1986; Schiebinger 1999). Research tracing and docu-menting women's absence from, or participation in, the history of specific technoscientific fields (Rossiter 1982, 1995; Abir-Am and Outram 1989) has informed these struggles.

In the early twenty-first century, although women are more fully inte-grated into the professions and institutions of Western science, men still predominate in its higher echelons. Also, women continue to be poorly rep-resented in many countries in some crucial technoscientific fields, including information and communication technologies (Wakeford 1997; Terry and Calvert 1997; Herman and Webster 2007). As long as such patterns of gen-der divisions and hierarchies persist, this kind of research will remain a key focus for FSTS research and intervention.

Extending their purview beyond gender relations, some feminists recog-nised that the natural sciences have also been implicated in other histori-cal patterns of inequality. Nancy Stephan (1982), Sandra Harding (1993) and others have exposed colonialist and imperialist skeletons in Western science's cupboard. Sandra Harding (1998) has been a leading figure in extending the call, not only for gender equality within the institutions and professional structures of the sciences, but also for more multicultural sci-ence. For Harding this means taking seriously non-Western traditions in knowledge production and instigating measures to improve the participa-tion, not only of women, but of other under-represented groups (especially non-white people) in crucial positions within the natural sciences. Feminists have borrowed from and contributed to postcolonial theory in trying to unfetter Western science from its imperial and colonial moorings.

Other scholars have highlighted the gendered imagery and language of the natural sciences. 'Mother nature' has been a powerful figure in Western culture. Long before second-wave feminism, Simone de Beauvoir (1988) alerted many to the persistent alignment of women with nature and of men with culture and technology in Western societies. However, it was only when Carolyn Merchant (1980) and Brian Easlea (1980) studied Francis Bacon's ambitions to intensify witch-hunting and vanquish nature in the sixteenth century as a key episode in the gender politics that forged modern science that the significance of this icon came under full critical scrutiny. Evelyn Fox Keller (1985) subjected the language of Bacon and other founding fathers of the Scientific Revolution to similar review. This research demonstrated that the foundations of modern science were forged in and through gendered imagery and language. It also inspired other scholars to investigate the gendered imagery of science and medicine in other eras and contexts (Jordanova 1989; Jacobus, Keller and Shuttleworth 1990).

Feminists have also led the way in forging cultural studies of science and technology (McNeil 2007, 2008). This has included challenging explorations of the imaginaries and visions which have informed and shaped modern Western science. Evelyn Fox Keller's (1992) use of psychoanalysis and anthropology to investigate the meeting of physics and the life sciences in the emergence of molecular biology is an interesting instance. Keller interrogates the motivation for scientific efforts to wrench the 'secrets of life' from nature and the harnessing of these for destructive purposes in the atomic bomb project. Likewise, Donna Haraway's (1985/1991) embrace of feminist science fiction as a rich resource for STS research pushed the boundaries and conventions of the field.

Health and illness is another space in which feminists have made notable contributions, in particular in rethinking patients' roles in contemporary biomedicine. Challenging the construction of women as passive (particularly in the face of male expertise), and inspired by the political interventions associated with the women's health movement, these scholars have studied and theorised how women experience themselves as patients. Studies of cancer survivors and activists (Spanier 1995; Stacey 1997; Cartwright 2000; Broom 2001; Gibbon 2007), psychiatric patients (Gremillion 2003; Singh 2004; Orr 2005), cosmetic surgery consumers (Davis 1995; Fraser 2003; Braun 2005), women taking hormone replacement therapy (Martin 1992; Lock 1993; Guillemin 2000; Henwood et al. 2003; Roberts 2007) and women engaging with new reproductive and/or genetic technologies (Franklin 1997; Rapp 1999; Mamo and Fishman 2001; Heath, Rapp and Taussig 2004; Throsby 2004; Thompson 2005; Franklin and Roberts 2006; Duden and Samerski 2007; McNeil 2007, chapters 5 and 6) have reframed the patient/consumer as at least partially active in their engagement with biomedicine and technoscience. Regarding women as passive 'victims' of science and medicine, they argue, produces an inaccurate and paralysing figuration in which women's individual and collective decisions are rendered strangely redundant or incomprehensible. Charis Thompson's (2005) analysis of women's experiences in an IVF clinic, for example, suggests that women strategically allow themselves to become 'objects' for clinicians and nurses in their efforts to realise personal goals.

These studies are situated within a wider strand of STS that analyses patient experiences, insisting on the relevance of sex/gender to these. It is seriously limiting, they suggest, for social scientists to understand the contemporary patient as 'gender neutral.' Instead, they show contemporary patients in their engagements with technoscience and biomedicine as sexed/ gendered bodies within institutions (clinics, Internet chat rooms, activist groups, GP surgeries) that constantly (re)produce gender.

Feminists researching science and medicine have produced detailed accounts of the ways in which bodies are made, performed or enacted rather than simply unfolded in a biological sense. Work on bodies deemed 'pathological' in terms of sex/gender (transsexual and intersexed bodies, for example) has described the ways in which medical and scientific discourses shape bodies, both materially (through surgery and pharmaceuticals) and discursively (through observing, counting and measuring and producing descriptions of norms and deviations; Fausto-Sterling 1992; Balsamo 1996; Terry 1999). Historical studies of bodies have been particularly important in demonstrating their social and cultural production. So, for example, Londa Schiebinger (1989) highlights the ways in which, during the eighteenth and nineteenth centuries, bodies came to be understood and lived as belonging to one of two distinct yet 'complementary' sexes. Representations of skeletons developed in the eighteenth century, Schiebinger argues, are evidence of a sexist (yet contested) worldview in which women were said to have smaller brains and to be naturally suited to child-rearing. Such representations, Schiebinger and others contend, also demonstrate the intersection of discourses of sex and race: scientific and medical arguments about the superiority of men over women were often interwoven with arguments about the superiority of white people over racialised 'others.'

WHAT DO FSTS THEORISTS FIND OF MOST INTEREST IN STS?

Science and technology studies offers feminists a range of tools for understanding, problematising, and undermining the naturalisation of the gendering of identities, practices, and social relations. While raising critical questions about the nature-culture distinction has not been the exclusive prerogative of this field, it has been a crucial, recurring trope in recent research. Moreover, detailed examinations of nature as an historically variable and culturally specific signifier has become part of STS stock-in-trade.

For some feminists it was the studies of technoscientific labour processes which first captured their attention. Influenced by Marxist theories and, in particular, by the studies of technological innovation and deskilling undertaken by Harry Braverman (1975), some feminist researchers launched investigations of women's work. Judy Wajcman, Wendy Faulkner, Anne-Jorunn Berg, Merete Lie and Marja Vehvilainen are just a few of the many feminist scholars who pursued this track (see for example, Wajcman 1991, 2000, 2004; Berg and Lie 1995; Lie 1995; Vehvilainen 1999; Faulkner 2000). Since the early 1980s, their research has enriched and complexified this strand of STS. So, for instance, studies of masculinity have become important in unravelling the gender relations of engineering (Faulkner 2000). Moreover, critical calls to employ queer theory have been a more recent intervention in this field (Landström 2007).

Concern for everyday life and the quotidian engagement with technology in contemporary Western societies rendered the concept of 'the domestication of technology' attractive to a number of FSTS researchers. Originally formulated by Roger Silverstone (1992, 2006) the term refers to a range of social processes through which technologies are integrated into and adapted in daily usage. Nelly Oudshoorn, Merete Lie and others have treated this concept as a methodological invitation to undertake detailed studies of how users can extend or change the expectations for and the meanings of particular technologies (including reproductive, information and communication technologies in specific situations and settings; Oudshoorn and Pinch 2003). For example, the patterns of use of personal computers and of mobile telephones have been varied and complex and by no means anticipated by their original designers. This work demonstrates that the meanings of technology are not fixed at production. Instead, this research has yielded detailed studies of the agency of users in transforming the meaning of specific technologies.

Feminists working in STS have employed other key concepts and tools from the field. One of the most significant of these in the area of health and medicine is Paul Rabinow's 'biosociality,' a term that references Michel Foucault's concept of 'biopower.' 'Biosociality' refers to contemporary forms of social collectivity organised around shared biological experiences or identities, such as testing positive for the HIV virus or being at risk of a particular genetic condition. Some feminists have taken up this term to discuss new collectives emerging in the area of disability (Rapp, Heath and Taussig 2001), whilst others have reflected on the gendering of the new forms of responsibility arising from biosocialities (Roberts 2006; Plows and Boddington 2007). In work on the Visible Human Project (a digital database produced by the reduction of a human corpse into thousands of tiny slices), Catherine Waldby (2000) introduced the related term 'biovalue' to designate the extraction of surplus value from biological matter that has become increasingly common in contemporary technoscience. This term has been applied and developed in a wide range of research on biotechnical phenomena, including stem cells and embryo and oocyte donation.

Actor-network theory (ANT), an important strand of STS theory and research since the 1990s, has produced several key terms that have been employed and developed by feminists, including distributed agency, configured users and the politics of nature. ANT has been associated with the investigation of the relational positioning of entities which comprise particular forms of technoscience. It has concomitantly challenged human-centric accounts of technoscientific systems and activities, emphasising distributed agency. For example, in research on the ways in which disabled people manage daily activities, Ingunn Moser (2006) describes the complex patterns through which technologies become agentic or active in constituting disabled bodies. Employing ANT and highlighting distributed agency in the operations of technologies and of practice, Moser invites disabled interviewees to trace their everyday interactions with technologies. Such technologies, Moser shows, can affirm conventional practices of masculinity or femininity. She contends that other technology-body interactions may challenge conventional gender alignments, producing new forms of subjectivity and new ways of doing gender.

Vicky Singleton's (Singleton and Michael 1993) research on cervical screening was an early and influential bringing together of ANT and feminist perspectives to explore this particular technology. The term 'configured user' refers to the ways in which the design, production and circulation of any particular technology involves an imagined or preferred ('configured') user. Madeleine Akrich and Bernike Pasveer's (2004) study of obstetric practices, for example, examines the ways in which the use of different technologies and practices creates radically different experiences of birth in France and the Netherlands.

Lucy Suchman's work on affective machines (robots and other devices) traces the distribution of agency within networks of human-machine interactions which reproduce (gendered) fantasies of independent emotional states. Suchman (2007b) employs both ethnomethodology and ANT in her investigations of the information and communication industry, artificial intelligence and robotics. She has recently turned her attention (2007a) to the ways in which feminist theories and research can enrich understandings of robotics and artificial intelligence.

WHAT DO FEMINISTS WORKING IN OTHER FIELDS TAKE FROM FSTS?

As the preceding account indicates, FSTS has brought valued perspectives and resources to feminism. FSTS has helped to destabilise the naturalisation of gender differences and inequalities through the critical gaze it casts on the legitimating and constitutive role of the sciences in these patterns.

Moreover, since the natural sciences have also informed the models and norms of knowledge production in Western culture more generally, the epistemological insights of FSTS have attracted other feminists. Beyond this, Western feminists' awareness of and concern about the technoscientific nature of twenty-first-century daily lives may draw them to this body of feminist research.

In addition to these broad motivations drawing feminists to STS, key feminist researchers in this field have forged concepts which have gained currency. Some of the most diffused concepts emerging from FSTS have come from the writing of Donna Haraway. Haraway's work is widely read outside of STS, and some of her terms have an active life in and beyond feminist and other research fields. Most notable amongst these are 'situated knowledges,' 'modest witness,' 'cyborg' and 'material-semiotic actor.' These terms are tools in Haraway's multi-dimensional analyses of the production of technoscientific knowledge as historically and culturally specific. The term 'situated knowledges' encapsulates her argument that science involves a set of material practices undertaken by particular groups of people in specific times and locations. It underscores the notion that scientific knowledge (like all forms of knowledge) is specific and not transcendent.

In a related argument, Haraway reworks Steven Shapin and Simon Schaffer's (1985) argument (made in the STS 'classic,' *Leviathan and the Air Pump*) that only particular people (i.e., 'gentlemen') in the seventeenth century were allowed to participate in the experimental method which became the lynchpin of modern natural science. Shapin and Schaffer label these men 'modest witnesses,' indicating that they positioned themselves as objective, disembodied observers of the natural world. Haraway argues that it is important to register the simultaneous making of both science and gender within scientific practices. She regards this as a way of opening science to those traditionally excluded from it (see also Harding 1993) and of grasping more fully the specificities and limitations of any particular epistemological perspective thereby refusing 'self-invisibility' and 'transparency' (Haraway 1997, 32).

Although developed specifically through and for analyses of technoscience, these terms have obvious value for other disciplines claiming to produce objective knowledge. Haraway's emphasis on understanding situatedness and modest witnessing provides tools for reconsidering the position of the analyst, theorist or knowledge producer without dismissing the practices of the discipline itself. She is not arguing that the knowledge produced by the natural sciences—or history or economics—is 'wrong'; rather, she demonstrates that the knowledge produced (like all forms of knowledge) is always partial and thus, in some ways, 'interested.'

Haraway does not bemoan the loss of traditional objectivity, nor does she believe that acknowledging the 'situatedness'of knowledge diminishes it. Rather, knowledge produced by genuinely modest witnesses is more likely to be reliable and functional, as it is does not entail pretensions to universality or timelessness. Unlike Haraway, who describes technoscience as telling 'stories,' Sandra Harding (1993) prefers to retain the term 'objectivity' in her analysis of knowledge production. 'Strong objectivity' for her denotes a superior form of knowledge resulting when the position of the knowledge producer is taken into account and when diverse social groups are involved in its generation. For Harding, science produced with such awareness, particularly that produced by those who are not privileged, will yield more effective and valuable knowledge of the world.

The terms 'cyborg' and 'material-semiotic actor' bookmark Haraway's attempts to theorise the role of both human and nonhuman actors in the production of particular worlds, objects, practices and knowledges. Both terms conjoin two seemingly incompatible 'opposites' (the cybernetic and the organic, the material and the semiotic) in explorations of nonbinarised thinking. Haraway's assertion in her 'Cyborg Manifesto' (1985/1991) that 'we are all cyborgs' has been widely discussed and used to explore multiple facets of contemporary life—from cosmetic surgery to factory work, from theatre to comic books. These terms are tools for thinking critically about historically conventional oppositions and for developing ways of disturbing established boundaries between nature and culture, humans and animals or machines and life.

Haraway also uses the terms 'diffraction' and 'implosion' to describe the relationship between science, nature and culture. Refusing a conception of science as simply reflecting or describing nature from a neutral position, she deploys these terms, borrowed from physics, to figure scientific practice and knowledge making as involving a messier, more complex relationship between 'the world or nature' and culture or science. Haraway perceives science as operating like light entering a prism. In this framing, science 'diffracts' the world; scientists do not merely describe nor do they fabricate the world. As these terms suggest, Haraway argues that the world we know is lived through scientific knowledge-making practices; it is changed by technoscience and, indeed, constituted in and through this relation.

Physicist and feminist theorist Karen Barad explores related issues in *Meeting the Universe Halfway* (2007). Engaging with the theories and experiments of physicist Niels Bohr, Barad employs the notion of 'intra-action' to suggest that subjects and objects are not ontologically distinct, but rather emerge through their encounters with each other. Her book traces the detailed technoscientific practices constituting forms of 'intra-action' that realise particular subject/object configurations. (For more elaborate discussions of Barad's contributions to feminist theory and epistemology, see also chapters 1 and 9, this volume.)

The conceptualisations and terms provided by Haraway and Barad have proved useful to feminist researchers investigating particular aspects of contemporary social experience. Claudia Castañeda and Lucy Suchman (forthcoming), for example, morph Haraway's 'primate visions' to talk about 'robot visions' and the fantasies of designers hoping to build affective machines.

Another term developed within FSTS that has had extensive currency is Charis Thompson's (2005) notion of 'ontological choreography.' Emerging from Thompson's ethnographic observations of women in IVF clinics the term highlights the ways in which subjectivities are made and unmade over time (a course of treatment, for example). Women patients in IVF clinics, Thompson argues, are sometimes positioned as 'objects': their bodies become sites of work for nurses, clinicians and medical technologies. At other times, women can act more easily as subjects. This argument highlights the activity of women engaging with biomedicine in their attempts to realise certain desired goals (in this case, to try to have a child and/or to ameliorate the suffering of infertility).

The concept of 'ontological choreography' has much to offer feminists puzzling over women's relationships with what might be understood as 'patriarchal' institutions or practices. Rather than framing such relationships as collusion or delusion, this concept indicates that researchers would be well advised to undertake detailed analyses of exactly how and why women engage in the way they do. Such research may involve some critique of the practices or institutions in question, but most notably, it offers a path out of conventional pathologisations of women.

The research described above that deals directly with the biological body has much to offer what has been called 'corporeal feminism' and, indeed, speaks to long-term feminist interests in body politics. Many feminists are engaged in thinking about the body and have debated how we can theorise the fleshiness or materiality of lived bodies. FSTS' analyses of the discourses that promise 'knowledge' about this materiality (for example, endocrinology, genetics, physiology, biology, immunology, neurology) provide other feminists with insights about bodies (about what they can do, how they are currently understood and so on). In addition, they offer distinctive critical approaches to truth claims about bodies, including those which pronounce the limits of (gendered and other specified) bodily capabilities. Hence, leading feminist theorists including Rosi Braidotti and Judith Butler have drawn upon FSTS in explicating their philosophical work on the body, subjectivity and sex/gender.

CONCLUSION

The field of FSTS is rich in both empirical detail and theoretical conceptualisations. It is also one of the most productive arenas of feminist work in which these two strands of research are brought together: many STS scholars see themselves both as empirical researchers and theorists. As we have suggested, this field is one of (at least) two-way traffic between FSTS and gender and women's studies. These contributions centre on core questions for the humanities and social sciences: how can we rethink the nature/ culture distinction? How might we theorise bodies as lived and/or socially situated? What is knowledge and how might we best make and analyse it? What is the signficance of sex/gender, race/ethnicity and other alignments of difference in shaping human experience and identities? How can we make sense of and live well (enough) in our increasingly technological and scientific worlds? FSTS has pursued such questions both empirically and conceptually. We hope this piece will be a useful roadmap for those concerned with these and related questions.

REFERENCES

Abir-Am, P.G., and D. Outram, eds. 1989. *Uneasy Careers and Intimate Lives: Women in Science, 1789–1979.* New Brunswick, NJ: Rutgers University Press.

Akrich, M., and B. Pasveer. 2004. Embodiment and Disembodiment in Childbirth Narratives. *Body and Society* 10 (2–3): 63–84.

Asdal, K., B. Brenna and I Moser. 2007. The Politics of Interventions: A History of STS. In *Technoscience: The Politics of Interventions*, ed. K. Asdal, B. Brenna and I. Moser, 7–53. Oslo: Oslo Academic Press.

Balsamo, A. 1996. *Technologies of the Gendered Body: Reading Cyborg Women.* Durham, NC: Duke University Press.

Barad, K. 2007. *Meeting the Universe Halfway: Quantum Physics and the Entanglement of Matter and Meaning.* Durham, NC: Duke University Press.

Beauvoir, S. de. 1988. *The Second Sex.* Trans. and ed. H. M. Parshley. London: Pan.

Berg, A. J., and M. Lie. 1995. Feminism and Constructionism: Do Artifacts Have Gender? *Science, Technology and Human Values* 20 (3): 332–51.

Birke, L. 2000. *Feminism and the Biological Body.* Edinburgh: Edinburgh University Press.

Braverman, H. 1975. *Labor and Monopoly Capital: The Degradation of Work in the Twentieth Century.* New York: Monthly Review Press.

Broom, D. 2001. Reading Breast Cancer: Reflections on a Dangerous Intersection. *Health* 5 (2): 249–68.

Braun, V. 2005. In Search of (Better) Sexual Pleasure: Female Genital 'Cosmetic' Surgery. *Sexualities* 8 (4): 407–24.

Cartwright, L. 2000. Community and the Public Body in Breast Cancer Media. In *Wild Science: Reading Feminism, Medicine and the Media*, ed. J. Marchessault and K. Sawchuk, 120–38. London and New York: Routledge.

Castañeda, C., and L. Suchman. Forthcoming. Robot Visions. In *Thinking with Haraway*, ed. S. Ghamari-Tabrizi.

Clarke, A. 1998. *Disciplining Reproduction.* Berkeley and London: University of California Press.

Davis, K. 1995. *Reshaping the Female Body: The Dilemma of Cosmetic Surgery.* London: Routledge.

Duden, B., and S. Samerski. 2007. 'Pop Genes': An Investigation of 'The Gene' in Popular Parlance. In *Biomedicine as Culture: Instrumental Practices, Technoscientific Knowledge and New Modes of Life*, ed. R. V. Burri and J. Dumit, 167–89. New York and London: Routledge.

Easlea, B. 1980. *Witch-hunting, Magic and the New Philosophy.* Brighton: Harvester.

Faulkner, W. 2000. The Power and the Pleasure? A Research Agenda for 'Making Gender Stick' to Engineers. *Science, Technology and Human Values* 25 (1): 87–119.

Fausto-Sterling, A. 1992. *Myths of Gender: Biological Theories about Women and Men*. Rev. ed. New York: Basic Books.

Franklin, S. 1997. *Embodied Progress: A Cultural Account of Assisted Reproduction*. London and New York: Routledge.

Franklin, S., and Roberts, C. 2006. *Born and Made: An Ethnography of Preimplantation Genetic Diagnosis*. Princeton, NJ: Princeton University Press.

Fraser, S. 2003. *Cosmetic Surgery, Gender and Culture*. London: Palgrave.

Gibbon, S. 2007. *Breast Cancer Genes and the Gendering of Knowledge*. London: Palgrave Macmillan.

Gremillion, H. 2003. *Feeding Anorexia: Gender and Power at a Treatment Center*. Durham and London: Duke University Press.

Guillemin, M. 2000. Working Practices of the Menopause Clinic. *Science, Technology and Human Values* 25 (4): 448–70.

Haraway, D. J. 1985/1991. A Cyborg Manifesto: Science, Technology, and Socialist-Feminism in the Late Twentieth Century. In *Simians, Cyborgs, and Women: The Reinvention of Nature*, 149–81. London: Free Association Books.

———. 1997. *Modest Witness@Second_Millennium: FemaleMan©_Meets_ OncoMouse™*. New York: Routledge.

Harding, S. 1986. *The Science Question in Feminism*. Milton Keynes: Open University Press.

———, ed. 1993. *The 'Racial Economy of Science': Toward a Democratic Future*. Bloomington: Indiana University Press.

———. 1998. *Is Science Multicultural? Postcolonialism, Feminism and Epistemologies*. Bloomington: Indiana University Press.

Heath, D., R. Rapp and K. Taussig. 2004. Genetic Citizenship. In *A Companion to the Anthropology of Politics*, ed. D. Nugent and J. Vincent, 152–67. London: Blackwell.

Henwood, F., S. Wyatt, A. Hart and J. Smith. 2003. 'Ignorance Is Bliss Sometimes': Constraints on the Emergence of the 'Informed Patient' in the Changing Landscape of Health Information. *Sociology of Health and Illness* 25 (6): 589–607.

Herman, C., and J. Webster. 2007. Gender and ICT Editorial. Special issue, *Information, Communication & Society* 10 (3): 279–86.

Hird, M. 2004. *Sex, Gender and Science*. London: Palgrave Macmillan.

Jacobus, M., E. F. Keller and S. Shuttleworth. 1990. *Body/Politics: Women and the Discourses of Science*. New York: Routledge.

Jordanova, L. 1989 *Sexual Visions: Images of Gender in Science and Medicine between the Eighteenth and Twentieth Centuries*. Hemel Hempstead: Harvester Wheatsheaf.

Keller, E. F. 1985. *Reflections on Gender and Science*. New Haven, CT and London: Yale University Press.

———. 1992. From Secrets of Life to Secrets of Death. In *Secrets of Life/Secrets of Death: Essays on Language, Gender and Science*, 39–55. New York and London: Routledge.

Landström, C. 2007. Queering Feminist Technology Studies. *Feminist Theory* 8 (1): 7–26.

Lie, M. 1995. Technology and Masculinity: The Case of the Computer. *European Journal of Women's Studies* 2 (3): 379–94.

Lock, M. 1993. *Encounters with Aging: Mythologies of Menopause in Japan and North America*. Berkeley and Los Angeles: University of California Press.

Lykke, N. 2008. Feminist Cultural Studies of Technoscience. *In Bits of Life: Feminism at the Intersections of Media, Bioscience and Technology*, ed. A. Smelik and N. Lykke, 3–15. Seattle: University of Washington Press.

McNeil, M. 2007. *Feminist Cultural Studies of Science and Technology*. London: Routledge.

———. 2008. Roots and Routes: The Making of Feminist Cultural Studies of Technoscience. In *Bits of Life: Feminist Studies of Media, Bioculture and Technoscience*, ed. A. Smelik and N. Lykke, 16–31. Seattle: Washington University Press.

Mamo, L., and J. Fishman. 2001. Potency in All the Right Places: Viagra as a Gendered Technology of the Body. *Body and Society* 7 (4): 13–35.

Martin, E. 1992. *The Woman in the Body: A Cultural Analysis of Reproduction.* 2nd ed. Milton Keynes: Open University Press.

Merchant, C. 1980. *The Death of Nature: Women, Ecology and the Scientific Revolution.* San Francisco: Harper and Row.

Moser, I. 2006. Sociotechnical Practices and Difference: On the Interferences between Disability, Gender and Class. *Science, Technology and Human Values* 31 (5): 537–65.

Noble, D. 1992. *A World without Women: The Christian Clerical Culture of Western Science.* New York: Alfred A. Knopf.

Orr, J. 2005. *Panic Diaries: A Genealogy of Panic Disorder.* Durham, NC: Duke University Press.

Oudshoorn, N., and T. Pinch, eds. 2003. *How Users Matter: The Co-construction of Users and Technologies.* Cambridge, MA: MIT Press.

Plows, A., and P. Boddington. 2007. Troubles with Biocitizenship? *Genomics, Society and Policy* 2 (3): 115–35.

Rapp, R. 1999. *Testing Women, Testing the Fetus.* New York and London: Routledge.

Rapp, R., D. Heath and K. Taussig. 2001. Genealogical Dis-Ease: Where Hereditary Abnormality, Biomedical Explanation, and Family Responsibility Meet. In *Relative Values: Reconfiguring Kinship Studies*, ed. S. Franklin and S. McKinnon, 384–409. Durham, NC: Duke University Press.

Roberts, C. 2006. 'What Can I Do to Help Myself?': Somatic Individuality and Contemporary Hormonal Bodies. *Science Studies* 19 (2): 54–76.

———. 2007. *Messengers of Sex: Hormones, Biomedicine and Feminism.* Cambridge: Cambridge University Press.

Rossiter, M. W. 1982. *Women Scientists in America: Struggles and Strategies to 1940.* Baltimore: Johns Hopkins University Press.

———. 1995. *Women Scientists in America: Before Affirmative Action 1940–1972.* Baltimore: Johns Hopkins University Press.

Russett, C. E. 1989. *Sexual Science: The Victorian Construction of Womanhood.* Cambridge, MA: Harvard University Press.

Schiebinger, L. 1989. *The Mind Has No Sex? Women in the Origins of Modern Science.* Cambridge, MA.: Harvard University Press.

———. 1999. *Has Feminism Changed Science?* Cambridge, MA: Harvard University Press.

Shapin, S., and S. Schaffer. 1985. *Leviathan and the Air-pump: Hobbes, Boyle and the Experimental Life.* Princeton, NJ: Princeton University Press.

Silverstone, R. 1992. *Consuming Technologies: Media and Information in Domestic Space.* London: Routledge.

———. 2006. Domesticating Domestication: Reflections on the Life of a Concept. In *Domestication of Media and Technology*, ed. T. Berker, M. Hartmann, Y. Punie and K. J. Ward, 229–48. Milton Keynes: Open University Press.

Singh, I. 2004. Doing Their Jobs: Mothering with Ritalin in a Culture of Mother-blame. *Social Science and Medicine* 59 (6): 1193–1205.

Singleton, V., and M. Michael. 1993. Actor Network and Ambivalence: General Practitioners and the UK Cervical Screening Programme. *Social Studies of Science* 23 (2): 227–64.

Spanier, B. B. 1995. *Im/partial Science: Gender Ideology in Molecular Biology.* Bloomington: Indiana University Press.

Stacey, J. 1997. *Teratologies: A Cultural Study of Cancer.* London and New York: Routledge.

Stephan, N. 1982. *The Idea of Race in Science: Great Britain 1800–1960.* London: Macmillan.

Suchman, L. 2007a. Feminist STS and the Sciences of the Artificial. In *The Handbook of Science and Technology Studies*, ed. E. J. Hackett, O. Amsterdamska, M. Lynch and J. Wajcman, 139–64. 3rd ed. Cambridge, MA: MIT Press.

———. 2007b. *Human-Machine Reconfigurations: Plans and Situated Actions.* 2nd. ed. Cambridge: Cambridge University Press.

Terry, J. 1999. *An American Obsession: Science, Medicine and Homosexuality in Modern Society.* Chicago: Chicago University Press.

Terry, J., and M. Calvert, eds. 1997. *Processed Lives: Gender and Technology in Everyday Life.* London: Routledge.

Thompson, C. 2005. *Making Parents: The Ontological Choreography of Reproductive Technologies.* Cambridge, MA: MIT Press.

Throsby, K. 2004. *When IVF Fails: Feminism, Infertility and the Negotiation of Normality.* Basingstoke: Palgrave Macmillan.

Vehvilainen, M. 1999. Gender and Computing in Retrospect: The Case of Finland. *Annals of the History of Computing* 21 (2): 44–51.

Wakeford, N. 1997. Networking Women and Grrrls with Information/Communication Technology: Surfing Tales of the World Wide Web. In *Processed Lives: Gender and Technology in Everyday Life*, ed. J. Terry and M. Calvert, 35–46. London: Routledge.

Wajcman, J. 1991. *Feminism Confronts Technology.* Cambridge: Polity Press.

———. 2000. Reflections on Gender and Technology Studies: In What State Is the Art? *Social Studies of Science* 30 (3): 447–64.

———. 2004. *Technofeminism.* Milton Keynes: Open University Press.

Waldby, C. 2000. *The Visible Human Project: Informatic Bodies and Posthuman Medicine.* London: Routledge.

Wilson, E. A. 1998. *Neural Geographies: Feminism and the Microstructure of Cognition.* New York: Routledge.

Part II
Methodologies

3 Intersectionality
A Theoretical Adjustment

Dorthe Staunæs and Dorte Marie Søndergaard

What could intersectionality mean? Does it always refer to the same thing when the term is used in scholarly texts? And in what ways might concepts like 'corporate masculinity' and 'coaching management style' be helpful in a theoretical adjustment of intersectionality?

Intersectionality has become a central concept in the understanding of inter-relations among sociocultural identification and differentiation categories such as gender, ethnicity, sexuality, race, age and dis/ability. The concept emphasises that the effects of these categories cannot be understood in isolation from each other. A variety of metaphors has been taken up to illustrate the nature of these interrelations—to name but a few: 'weaving,' 'entangling,' 'interplay,' 'tinting,' 'toning,' 'imbuing,' 'interlocking' and 'crosswise and overlapping movements.' This chapter will focus on the concept of intersectionality and some of its theoretical calibrations, which we see as productive in relation to analytical usage of the term in the sociopsychological exploration of diversity with regard to gender, more specifically in connection with the paths to high-ranking managerial appointment.

Between 2002 and 2004 we produced empirical material for the research project *Diversity, Gender and Top Management*. The project was conducted in a private business, here called X-Company, which had already developed and integrated a range of initiatives to promote gender equality at the structural level such as mentor schemes, equal opportunities committees, bonus schemes, various branding and equal opportunities campaigns. With an eye to both the risks of a democratic deficit and the possibility of a financial profit, the company wished to accelerate the recruitment of women to positions in top management.

Our approach to the project was to analyse the more complex and subtle aspects of both conceptualisations of gender and the gender practices at play amongst staff, as well as management of the firm's recruitment, selection and decision-making practices, and in their general interaction. Our aim was to develop discursive and theoretical aids to effect change in these conceptions and practices within the company. The project set out to investigate discursive patterns and dynamics which contributed to establishing the grounds for the recruitment routes, career paths, decision lines, networks, assessments and so on at the various organisational levels and in the various departments.[1] We focussed on how sociocultural identification and differentiation categories interacted to form the employees' meaning-making processes (Bruner 1990). In connection with these processes, we were also interested in how sociocultural categories interacted in the employees' perceptions and assessments of such issues as 'who has talent,' 'what kind of management style is appropriate' and 'who can successfully satisfy the expectations of the management.'

In this chapter we raise the questions: how may the concept of intersectionality be helpful in this type of research—and what adjustments to the concept may be suggested in order to enhance its analytical productivity? This chapter aims to establish a platform for adjusting the concept, and we use our work with 'corporate masculinity' and 'coaching management styles' to improve its potential. Central to this is the emphasis we place on the adjustment as situated within particular disciplines and fields of study, as is the assessment of the analytic value of the concept.

A USEFUL AND PRODUCTIVE CONCEPT?

Is intersectionality an analytically productive concept? Well, that depends. A number of different and often very discipline-specific versions of the meaning of the term seem to be in circulation. Examining the literature in the area one notices how the celebration, rejection, use and transformation of the concept are closely connected to the solidarities, loyalties, interests and ambitions of the different disciplines and fields of study which gave rise to it.

The term intersectionality is usually ascribed to the black feminist movement in North America, with its roots in identity and standpoint theory (Crenshaw 1991; Collins 1998; Lykke 2003). Acknowledging its historical roots in critical feminist race theory (Brah and Phoenix 2004), the term was launched by law professor Kimberlé Crenshaw in an analysis of the invisibility of black women in the American legal system. The concept was born of a commitment to demonstrate the positioning of black women as outsiders within in a matrix of domination (Collins 1998), i.e., in a structural system which favours the categories male, Christian, white, affluent, heterosexual, slim and young. It was the favouring of certain categories, and the marginalisation of the bearers of other sociocultural categories of identification and differentiation, which gave the concept relevance as a tool of political analysis. Here intersectionality dealt with the synchronicity between and interaction among (hetero)sexism, racism, class marginalisation and other classic 'isms' linked to sociocultural categories. The term was, and still is, used in the context of political science and juridical discussions on civil rights for women, ethnic and racial minorities, people with disabilities and LGBT people. It is used with the aim of accentuating how people who fall into a particular combination of categories frequently lack the rights, protection and privileges enjoyed by (certain) others.

Like many other theoretical concepts, intersectionality speedily crossed the Atlantic to enter European and Scandinavian contexts (Knapp 2005), where it has been adopted for use in areas as varied as education, employment, integration, diversity management, politics, migration, trafficking and hip-hop culture. The concept has travelled from social science disciplines like law and political science to cultural and humanistic fields such as anthropology, psychology, cultural studies, literary and media studies. In some areas its roots in standpoint theory and identity politics are preserved. In others the concept is coupled with postcolonialism (de los Reyes and Mulinari 2005) or with cultural studies and anthropology, as for instance in connection with conceptualisations of creolisation and hybrid cultures (Mørck 1998). In other contexts these roots are discussed and transformed using theoretical filters such as queer theory, poststructuralism, science and technology studies, actor-network theory and postconstructionism (Moser 2003; Staunæs 2003, 2005; Søndergaard 2005a, 2005b; Kofoed 2008; Lykke 2010).

In what ways is the concept analytically useful? According to the gender scholar Nina Lykke (2003, 2010), the concept of intersectionality can function as a meeting point for many different discursive endeavours to achieve sensitivity in relation to complexity. For some, the concept is a long-awaited answer to a scholarly need for an analytical approach to variation, complexity, confusion, ambivalence and change in connection with sociocultural categories of identification and differentiation, and it is thus welcomed by many (who also extend and develop it) as a collective term for something they have long been working on. In these contexts it is introduced into decentred and pluralising analyses, which aim at challenging existing regimes of power and dominance. This celebration coexists with criticism from others, who point out dryly that there is no need to reinvent the wheel; existing terms like 'transversalism' (Yuval-Davis 1997, 2006), 'nomadic subjects' (Braidotti 1994) and 'inappropriate/d Others' (Minh-ha 1989; Haraway 1992) may capture transgressive and complex identities and categories in a far more subtle way than intersectionality can. What worries some researchers about the concept is its tendency to reduce and fix identities and categories, and potentially re-establish forms of colonial power based on white hegemony. In this sense, an evaluation of the applicability of the concept of intersectionality is coloured by academic, activist and political interests. Antiracist scholarship (Scheurich 2002), in fact, puts forward a case for minimising focus on the intersection and heterogeneity of categories on the grounds that an analysis which is sensitive to sociocultural complexity may have political repercussions, for instance in the context of rights and identity politics.

In political science, economic and social science contexts, however, the term is discussed as a challenge to white hegemonic feminism and thus applied as a counterpoint to colonial tendencies in gender research (de los Reyes and Mulinari 2005). Contrary to this, though, it is the lack of challenge to white hegemonic feminism which has bothered younger Swedish feminists in connection with the concept. They write of intersectionality as a potential cover-up manoeuvre for white normativity (Carbin and Tornhill 2005), a means to carry on 'business as usual.' According to their understanding of the concept, the category of woman remains intact as a universal, simply varnished with a little (racialised) ethnicity.

Obviously a variety of academic ambitions and interests play their part in assessing the potential of the concept. In law, for instance, there is the need to stabilise categories in order to assign rights and responsibilities. Consequently the clearest understanding of intersectionality as reciprocal systems of oppression and converging axes of sexism, racism and social marginalisation is to be found in juridical and political science texts on questions of conflict.

In our own field, psychology, a number of researchers work with experienced and lived human subjectivities and sociocultural processes of formation. This kind of work focuses on, for example, the flexibility and variability of identities and categories, as was the case in our research on gender and management. Our ambition to investigate processes associated with meaning making among the employees of a company rather than to investigate the company's structural conditions marks our position as situated within a particular academic discipline. In this case it meant a social-psychological concern with the ways in which people understand and think, their processes of becoming and producing 'themselves' and their 'worlds' whilst being formed and disciplined by these 'worlds.' In other words, this is an example of an academic interest in, and attention to, the ways in which people's meanings and discursive experiences emerge in interaction with each other and in interplay with (interacting) physical and material frames and phenomena (Barad 2007; Højgaard and Søndergaard, forthcoming).

Conditions and processes of this type form some of the premises for individual opportunities in an organisation. Thus it is important to investigate how the local nuancing of categories in specific companies enhances or hampers opportunities and limitations. The sociocultural categories set important premises for a range of understandings and interpretations, which are used by staff and managers in their efforts to make sense and to manoeuvre in an organisation. The sociocultural categories are re/created, or revised, through the reflections and interpretations encountered by individuals in the organisation. Individuals carry signs, marks on the body which are eagerly read by others (and by themselves) in the ongoing effort to reiterate and negotiate social order with its promises of positional predictability and legitimacy in relation to behaviour, desires, belongings, ideas, fears and whatever other kinds of 'phenomena' people invite in their efforts to understand subjective, material and social becoming. These interpretations are a crucial part of the expectations and consequences of organisational positioning. They set the premises for what is regarded as natural for whom, and for what is regarded as unnatural or incredible, and by whom. These are the patterns of appropriate and inappropriate becoming, doing and being (Butler 1990, 1993; Søndergaard 1996; Davies 2000; Søndergaard 2002, 2005a).

When one is concerned with people's experiences, the versions of the intersectionality concept that come from, for instance, the field of law may stand in the way of a more complexity-sensitive analysis of how social categories function as mechanisms within organisation, how they work to reproduce social order and legitimise and demarcate the subjective horizons of experience. Furthermore, the 'classical' version of the concept may nurture a tendency for deterministic thinking and even cause the researcher to overlook exceptions and ruptures in the social order under scrutiny; these exceptions and ruptures may perhaps be precisely the kind of elements that might be interesting to include in the investigation, if one takes up a subject-oriented perspective.

In this sense it is necessary to bear in mind the variations amongst academic disciplines or fields when assessing and possibly exploring the potential of the following suggestions for an adjustment of the concept of intersectionality. In this chapter the adjustment is related to social psychology, and it should not be seen as an argument for the predominance of one particular specification of the concept; this would amount to a theory imperialism which neglects the fruitfulness of other conceptualisations. We do not subscribe to the one-size-fits-all paradigm (Oudshoorn 1996) but prefer concepts to be developed with a sensitivity closely related to the specific field of enquiry. In line with Donna Haraway's (1991) idea of partial and situated knowledges, our claim is that it is far more productive to make use of different conceptual specifications for varying kinds of difference, social mechanisms and ways of relating. On the other hand the partial perspective should not lead to the idea that all conceptions of intersectionality are basically equally valuable. This would amount to multilateral theory imperialism combined with a kind of amnesia at the expense of professional humility. Theoretical concepts can neither comprehend the whole world, nor should they. Researchers should desist from assuming an either/or approach to intersectionality analyses and instead reveal their aims, ambitions and following reflections on the definition of how they are applying the concept.

The adjustments suggested in this chapter may help to inspire more explicit formulations of the concept in other disciplines. They may contribute to more specific transdisciplinary reflections and should in any case encourage researchers to maintain their own academic standards.

A METAPHOR FOR INTERACTING FORCES

The literature concerning intersectionality makes use of a wealth of different metaphors to make explicit the potential of the concept. Metaphors present sensory imagery which can intensify the analytical gaze, thus contributing to analytical insights. Metaphors can support an analytical system, which allows one to follow the connections and building blocks in a figure, thereby turning the analysis in unexpected directions. At the same time, tracing the logic of the metaphor can enable an analytical estrangement of the gaze on the empirical material. 'Estrangement' means that you make the familiar appear unfamiliar (Bryld and Lykke 2000, 50–71). The point we want to make here is that metaphors can act as agents of estrangement, i.e., when used reflexively, they can help us to elicit new and different associations and connotations, and thus to test the established pictures of a given field and the questions which can be put to it.

The question is: which metaphors may be productive in capturing the character of the interacting forces and of their processes, their repetitions, breaches and upheavals—and in what ways? Is it conceivable that varying types of interacting forces require varying types of metaphors to support varying definitions and applications of the same concept? Crenshaw uses the metaphor of a crossroads to illustrate how particular categories can be envisaged as main and secondary roads which converge and interact (Crenshaw and Harris 2010, 4). At the same time, the concept of intersectionality has been rejected on the grounds of precisely this metaphor. 'Crossroads' may indicate two roads which meet for a split second only to part and never meet again. Some researchers regard this as a misleading image which suggests that the roads were constructed without any reference to each other (Carbin and Tornhill 2005; Yuval-Davies 2006).

Viewing the chains of association formed around the metaphor of the crossroads in various articles, it is striking that the auxiliary concepts apparently elicited by the metaphor are structurally informed: axes, lines, addition, subtraction, systems and structures. Seen through the lens of a social psychology preoccupied with change and action, this metaphor becomes problematic, dealing as it does with an intersection in a system of coordinates, with an encounter, a central point, a brief contact, possibly a collision. The crossroads metaphor provides an interpretive frame which offers the chance to observe the intersection of two, three or even more roads, but it does not hint at what takes place at the intersections, what is moving, emerging, disappearing or perhaps even changed by the encounter. In this metaphorical view, power disappears to a more subtle level, which certainly could not have been the intention: how can the image of the crossroads produce understandings of the process of becoming *main road* and *secondary road*, of majoritising and minoritising, which with a change of terminology provides the potential for change and subversion? Using the image of a crossroads makes it more difficult to conduct an analysis of change, subversion and life as it is lived.

Another question that has occupied intersectionality researchers discussing the crossroad metaphor's rather one-dimensional character has to do with the obligation to reflect as many categories as possible and to avoid giving priority to any one in particular. The question is: is it analytically productive to remove categories, on the pretext that they are less significant? Our somewhat provocative answer is yes; in empirical contexts there actually are situations where a sociocultural category like gender is surpassed by other categories, for example ethnicity. 'Surpassed' does not mean that 'gender' doesn't mean anything at all, but it means that other categories might be more pivotal. A concept used to capture fluid forms and power asymmetries should be able to grasp what is incomplete, vague and confused. It will therefore be necessary to develop a concept which is prepared to grasp such phenomena and situations, but which does not start the analysis by hailing a model which fixes the number and character of categories in an effort to obey particular theoretical obligations. Analyses have to reflect the empirical setting, and concepts must be sensitive enough to help researchers do so. The concept should be analytically flexible and help us to see the unexpected, and potentially, question the expected. On the other hand, one must also balance one's eagerness for complexity with the research capacity to handle an undreamt-of number of intersections, thereby maintaining that one's own professional limitations are not the entire expression of a given field or case but only *one* way of framing it.

What if categories and hierarchies were thought of as in motion, as mobile and emerging, only momentarily marked and 'pure,' but as a rule diffused and nonpurified? What kind of metaphor would it require to capture that kind of phenomena? Is a crossroads the best way of understanding the intersecting processes under analysis? What happens if we change the metaphoric repertoire and move from images of lines and axes to images of space, light, sound and motion? Is the metaphor most productive when it indicates auditory, visual, tactile or physical aspects? Should it appeal to the sense of hearing, sight, taste or scent?

The idea here is not to find an ingenious metaphor which can express the essence of intersectionality but to encourage attempts to evolve different types of metaphors and test their effects in capturing a given field and its mechanisms, thereby taking note of how they work.

MAJORITY EXCLUSION

When working to develop the concept of intersectionality it is important to consider power and dominance, majority and minority positionings. However, we may not always think about these aspects in quite the way that is presumed in more standpoint-inspired approaches to intersectionality. Most intersectionality researchers agree that intersectionality is an analytical concept used to grasp the complex, ambivalent and relational nature of identities and sociocultural categories, and that the concept contributes to an understanding of how social and material forces organise sociocultural diversity by means of what we, the authors of this chapter, would term minoritising and majoritising movements, or what some researchers would call oppression, dominance and underprivilege.

The strength of the classical version of the concept of intersectionality (Crenshaw 1991; Collins 1998) is to be found in its underlining of the point that the many different systems of oppression cannot be understood separately but must be seen as interwoven and reciprocally interacting and interlocking systems which do not simply marginalise minorities but also marginalise subcategories among these minorities, such as black and economically underprivileged women in relation to black men. With this particular kind of power-critical concept it becomes possible to create an identity politics in which the focus of research as well as the political concern and loyalty are reserved for the minoritised. In so doing, however, the classic power-critical intersectionality approach may establish a minority perspective, which tends to reduce reflexivity in relation to the majority and to silence how the majority is constituted (Staunæs 2003). This is where the classical concept of intersectionality, with its focus on power as primarily oppressive and with its relatively stable sociocultural categories, may need an adjustment to enable a productive analytic encounter with the kind of sociopsychological research that is committed to complexity.

INTERSECTION AS A DISORDERLY SPACE OF EMERGENCE

If we had applied the classic intersectionality approach in our research project on gender and management, we would have retained the focus on the category of woman and on this group's difficult conditions, leaving largely unnoticed what was going on among the men above the glass ceiling. Michel Foucault's concept of power involves an understanding of the emergence of the subject as a two-sided process, a process of subject-formation (Foucault 1980, 1983). Discursive power disciplines the subject, imposing upon it certain conditions of formation. At the same time it is precisely through this process of subjection that the subject emerges as agentic and capable of negotiating the conditions of formation. Through this understanding of subjectivity and agency the dynamic and never finalised nature of these categories becomes prominent. By conceptualising power as not merely a question of oppression, but of multiple and fluid positionings with minoritising as well as majoritising effects, it becomes obvious that power creates categories and that categories exist when power 'does' them (West and Zimmerman 1987). Analytically, categories must be understood as having perforated lines for boundaries. Because sociocultural categories are constantly open to be challenged, activated or closed down, it seems most productive to grasp the character of their boundaries as permeable. The point is to underline the simultaneous emergence and movement of the sociocultural categories as an effect of the productive exercise of power. It requires concrete empirical investigation to decide on which categories to focus analytically in any specific context.

With a different linguistic slant, and relying on a less structuralist but rather more Foucauldian approach to power and the conditions of emergence, it becomes possible to use the term *intersection* without thinking of crossroads but with focus on a place or space between sections (inter sections) which is productive of sociocultural phenomena. Twisting the concept in this way, one can inquire whether intersection takes place between entities that are already fixed? Or is it the place that creates the entities? Or is it a both/and, i.e., a space for interaction where things that already exist (for a while) meet and (for a while) become something that does not yet exist? One can think of intersectionality as a concept which should grasp what is going on in and between sections: in and between nonlinear, confused and fugitive connections, and in and between places which may be slumbering but are never static, where entities emerge and where power and hierarchies are created, cited and overturned. With such a lens one could focus, on the one hand, on how something already given 'intersects' and becomes transformed. On the other hand one could follow an emerging process and, reapplying Candace West and Don Zimmerman's (1987) 'doing gender,' trace how it is done.[2]

From this perspective, intersection can be understood as a productive place for the emergence of (not only oppression but also) new possibilities of identity and agency, an ambivalent place also endowed with emancipatory potential, a place for the development of strategies (not only of subjugation but also) of resistance and transgressive subject positions (May and Ferri 2002). From a social-psychological perspective this means that intersections can both be places for the realisation of awkward subject positions whose effects are reluctance, conflict, awkwardness, unpleasantness and misunderstanding (Wetherell 1998; Staunæs 2003), but also places which appear to result in more comfortable subject positions which are amenable, easy, unproblematic and liveable (Staunæs 2005).

INTERSECTIONS WHICH PRIVILEGE CORPORATE MASCULINITY

The Foucauldian 'take' on power, coupled with the concept of intersectionality understood as a disorderly space of emergence, can result in an approach which includes the majority in the analyses in ways that take both men and women into account, thus seeing men as gendered individuals. Those in dominant and/or majoritised positions are also disciplined, in the Foucauldian sense. Where classic thinking on power tends to presume to know who takes the dominated position and who becomes the minoritised Other, our conceptual adjustment permits an ongoing review of the minoritising and majoritising processes and investigates who is—at that specific point in time and space—cast as the Other, and how, in specific situations, the dominant may momentarily become the dominated Other.

In our project on X-Company, therefore, we conducted an analysis of majoritising processes in the organisation, i.e., of the prevailing normativities; the figures and subjects which signalled these normativities; and the specific subjects who inhabited powerful, generally and implicitly appropriate positions. We were particularly interested in the ways in which all these processes, positionings and signals were constituted by different reciprocally interacting hierarchical systems of categories. The point of this analytical strategy was to investigate the constitution of dominance; in focussing on dominance one still keeps an analytic eye on those positioned as Other or as minority, those occupying the more troubled positionings. The point is to investigate the contingent nature of dominance. Those who are dominating can become dominated and vice versa, depending on how they are constructed in their—in principle temporary but in practice inert—constituent form. This implies a necessity to include such analytical questions as: when, and in which contexts, do which men no longer belong to the dominating majority? When, and in which contexts, do which women no longer belong to the dominated minority?

In intersectionality analyses class is often used as a perspective to clarify the systems of oppression which have become the lot of the working/underclass (Skeggs 2004; de los Reyes and Mulinari 2005). When we do intersectionality analysis, however, it is important to remember that the category of class does not only deal with those marked as Other. Class, like gender, is indeed, but not only, a matter of the underprivileged. Class is also a category of differentiation and disciplining which must be taken into account when investigating the higher echelons of business. As Pierre Bourdieu and other theorists of class have demonstrated, the higher echelons have emerged by means of significant class-based networks, performativity and experiences of physical presence like clothing and other items of self-presentation, particular kinds of education at particular schools and colleges, sport, sexual preference and marital constellations. Thus the higher echelons have also been disciplined in particular ways which seem to pay premiums in the corridors of power. The same goes for racialised ethnicity: these categories are not reserved for the ethnically racialised minorities but work precisely to privilege and discipline the majority, equally ethnically racialised, no matter how taken for granted and invisible this racialisation may have become (Frankenberg 1993; Afsar and Maynard 1994; Staunæs 2003).

Scrutinising the interacting gendered, ethnically racialised and class privileges in the project on gender and top management we reached the conclusion that the implicit normativity reigning above the glass ceiling is much narrower and more specific than we had at first assumed. The relation between gender and top management was not merely a matter of different career access for men and women, but of the continual constitution of an obligatory management normativity interwoven with a specific form of masculinity, which was itself saturated by specific class and ethnic-racial references (Collinson and Hearn 1996).

Corporate masculinity—a form of masculinity orientated towards organisations and businesses (or, as a corresponding phenomenon is called by Connell, 'globalised business-oriented masculinity' (Connell 1998; Connell and Wood 2005)—is thus a phenomenon within business culture which is reproduced daily. It is supported by a number of reciprocally interacting forces sedimented as heterosexual, white and upper-middle class, and in relationally generated processes like male bonding and heterosexualisation. Other forms of masculinity appear to be subordinated to corporate masculinity, with the effect that not only women are subordinated but also other ethnically racialised masculinities (Staunæs and Søndergaard 2006, 2008a, 2008b). On the other hand, corporate masculinity is also an expression of precarious dominance as its continued existence requires daily repetition and acknowledgement. Perhaps it is through attention to precisely this vulnerability, this possibility of rupture and to the relative subordination of other ethnically racialised masculinities, that the road to a potential change in the gendered order in organisations may be glimpsed. If indeed that is what is desired.

INTERSECTIONS BETWEEN COMPONENTS YET UNKNOWN

The North American usage of the concept of intersectionality in the tradition of critical feminist race theory deals with familiar and comparatively well-defined classical background categories such as gender, class, race and ethnicity. The analyses of intersectionality which are inspired by poststructuralist social psychology, however, seem to clear the way for more complicated analyses of the interplay among not merely the classic categories but also other modes of relating.

In the analysis of X-Company it was possible to work with the problem of how less considered categories such as 'manager,' 'administrative director,' 'human resource manager,'[3] 'high jumper,' 'comet,' 'consultant' and 'equal opportunities coordinator' interacted with the subjectivities alive in the company. It was similarly possible to theorise the intertwining of the discursive normativities associated with these categories. This meant paying attention to the organisation's narrative presentation of 'the good leader' and to normative imperatives concerning 'good leadership.'

X-Company was in the midst of a change of managerial style, moving from the previous bureaucratic (ordering and controlling) leader to the modern, involving and coaching, type. The 'old' managerial form lived as a phenomenon with mainly masculine connotations. The new coaching managerial style did not yet appear to have taken on completely stable gender connotations but still had feminine connotations and white, middle-class nuancing. The appointment of women to managerial positions was largely justified by the assumption that women would be able to contribute something special and different from the men—something which would only be desirable, however, in appropriately controlled doses. According to meaning making in the company, the proper kind of femininity should not involve too much female vivacity, emotional appeal or fluttering of eyelashes (Staunæs and Søndergaard 2008b). The special quality which women could be supposed to offer might, for instance, be a professional form of emotional orientation to help the new coaching managerial style find its feet in understanding the emotions of others and mastering the dialogic basis for forming and directing other people.

However, unrest in the X-Company's culture and top talent worked to pull the new managerial form towards a masculine tone. This unrest can be perceived in some of the (also active) ideas which were formulated concerning how this new and partially femininely connoted form of leadership could best be controlled, rationed and limited by the leaders who were assumed to have a natural access to tough forms of action—i.e., men. Where these discursive practices were active, managers in female bodies who wished to profile themselves as modern coaching managerial types bore the burden of convincingly demonstrating their own capacity to control a presumed 'softness.' Alternatively, they could seize the opportunity to profile themselves as the more old-fashioned 'hard' managerial type as a stage in legitimising themselves as management material.

LIMITATIONS AND DIFFICULTIES

The revisions we have suggested to the concept of intersectionality reject any easy identification of the nature of a relevant relation and a relevant 'section' of what we should look for and which interacting forces and movements we should analyse. It is likely that there may be other or more categories and other or more components active in the field under analysis than those we originally supposed. We may need to follow up on other mechanisms of differentiation and other power structures than were possible to imagine in advance. Intersectionality in its theoretical and academic turn is thus not simply a term denoting the transgressing of categories but rather a matter of transgressive research guided by a transgressive methodology. That sort of thing can stir up a lot of noise in the researcher's workshop. Some people find that kind of noise productive whilst others will probably prefer to surpass the noise and reserve the concept for familiar social distinctions and systems of oppression. The angle on the concept, which presents intersections as disorderly spaces for emergence, is (at present) a fairly useful analytical tool for sociopsychological research into people's meaning-making processes and in connection with the social-constructionist preoccupation with noticing the small cracks from which change can emerge. However, levelling academic and objective differences to import this conceptualisation without contest into all other disciplines and fields would be to risk a short circuit.

What is awkward about working with a concept like intersectionality in the way that we have done is that in many ways the concept is restricted to a very clear paradigm, that of identity politics, and to academic areas like law and political science. Is it possible to challenge the power of definition? Obviously, a number of unwanted, historically founded connotations might be drawn into the reading of our analysis, meanings we would prefer to avoid and which confuse our message. There may, for example, be associations of dogmatic group solidarity, which get in the way of ambitions to trace the movements of minoritising processes and not stop with the discovery of interacting mechanisms which clarify the marginalisation of just one group. The danger of unilateral interests can be promoted here. On the other hand, it may be necessary to be attentive to categories, and even guard them to some extent in a more mobile form than is found in identity politics, in a world which over and over again is not only seen to have gendered, ethnic, racial, religious, sexual and geopolitical divisions and hierarchies on its agenda but also to have these divisions on the agenda in constantly new versions and camouflaged transformations, sometimes with minoritising and majoritising effects. However, as the shifting of categories accelerates, perhaps there *is* a need for a more sensitive strategy of analysis of categorisation.

NOTES

1. We collected documents, brochures and folders related to personnel policies, recruiting, tests and so on and concurrently made a number of observations from the company's intranet and notice boards, attended different types of meetings and were introduced to different types of evaluating and testing instruments.
2. Similar ideas can be found in McCall (2003), who in her discussion of the methodological challenges associated with the concept of intersectionality speaks of intracategorical complexity, and in Lykke (2005) who uses Karen Barad (2003) to advance the concept of intersectionality.
3. Human resource management signifies the strategic attempts to optimise human resources using goal-oriented educational planning and the development of the organisational structure, work environment, tasks, incentives, training courses and so on.

REFERENCES

Afsar, H., and M. Maynard, eds. 1994. *The Dynamics of 'Race' and Gender—Some Feminist Interventions*. London: Taylor and Francis.

Barad, K. 2003. Posthumanist Performativity: Toward an Understanding of How Matter Comes to Matter. *Signs: Journal of Women in Culture and Society* 28 (3): 801–31.

———. 2007. *Meeting the Universe Halfway: Quantum Physics and the Entanglement of Matter and Meaning.* Durham, NC: Duke University Press.

Brah, A., and A. Phoenix. 2004. Ain't I a Woman: Intersectionality Revisited. *Journal of International Women Studies* 5 (3): 75–86.

Braidotti, R. 1994. *Nomadic Subjects: Embodiment and Sexual Difference in Contemporary Feminist Theory.* New York: Columbia University Press

Bruner, J. 1990. *Acts of Meaning.* Cambridge, MA: Harvard University Press.

Bryld, M., and N. Lykke. 2000. *Cosmodolphins: Feminist Cultural Studies of Technology, Animals and the Sacred.* London: Zed Books.

Butler, J. 1990. *Gender Trouble: Feminism and the Subversion of Identity.* London: Routledge.

———. 1993. *Bodies That Matter: On the Discursive Limits of 'Sex.'* London: Routledge.

Carbin, M., and S. Tornhill. 2005. Intersektionalitet'ett oanvändbart begrepp? *Kvinnovetenskaplig tidskrift* 24 (3): 111–14.

Collins, P. H. 1998. It Is All in the Family: Intersections of Gender, Race, and Nation. *Hypatia* 13 (3): 62–82.

Collinson, D. L., and J. Hearn. 1996. Breaking the Silence: On Men, Masculinities and Managements. In *Men as Masculinities, Masculinities as Men: Critical Perspectives on Men, Masculinities and Management,* ed. D. L. Collison and J. Hearn, 1–24. London: Sage.

Connell, R. W. 1998. Masculinities and Globalisation. *Men and Masculinities* 1 (1): 3–23.

Connell, R. W., and J. Wood. 2005. Globalization and Business Masculinities. *Men and Masculinities* 7 (4): 347–64.

Crenshaw, K. 1991. Mapping the Margins: Intersectionality, Identity Politics, and Violence against Women of Color. *Stanford Law Review* 43 (6): 1241–79.

Crenshaw, K. W., and L. C. Harris. 2010. *A Primer on Intersectionality Booklet.* African American Policy Forum, Vassar College, Columbia Law School, Poughkeepsie, NY. http://aapf.org/tool_to_speak_out/intersectionality-primer/ (accessed June 18, 2010).

Davies, B. 2000. *A Body of Writing.* Oxford: AltaMira Press.

de los Reyes, P., and D. Mulinari. 2005. *Intersektionalitet: Kritiska refleksioner över (o)jämlikhetens landskab.* Malmø: Liber.

Foucault, M. 1980. *Power/Knowledge: Selected interviews and Other Writings 1972–1977,* ed. C. Gordon, trans. C. Gordon, L. Marshall, J. Mepham and K. Soper. New York: Pantheon.

———. 1983. The Subject and Power. In *The Foucault Reader,* ed. H. Dreyfus and P. Rabinow, 208–26. Harmondsworth: Penguin.

Frankenberg, R. 1993. *White Women—Race matters: The Social Construction of Whiteness.* Minneapolis: University of Minnesota Press.

Haraway, D. 1991. Situated Knowledges: The Science Question in Feminism and the Privilege of Partial Perspective. In *Simians, Cyborgs, and Women: The Reinvention of Nature,* 183–202. London: Free Association Books.

———. 1992. The Promises of Monsters: A Regenerative Politics for inappropriate/d Others. In *Cultural Studies,* ed. L. Grossberg, C. Nelson and P. Treichler, 295–337. New York and London: Routledge.

Højgaard, L., and D. M. Søndergaard. (Forthcoming). Theorizing the Complexities of Discursive and Material Subjectivity: Agential Realism and Poststructural Analyses. *Theory and Psychology.*

Knapp, G. A. 2005. Race, Class, Gender: Reclaiming Baggage in Fast Travelling Theories. *European Journal of Women's Studies* 12 (12): 249–65.

Kofoed, J. 2008. Appropriate Pupilness: Social Categories Intersecting in School. *Childhood* 15 (3): 415–30.

Lykke, N. 2003. Intersektionalitet'ett användbart begrepp för genusforskningen. *Kvinnovetenskaplig tidskrift* 23 (1): 47–57.

———. 2005. Nya perspektiv på intersektionalitet. *Kvinnovetenskaplig tidskrift* 26 (2–3): 7–17.

———. 2010. *Feminist Studies, A Guide to Intersectional Theory, Methodology and Writing*. New York: Routledge.

May, V. M., and B. A. Ferri. 2002. I'm a Wheelchair Girl Now: Abjection, Intersectionality, and Subjectivity in Atom Egoyan's *The Sweet Hereafter*. *Women's Quarterly* 30 (1/2): 131–50.

McCall, L. 2003. Managing the Complexity of Intersectionality. *Signs: Journal of Women in Culture and Society* 30 (3): 1771–1800.

Minh-ha, T. T. 1989. *Woman, Native, Other. Writing Postcoloniality and Feminism*. Bloomington: Indiana University Press.

Moser, I. 2003. *Road Traffic Accidents: The Ordering of Subjects, Bodies and Disability*. Oslo: Unipub Forlag.

Mørck, Y. 1998. *Bindestregsdanskere–fortællinger om køn, generationer og etnicitet*. Frederiksberg: Forlaget Sociologi.

Oudshoorn, N. 1996. The Decline of the One-Size-Fits-All Paradigm, or How Reproductive Scientists Try to Cope with Postmodernity. In *Between Monsters, Goddesses, and Cyborgs. Feminist Confrontations with Science, Medicine, and Cyberspace*, ed. N. Lykke and R. Braidotti, 153–72. London: Zed Books.

Scheurich, J. J. 2002. *Antiracist Scholarship—an Advocacy*. New York: State University of New York Press.

Skeggs, B. 2004. *Class, Self, Culture*. London: Routledge.

Staunæs, D. 2003. Where Have All the Subjects Gone? Bringing Together the Concepts of Intersectionality and Subjectification. *NORA—Nordic Journal of Women Studies* 11 (2): 101–10.

———. 2005. From Culturally Avant-garde to Sexually Promiscuous: Troubling Subjectivities and Intersections in the Transition from Childhood into Youth. *Feminism and Psychology* 15 (2): 149–67.

Staunæs, D., and D. M. Søndergaard. 2006. Corporate Fictions. *Tidsskrift for Kjønnsforskning* (3): 69–87.

———. 2008a. Who Is Ready for the Results? Reflections on the Multivoicedness of Useful Research. *Journal of Qualitative Studies in Education* 21 (1): 3–18.

———. 2008b. Management and Gender Diversity: Intertwining Categories and Paradoxes. In *Critical Studies of Gender Equalities*, ed. E. Magnusson, M. Rönnblom and H. Silius, 135–71. Halmstad: Makadam Förlag.

Søndergaard, D. M. 1996. *Tegnet på kroppen. Køn: Koder og konstruktioner i akademia*. København: Museum Tusculanum.

———. 2002. Poststructuralist Approaches to Empirical Analysis. *International Journal of Qualitative Studies in Education* 15 (2): 187–204.

———. 2005a. Making Sense of Gender, Age, Power and Disciplinary Position: Intersecting Discourses in the Academy. *Feminism and Psychology* 15 (2): 189–208.

———. 2005b. Academic Desire Trajectories: Retooling the Concepts of Subject, Desire and Biography. *European Journal of Women's Studies* 12 (3): 297–313.

Yuval-Davis, N. 1997. *Gender and Nation*. London: Sage Publications.

———. 2006. Intersectionality and Feminist Politics. *European Journal of Women's Studies* 13 (3): 193–209.

West, C., and D. Zimmerman. 1987. Doing Gender. *Gender and Society* 1 (2): 125–51.

Wetherell, M. 1998. Positioning and Interpretative Repertoires: Conversation Analysis and Poststructuralism in Dialogue. *Disourse and Society* 9 (3): 387–412.

4 What to Make of Identity and Experience in Twenty-first-century Feminist Research

Allaine Cerwonka

Developing research insights from the study of people's 'experience' has come to serve as a kind of foundational epistemology for women's and gender studies. It is the cornerstone of a number of popular feminist research approaches, including oral life history, ethnography, standpoint theory, critical race and postcolonial research, to name but a few. Each of these approaches generates knowledge claims from people's accounts of their own experiences and understandings of the world in which they live. The use of experience within feminist research has its roots in the mid-twentieth-century tradition of consciousness raising as well as feminist critiques of positivism. As such, drawing on people's experience (especially those of marginalised groups) is a methodological approach which feminist researchers rarely are called on to defend by other feminist researchers. It has a certain moral status that would be worth discussing if space permitted.

In this chapter, I focus on my concerns about the use of experience for feminist knowledge claims. Broadly speaking, my concerns follow from a sense that the methodological use of experience often relies upon and reinstates a notion of identity that reproduces humanist notions of the subject and contains assumptions about agency, resistance and the liberatory potential of research. These latent humanist ideas in the research design are somewhat perplexing given that women's and gender studies students, as well as many seasoned academics, draw on poststructural theories about power. It is standard for women's and gender studies research to begin from the idea of (gender) identity as socially constructed. After all, Judith Butler is one of the most-cited feminist scholars in Europe. However, when it comes to methodology, many researchers produce a research design that actually stands in tension with the theories they find most convincing in other contexts. It is this tension that I wish to interrogate in this chapter. To this end, I will review the logic underpinning the use of experience for knowledge claims.

Although the approaches I mentioned earlier do differ in various ways, their uses of experience share certain compatible ideas about the political value of building knowledge claims from people's lived reality and the value of experience (standpoint) to provide alternative explanations of power relations, ideology and dominant discourses. Standpoint theorists have offered the most elaborate discussion of the benefit of experience for feminist research. Therefore, I draw a significant amount from their writings in my review of key ideas about the use of experience in research. However, I also draw from others in my analysis, including anthropologists and critical-race theorists in order to explicate the goals which animate much feminist social science research. My analysis raises certain questions about the latent assumptions embedded in such methodological approaches, paying particular attention to the (liberal) assumptions about identity and power such research reproduces. Finally, I suggest alternative ways for feminist researchers to conceptualise identity and experience in their methodological practices, ways which are more consistent with the theoretical ideas informing much European feminist research today about subjectivity as socially constructed (see also Cerwonka and Malkki 2007).

RENOUNCING 'POWER' IN FEMINIST RESEARCH

Many feminist researchers who conduct research among marginalised communities or groups see their role, in large part, as giving voice to members of the community. They also see their work as potentially exposing how hegemonic structures have historically and/or currently disempowered some groups. In so doing, they seek to avoid the perceived elitism and universalism of much theory and positivist research and to avoid the imperialism of what some fear to be an act of speaking for others. Dorothy Smith,[1] one of the key architects of feminist standpoint theory, launches a critique of mainstream sociological methods that echoes the larger feminist attack on positivism:

> The constitution of an objective sociology is an authoritative version of how things are done from a position and as part of the practices of ruling in our kind of society. It has depended upon class and sex bases which make it possible for sociology to evade the problem that our kind of society is known and experienced rather differently from different positions within it. (Smith 2004, 30)

Given the way certain groups (women, people of colour, homosexuals, the poor and so on) have been ignored or otherwise denied voice in scholarly research, it is not surprising that one of the first steps of feminist research was to assert the situated experience of members of these and other groups. Andrea Pető and Berteke Waaldijk (see chapter 5, this volume) discuss the disciplinary factors that can prompt feminist scholars to create nostalgic descriptions of gender solidarity and fail to complicate unflattering complicities between women and nonprogressive forces (e.g., imperialism, racism and so on) that the researcher might discover in women's experiences historically. Additionally, the consciousness raising of the 1960s and 1970s promoted a kind of epistemology that continues to influence feminist scholarship today. Consciousness raising was based on the idea that identifying and comparing lived experience facilitated new ways to understand one's own life, analyse social structures and identify collective political interests. The insights that developed within and from consciousness-raising groups—of speaking to others about one's own emotional and material experience—were treated as an unproblematic form of knowledge about the social conditions of women's lives. It operated on the assumption that women's 'reality' provided a truth about the functioning and costs of patriarchy. In other words, such sessions provided an alternative framework for interpreting society for both the group members and for the larger political movement.

Particularly within women's studies and ethnic studies, experience offers a kind of truth that allows insight into the terms of oppression. As such, it is treated by many as an unproblematic expression of truth (identity, political perspective, history) that exists intact, just beyond power's reach and available to the scholar who wants to excavate forgotten or silenced histories. Anthropologist Ruth Behar, for instance, whose ethnographic work and coedited volume *Women Writing Culture* (Behar and Gordon 1995) has inspired many feminist researchers, articulates an understanding of the value of experience for knowledge production. She describes the task of empirical work (ethnography in particular) as bearing witness and providing testimony of the experience (pain and hardship in most cases) of others. In *The Vulnerable Observer*, she writes:

> In our time, in this special period, the periodo especial, where bearing testimony and witnessing offer the only, and still slippery, hold on truth, every form of representation must pay homage to its roots in the ethnographic experience of talking, listening, transcribing, translating, and interpreting. . . . Anthropology, to give my Aunt Rebeca a grandiose reply, is the most fascinating, bizarre, disturbing, and necessary form of witnessing left to us at the end of the twentieth century. (Behar 1996, 162–63, 165)

Behar's approach reflects a larger trend within feminist research that takes experience and identity of disempowered groups as a fairly transparent (albeit slippery) truth about identity, history and various kinds of subaltern perspectives which have been omitted from dominant theories and histories. Sociologist Dorothy Smith describes in more detail the epistemological value of understanding the experience of others who occupy a location in the social landscape that differs from the dominant group. The 'standpoint' of different groups introduces the researcher to analytical frameworks that s/he could not necessarily know from the researcher's own social location. In her seminal article on standpoint theory, Smith writes:

Riding a train not long ago in Ontario I saw a family of Indians, woman, man, and three children standing together on a spur above a river watching the train go by. There was (for me) that moment—the train, those five people seen on the other side of the glass. I saw first that I could tell this incident as it was, but that telling as a description built in my position and my interpretations. I have called them a family; I have said they were watching the train. My understanding has already subsumed theirs. Everything may have been quite other for them. My description is privileged to stand as what actually happened, because theirs is not heard in the contexts in which I may speak. If we begin from the world as we actually experience it, it is at least possible to see that we are located and that what we know of the other is conditional upon that location as part of a relation comprehending the other's location also. There are and must be different experiences of the world and different bases of experience. We must not do away with them by taking advantage of our privileged speaking to construct a sociological version which is then imposed upon them as their reality. We may not rewrite the other's world or impose upon it a conceptual framework which extracts from it what fits with ours. Our conceptual procedures should be capable of explicating and analyzing the properties of their experienced world rather than administrating it. Their reality, their varieties of experience must be an unconditional datum. (Smith 2004, 30)

In bell hooks' discussion of the value of her own and other's marginalised standpoints, we see that being 'located in the margin' can be personally empowering for oppressed people and politically important for the transformation of society more broadly:

I am located in the margin. I make a definite distinction between that marginality which is imposed by oppressive structures and that marginality one chooses as a site of resistance—as a location of radical openness and possibility. This site of resistance is continually formed in that segregated culture of opposition that is our critical response to domination. We come to this space through suffering and pain, through struggle. We know struggle to be that which pleasures, delights, and fulfills desire. We are transformed, individually, collectively, as we make radical collective space which affirms and sustains our subjectivity, which gives us a new location from which to articulate our sense of the world. (hooks 2004, 159)

Thus, for its advocates, the method of producing scholarly knowledge from people's experiences holds a liberatory potential in a number of ways.

Additionally, one evident priority for scholars who methodologically employ experience and standpoint is a concern to avoid doing violence to another (especially marginalised group) by speaking *for* them. Thus, it is perhaps not surprising that feminist researchers would want to avoid analysing, deconstructing, explaining the terms of the experience of marginalised people. While indeed there is a fair amount of feminist research that takes as its aim to present simply the experience and views of others without 'imposing' theoretical or significant analytical framing on the material, feminist standpoint theorists offer an epistemological rationale for knowledge gained about social structures and power from people's accounts of their own situation. Importantly, Smith clarifies that experience cannot be reduced to 'perspective':

> Let me make it clear that when I speak of 'experience' I do not use the term as a synonym for 'perspective.' Nor in proposing a sociology grounded in the sociologist's actual experience, am I recommending the self-indulgence of inner exploration or any other enterprise with the self as the sole focus and object. (Smith 2004, 29)

She also identifies the goal of research stating, "The aim of an alternative sociology would be to develop precisely that capacity from that beginning so that it might be a means to anyone of understanding how the world comes about for her and how it is organized so that it happens to her as it does in her experience" (Smith 2004, 32).

Although Smith rejects the idea of experience as perspective, it is difficult to see how positionality is different from perspective. Nancy Hartsock offers further arguments that are consistent with and productively extend Smith's explanation. Hartsock argues that we need to understand how experience is created out of material circumstances. She relates experience to social structure, indicating the indebtedness of standpoint theory to Marxism, writing:

> I hold that the powerful vision of both the perverseness and reality of class domination made possible by Marx's adoption of the standpoint of the proletariat suggests that a specifically feminist standpoint would allow for a much more profound critique of phallocentric ideologies and institutions that has yet to be achieved. . . . But rather than beginning with men's labor, I will focus on women's life activity and on the institutions which structure that activity in order to raise the question of whether this activity can form the ground for a distinctive standpoint, that is, to determine whether it meets the requirements for a feminist standpoint. (Hartsock 2004, 40)[2]

Both Smith and Hartsock distance themselves from a psychological or a fully experiential account. Nevertheless their approaches continue to use the positionality of the speaker (that is, experience) as a lens through which to understand social structure. They don't take identity or experience as part of the dynamic of power relations—except as their end product or consequence. In this regard, standpoint theory and other methods which draw on experience for analytical insights are reproducing a Marxist approach toward the production of subjectivity. Standpoint theory is but the clearest example of viewing people's life experiences as simultaneously *structured* by power relations but in some way transcendent of power. The aim of the researcher is to gain an alternative reading of social structures that, ideally, captures some of power's contradictions and vulnerabilities.

In contrast, poststructural theories on identity emphasise that the subject does not stand in clear distinction from the power structures that produce it. This discourages researchers from the (humanist) project of looking for an individuated consciousness and an unfettered self that exists prior to the power relations that limit her full humanity. As underlined in the previous chapter by Staunæs and Søndergaard (chapter 3, this volume), Foucault and Butler, for instance, emphasise the paradox of subjectification whereby the practices which subordinate people shape the consciousness of and possibilities for the self's identity (Butler 1990; Foucault 1990). Given this understanding of the highly intertwined nature of identity and power, the move to read 'experience' as a way of gaining some alternative understanding of social structures invites us to see the self in much more individuated and humanist terms than is appropriate. Instead, we would be better off aiming to understand the processes by which certain social relations produce identity and other effects. While this would include a consideration of how the subject articulates her/his self, it would understand those articulations as one moment in a larger process of practices of power and self.

Even the more careful discussions of the epistemological uses of experience seem to suffer from the problem that Joan W. Scott so powerfully deconstructs in her important essay 'Experience' (Scott 1992). Her analysis of the problems of popular uses of experience is relevant to the approach of scholars such as Ruth Behar and bell hooks, as well as to standpoint theory and oral life history. Scott cautions against treating subaltern identities and experience as independent of social processes. Her critique suggests that while many feminist scholars may successfully avoid reducing experience to simply psychological states and viewpoints by embedding experience in social positionality, they still do not complicate the very notion of experience. Consequently, identity and experience themselves are not explained but rather are taken as givens:

> When experience is taken as the origin of knowledge, the vision of the individual subject (the person who had the experience or the historian who recounts it) becomes the bedrock of evidence upon which explanation is built. Questions about the constructed nature of experience, about how one's vision is structured—about language (or discourse) and history—are left aside. The evidence of experience then becomes evidence for the fact of difference, rather than a way of exploring how

difference is established, how it operates, how and in what ways it constitutes the subjects who see and act in the world. (Scott 1992, 25)

Scott reminds us that experience, even the experience of oppression or resistance, needs to be explained; it is but one factor among others to consider in understanding the processes by which certain identities, or 'difference' more generally, are constructed. Therefore, instead of looking to the experience to provide intact 'standpoints' from which to generate accounts of the world, we must ask what factors constituted the experience and identities, and how the positionality—even of marginalised people—is relational to a range of influences (some of them unflattering even). Such a task is different from, and more analytically and politically productive than, the gesture of giving voice to or bearing witness to others' experience of marginality or oppression. If we take identity (or standpoint) as the starting point of analysis, we risk reifying and naturalising the very things we seek to explain.

One might worry that explaining people's experience in a way different to their own explanations is an arrogant enterprise on the part of the researcher. It suggests that researchers know things about the people whom they research that these people do not know about themselves. It suggests that the people we research have a false consciousness or self-deception about their own lives and require us to tell the real story about their experience or identity. Of course, one might reasonably ask, 'Is this not the approach to research (sometimes labelled masculinist or imperialist) that feminists seek to reject?' This concern is understandable. However, tracing self-understandings or experience to structural or institutional arrangements (in a move that will also explain the identity or experience) is more than an exercise in revealing the self-deception of the people among whom we conduct research. Rather, it involves tracing the genesis, and analysing the terms, of these structures of feelings (Williams 1977), discourses (Foucault 1972) and ideascapes (Appadurai 1996) in order to show how, and in what form, self-understandings and experience are produced. Certainly, disempowered people are often in a position to provide an alternative interpretation of structures of power such as race or patriarchy, as feminist standpoint theorists argue (Hill Collins 1991; Mohanty 2003; Naples 2003; Hartsock 2004; Smith 2004). Yet, it does not logically follow that there are social locations outside of socially constructed self-understandings from which certain groups can offer a critique and which therefore require no additional interrogation and analysis from the scholar. Simply *representing* a marginalised group's experiences (and building a critique of power from it) does not provide an undistorted window onto how structures of power work. They tell us one group's reading of it, but they do not tell us necessarily the terms that created it.

A final way in which the feminist approach to 'experience' in research creates overly simplistic notions of identity is by treating experience and the self as fairly transparent and something for which we can account. The humanist approach (with liberalism being an important example of the humanist approach to the subject, but others as well), takes identity as something fairly stable; identity might be shaped by external factors, but there is a fairly stable self which is knowable. Despite widespread critique of such theories (general acceptance of a notion of 'social construction-ism'), research designs that build from 'experience' too often overlook that the core of the antihumanist critique. What they ignore is the fact that identity and experience are unstable, fluid and mainly unconscious prod-ucts of social negotiations that speak us, rather than things which are eas-ily intelligible to us. All of these factors call into question taking someone's account of their experience as the window onto social reality—rather than reading this account as just one piece of a complex social location, as I argue we should.

If we take seriously psychoanalysis and/or the idea of social construc-tion, we cannot presume that any of us can easily or competently explain our subjective experience of life. Anthropologist Emily Martin reminds us of the limited capacity of people to fully articulate their situation: "The task is complicated because people cannot be aware of all aspects of their behavior. A great deal of what people communicate in their words and behavior is inchoate, beyond articulation in words" (Martin 2007, 9). This is neither the problem of people lying or deliberately withholding informa-tion from the researcher, nor that of faulty memory. It is rather that people often do not fully understand those things that are most important to them. It also echoes the insights of psychoanalytic theory and fiction: much of what we as humans feel most deeply is beyond our ability to explain or be fully aware of. Thus, our personal narratives and analyses of our experi-ence are at best partial and usually cannot provide a full analytical portrait (leaving aside any desire for totality in our research explanations, of course) of the social world or even of ourselves.

TOWARD A RELATIONAL APPROACH
TO IDENTITY AND EXPERIENCE

We might contrast the popular treatment of experience in research I have been describing with Ella Shohat's call for a 'relational approach' to expe-rience and identities (Kaplan and Grewal 2002, 76). Looking at identity *relationally* means understanding how experience and identity are con-structed in relation to other identities and social categories or experiences (see also Cerwonka 2008). Therefore, one could not take categories like 'Croatian women's experience' or 'black women's standpoint' as a given. Instead, we would need to enquire into how Croatian women's experience is produced relationally. We need to do so with an eye to the very fluid his-torical and political contexts out of which any identity is generated, rather than simply add on other categories, like race, class, sexuality, nationality or religion—which are often taken as stable and obvious categories. As feminist philosopher Diane Fuss argues, "[I]dentification is the detour through the other that defines the self. This detour through the other follows no predetermined developmental path, nor does it travel outside history and culture. Identification names the entry of history and culture into the subject" (1995, 3 cited in Nelson 1999, 29). Most feminist researchers who make knowledge claims from the experience of people whom they interview do see identity as sociohistorically produced. Yet many foreclose what 'developmental path' people's identity takes in so far as they use fairly standard identity categories as the parameters demarcating experience.

Anthropologist Diane Nelson's analysis of solidarity politics in Guatemala provides a useful example of a complex approach to reading identity and power structures. Drawing on the experiences of Guatemalan leftists, as well as her own experiences as a *gringa* (white American) researcher, she reads the way race, gender and solidarity are shifting terms shaped by local and transnational discourses and institutions. She describes this research approach not in terms of a static 'standpoint' but instead develops the concept of 'fluidarity analysis' to highlight the relational quality of her analytical lens. She writes:

> My tactic in writing about years of conversations, events, written and spoken polemics, and observed and experienced emotions is to acknowledge that the interrelations of ethnic, gender, and national identities in Guatemala are quite fluid and always in recombinant articulation with me, the gringa anthropologist . . . these not very solid identifications may call for a methodology of fluidarity. (Nelson 1999, 31)

Nelson succeeds in drawing on important theoretical insights about the instability of identity and the complexity of political position that both the researcher and researched occupy ('neither innocent nor transcendent'). In so doing she begins to develop a method that better reflects the theoretical subtleties underpinning many of our research projects. She explains:

> Rather than being 'solid,' a gringa in relation to Guatemala is overdetermined by complex plays of identification and difference over what Liisa Malkki terms 'bleeding boundaries' (1992, 26). . . . This chapter explores these contradictory articulations of gringa identity as a site that is neither innocent nor transcendent (Visweswaran 1994), that is both complicitous and inescapable, but through its very relationality and vulnerability—its unstable desire-driven articulation—may be the only site from which to launch a fluidarity analysis. (Nelson 1999, 48)

I will further elaborate on Nelson's approach by drawing on some specific moments in her analysis. Nelson describes a moment from her fieldwork related to the human rights activism in which she was involved in Mexico City in 1988. She describes being invited to bear witness to the evidence of acid burns and other scarring on the body of an exiled Guatemalan man who had been tortured for his activism. In addition to the powerful experience of witnessing what she describes as "the new geographies of his body, where the deltas and rivulets of acid had left their scars," (1999, 207) this moment in fieldwork taught her about how experience (her own and the torture victim's) was profoundly shaped by desires and discourses within a complex racial, gender and national politics in Guatemala and beyond. Nelson describes how, a month or so after initially meeting this man to help write a report about his experience of torture, she unexpectedly ran into him on the subway. She was surprised and embarrassed when, after some conversation, this man whom she barely knew described how he constantly thought about her and proclaimed his love for her. Nelson uses this incident to discuss the way in which, contrary to being stable or transparent, experience, identity and even bodily desire is embedded in larger political and discursive structures that shaped his desexualisation in Nelson's eyes as 'the innocent victim' and his eroticisation of her as a *gringa*:

> This scene—the body I had seen, my body that he saw—was shot through with ambivalences that disrupted the straightforward human- itarian and ethnographic gesture I thought I was involved in. . . . So rather than being a solid ground for bodies politic, bodies are produced (and aroused) in complex and often contradictory ways through desire and racial discourses like *mestizaje*. (Nelson 1999, 209)

With this incident, Nelson makes a number of rich points about identity and bodies. However, the value of her analysis for our present discussion is the way in which she models a complex reading of experience and per- spective, both her informant's and her own, in this research context. She engages in this research for many of the same intellectual and political reasons that many other feminist researchers engage in interviews and participant observation. She states explicitly that she hoped to support a progressive politics for those with less power in Guatemala. She explains, "I have understood my relation to Guatemala as being *in solidarity* as a researcher and activist. This has meant forming alliances with Guatema- lans and like-minded gringos and producing 'partial' accounts that take the side of the oppressed" (1999, 42).

Although with time she came to have a more complex understanding of social change, her ideas about solidarity, identity and experience as fluid and relational were not a product of disillusionment. Her analysis illus- trates nicely the many national and transnational factors that shape intan- gibles, such as identity as well as the body and its desires. The perspective and desires of the man whose scars and experience she bore witness to and her own constellation of sympathy, desires and expectations do not provide a transparent window onto some larger positionality. They can only be understood in relation to the power relations that produce them. This isn't to minimise the affective or political importance of either of their experiences. Rather, it perhaps takes them more seriously by understanding the complex set of relations (economic, cultural, gendered and so forth) that shape a given experience. A given experience is but one node of many that must be read to decipher social power relations. Additionally, the experience is constituted within a wider set of relationships (economic, political, racial, gendered). Thus, it is not enough to use people's experience primarily to understand something else (class or race relations, for instance). Rather, in order to construct even a partial understanding of the experience (and the things it gives us insight into), we also need to analyse carefully how any number of other relations have constituted that experience. To think this is disrespectful of another's humanity, suffering or experience is in essence to work with a tacit humanist understanding of identity; it rests on the idea that identities are unique and deeply personal and they need to be validated and honoured. I recognise that it is difficult for many to relinquish such tacit understandings of identity. One's own identity, after all, feels profoundly personal and individual. Additionally, the discourse of liberalism that permeates democratic capitalist societies invites us in innumerable ways to understand ourselves and others in terms of 'individuality.' However, it is important to ask why we presume that inviting people to speak about their experience, and the researcher's witnessing of this, is necessarily politically progressive and empowering. It may well be that the idea of 'bearing witness' as a researcher actually functions to reproduce liberal individualist ideologies. Insofar as it does, it potentially participates in the very ideological structures that operate to blame and hold disempowered people responsible for their own 'failings.' These are the very ideological structures obscuring the structural causes which result in some groups of people systematically losing out in social hierarchies and institutions. Therefore, although taking a person or disempowered group's experience as something to be analysed rather than witnessed might feel 'disrespectful,' one can argue that it helps dislodge the liberal (capitalist) power structures that justify and legitimate inequalities.

CONCLUSION

In this chapter, I have engaged with the writings of numerous feminist researchers who describe the value of using the 'experience' of (marginalised) people for developing analytical insights into relations of domination. One of the goals within such a methodological approach has been to provide a forum for suppressed voices. For many feminist historians, sociologists and other researchers, giving voice to the oppressed or forgotten is a vital corrective to dominant history and other forms of research. Indeed, there is much value in trying to produce research that deconstructs social injustices. However, I argue that at the same time much research that builds from others' 'experience' is incompatible with the theories of identity and power that many of the same researchers find convincing. If identity is socially produced from power relations, then in addition to accounting for alternative standpoints or identities, qualitative research must also explain the terms on which identities and experience rest, and it should explain how they incorporate, reflect, stand in tension with dominant ideologies or discourses. I argue this is a more fruitful trajectory for analysis than proceeding methodologically as if alternative viewpoints or identities exist *despite* dominant structures and that our role as researchers is to affirm/testify to their value.

I think there is an important political and intellectual reason for pushing what some might see as a petty point. Having relinquished the positivist fantasy privileged insight as 'neutral' researchers, feminists are now challenged to go even further in their development of alternative research frameworks. This involves more than acknowledging that there is no one position or universal explanation and that positionality matters. I argue that it is not enough for researchers to advertise different standpoints on a given issue, emphasising subordinated readings of the social world. Researchers also need to offer arguments and explanations of how and why things have come to be as they are, even if we accept that those arguments are provisional and partial. In an effort not to speak *for* others, many researchers have decided that they can instead only comfortably provide a vehicle for marginalised people to speak for themselves (through interview material, for example). Of course, work on the politics of representation in research suggests there is no unproblematic, neutral way to allow others to speak for themselves (for instance, the research still remains the author's, who receives the professional acclaim for it). Although some have tried to find ways to avoid these political problems (by listing the interviewees as co-authors or giving something back to their research community), it only defers an important epistemological issue. Feminist researchers need to return to the fundamental question of how, and by what right, a researcher can produce research that rests on the experiences, identity, views, times and so forth of other people, especially disempowered people. Is there something between the traditional positivist ideal of the researcher as a neutral expert who simply produces Truth and the idea of the researcher as sympathetic vehicle for the undocumented views of marginalised groups? Clearly there is, and researchers across the disciplines are engaged in developing new models. However, surprisingly, much feminist research and discussion of methods spends a great deal of time discussing the problems of disempowering others through research representations and very little time thinking about what researchers' creative, analytical arguments about various objects of inquiry might look like.

Women's and gender studies was at the forefront of reconceptualising the links between identity, experience and knowledge, and feminist research has helped to lead an epistemic revolution in the social sciences. However, there remains work to be done to enrich the dialogue between theories of identity (especially theories that challenge humanist assumptions) and methodology. It is important not only in order to 'get the theory right' but also because the rich empirical insights we can gain from qualitative research are potentially very productive for further complicating the theoretical concepts animating a great deal of feminist research.

NOTES

1. When discussing feminist standpoint theory, I engage most directly with two influential essays by Dorothy Smith and Nancy Hartsock. Smith's essay appeared originally as a conference paper in 1972 and Hartsock's essay was originally published in 1980. My engagement with standpoint theory is also informed by Patricia Hill Collins, Nancy Naples and Chandra Talpade Mohanty.
2. Smith also retains the Marxist faith in the transformative power of the underclass revealing the true nature of social relations: "As an engaged vision, the understanding of the oppressed, the adoption of a standpoint exposes the real relations among human beings as inhuman, points beyond the present, and carries a historically liberatory role" (Smith 2004, 37). In other words, feminist research can demystify relations of domination and thus help facilitate political change.

REFERENCES

Appadurai, A. 1996. Difference and Disjuncture in the Global Cultural Economy. In *Modernity at Large: Cultural Dimensions of Globalization*, 27–47. Minneapolis: University of Minnesota Press.

Behar, R. 1996. *The Vulnerable Observer: Anthropology That Breaks Your Heart*. Boston: Beacon Press.

Behar, R., and D. Gordon, eds. 1995. *Women Writing Culture*. Berkeley and Los Angeles: University of California Press.

Butler, J. 1990. *Gender Trouble: Feminism and the Subversion of Identity*. New York: Routledge.

Cerwonka, A. 2008. Traveling Feminist Thought: 'Difference' and Transculturation in Central and Eastern European Feminism. *Signs: Journal of Women and Culture* 33 (4): 809–32.

Cerwonka, A., and L. Malkki. 2007. *Improvising Theory: Process and Temporality in Ethnographic Fieldwork*. Chicago: University of Chicago Press.

Foucault, M. 1972. *The Archaeology of Knowledge and the Discourse on Language*. New York: Pantheon.

———. 1990. *The History of Sexuality*. Vol. 1, *An Introduction*. New York: Vintage Books.

Fuss, D. 1995. *Identification Papers: Readings on Psychoanalysis, Sexuality, and Culture*. New York: Routledge.

Hartsock, N. C. M. 2004. The Feminist Standpoint: Developing the Ground for a Specifically Feminist Historical Materialism. In *The Feminist Standpoint Theory Reader: Intellectual and Political Controversies*, ed. S. Harding, 35–53. New York: Routledge.

Hill Collins, P. 1991. *Black Feminist Thought: Knowledge, Consciousness, and the Politics of Empowerment.* New York: Routledge.

hooks, b. 2004. Choosing the Margin as a Space of Radical Openness. In *The Feminist Standpoint Theory Reader: Intellectual and Political Controversies,* ed. S. Harding, 153–59. New York: Routledge.

Kaplan, C., and I. Grewal. 2002. Transnational practices and Interdisciplinary Feminist Scholarship: Refiguring Women's and Gender Studies. In *Women's Studies On Its Own: A Next Wave Reader in Institutional Change,* ed. R. Wiegman, 66–81. Durham, NC: Duke University Press.

Martin, E. 2007. *Bipolar Expeditions: Mania and Depression in American Culture.* Princeton, NJ: Princeton University Press.

Mohanty, C. T. 2003. *Feminism Without Borders: Decolonizing Theory, Practicing Solidarity.* Durham, NC: Duke University Press.

Naples, N. 2003. *Feminism and Method: Ethnography, Discourse Analysis, and Activist Research.* New York: Routledge.

Nelson, D. M. 1999. *A Finger in the Wound: Body Politics in Quincentennial Guatemala.* Berkeley and Los Angeles: University of California Press.

Scott, J. W. 1992. Experience. In *Feminists Theorize the Political,* ed. J. Butler and J. W. Scott, 22–40. New York: Routledge.

Smith, D. 2004. Women's Perspective as a Radical Critique of Sociology. In *The Feminist Standpoint Theory Reader: Intellectual and Political Controversies,* ed. S. Harding, 21–34. New York: Routledge.

Visweswaran, K. 1994. *Fictions of Feminist Ethnography.* Minneapolis: University of Minnesota Press.

Williams, R. 1977. *Marxism and Literature.* Oxford: Oxford University Press.

5　Histories and Memories in Feminist Research

Andrea Pető and Berteke Waaldijk

COMPLICATED RELATIONSHIPS: PASTS AND FEMINISM

Historical Angels and the Angel of History

According to Virginia Woolf in 'Professions for Women,' every woman author has to kill the angel in the house in order to deal "freely and openly" with "what you think to be the truth about human relations, morality, sex" (Woolf 1972, 286). The "angel in the house" tempts her to be "utterly self-less," to "charm and . . . conciliate," and to comfort rather than confront. Only when this angel is no longer there can a woman truly write.

For graduate students and researchers in women's/gender studies, there are many such angels. They ask students to adapt to the expectations of academic writing, not to subvert the basic requirements of a discipline, to normalise writing and to follow the disciplinary rules. The voices of these angels come in many different forms. Some of the angelic voices we want to discuss in this chapter are those of what we will call the 'Historical Angels.' These angels speak the voice of chronological 'common sense' ('but this was just part of the general emancipation movement of that period'); they refer to economic backgrounds as a dismissal of radical politics (about nineteenth-century feminists: 'oh, but these women were all upper-class women'); they describe social conditions as an excuse for violence (about rape: 'this sexual practice was widespread'); and they deny feminist interventions with references to 'broader' cultural history ('the writing of Virginia Woolf has nothing to do with feminism; she is a modernist').

The Historical Angels urge feminist scholars to make the story about their research understandable to the mainstream and to provide historical perspectives that allow readers and colleagues to understand the text without having to understand gender or sexual difference. Historical continuity, simple causal explanations and a story line of gradual improvement in the position of women form an accessible way of writing about the past of women. With such an historical perspective, the report about your research fits into a larger perspective shared by the mainstream: it can make your research normal; it will be understood by those who do not share your background in women's/gender studies or feminist research.

In this chapter we want to address the risks involved in listening to these Historical Angels.

It is no surprise that feminist researchers have a complicated relationship with and a justified ambivalence towards writing about the past of women. Writing history or including historical perspectives in the context of feminist research projects carries two connotations. On the one hand, history provides a comfortable way to be understood and accepted. On the other hand, historical perspectives for many suggest acceptance of narratives about 'facts' and 'objectivity,' of 'truth' and undisputed national progress. Such narratives themselves have contributed to the exclusion of women, the defence of European imperialism and the advocacy of 'Western' supremacy. The interdisciplinary field of women's/gender studies aspires to combine and integrate different academic disciplines in creating new ways to think about gender. However, the discipline of academic history is not easily integrated into this interdisciplinary project, but it is nonetheless crucial to think about the way historical scholarship can be incorporated in feminist research.

Therefore, whether you do a research project about history or one that is in itself not about history but, for example, about fictional texts, artistic practices, philosophical debates, women's experiences or contested sexualities, we would like to encourage you to 'kill' the Historical Angels who would comfortingly historicise your topic and instead let yourself be inspired by an alternative angel: the 'Angel of History' as described by Walter Benjamin in 1940 (Benjamin 1973, 259). The 'Angel of History' is the opposite of reasonable progress viewed as a continuous chain of past events. This angel sees in the past the catastrophes that pile wreckage upon wreckage. Rather than a comfortable place of identification and explanation, the past is a place where the Angel of History would like to stay to awaken the dead, to make whole what has been smashed. This angel suggests another way— and we would argue one more inspiring for feminist research projects—of relating to the past: passionate, uncomforting and unaccepting. We want to distinguish this 'Angel of History' from the 'Historical Angels' that ask for comforting historical contextualisation, like historians who remove their 'I' when they write.

The Historical Angels of chronology and objectivity will ask researchers to be clear and reassuring about the past. They ask historical writers to remove discomfort by making things clear and simple through providing objective and chronological facts about the age of the interviewees, about the social and economic circumstances of a women's project, and about the sexual practices or philosophical debates that they describe in the research project. One way to deal with such demands is to devote a separate chapter to the historical context, the chronological order, and then start the 'real work' of feminist or gender analysis that will take the reader beyond chronology and factuality. We call this strategy 'add history and do not stir.' In an ironic way it resembles the way in which categories such as gender, race and ethnicity were added to traditional research: one separate chapter about women and/or one separate chapter about race and ethnicity; some facts are added, but the story and the categories of interpretation are not changed.

In this chapter we will:

1) explore ways in which feminist historians have challenged practices in the field of history,
2) suggest strategies for critical feminist inclusion of historical perspectives and
3) address ways in which history could be integrated in nonhistorical gender projects.

HOW FEMINIST HISTORIANS HAVE CHALLENGED PRACTICES IN THE FIELD OF HISTORY

History understood as the telling of stories about the past is as old as language, but history as an academic discipline began in the 1830s (Smith 1998), and it has always been closely connected to public and national purposes. History as a discipline started as national history and helped national political and nationalist movements to write their narratives, to whip up popular support. An important consequence of this genealogy of the historical discipline has been that certain topics 'belonged' in history books whereas others did not. A crucial contribution by feminist historians to traditional history as well as to women's/gender studies was the insight that the distinction between public and private was gendered and has limited the field of political national history (Scott 1986). By excluding the private from scientific history, the discipline could live up to its nationalist promises. This strategy was used by history writers to speak about political history, and it has had very different meanings and consequences for women both as objects of historical enquiry and as writers of histories.

The topics which emerged from traditional history books are rarely encouraging, seen from a feminist point of view. Jane Austen's complaint in 1803, voiced by one of the female characters in *Northanger Abbey*, that history was boring and uninspiring because it was all about "[t]he quarrels of popes and kings, with wars and pestilences, in every page; the men all so good for nothing, and hardly any woman at all" (Austen 1985, 123) could also have been made about some historical scholarship. Trying to find alternatives to topics that do not offer much possibility of identification, feminist historians started to look at the past to find their 'missing history.' When women started to write up histories of women they could only make visible that which was already visible in the sources: the history of queens, witches and prostitutes, that is, of women defined in the language of public political history as exceptions and outsiders. An important reason for the mixed feelings feminist researchers have towards historical writing is the perceived absence of gender perspectives in academic history, in popular culture and in public history. "The past is a foreign country: they do things differently there." L. P. Hartley's (1997) proverbial beginning to his novel *The Go-Between* is true for many gender specialists: the past feels indeed like a foreign country, a country where they have no citizenship.

The focus on public and national history has impacted the design of methods and methodology. The history of the public sphere was considered to deal with objective facts, while the private and personal is seen as 'subjective' (Smith 1998). Writing about the past in an impersonal way, letting the primary sources speak without the intervention of the historical researcher and striving for objectivity became the benchmarks of professional political history. However, these are rarely inviting to contemporary women's/gender studies graduate students and researchers. Added to this methodological hesitance is the problem of 'missing sources': it is very difficult to find 'real historical' sources for topics and themes that allow exciting gender interpretations. It therefore may seem impossible to include a historical context in research that does justice to women's perspectives.

Of course, the nineteenth-century ideals of history as an academic discipline that should celebrate nationhood have long been contested. The twentieth century witnessed a crisis in the humanities that resulted from, and contributed to, a growing awareness that history is more than national history. The fragmentation of what was previously called 'history' started with the rise of social history, labour history, and cultural history. Knowledge about history became contested, and counterhistories were written. This uneasy relationship was developing amid the general crisis of the humanities (Said 2004; Waaldijk 2005; Grever 2007; Mak and Waaldijk 2009; Petö 2009; Van der Sanden 2010). The reaction against this democratisation of history was swift and strong. In the culture wars in the US those who wanted history to be more inclusive of gender, race and class were 'accused' of 'political correctness' and of jeopardising the objectivity of history. In Europe, critiques of the new forms of history writing were expressed as general complaints that people know less and less about 'history,' understood as the canonised version of history. In the early twenty-first century national governments are setting up programmess and educational systems to encourage the population to share official national history; knowledge about national pasts is thus turned into a prerequisite for citizenship.

In a way, this is paradoxical because 'history'—understood as 'studying the past'—has never been more popular. Several popular journals are devoted to history, and there are Web sites and TV channels devoted to it as well. Political movements from both the Right and the Left are turning to the past to justify their political demands. Private citizens write histories of their families, create Web sites of family genealogy, read biographies and watch movies that bring to life histories from the distant and not too distant pasts (Petö and Schrijvers 2009).

The integration of popular history within mass culture makes reconceptu-alising the relationship between feminism and historical research a political imperative. The question of whether and how feminist graduate students and researchers include references to the past is not just about history as an aca-demic discipline, but about public debates on identity, inclusion and exclu-sion. It should be noted that academic history plays an important role in the construction of history as part of popular culture and political debates. The tradition of respectable senior (men) academics and some women histori-ans explaining history in a popular way was always present in Anglo-Saxon history writing, from R. H. Tawney to Eric Hobsbawn. This tradition was revived in the late twentieth century due to the uncertainty caused by the paradigm change after the collapse of communism. Millions were reading paperback editions of Samuel P. Huntington's *Clash of Civilizations and the Remaking of World Order* (1996) and Francis Fukuyama's *The End of His-tory and the Last Man* (1992), not to mention the success of stories about the safely distant Middle Ages, such as Umberto Eco's *The Name of the Rose* (1983) and Dan Brown's *The Da Vinci Code* (2003), which in the globalised world reached an audience far wider than that of which any professional historian might have dreamt. This makes us aware that historical narratives reached audiences in many different genres. Writing the past is not solely the prerogative of historians; rather, historical perspectives are visible in virtu-ally all genres: biography, literary studies, romantic fiction, science fiction and crime fiction—a genre to which we will return at the end of this article.

For feminist scholars there is a further genre wherein history plays an enormous role, and that is the discourse about women's liberation or eman-cipation. That history is crucial for these discourses and has to do with the ambiguity of historical findings and future-related expectations and pro-jections. The definition of history as a positivist listing of a chain of events limited researchers of women's pasts to imagining these pasts as a linear development and as a normative project which will lead to a 'new begin-ning' (Felski 1995, 145–73). Feminist historians often construct a narra-tive that competes with the canonised story in the positivist terms of that history. Historical research on women has always had a strong link with the women's movement. Simone de Beauvoir's adage that one is not born but rather becomes a woman is a way of putting history before biology. For women's movements the past has often been a treasure chest of inspi-ration and identification: to imagine that long ago women were not only oppressed, but were also strong and decisive was politically valuable. What was often forgotten was that such narratives of liberation, in common with those of the labour movement and antislavery movements, are embedded in a meta-narrative of progress and increasing freedom either through revolu-tions or through steady democratisation. In this sense histories of feminism and women's liberation are closely linked in form to political histories of nation states and empires. The history of women then becomes a narrative of progress and identification. This means that every remark about women in the past can be turned into a political argument. Every political argument contains an implicit reference to the past.

It is no surprise that in the early stages of women's/gender studies as an academic field, historical arguments played a key role. However, it is worrying to see how in many countries the institutionalisation of interdisciplinary women's/gender studies takes place either as a social science project or as part of literary and media studies. The absence of history departments and history in the institutionalisation of women's/gender studies in the past decades is indeed painful (Griffin 2005). In this chapter we plead for a critical integration of historical perspectives in interdisciplinary gender projects.

With that said, it is not easy to include historical perspectives in interdisciplinary projects. We propose looking at the work of feminist historians to see how this may be possible. Feminist historians arguing with the historical discipline have tended to focus on the idea of a separate history for women. There is a long and strong tradition of conceiving women's history as a form of memorialisation of women's pasts. The idea that women have a genealogy that differs from the history that has been written by men about their male ancestors has a long tradition in feminism and dominated the field of women's history in its developing phases as an academic specialisation. For feminists the retrieval of the personal meant that they could write women's history and restore women to history. This strategy, which discovered and emphasised the gap between public male history and the private realm of women, reinforced the distance between gender history and 'scientific' history.

Important as this approach to the past may be, the idea that the history of women is by definition different from historical writing about men has notable disadvantages. It can blind feminist historians to the themes and mechanisms of inclusion and exclusion that the writing of women's history shares with 'male' history. It may result in over-nostalgic descriptions of gender based solidarity, neglect differences in power and authority between women or overlook the ways in which the history of various forms of feminism is intertwined with histories of exploitation, imperialism and suppression. Conceiving women's history as separate and different misses the intersections of gender with other categories of exclusion, what Dorthe Staunæs and Dorte Marie Søndergaard discuss as a "matter of transgressive research guided by a transgressive methodology" (chapter 3, this volume). Such a separation limits the possibilities of including critical historical perspectives in interdisciplinary research. For Woolf, the angel of the house provided safety and comfort instead of critical contestation; the self-effacing angel made invisible the work she had to do to provide homely comfort. This image resonates with impersonal objective historical knowledge which is separate from the scholar. Such a view of historical knowledge alienates feminist scholars and PhD students from their deep and political engagement.

Does this mean graduate students and other researchers working in women's/gender studies should leave the field of history to its own devices and not refer to the past? On the contrary, it is precisely because referring to the past can take such powerful and seductive forms that it is crucial gender scholars address history as the construction of the past with a projection of the future. When we define history as a site offering space for the articulation of different and alternative futures by subordinate groups, it will be possible to include historical perspectives in gender research projects in a productive and affirmative way (Van der Tuin, chapter 1, this volume).

With the aim of making critical historical perspectives a part of the interdisciplinary gender studies project, we will now identify alternative strategies pursued by feminist historians and discuss how women's/gender studies scholars not working in the field of history can profit from these insights.

STRATEGIES FOR CRITICAL FEMINIST INCLUSION OF HISTORICAL PERSPECTIVES: NEW NARRATIVES, NEW TEXTS AND NEW CLUES

The following examples of strategies for the critical inclusion of historical perspectives are what we call 'looking for history in unexpected places.'

We indicated earlier the difficulties for feminist researchers stemming from disciplinary rules and the genres of academic writing. Here it is crucial to remember that talking about the past is not limited to professional academic history. Women and men throughout the world and throughout the ages have composed stories, texts, observations, songs and practices that referred to events from their pasts. There was a great variety of often gendered genres which kept alive memories of the past: from telling and retelling stories, singing songs and making quilts to writing novels, family memoirs and academic dissertations (Levine 1977; Zemon Davis 1980; Carby 1987; Pomata 1993; Grever 1994; O'Dowd and Porciani 2004). Feminist historians look to these sources when teaching feminist history in order to challenge the hegemony of positivist epistemology, one of the causes of the troubled relationship between gender research and history (Petö and Waaldijk 2006). In this section we explore some unorthodox sources and point out their heuristic and political possibilities for feminist research.

Oral Histories and Memories

Oral history is both a critical method and a genre of enquiry. As such, it is the perfect means to analyse new approaches to our pasts. If we take, for example, the research on migration, we find that migrants' stories about their education and what they tell us in the form of family stories as private stories often use the available narrative toolkit of public histories. However, if you do research on migration and interview migrants, you can also ask your informants how they perceive this history; you can ask them to speak about the history they have been taught at school, in political speeches, in adult educational projects. This way a differentiation is made, and the interaction between private memories and official and public histories becomes visible. The question of memory concerns looking at how readings of the present can be translated into projections for the future. One example is writing about the experiences of women raped by Red Army soldiers and the way in which those memories have been muted or used in public histories in different historical periods. By asking women to speak not only about their memories but also about their perceptions of how public and official histories dealt with this part of their lives, you may get a better understanding of the ways in which historical narratives allow some experiences to be remembered and others to be repressed (Petö 2003, 129–49). Another example is work on the ways in which contemporary political circumstances and different migrant settings influence how migrants construct their subjectivity. By taking into account how the history of migration has been portrayed in public texts (history books, policy papers, journalism) you may understand how personal narratives about migration experiences are impacted by them. It may help you, for example, to understand and discuss why some women can and do speak about themselves as political refugees whereas others stress economic or family reasons for their migration (Passerini et al. 2007).

Diaries

Diaries have been a favourite subject of feminist research. Historians, literary scholars, psychologists and social scientists can sometimes get access to diaries written by men and women involved in the projects they study. This genre seems to offer access to the private thoughts of women, and it is tempting to think, and historical training encourages us to do so, that a diary contains the truth about a woman's life. Sometimes diaries have been written with a sideways glance to potential audiences; in other cases it seems as if their words are supposed to be read by no one other than the author herself (although you as someone from years/centuries later do read them). However, many diaries do not only contain extremely personal stories. They refer to and are influenced by political, ideological and economic circumstances. One of the more famous examples is the diary of Anne Frank, in which she wrote not only about personal feelings but also about the role of women in history (Waaldijk 1994). In diaries it may become clear how the historical developments of the time were perceived or not perceived.

Fiction

Novels, whether works of popular fiction (e.g., romances or crime fiction) or belonging to the realm of literature, often tell stories about topics and themes on which gender scholars carry out research (sexuality, the self, women's work, migration, colonialism, persecution). We have been trained to read such texts as subjective nontrue (fictional) narratives. However, one way of incorporating historical perspectives into your research project may be to examine whether there are also historical narratives integrated into these texts. Novels refer to historical circumstances; they structure the possibilities of agency open to the characters. Novels reflect ideas about women's roles in the period the novel was written. When you want to integrate novels in your research we suggest that you not only access them using feminist literary criticism tools, but that you also look out for the historical perspectives implied in the stories. Information about women's agency and sexuality provide you, as a researcher, with historical perspectives on your topic. This type of looking for history does not help you with the 'background' and 'facts,' but it does help you to recognise historical narratives: stories of progress or of tragic loss, stories about found identity or about lost connections. These narratives are not the truth, but they will help you to formulate different interpretations of your topic and to recognise the narratives in the other texts about the topic. One example of this is Mary Poovey's work on Charlotte Bronte's *Jane Eyre*. Poovey argues that this novel tells us how the job of governess was being perceived in new terms (Poovey 1988, 126–62). Toni Morrison's 1987 novel, *Beloved*, about the end of slavery in the US says more, in a way, about the historical perspective of the 1980s on slavery than about the post–Civil War period. It is exactly this contemporary historical perspective that makes novels so interesting; it allows you to see how public history and private memory are intertwined, and it shows how narratives travel from one genre to another.

Alternative narratives

A more explicit way of defining history as a site where alternative futures can be imagined comes from Polish feminist historian Ewa Domanska. She argues that the stories we find in the past are the stories of oppression and violence. When researchers look around in the present world they also find 'unfinished history' full of oppression and violence. A 'history' that is permeated by so much violence, dictatorship and exploitation needs students who feel they can tell other stories and formulate alternatives (Domanska 2005, 389–413). Dutch historian Geertje Mak suggests that the historical meta-narrative of events and development (progress) excludes women's experiences, and women's history can only be written when other narratives are chosen (Mak 2007, 128–42). They may thus contribute to the alternatives that have also been part of the European past: protest and idealism.

THE ROLE OF HISTORY IN NONHISTORICAL GENDER PROJECTS

An often employed strategy for including history is to write a 'historical chapter' listing works dealing with the topic in question. There is nothing wrong with this strategy in itself. When you are not trained as a historian, you will have to ask advice from historians and use overviews and general textbooks. You will not be in a position to criticise those works as you are not writing a history book; rather, you want to inform the reader, who may not know about the national, regional or global context of the texts, women, experiences and debates you want to describe and analyse. Looking for such history books and articles about your topic implies that you are already using existing narratives of the past. In a way you strengthen the distinction between the objective facts surrounding your topic and the interactive subject treatment you give to your topic. However, there is a real risk here. By dividing your story into background (undisputed, real, factual) and centrepiece (interactive analysed, subjectively interrogated) you reinforce the presuppositions of traditional history (White 2005, 147–57). This approach resembles that of the 'Historical Angels': it provides readers with a comforting sense of where to locate your story in time, connecting it to well-known themes from widely available historical discourse. The risk of this approach is huge. You run the risk of failing to promote the construction of critical 'intellectual biographies' (Stanley 1993, 41–52) or the appreciation of already existing feminist scholarship.

When writing about the past it is crucial to use the work of feminist historians: this will make visible the structures and assists in setting up feminist genealogies. Find out what feminist historians have written about 'your' topic and about 'your' period, and how they have criticised general histories and overviews of the period. See how you can make your research project relate to their argumentation to produce a different view of history. Instead of using their work as a 'fundgrube' (finding place) for facts and figures, do justice to the critical dialogue they are having with their discipline. For example, when your dissertation is about the work of a woman writer in the early twentieth century, refer to the work of feminist literary scholars Sandra M. Gilbert and Susan Gubar (Gilbert and Gubar 1988), not simply to include details about the number of women publishing novels in that period, but also to cite their argument about the gendered nature of modernism. Or, when writing about women's memories of World War II, analyse the narrative frameworks which construct gendered spaces of narration. Yet another strategy asks you to experience the seductive power of traditional historical narratives while writing about the human hero/heroine against a historical background of harsh conditions. This strategy requires more time and reflection, but if you take the time to pursue it properly, you will note that women's stories are not always 'absent' from history; sometimes they are indeed present—and exploited or even celebrated. They interact with other stories. To pursue this strategy those who are not historians in women's/gender studies should read work by feminist historians who have addressed the issue, i.e., moved beyond the approach that women simply have been excluded from history. When working on gender, fascism and nationalism, for example, it is important to read not only historical research about the way national citizenship excluded women but also to use the work of feminist historians who point out how some women have profited from nationalist and fascist movements and have been put on a pedestal as 'Mothers in the Fatherland' or as 'Republican mothers' (Koonz 1988; Kerber 1997).

What should you do when you are writing about theory or theoretical developments in your dissertation? Whether your whole research project is about theory or only one of its chapters summarises theoretical developments, we suggest deconstructing the chronological stories about the development of theory. Such narratives describe changes over time, and you can learn from feminist historians how meta-narratives not only provide chronological order but also determine what can be a subject and what belongs to the margins. How tempting it is to describe the beginnings of theory as naïve and later developments as acquiring more sophistication. Feminist theorist Clare Hemmings has shown how different theoretical approaches in women's/gender studies are often introduced in a chronological model that constructs a continuous progression towards more complete and sophisticated insights. She points out how the choice of such a narrative of progress divides the actors into insiders and outsiders, those who grow and develop and those who remain in the margins of that history (Hemmings 2005). Feminist scholar Iris van der Tuin has introduced the concept of 'jumping generations' to allow a break with traditional chronologies. The past is a site for inventing futures. She argues that feminist theory requires a different connection to the past, not one of overcoming its deficits, but of an active dialogue (see Van der Tuin 2008; and chapter 1, this volume). Feminist philosopher Claire Colebrook wrote, "Rehearsing feminism's past is, then, not merely a sanctimonious exercise of self-congratulation for having overcome the blindness of a past; it is also an awareness that the past may harbor potentials to which we are not yet attuned" (2009, 12). This attitude resembles that of the Angel of History of Walter Benjamin, whom we introduced in the beginning, i.e., the angel who will not accept the inevitable outcome of the past, but rather engages in a passionate dialogue with that past.

CONCLUSION: HISTORY AND CRIME FICTION

We started this chapter with Virginia Woolf inviting women to kill the angel in the house and with Walter Benjamin, who described how that other angel, the Angel of History, looks back at the past and does not see a 'chain of events' but 'wreckage piled on wreckage' and wants to 'make whole what has been smashed.' These references to killing and 'making whole' bring us to the image of the detective in crime fiction. We are aware that historians traditionally like to compare themselves to detectives who find out the truth of what has happened. To end, then, we want to explore the parallel of writing history and writing detective stories.

The historical narrative is chronological as is the story in crime fiction: the researcher is looking for clues of past events, their reflections in memory, which necessarily differs from person to person. It is the historian who has the power and the hegemony to construct one narrative from all the versions of the clues. Solving a crime resembles doing historical research, whereas writing a historiographical chapter in a feminist paper requires the skills of a crime fiction writer in order to unfold an enigma of the research topic (Strout 1994).

The genre of crime fiction follows a well-known formula, culminating in solving of the crime. The changes in the genre in recent decades have run parallel with changes in history writing: a genre where omnipotent male detectives interpreted the clues and created narratives about crime events has undergone change. Female detectives have faced the dilemma of 'not fitting into' the male world, just as the first female historians had to suffer isolation and humiliation (O'Dowd and Porciani 2004). There are important similarities between the manner in which crime fiction as a genre has been gendered in recent decades and how history has explored gendered stories of the past. Both are translating signs and clues into narrative. This closeness and the possibility of breaking the code of the formula are debated in the literature and can be a starting point for thinking about how to break the codes of history writing while doing feminist research. The genre of crime fiction offers three possibilities for breaking the code, insofar as the first task is not to solve the mystery but to decode the language in which the mystery itself is written. Firstly, we need to identify the possibilities and also the limitations of a chronological narrative. Second, to understand the stories it is necessary to break the cultural codes, and at the end of the code breaking process a new text, an explanatory narrative, should be constructed where the events are understood and reconceptualised. The narrow path between academic writing and fiction offers space for a reconceptualisation of the relationship between the author and the audience. History as an unfinished project is constructed in crime stories through stories and testimonies about events that challenge the concept of the 'one' and 'true' narrative. Those who are researching differently should not easily give away the agency of the researcher to decide what is a clue.

REFERENCES

Austen, J. 1985. *Northanger Abbey*. Hammondsworth: Penguin Books.

Benjamin, W. 1973. *Illuminations*. London: Fontana.

Carby, H. V. 1987. *Reconstructing Womanhood: The Emergence of the Afro-American Woman Novelist*. New York: Oxford University Press.

Colebrook, C. 2009. Stratigraphic Time, Women's Time. *Australian Feminist Studies* 24 (59): 11–16.

Domanska, E. 2005. Toward the Archaeontology of the Dead Body. *Rethinking History* 9 (4): 389–413.

Felski, R. 1995. The Gender of Modernity. Cambridge, MA: Harvard University Press.

Gilbert, S., and S. Gubar. 1988. No Man's Land: The Place of the Woman Writer in the Twentieth Century. Vol. 1, The War of the Words. New Haven, CT: Yale University Press.

Grever, M. 1994. Strijd tegen de Stilte: Johanna Naber (1859–1941) en de vrouwenstem in de geschiedenis [Struggle Against the Silence: Johanna Naber (1859–1941) and the Women's Voice in History]. Hilversum: Verloren.

———. 2007. Plurality, Narrative and the Historical Canon. In Beyond the Canon: History for the Twenty First Century, ed. S. Stuurman and M. Grever, 31–47. Houndmills: Palgrave Macmillan.

Griffin, G., ed. 2005. Doing Women's Studies: Employment Opportunities, Personal Impacts and Social Consequences. London and New York: Zed Books.

Hartley, L. P. 1997. The Go-Between. London: Penguin.

Hemmings, C. 2005. Telling Feminist Stories. Feminist Theory 6 (2): 115–39.

Kerber, L. K. 1997. The Republican Mother: Women and the Enlightenment—An American Perspective. In Toward an Intellectual History of Women: Essays by Linda K. Kerber, 41–62. Chapel Hill: University of North Carolina Press.

Koonz, C. 1988. Mothers in the Fatherland: Women, the Family and Nazi Politics. London: Methuan.

Levine, L. W. 1977. Black Culture and Black Consciousness: Afro-American Folk Thought from Slavery to Freedom. New York and Oxford: Oxford University Press.

Mak, G. 2007. Moving History: How Gender Has Touched the Canon. In Beyond the Canon: History for the Twenty First Century, ed. S. Stuurman and M. Grever, 128–42. Houndmills: Palgrave Macmillan.

Mak, G., and B. Waaldijk. 2009. Gender, History and the Politics of Florence Nightingale. In Doing Gender in Media, Art and Culture, ed. R. Buikema and I. van der Tuin, 207–22. New York: Routledge.

Morrison, T. 1987. Beloved: A Novel. New York: Alfred Knopf.

O'Dowd, M., and I. Porciani, eds. 2004. History Women. Special issue, Storia della Storiografia 46: 3–202.

Passerini, L., D. Lyon, E. Capussotti and I. Laliotou, eds. 2007. Women Migrants from East to West: Gender, Mobility and Belonging in Contemporary Europe. Oxford and New York: Berghahn Books.

Pető, A. 2003. Memory and the Narrative of Rape in Budapest and Vienna. In Life after Death: Approaches to a Cultural and Social History of Europe, ed. D. Schumann and R. Bessel, 129–49. Cambridge: Cambridge University Press.

———. 2009. From Visibility to Analysis: Gender and History. In Paths to Gender: European Historical Perspectives on Women and Men, ed. C. Salvaterra and B. Waaldijk, 1–9. Pisa: Pisa University Press.

Pető, A., and B. Waaldijk, eds. 2006. Teaching with Memories: European Women's Histories in International and Interdisciplinary Classrooms. Galway: Women's Studies Centre, University of Galway Press.

Pető, A., and K. Schrijvers, eds. 2009. Faces of Death: Visualising History. Pisa: Pisa University Press.

Pomata, G. 1993. History, Particular and Universal: Some Recent Women's History Textbooks. Feminist Studies 19 (1): 7–50.

Poovey, M. 1988. Uneven Developments: The Ideological Work of Gender in Mid-Victorian England. Chicago: University of Chicago Press.

Said, E. W. 2004. Humanism and Democratic Criticism. New York: Columbia University Press.

Sanden, J. van der. 2010. Transferring Knowledge about Sex and Gender: Dutch Case Studies. Pisa: Pisa University Press.

Scott, J. 1986. Gender: A Useful Category of Historical Analysis. *American Historical Review* 91 (5): 1053–75.

Smith, B. G. 1998. *The Gender of History: Men, Women, and Historical Practice.* Cambridge, MA: Harvard University Press.

Stanley, L. 1993. On Auto/biography in Sociology *Sociology* 27 (1): 41–52.

Strout, C. 1994. The Historian and the Detective. *Partisan Review* 61 (4): 666–74.

Tuin, I. van der. 2008. *Third Wave Materialism: New Feminist Epistemologies and the Generation of European Women's Studies.* Dissertation, University of Utrecht.

Waaldijk, B. 1994. Reading Anne Frank as a Woman. *Women's Studies International Forum* 16 (4): 327–36.

———. 2005. *Yearning for Culture: Citizenship and the Humanities.* Utrecht: Utrecht University Press.

White, H. 2005. Historical Fiction, Fictional History, and Historical Reality. *Rethinking History* 9 (2–3): 147–57.

Woolf, V. 1972. Professions for Women. In *Collected Essays.* Vol. 2, 284–90. London: Hogarth Press.

Zemon Davis, N. 1980. Gender and Genre: Women as Historical Writers, 1400–1820. In *Beyond Their Sex: Learned Women of the European Past,* ed. P. H. Labalme, 153–82. New York: New York University Press.

Part III
Research Methods

6 Writing about Research Methods in the Arts and Humanities

Gabriele Griffin

Writing about research methods in the arts and humanities is not easy, in part because of the history of silence (of which more below) surrounding the research process in certain arts/humanities disciplines,[1] and in part because what we understand by 'arts and humanities' is a contested terrain, increasingly so in a research age when interdisciplinarity is on the rise. From the point of view of a researcher, however, it is important to be able to articulate what research processes she has undertaken, not least because research funders, including for the arts/humanities, increasingly require that one discuss in detail the method/ologies underpinning one's research. In the following I shall therefore first discuss the relationship of the arts/humanities to research method/ologies more generally, then discuss specific ways of articulating research methods in arts/humanities from a researcher's point of view.

The phrase 'arts and humanities' covers a wide range of disciplines which are differently grouped together in diverse countries and research contexts. History, for instance, may be regarded as a social science or as a humanities subject depending on the country, institution or organization you are dealing with and also on the kind of history one does, e.g. economic history or cultural history.[2] Given this diversity, I shall refrain from specifying a single definition but instead use a (slightly modified) version of the UK Arts and Humanities Research Council's subject domains in the first instance which include classics, ancient history, archaeology; visual arts and media; literature and languages; medieval and modern history; linguistics; librarianship, information and museum studies; music and performing arts; philosophy, religious studies and law.

These very diverse subjects have very different histories of acknowledging and recording (or not) research processes. Until very recently, research methods were not widely discussed in many of the arts/humanities subjects. In English studies[3] or literature as a research area in the 1980s, when I was a postgraduate student, they did not figure at all; research was what you did, and the best you could hope for was a brief introduction to the vagaries of the library. There was no sense that you needed to know about the process of conducting research or that how you did it might influence the outcome—though you might find yourself held to account during your *viva* (final examination) for the sources you had used as the basis for your research. During the second half of the 1990s when the issue of research training began to creep up on public and institutional agendas in the UK, research methods were what academics got others to deliver to their students—mostly in the form of a basic library introduction (always unwelcome by those who had used that particular library already and felt they knew it) and basic computing skills (also frequently unwelcome, especially among younger students who had grown up with computers and had certain basic word-processing skills).[4] The ethos remained that research methods, here actually research skills, were divorced from the academic enquiry into the subject; that it was librarians' and computer technicians' job to deliver any relevant training (the word 'training' itself viewed as detracting from higher-order intellectual endeavour)[5] and that it was a necessary evil rather than a positive good.

METHODS IN ARTS/HUMANITIES
RESEARCH: A QUESTION OF SILENCE?

This is in some respects strange, considering that significant numbers of arts/humanities academics in the UK—as in other countries—are active researchers who clearly employ research methods to produce their often stunning and paradigm-shifting results.[6] Yet they have remained surprisingly silent about what it is that they do to achieve these results. One prevailing view is that "[a] lot of research methods can't be taught. You pick it up by doing it" (Williams 2002, 27). The corresponding view from a student who had undertaken research methods training was: "Everyone in my group hated it and didn't learn anything. The only thing you learnt was from working with my supervisor." And from another: "The most useful part was going around by myself, finding out what I needed to know" (Williams 2002, 35). Such views are unsurprising in a research environment where the emphasis is on learning by doing; where supervisors themselves have no history of research training as a function of when they undertook their own postgraduate research; where students and staff work in disciplines, indeed countries, that have no significant history of providing such training; and where—as both the UK English Subject Centre's report on this issue (Williams 2002) and the Arts and Humanities Research Board's *Postgraduate Review* (2002) indicate—notions of radical individualism in research rather than research collaboration prevail. To this day, and unlike research degrees in the social sciences, for instance, PhD's in literature but also in other arts and humanities disciplines do not require a method/ology section—something that is absolutely commonplace, not to say *de rigueur*, in other subjects.

This situation has shifted dramatically since the turn of this century. In November 2002, the English Subject Centre in the UK published a research report on *Postgraduate Training in Research Methods: Current Practice and Future Needs in English* (Williams 2002). It followed hot on the heels of the Arts and Humanities Research Board (AHRB; from 2006 AHRC) *Postgraduate Review* which had appeared in January 2002. Given the vast range of postgraduate degree courses across the UK and the intense competition for resources to support them, the AHRB's review recognised the need "to nurture research cultures" and "to encourage best practice in research training" (3). In this it followed the already existent research councils in the UK such as the Economic and Social Research Council (ESRC) which have well-developed, if in some ways contested,[7] research training requirements that must be explicitly and mandatorily incorporated into postgraduate schemes in order for these to receive funded studentships. Similar moves can be observed across other European countries, facilitated in part by the so-called Bologna Process (see special issue of *NORA*, *(Inter) disciplinarity and the Bologna Process* 2006) that seeks to 'harmonise' the European Higher Education Area by creating comparable structures, not least in postgraduate education.

Increasingly it has been recognised that learning about research methods should form part of one's research training. Since 2004 the AHRB (now AHRC) has required the provision of a 'Departmental Research Training' statement as part of every application for a funded studentship. As one student said, "It's important to have the discourse so that you can communicate knowledgably in your own subject" (Williams 2002, 14).

The issue is becoming increasingly more complex because of two further factors. One is the move, at least in the UK, towards practice-based research degrees in certain arts and humanities disciplines, e.g. postgraduate degrees in creative writing. These require research students to produce a work of fine art, a piece of creative writing or some other cultural artefact and at the same time document its research component, i.e. articulate what 'conducting practice-based research' entails. This is a very new area of research methodological consideration, effectively postdating the turn of the millennium. Unsurprisingly, Jon Cook (2005) begins his exploration of the issue of practice-based research by stating, "The idea of creativity or creative writing as a research method may seem a contradiction in terms. Long-held beliefs about the nature of creativity identify it as something that is outside or beyond methical thought" (195). Cook talks of 'methical' rather than 'methodological' thought, but the two go together: both require systematic deliberation and metadiscursive reflection on the research process. Current academics in the arts and humanities, however, have themselves not had 'training' in such matters and are, in a sense, 'making it up as they go along,' in other words, beginning to produce texts that explain how one might discuss the research process involved in practice-based research. Current new researchers thus have the opportunity to shape the newly emerging field of practice-based research methods.

The second factor that complicates issues of research methods in the arts and humanities is the increasing drive towards interdisciplinarity. This almost always requires working in research teams (as opposed to researching by oneself, the more traditional form of much arts and humanities research) involving people from different disciplinary backgrounds. Many of the thematic research priorities such as 'landscapes and environment,' 'security,' 'sustainability,' 'migration' or 'gender' require researching not only across arts/humanities, but involve different kinds of knowledge domains such as the social sciences or engineering and so forth. Human-computer interaction (HCI), for instance, integrates designers with engineers, mathematicians, computer specialists and others. These have very different ideas about how to do research, what constitutes 'good' research, what counts as evidence and how to present research. Here the need to be able to articulate one's own research method/ologies is only too evident: if one cannot explain what one does and how one does it as the starting point for collaboration, such collaboration becomes very difficult. An associated dimension is that the 'cultural turn' in the social sciences has meant that social sciences researchers (and others) are increasingly interested in arts/ humanities methods and work, and have turned their research eye to examining how arts and humanities scholars operate, for instance, utilising network theories and the work of people such as Bruno Latour to examine the 'cultural industries.' This has partly been driven by an increasing demand that the (economic) contribution which the arts/humanities make to European economies be better understood.

Unlike other research councils in the UK, the AHRC has not become prescriptive in what content it requires from research training courses, but it has produced a 'Joint Statement of the Research Councils Skills Training Requirements for Research Students' which is intended to reemphasise "that training in research skills and techniques is the key element in the development of a research student" (AHRC 2001, 41). This statement lists an extended number of research skills, techniques and competencies which the AHRC considers necessary for the adequate training of research students.

Much arts/humanities research, especially at postgraduate level, continues to be done by individual scholars working alone. Where research training is then focused on 'individual need,' it delivers a particular view of research. It is a responsive model focusing on the identification of/response to individual needs as they arise from a specific research project; it assumes implicitly that the research methods relevant to that particular research project are *the only ones* a research student needs to acquire, presumably because it is assumed to be the kind of research that the scholar will continue to re/produce throughout her academic life. However, both disciplinary and research technological developments over time in fact require changes in research practice; one need only think of the impact of the advance in computer technologies on textual editing (Short and Deegan 2005).

The research methods we employ impact on the research findings we generate. In literary studies it is common practice to assume that "in the end it's about reading" (Williams 2002, 14). Such a view admits only to the notion of text-based research as the proper domain of literary research. But as the 2001 research evaluation panel's definition of its domain showed, literary research is much more than textual analysis.[8] The failure to recognise this is a failure of the research imagination.[9] Knowledge of a range of methods enables researchers to ask different research questions.

METHODS AND SKILLS

A word about research methods/skills/methodologies: Sadie Williams uses the word 'skills' to describe what postgraduates need "to undertake PhD work in English" (2002, 58). However, a distinction needs to be made between research skills, methods and methodologies, a differentiation that is common in many disciplines. Research skills are techniques for handling material. In literary studies, they include library search skills, editorial skills, bibliographic skills, IT skills, period-specific skills (such as learning to read secretary script or how to record variants amongst different manuscripts), and professional skills such as how to present papers at a conference (Williams 2002, 58–59). Many of these skills are also required in other arts and humanities disciplines.

Such skills may be distinguished from research methods, concerned with how one carries out one's research. Here choice of method depends on the kind of research one wants to conduct. Thus the interpretation of artefacts (be they texts or objects) requires different methods—textual, visual—depending on the kind of artefact one is dealing with. Methodologies are the perspectives one brings to bear on one's research, such as feminist or postcolonialist ones, for example. The many different critical interpretations of diverse artefacts are possible not least because different people bring different perspectives to bear on their analyses of a given object. A feminist reading of Jane Austen's *Mansfield Park* might consider how space is differently assigned to women and men in the text, and the trait in Austen's novels of confining women to house and garden (they fall in every sense of that word if they leave that space), whilst a postcolonial reading might focus on the role which Sir Bertram's ownership of plantations in Antigua plays in the novel's portrayal of male authority. Different methodological perspectives will thus yield quite different insights into one's material (see also Lukić and Sánchez Espinosa's discussion of different feminist close readings of Charlotte Brontë's *Jane Eyre*, chapter 7, this volume).

This brief description of the differences between bringing a feminist or a postcolonial perspective to bear on a text indicates one important aspect of conducting a research project: selection. Deciding on a particular research project is to a significant extent about deciding on the specific research skills, methods and methodologies necessary and appropriate to conduct that research. When examiners read PhD theses or panels assess research applications, they consider how appropriate that selection is.

Such selection implies a narrowing down of the vast array of skills, methods and methodologies available to a researcher. This should not, however, blind one to the fact that all research requires more than one research skill or method (though not usually methodology). For instance, if one decides to write a biography, one might conduct archival research, textual and document analyses, interviews, discourse analysis, employ visual methods and possibly even quantitative methods to arrive at the final product. Researchers never employ just one research skill or method but work with a combination of these. This is evident in the traces of research made increasingly explicit by writers of historical novels and of auto/biography, for example. Even Margaret Forster starts her postfixed 'Author's Note' on her family memoir *Hidden Lives* with the sentence: "In one sense there was no real research . . . for this book since it relies so heavily on personal memory . . . but attempting to place these memories . . . in some historical context did lead to a great deal of delving into the Cumbria County Council Archives" (1995, 308). Such disavowal, followed by an acknowledgment of a research process, is very interesting, and research might be undertaken into how and why literary authors articulate the research process underpinning their writing.

The distinction between research skills, methods and methodologies is useful for understanding different aspects of the research process, but it is also a distinction that is in some respects artificial because the three are interdependent and are equally necessary to the successful completion of a research project. Carolyn Steedman's (2005) 'Archival Methods' includes very practical advice such as the need for pencils in archives (don't bring a biro—you may not be allowed to use it) and the smallest handbag possible (bags are also not usually allowed); methodological reflections, here on the nature of archives, for example, and on the fact that the agenda underlying their establishment is different from that of visiting researchers'; and method-related ones such as the incompleteness of any archive, and the search for the 'lost' object within these. All of these influence the outcome of using archival methods to conduct research; understanding the incompleteness of archives, for instance, impacts on what other archives or sources one decides to use to 'complete' (if this is ever possible) the information one has. Similarly, understanding the reason why an archive was established helps one to assess its contents; the desire to preserve a particular memory of a specific person, for instance, may lead to the destruction—not necessarily immediately evident to the researcher—of all materials (letters, diaries and so forth) that detract from that particular memory.

This understanding of the partiality of research findings (which is not particular to the conduct of auto/biographical research) has, in some disciplines, led to a discussion of what constitutes 'good' research. Auto/biographies, for instance, are notoriously slated by critics—when they are criticised—for their incompleteness, for failure to include certain kinds of information. In the (hard/natural) sciences, criteria such as verifiability of data (can one independently produce the same results), falsifiability (can the results be proved wrong), reliability (can the results be independently reproduced time and again), generalisibility (is what is found true of all texts/ people and the rest belonging to the category for which claims are made) and so on have been invoked to establish if something constitutes 'good' research. But the nature of much arts/humanities research and our changing understanding of what research can and cannot do/be, has increasingly led to the interrogation of the validity and appropriateness of those criteria (e.g., Peräkylä 1997; Phillips and Jørgensen 2002, 182–212; M. M. Gergen and K. J. Gergen 2003) which are, in any event, clearly not equally applicable across all research and knowledge domains. Instead, writers on research methods increasingly invoke criteria such as plausibility (i.e., how persuasive a set of findings are to a given community of readers), reflexivity (how much awareness of the particularities of the research process and its impacts on the findings are articulated by the author) and comprehensiveness (how extensive and exhaustive was the research conducted) to evaluate what constitutes 'good' research (Hollway and Jefferson 2000; Smith and Deemer 2003).

A CATALOGUE OF HUMANITIES/ARTS METHODS

These are useful criteria to bear in mind in undertaking *oral history* projects (see Pető and Waaldijk, chapter 5, this volume) where information provided by interviewees has to be triangulated with other evidence to understand the workings of personal memory (see also Cerwonka's discussion of feminist debates on the notion of 'experience,' chapter 4, this volume). Penny Summerfield (2005) utilises her experience of such projects to show how the narratives of 'ordinary' people can modify public records of events—in this instance, of women's role in the Home Guards during World War II. Summerfield's account of the imbrication of personal memory in the reproduction of cultural narratives (revealed in one of her interviewee's critical engagement, through the lens of her own experiences, with the popular UK TV programme *Dad's Army*) suggests the use of oral history as a means of understanding the workings of, for example, literary and cultural phenomena in and on people's imagination.

Like oral history, *visual methods* are vital for the arts/humanities because visual signs are a dominant aspect of our cultural world. As Gillian Rose (2005) suggests, all art forms from art images to graphic novels or stage designs produce a rich visual research world (see also Buikema and Zarzycka, chapter 8, this volume). Yet in certain arts/humanities subjects we either tend to ignore them or treat them in a positivistic manner as if their meanings were self-evident and required no specific engagement. Rose (2005) details three different ways in which visual signs might be approached methodologically, namely, via compositional interpretation, semiology and discourse analysis. She argues that these different approaches draw attention to diverse aspects of visual images such as the detail of the image itself and its context of production and/or reproduction. She also importantly points out that visual images do not only accompany texts; frequently, the reverse is true, i.e. texts accompany visual images as captions to photographs or explanations for exhibits in museums. Implicit in this is frequently a hierarchization of sign systems, where one sign system is privileged over another although their interplay operates to question that structure. Obvious examples of this are textual explanations in art galleries. Such sites privilege the visual image but viewers frequently bend first to read the caption, all the better to 'understand' the image.

In discussing *discourse analysis* as a method for exploring visual material, Rose draws on Michel Foucault's notion of discourse as a form of discipline that produces subjects. Visual images, such as signs in libraries telling us to turn off mobile phones and not to smoke, effect such disciplining, thus constructing us as particular subjects. Rose argues that discourse analysis can be used as a research method to show how images construct specific views of the world. The same is true of the use of discourse analysis for textual interpretations. Discourse analysis, particularly as critical discourse analysis (CDA) simultaneously references a theory of language, namely, of language as *invested* and a method for researching written and oral language as it is actually used. CDA is centrally concerned with analysing patterns in language use in order to uncover the workings of ideology or investment within/through it, and thus to be able to resist it. As discourse analysis entails selection of focus—we may, for instance, concentrate on the verb forms used in a given text in order to highlight how that text constructs agency—it can never be complete.

One way in which it may be conducted is with the use of computer programs such Atlas.ti or NUDIST (Short and Deegan 2005). *Computer-aided discourse analysis* is carried out by an increasing number of researchers within the arts and humanities; it is part of the amazing IT revolution which is set to produce new ways, and change some of the existent ways, in which we conduct research in all disciplines. It requires a change in disposition among researchers; learning to use computer programs to conduct discourse analysis demands time and effort, something frequently not built into individuals' research plans. This, however, may change as requirements for much more explicit research training programs for research students become imperative.

Where discourse analysis centres on language, *ethnographic research methods* extend that concern to cultural and social practices. Rachel Alsop (2005) offers a brief exposition of ethnographic methods and changes in understanding of those methods as a means of recognising that ethnographic accounts constitute 'fictions' about an experience (and are thus of course amenable to the kinds of literary analyses that we might subject other fictional accounts to regarding, for instance, narrative structure) and reflect particular dispositions regarding those written about. Alsop further engages with the recent rise in reading groups to discuss how these offer a site for ethnographic research in English studies. Audience research, too, in the theatre, cinema and at performance sites such as literature festivals, might be done utilizing ethnographic methods to create what have become known as microethnographies.

Quite different opportunities exist through the use of *quantitative methods* in the study of literature. Pat Hudson (2005) asks why scholars of literary texts have tended to ignore the numbers they encounter in such texts, for instance, in the detailing of wealth in eighteenth-century novels. She suggests that this is partly attributable to the different values we attach to words and numbers—crudely, viewing the former as subjective and the latter as objective. Hudson argues that this distinction is misguided and outlines how numbers may be used both as interpretive tools and as a means of conveying sets of information not readily producible in another form. In particular she shows that computational methods for calculating the frequency with which certain words occur and the contexts in which they are set can act as a useful tool for interpreting the meaning of a text and for the purposes of authorship attribution. Second, Hudson shows how statistical methods can be useful for displaying information about texts, audiences, the production and consumption of texts and so forth.

Textual analysis is, of course, a staple of much arts/humanities research. It is about the close reading of cultural artefacts (for a discussion of close reading, see also chapter 7, this volume). Catherine Belsey (2005) bases her empirical account of how one conducts textual analysis on a painting, Titian's *Tarquin and Lucretia*. Taking the reader through a close analysis of that work and thus laying bare her methods, Belsey highlights how textual analysis relies on other and additional research methods as well as a methodology or perspective (here a feminist one) to give focus to the reading one produces. Textual analysis thus has to be informed by background research into the context of a given culture, the context of its production, content, and consumption. Belsey encourages the researcher's need to consult original sources. She suggests that understanding meaning making, differently understood in different historical periods and by different theoreticians, is key to undertaking textual analyses. She understands meaning making as a relational process, between cultural artefact and consumer, but also between the consumer (viewer, reader) and those to whom consumers communicate the meanings they have established for a given artefact. This understanding relativises meaning; it reiterates the situatedness of knowledge, its partiality and specificity, already highlighted in connection with other research methods discussed.

Situatedness is important when considering *interviewing* as a research method. The representation of interviews with living authors, one of the more common kinds of interview conducted in literary studies research, tends to obscure the interview process. Interviewing requires a series of practical skills, a clear understanding of the different kinds of interview one might conduct and their underlying assumptions, knowledge of the different ways in which interviews can be transcribed and how these constitute and influence interpretations of interview material. Interviewing as a research method often combines with, or is part of, other research methods, including auto/biographical methods, ethnographic methods, oral history and, indeed, textual analysis or discourse analysis at the point where the interview material is interpreted. It thus forms a central plank of many arts/humanities research processes.

Whereas interviewing may be viewed as uncontentiously representing a research method, *creative work* as research has only recently been considered in that light. The 2001 Research Assessment Exercise panel in the UK, for example, saw creative writing "as an important element within English departments" to be "assessed . . . in so far as it represents 'the invention and generation of ideas, images, performances where these lead to new or substantially improved insights'" (UK Research Assessment Exercise 2001a, 1–2). This was substantially repeated in the 2008 Research Assessment Exercise (see UK Research Assessment Exercise 2006).

Cook (2005) engages with the issue of how to define creative writing as a research method *inter alia* in the light of public funding bodies' attempts to grapple with this particular issue. Across the creative arts, from creative writing to music, performance, dance, film, video and digital work and fine art, debates are occurring about the assessment of creative work as research. In consequence, Edinburgh University Press brought out a volume on this issue as part of its Research Methods for the Arts and Humanities series.[10] To qualify as research, creative work is frequently required to be accompanied by a theoretical piece of writing, detailing its research dimension.

The articulation at metadiscursive level of how the research process underpinning creative work is embedded within it constitutes one way of establishing creative work as research. Cook (2005) takes another approach, focusing on the notion of creative writing as discovery, through utilizing essays by Seamus Heaney and Mark Schorer to explore how writing skills, or craft, and technique materialise subject matter. He juxtaposes these positions with Denise Riley's who regards writing not as active discovery but as a form of passivity before the assault of language that rushes at us from outside. A distinction emerges between the work of language and the work of the writer, resulting in creative writing as "a mode of research into the nature of literary form and language" (Cook 2005, 205). Cook links this insight into the practice of rewriting as the process through which research into form takes place, re/producing the process of discovery at every draft. Cook relates this process to the need for reading, as the activity through which writing as discovery both of content and form may be informed. His assertion that these interrelated processes and activities can be documented and critically analysed, that is, a metanarrative about the research process informing creative activity can be derived from these, is an important contribution to the question of how to understand creative writing as a research method.

In 'ICT as a Research Method' Harold Short and Marilyn Deegan (2005) tread on relatively new ground in that ICT methods in the humanities are a recent phenomenon, to date still carried out mainly by specialist researchers in particular fields of textual analysis and in linguistics. However, as they make clear, the advent of more and more, and more easily useable, computer software and hardware has greatly enhanced opportunities for researchers in arts/humanities to work on literary and other texts. Short and Deegan offer a brief history of textual computing, then examine how it has been used to store and analyse literary texts. They discuss the issues involved in creating digital archives of manuscript sources and provide information about some of the most interesting literature digitization projects and what these involve. They analyse how computers as a medium change our relations to texts and the implications this has for literary criticism, for theories of the text and for interactions with texts including in the area of scholarly editions. Importantly, they highlight the implications of this for possibilities of collaborative research.

CONCLUDING REMARKS

In contrast to the explosion of research methods texts in the social sciences over the past twenty-five years, in the arts/humanities there is still very little in certain disciplines (compare, for example, the wealth of texts on historical research methods relative to the paucity of such texts for literature or film studies). Importantly, the 'cultural turn' in the social sciences, as any perusal of 'Research Methods' catalogues by publishers such as Sage or Blackwell shows, has led to an extensive appropriation of research methods entirely derived from the arts/humanities, a fact that surprisingly has gone largely unremarked upon by the arts/humanities communities themselves. Thus instead of thinking of research methods as an alien graft upon arts/humanities disciplines, we should be proudly reclaiming those methods and making them more explicitly our own. We should also recognise that such reclamation will aid dialogue and collaboration across disciplines and will encourage researchers to think divergently about the kinds of research they might engage in. Within many arts/humanities disciplines the process of articulating research methods is only just beginning. There is a significant need to move this process forward and for the arts/humanities to re/claim the methods that have underpinned research in these fields.

NOTES

1. For the purposes of this chapter I use 'discipline' and 'subject' interchangeably.
2. In an EU-funded research project on integrated research methods in the humanities and social sciences (2004–2007) we found that different European countries had very different ways of classifying disciplines (*ResearchIntegration*).
3. Eliot and Owens' *A Handbook to Literary Research* (1998), designed to accompany the Open University's MA in literature, is one of the very few books that has appeared on the subject.
4. It should be pointed out that the rapidly increasing sophistication of computer software and the introduction of programmes such as Masterfile and Endnote, designed to enable the production of large documents such as theses with automatically generated lists of contents, indexes, bibliographies and so forth means that both practising academics and research students need training in the use of these advanced technologies. Many academics still tend to use their computers as a superior form of typewriter. As someone whose first computer was the earliest Amstrad onto which one had to load the software programme every time one wanted to use the computer, I am keenly aware of the discrepancy between technologies available in the 1970s and 1980s and those available now to aid research.
5. See Williams (2002), par. 4.1.1 on the rejection of that terminology.
6. According to the 2001 RAE English Panel's Overview Report (UK Research Assessment Exercise 2001b), eighty-nine institutions submitted a total of 1,526 full-time equivalent numbers of staff under English language and literature (Unit 50 of the RAE 2001).
7. One of the frequent complaints about the ESRC research training requirements is that, at Masters level, they are so extensive that they leave little room for the substantive content of a given Masters course and that they are too heavily weighted in favour of quantitative methods which many social scientists do not routinely employ.
8. Thus the 2001 RAE English Panel's Criteria and Working Methods stated: "The Panel recognises that English includes a very broad range of approaches and is by its nature frequently interdisciplinary, and it will take a broad view of what constitutes English" (3.41.3).
9. It is also a function of long histories of disciplinisation which engage in active boundary patrols regarding their domains. When I submitted a research application of text-based research on women playwrights to a subject panel on 'Drama and Theatre Studies,' I was advised to resubmit the proposal to the 'Language and Literature' panel because my research was text- rather than performance-based—despite being focused entirely on contemporary theatre work. Irrespective of the relative merit of my application, it is interesting to note that this advice constitutes research-methods-based policing of disciplinary boundaries where it is not so much what you work on, but how you work on it, which determines your categorisation for funding purposes.
10. See Dean, Smith and Dean (2009). A current volume in process, Baz Kershaw and Helen Nicholson's *Research Methods in Theatre and Performance* (EUP 2011) also takes a practice-as-performance approach.

REFERENCES

Arts and Humanities Research Board (AHRB). 2002. *Review of Postgraduate Programmes*. http://www.ccue.ac.uk/fileadmin/documents/AHRBreview_01. pdf (accessed August 25, 2010).

Arts and Humanities Research Council (AHRC). Joint Statement of the Research Councils Skills Training Requirements for Research Students. http://www.vitae. ac.uk/cms/files/RCUK-Joint-Skills-Statement-2001.pdf (accessed August 25, 2010).

Alsop, R. 2005. The Uses of Ethnography. In *Research Methods for English Studies*, ed. G. Griffin, 111–30. Edinburgh: Edinburgh University Press.

Belsey, C. 2005. Textual Analysis as a Research Method. In *Research Methods for English Studies*, ed. G. Griffin, 157–74. Edinburgh: Edinburgh University Press.

Cook, J. 2005. Creative Writing as a Research Method. In *Research Methods for English Studies*, ed. G. Griffin, 195–211. Edinburgh: Edinburgh University Press.

Dean, R., H. Smith and R. T. Dean, eds. 2009. *Practice-led Research, Research-led Practice in the Creative Arts*. Edinburgh: Edinburgh University Press.

Eliot, S., and W. R. Owens, eds. 1998. *A Handbook to Literary Research*. London: Routledge.

Forster, M. 1995. *Hidden Lives: A Family Memoir*. London: Penguin.

Gergen, M. M., and K. J. Gergen. 2003. Qualitative Inquiry: Tensions and Transformations. In *The Landscape of Qualitative Research*, ed. N. K. Denzin and Y. S. Lincoln, 575–610. London: Sage.

Hollway, W., and T. Jefferson. 2000. *Doing Qualitative Research Differently*. London: Sage.

Hudson, P. 2005. Numbers and Words: Quantitative Methods for Scholars of Texts.In *Research Methods for English Studies*, ed. G. Griffin, 131–56. Edinburgh: Edinburgh University Press.

NORA—Nordic Journal of Feminist and Gender Research 2 (14). Special issue, *(Inter)disciplinarity and the Bologna Process: Walk on the Wild Side?*

Peräkylä, A. 1997. Reliability and Validity in Research Based on Naturally Occurring Social Interaction. In *Qualitative Research: Theory, Method and Practice*, ed. D. Silverman, 283–304. London: Sage.

Phillips, L., and M. Jørgensen, eds. 2002. *Discourse Analysis as Theory and Method*. London: Sage.

Rose, G. 2005. Visual Methodologies. In *Research Methods for English Studies*, ed. G. Griffin, 67–90. Edinburgh: Edinburgh University Press.

Short, H., and M. Deegan. 2005. ICT as a Research Method. In *Research Methods for English Studies*, ed. G. Griffin, 213–36. Edinburgh: Edinburgh University Press.

Smith, J. K., and D. K. Deemer. 2003. The Problem of Criteria in the Age of Relativism. In *Collecting and Interpreting Qualitative Materials*, ed. N. K. Denzin and Y. S. Lincoln, 427–57. 2nd ed. Thousand Oaks: Sage.

Steedman, C. 2005. Archival Methods. In *Research Methods for English Studies*, ed. G. Griffin, 17–30. Edinburgh: Edinburgh University Press.

Summerfield, P. 2005. Oral History as a Research Method. In *Research Methods for English Studies*, ed. G. Griffin, 47–66. Edinburgh: Edinburgh University Press.

UK Research Assessment Exercise. 2001a. English Panel's Criteria and Working Methods. http://www.rae.ac.uk/2001/PanGuide/guide/guide2.htm (accessed August 19, 2010).

———. 2001b. English Panel's Overview Report. http://www.rae.ac.uk/2001/overview/docs/UoA50.pdf (accessed August 19, 2010).

———. 2006. English Panel's Definition of Research for the RAE, Annex 3. http://www.rae.ac.uk/pubs/2006/01/docs/m57.pdf (accessed August 18, 2010).

Williams, S. (2002) 2003. *Postgraduate Training in Research Methods: Current Practice and Future Needs in English*. London: English Subject Centre, Royal Holloway College.

WEB SITES

UK Arts and Humanities Research Council. http://www.ahrc.ac.uk (accessed August 18, 2010).

ResearchIntegration. http://www.york.ac.uk/res/researchintegration (accessed August 19, 2010).

7 Feminist Perspectives on Close Reading

Jasmina Lukić and Adelina Sánchez Espinosa

This chapter re/evaluates the importance of close reading while openly foregrounding gender as a critical concept. It sets out to show that far from being neutral as conventionally assumed, or alien to feminism because of its connections with so-called formalist approaches, close reading as a method of interpretation remains a useful tool for feminist analysis. After a brief look at the history of the method, this chapter moves on to investigate how the traditional strategies of close reading become modified, invigorated and renewed when adapted to the needs of feminist and gender studies methodological claims. We will illustrate our points with a critical insight of the ways in which a feminist favourite, Charlotte Brontë's novel *Jane Eyre* (1847), has been closely read by feminist scholars from a number of different critical positions.[1]

INTRODUCTION: CLOSE READING AND ITS REREADINGS

For several decades now strategies of close reading have not been discussed very much in academia, being seemingly abandoned together with New Criticism, an approach to literary studies which introduced close reading as its preferred interpretative method. As Ato Quayson outlines:

> Central to the close reading inspired by the New Criticism was an attempt to identify ambiguity, irony, and paradox as different levels at which the text signaled tensions within its structure. A methodological implication that derived from this focus was that the external world of politics and society was efficiently bracketed out of consideration. Furthermore, the aesthetic object, most often a poem, was elevated to a superior ontology and became the privileged gateway for knowing the world. (Quayson 2005, 122)

In describing the core of the New Critics' literary credo, Quayson also lists some of the central arguments against them from debates which started in the 1960s, namely, their ahistorical approach to the literary text, which is understood as a totalised self-contained entity that transcends its immediate social and historical context.

The paradigm shift which occurred in the following decade and brought poststructuralism and deconstruction to the centre of theoretical debates has gradually suppressed the influence of New Criticism, and more generally of formalist approaches, seemingly diminishing the importance of close reading as well. However, as Jane Gallop recently argued when speaking of the paradigm shift from the point of view of English studies, close reading can be seen as an important link between the two debating sides, the New Critics and the deconstructionists: "Looking back now at that period, I would emphasize not the debate about theory but the close reading practice appearing on both sides of the divide. Deconstructionism did not challenge the centrality of close reading to English; on the contrary, it infused it with new zeal" (Gallop 2007, 182).

What Gallop states here is also argued in a somewhat different manner by Frank Lentricchia and Andrew DuBois in their comprehensive anthology *Close Reading: The Reader* (2003). Starting from DuBois' claim that "there is no single influential manifesto or statement of purpose that insists on the term itself as the sole name for a particular practice" (Dubois 2003, 3), the editors frame the problems of close reading in a broader context as questions about the nature of reading in general. The anthology is organised in such a way as to "assert that a genuine (perhaps the central) debate in twentieth-century literary criticism is a debate between formalist and non-formalist methods of response" (Dubois 2003, 1). While an effort is made to reaffirm formalist strategies of reading, the collection more importantly shows the extent to which actual reading practices depend on the questions asked and on how much a supposedly 'objective' method of 'close reading' can produce very different results if applied in different interpretative frameworks. Thus, together with texts from Ransome and Brooks as founding figures of the method of close reading, and from Krieger and Lentricchia as critics who further developed and applied the method in a more traditional sense of the term, we also find articles representing poststructuralist strategies of close reading (de Man and Barthes), New Historicism (Gallagher and Greenblatt), feminism (Gilbert and Gubar; Kosofsky Sedgwick), and postcolonial criticism (Bhabha). Using close reading as a link between these different approaches, the anthology puts an emphasis on the *contextuality* and *historicity* of any reading, immanent ones included.

Quayson approaches the same problem from the other side. After several decades of predominance of reading methods that privilege social context over specific questions of the form, Quayson wants to bring back into consideration "a respect for the text as an aesthetic object" (Quayson 2005, 124), but in such a way as to keep an equally strong interest in social reality:

> [W]hile retaining a clearly Marxian vocabulary in *Callibrations*, I sought to elaborate a method that would not ascribe to either literature or society any prior or supervening causality. . . . The task I set

myself then was to elaborate a method of reading that would be replicated in relation to different literary and social contexts. (Quayson 2005, 126)

The basis for such a method is close reading, which for Quayson helps with understanding not only literary structures but also social reality:

For me objects to be analyzed are assumed to be constitutively woven out of heterogeneities in the first instance, the task then being to identify the specific *configuration* and *implications* of the coming together of these heterogeneities. And this counts for both literary as for the nonliterary objects. (Quayson 2005, 127)

FEMINIST APPROACHES TO CLOSE READING: AN OVERVIEW

Feminist methodologies have marginalised or disregarded close reading since the early days of the second wave. This marginalisation started with the rejection of intrinsic approaches to literary studies in the 1970s, and it remains visible nowadays. For example, in *A Handbook of Literary Feminisms* by Shari Benstock, Suzanne Ferriss and Susanne Woods (2002) there is a short but highly useful glossary of key terms in feminist literary studies. It is indicative, though, that 'close reading' is not one of them, nor is it listed in a number of other dictionaries, handbooks, casebooks and other popular reference works that help students orient themselves in feminist literary and cultural studies (Humm 1986; Eagleton 1991; Armstrong 1992; Belsey and Moore 1997; Belsey 2002; Moi 2002).

With that said, close reading, once detached from the restrictive theoretical framework of New Criticism, remains one of the much needed tools in feminist literary studies, cultural studies and beyond. As part of critical reading of different cultural texts, close reading is being used within a variety of feminist interpretative frameworks, including, amongst others, feminist stylistics, deconstruction, postcolonial readings and narratological interpretations. "For feminist narratologists 'close reading' is still very much a 'going concern' as we begin a new century," states Robyn Warhol, approaching narratology as a particular form of close reading (Warhol 2003, 25). Meanwhile, Sara Mills, following Peggy Kamuf, claims that "for many feminists teaching and reading, our own suspicious reading of texts may take the form of close reading" (Mills 1995, 15).

Indeed, both Mills and Kamuf, the former from a stylistic perspective and the latter from a deconstructionist one, serve as examples of the various facets of the reappropriation of close reading by contemporary feminist methodologies. Mills outlines her understanding of feminist close reading in the article 'Knowing Your Place: A Marxist Feminist Stylistic Analysis' (1992), the main ideas of which are later expanded in her book *Feminist Stylistics* (1995), where she elaborates in more detail concrete strategies of interpretation. Developing a feminist version of contextualised stylistics, Mills starts with a revision of the model of context as it was used in traditional linguistics. In her view, "textual production and reception are considered to be part of context, and not simply the context of production" (Mills 1992, 183). Thus she creates a model which in *Feminist Stylistics* is presented as a "feminist model of the text" (Mills 1995, 31), where context is introduced through a series of interrelated categories like textual antecedents, literary conventions, current literary trends, affiliation, publishing practice, sociohistorical factors and author: "Thus, texts are determined by a wide range of pressures on their processes of production and reception, and also have an effect on their audience and on the process of production of further texts" (1992, 185). This does not mean that the text has lost its centrality in the process of interpretation, and Mills underlines the importance of "dominant reading/s" without which there "would be no consensus whatsoever as to what texts meant" (1992, 189). At the same time, in the way it addresses its reader, the text opens a space for 'oppositional reading,' a concept which enables Mills to engender her model of the feminist text.

In the reading process, following Julie Rivkin and Tanya Modleski, Mills insists on multiple positionings: "[W]hat is required is a more complex notion of what 'reading as a woman/man' consists of, which would take account of other factors which interact with gender" (1995, 79). The actual text remains at the centre of this interrogation since, in practical terms, Mills separates three levels of analysis: of the word, of the phrase/sentence and of the discourse. In the actual analysis she is primarily interested in gender perspectives and in sexism in language. Following the main assumption of linguistic determinism that "language *produces* our perception of the world" (Mills 1992, 84), she wants not only to unmask different ways in which sexism works in language but also to propose strategies to oppose it.

Moving on to Peggy Kamuf, we actually have to go back to deconstructionist strategies of close reading, that is, to reading from the margin and through erasure of the borders that are set by the 'proper' signature and the institution of literary criticism. Kamuf uses as an example *Les Lettres Portugaises (The Letters of a Portuguese Nun;* 1669), a text which was initially published without any authorial name, and whose authorship has been differently attributed over several centuries, first to a woman and later to a man.

As a text without clear authorial attribution, *Les Lettres Portugaises* can be seen as an ideal example for the traditional stylistic or New Critical form of close reading. However, Kamuf uses the text to show how gender intervenes in the supposedly objective approaches of both older literary historians from earlier centuries, as well as of those who wrote in the 1950s, such as Leo Spitzer. Kamuf shows that even Spitzer's stylistic analysis is guided by the same principles of patriarchal logic which traditionally ascribes craftsmanship to men and only rough, unre-fined feelings to women. Kamuf manages to preserve an appreciation for Spitzer's knowledge and skills, whilst at the same time thoroughly undermining the whole system of values on which it is based, with its privileging of the male principle over anything recognised as 'female' or 'feminine.' Kamuf does not want, however, to change the privileging of one reading over the other:

> [T]o affix a signature—a determinate intentionality—to a text, whether as we read or as we write, is to attempt what Spitzer tries to do with this essay: contain an unlimited textual system, install a measure of protec-tion between this boundlessness and one's own power to know, to be this power and to know that one is this power. (Kamuf 1980, 297)

Thus, taking away the name from the text points to the inherent instabil-ity of the meaning and opens the text for all kinds of subversive readings. This early text by Kamuf indicates why deconstructionist practices of close reading with their emphasis on multiple, indeterminate meanings of the text are compatible with feminist approaches and why it was pos-sible for feminist theorists working in this frame to use it extensively. The discussion of 'parenthood' of the text in Kamuf's article is obviously historically contextualised in feminist debates of the time over the role of women in literature, and the ways in which patriarchy excludes them from the realm of creative writing. Kamuf questions the assumption that to write means to 'father' a text, radically reversing the claim by suggest-ing that "reading a text as written by a woman will be reading it *as if* it had no (determined) father, *as if*, in other words, it were illegitimate, recognized by its mother who can only give it a borrowed name" (Kamuf 1980, 298). Kamuf does not speak of a *biological* woman here, of a sexed writer's body and identity; she translates the problem to the domain of reading, into a reading position that can obviously be taken equally by anyone, but which has to be subversive towards the dominant logic of phallocentrism.

In her 2007 volume *Reading in Detail*, Naomi Schor proposes another version of close reading which uses deconstructionist tradition to an extent, but also feminist aesthetics grounded in practices of oppositional reading. In a preface to a recent edition of the book Ellen Rooney calls bringing gen-der into the study of textual details "an aesthetics of Bad Objects" (Rooney 2007, xiii). Schor raises the following questions:

> [I]s detail feminine? Are women—that is, females socialized as wom-en—as so many thinkers both male and female assert, more firmly grounded than men in the world of immanence? Do the works pro-duced by women artists exhibit a higher density of homey and/or orna-

mental details than those produced by their male counterparts? (Schor 2007, 116)

The answers lead her to move beyond the details to search for a wider social and ideological context in which women are forced to articulate their particular position:

> [T]here exists no reliable body of evidence to show that women's art is either more or less particularistic then men's. . . . Feminine specificity lies in the direction of a specifically feminine form of idealism, one that seeks to transcend not the sticky feminine world of prosaic details, but rather the deadly asperities of male violence and destruction. (Schor 2007, 116–17)

With such a conclusion Schor actually makes a shift from an abstract philosophical and aesthetic debate on the nature of the detail in literary studies, and its role in reading, to very immediate, socially grounded readings of both male and female texts that takes into account some very concrete devastating effects of patriarchy.

Likewise, Sara Ahmed's approach (1998) is most illuminating regarding the relationship between feminism and postmodernism; the attitude of feminism should be 'speaking back' to postmodernism. The differences defining postmodern constructions of rights, ethics, woman, subjectivity and so forth are those that matter and 'close reading' is used as a feminist methodology to exhibit those differences. Ahmed states that "a concern with what postmodernism is doing requires a commitment to close reading" (1998, 17), and like DuBois (2007), she insists that "this approach to closer readings is hence bound up with ethics, with the meta-discursive question of what makes some readings more just than others" (Ahmed 1998, 9).

While voicing feminism in rapport with postmodernism, Ahmed's close reading of postmodern texts helps her challenge the indeterminacy of the latter. Ahmed argues against reading postmodernism as a generalising and inclusive condition and calls for a closer reading of the differences within postmodernism. What are the implications for feminism if it is positioned within this generalised postmodernism? Would that positioning obliterate the differences, multifarious aspects and varieties within feminism itself? Ahmed responds with a close reading of some feminist postmodernist texts and by advocating a "transformative" feminist close reading of postmodernism which would be "speaking to postmodernism as a feminist works to destabilize both terms, pointing to the differences that matter which are located within (and not just between) the terms" (Ahmed 1998, 15).

Close reading is also the methodology used in Ahmed's approach to feminist theory, in which she claims that "critical readings need to pay attention to the authorization of certain theoretical texts within the academy" (1998, 17). Thus, a closer and more critical reading of authorised theoretical texts supports Ahmed's political position, transforming authorisation within the academy and voicing silenced feminist scholarship in this dialogue with postmodernism. Her close readings aim to produce the following results:

> [The judgments] will be re-worked as sites of critical potential for feminism: by locating problems, say, in how postmodern texts have dealt with the question of ethics, I will then provide an alternative way of dealing with such a question. Throughout, I will move from a particular judgment to a more general reflection on the differences that might matter for feminism. The closer readings of particular postmodern texts hence enable me to delineate a trans/formative feminist position. (Ahmed 1998, 20)

READINGS OF *JANE EYRE* AS A CASE IN POINT

As we have shown in the survey above, close reading can be used in different theoretical frameworks. To illustrate our point we are going to review here several feminist readings of *Jane Eyre* by Charlotte Brontë (1847) from the last decades. Jane Eyre is a canonical feminist text. We shall emphasise the differences between a number of feminist readings of it.

One of the early readings of *Jane Eyre* where close reading has been used to support specific feminist frames of interpretation was that of Elaine Showalter in *A Literature of Their Own* (1995). Showalter read *Jane Eyre* in accordance with her understanding of the development of the women's tradition in England, which she divides into three phases: *feminine*, *feminist* and *female* (Showalter 1995, 13). *Jane Eyre* belongs to the feminine phase, which is characterised by "*imitation* of the prevailing modes of the dominant tradition" (ibid., 13), and by "all-inclusive female realism, a broad, socially informed exploration of the daily lives and values of women within the family and the community" (ibid., 29). However, as Showalter remarks, "restrictive education and intensive conditioning" (ibid., 27) affected the way women wrote, making it difficult for them to surpass in their writings certain limits set by society. In her reading of *Jane Eyre* Showalter emphasises the richness of the psychological portrait of the heroine and the innovative narrative strategies used to achieve this richness. Brontë's most profound innovation "is the division of the Victorian female psyche into its extreme components of mind and body, which she externalizes as two characters, Helen Burns and Bertha Mason" (ibid., 113). As literary characters, both Helen and Bertha function on a realist level, but they are also polar personalities, extreme aspects of Jane Eyre herself, which have to be destroyed in order to give way to "the full strength and development of the central consciousness, for integration of the sprit and the body" (ibid., 113). Because Showalter reads the novel as a story of growing up and sexual maturation in Victorian England, Bertha Mason is more interesting to her than Helen Burns. Thus Showalter sees in Bertha Mason an image of untamed, uncontrolled sexuality which was generally perceived as a form of madness in women, supporting her claim with a series of quotes from notable physicians from the time of the publication of the book.

Showalter reads the plot of the novel as a series of interrelated seclusions, focusing her close reading on the episodes that confirm such a view. She starts the analysis of the novel with the episode of Jane Eyre being locked in the 'red room,' the first in a series of spaces used for disciplining the body and the mind of women who have excessive energy, and possibly excessive sexual appetite. Jane Eyre's time at Lowood School follows, and subsequently, her stay at Rochester's estate, complete with Bertha Mason's attic to demonstrate what happens to women who transgress the borders.

Behind Showalter's close reading of *Jane Eyre* lies primarily an attack on the patriarchal literary forces that reflected the Victorian concept of femininity, and also on a situation in which women's sexuality was a taboo to be expressed only in somatic metaphors of illness and madness, such as the 'madwoman in the attic.' Showalter's approach manifests, ultimately, this critic's recurrent concern with the penalisation and somatisation of women's sexuality in Victorian culture.[2]

The literary images behind the social oppression of Victorian women also inform both Adrienne Rich's and Sandra Gilbert's gynocritical close readings of *Jane Eyre*. Adrienne Rich's '*Jane Eyre*: The Temptations of a Motherless Woman' (1979) is now a classic text in which Rich's close reading follows the lines of her own interests in mothering, motherhood and the search for women's identity. Rich argues that the narrative in *Jane Eyre* is marked by a number of moments of female temptation to fall into madness, romantic love and self-destruction which Jane, motherless and powerless, can only resist and defeat with the help of the counteracting patterns of other strong women in whom she finds support and who, therefore, act as surrogate mothers whose model helps her grow into an independent self.

Rich 'close reads' the novel by framing it within the context of two central debates of early second-wave feminist literary criticism: passion and madness in women's writing. Thus, to Rich, Bertha is also Jane's alter ego, overpassionate to the point of madness, exemplifying the Victorian dichotomy between the freedom of sexual desire allowed to a fallen woman but forbidden to a married one. Rich concludes her analysis by proposing her own reading of women's liberation in which Brontë eventually castrates the patriarch, Rochester, and places him on an equal level with a woman who manages to preserve her sense of self-identity through the *bildungsroman*. The final marriage is, therefore, "a continuation of this woman's creation of herself" (Rich 1979, 483).

Sandra Gilbert's article on *Jane Eyre*, included in the well-known volume she coauthored with Susan Gubar titled *The Madwoman in the Attic* (1979), is probably the most influential analysis of the novel. In 'A Dialogue of Self and Soul: Plain Jane's Progress,' (1979) Gilbert uses the novel as an illustration of her two main concerns at the time: the canonising of literature by women and the difference in women's discourse. The locked-up Bertha now becomes a central metaphor for women's exclusion from the literary tradition and also for the palimpsestic nature of women's writing. Ultimately, in Gilbert's opinion, this novel is simply a case study of the difficulties every woman must negotiate in a patriarchal society: oppression, starvation, madness and, above all, "a secret dialogue of self and soul" (1979, 484)—a play between rational Jane and her irrational alter ego, Bertha, with the attic being the complex focal point of the conflict. Patriarchy exercises its power through Rochester's secret possession of the hidden details of sexuality, and it is this superiority of knowledge that undermines Jane's equality. Gilbert's reading is as liberating as Rich's, concluding that Jane's gradual awakening to her own needs makes for a final marriage of two minds.

Jane Eyre as an illustration of women's sexuality in the Victorian period is revisited by Gilbert twenty years later in '*Jane Eyre* and the Secrets of Furious Lovemaking' (1998). This article opens by referring back to her earlier impassioned reading of the novel as an example of how the literary is "both the personal and the political" (Gilbert 1998, 2). She qualifies that her fascination with the novel as arising from that which she sees as "the impassioned analysis of the multiple dramas of sexuality" (ibid., 5) so that Brontë's narrative "dramatizes a 'furious' yearning not just for political equality but for equality of desire" (ibid., 5). To Gilbert, Brontë's novel contributes to the public exposition of the need for a more equal view of women's sexuality, the madwoman fully qualified now as a metaphor of an uncontrolled sexuality which could be highly dangerous for the Victorian establishment of patriarchal power:

> From this perspective, the secret in the attic is not simply Brontë's rebellion and rage against the subordination of women, but also her intuition that the social enforcement of such subordination was grounded in widespread fears and yearnings that, if not properly controlled, could turn into insatiable and deadly sexual hungers. (Gilbert 1998, 10)

The theme of sexuality as that which should be read between the lines of some Victorian novels also lies at the core of another interesting 1978 close reading of *Jane Eyre*, contributed by the so-called Marxist-feminist Literature Collective, a large group including Cora Kaplan, Mary Jacobus and Michèle Barrett, among others. Their approaches to *Jane Eyre*, part of a larger contribution on women's writing in the nineteenth century, centre on the Machereyan concept of the 'not said,'[3] which they use for their readings of Victorian sexuality. They propose an interesting reading of the novel according to which the antagonistic forces that act as the motor of the novel are Jane's search for a kinship system, a family structure, and the opening of the tabooed subject locked in the attic, "the Pandora's box of unleashed female libido" (Marxist-feminist Literature Collective 1978, 119). In their opinion, *Jane Eyre* represents an insurgence of women's sexuality into the practice of literature so that, although the end seems to be a validation of the legitimised system, the 'not said' throughout the novel constitutes an active attempt to inscribe women as sexual subjects within the Victorian system.

A particularly influential text on *Jane Eyre* is Gayatri Chakravorty Spivak's 1985 comparative analysis of three women's texts which brings together critical readings of Brontë's text and Jean Rhys' *Wide Sargasso Sea* which can—as a creative rewriting, or 'reinscription' of *Jane Eyre*—also be seen as a kind of close reading of Brontë's novel. Together with these two novels, Spivak also reads Mary Shelley's *Frankenstein*, which is seen here as "an analysis—even a deconstruction—of a 'worlding' such as *Jane Eyre*'s" (Spivak 1985, 798).

Spivak is concerned with the 'printed book,' focusing on the text of the novel, excluding the author and moving away from deconstructionist versions of close reading. This reaffirmation of the unity of the text is needed here in order to support a very clear political message behind Spivak's analysis, a strong criticism of the logic of imperialism which she recognises in Brontë's book. The problem for Spivak is not so much that Brontë reproduces 'the axioms of imperialism' which were a part of her time, but that none of the feminist critics who have interpreted the novel have engaged with the relevance of that logic. Thus, however strongly focused on the novel, her analysis is actually meant to be in dialogue with a number of other feminist readings.

Spivak focuses on Bertha Mason, who is considered here to be "a figure produced by axiomatics of imperialism" (1993, 801), and in that sense she is not seen here as Jane's double but as a figure which indicates that behind Jane's personal project of creating a nuclear family for herself, there is also a "greater" project of "soul making beyond 'mere' sexual reproduction" (ibid., 802). Seen in this way, the story of Bertha Mason links with the narrative of St. John Rivers, which is the other central point in Spivak's reading of the novel. St. John Rivers is a character who wants to become a missionary, and he wants Jane to join him in this undertaking. Spivak emphasises that St. John "is granted the important task of concluding the *text*" so that

> [a]t the novel's end, the *allegorical* language of Christian psychobiography—rather than textually constituted a seemingly *private* grammar of the creative imagination which we noted at the novel's opening—marks the inaccessibility of the imperialist project as such to the nascent 'feminist' scenario. (Spivak 1985, 803)

In other words, it is the imperialist project which remains unquestioned in *Jane Eyre* that prevents the novel from developing its feminist potential. It is the criticism of this imperialist project in Jean Rhys's rewriting of *Jane Eyre* that liberates the critical approach to patriarchy in *Wide Sargasso Sea*.

Following Spivak, Susan Meyer also proposes a postcolonial reading of *Jane Eyre*, but she recognises in Brontë's novel a more complex approach to the issues of race, class and gender and to the British imperialist project. She claims that *"Jane Eyre* is characterized not by Spivak's 'unquestioned ideology' of imperialism but by an ideology of imperialism that is questioned—and then reaffirmed—in interesting and illuminating ways" (Meyer 1996, 66).

In Meyer's view, a critical attitude towards the imperial project is structurally built into the novel, and it occurs along the intersection of race, class and gender. In her rather detailed reading of the text, Meyer emphasises the ambiguous race identity of Bertha Mason, who is *becoming* black as the story develops through a series of details that emphasise her dark colour and particular facial features: "Bertha represents the 'dark races' in the empire, particularly African slaves, and gives them a human presence that lends a vividness to Brontë's metaphorical use of race" (1996, 72), which is openly related in the novel with gender and class issues. Meyer points to a variety of places where images of slavery are used to indicate the degraded position of Jane Eyre in a number of situations: in relation to her adoptive family, at the school in Lowood and in relation to Rochester, particularly but not exclusively at the time when she is a governess. Hence, Meyer's close reading focuses on particular scenes, on the language used and on the narrator's position towards what is being described.

When it comes to St. John's narrative Meyer's reading opposes Spivak's. Again using close reading, Meyer points out how negatively the narrator, that is, Jane Eyre, describes St. John. This in her view translates further into criticism of his imperial project as well (ibid., 87–89). However, Meyer also admits that the novel remains ambiguous in that respect, so that although "the ending of the novel punishes Rochester both for his figurative enslavement of women and for his acquisition of colonial wealth" (ibid., 91), it does not offer a resolution of colonial relations. Jane's own property, which enables her to say, "I am my own mistress," is also grounded in colonial relations of power and imperial practices and the whole of society and its everyday practices (represented here as 'Indian ink' and 'Morocco pocketbook') are permeated with them. That is why the line of criticism concerning imperialism is the only one which, in the end, lacks closure in the novel (ibid., 93–95).

A detailed critical analysis of Spivak's and Meyer's texts is offered by Rosemarie Buikema (1999), who has made an overview of feminist readings of *Jane Eyre* primarily looking into the ways feminist criticism has addressed configurations of gender, class and ethnicity. Buikema points to a shift in understanding and interpreting the feminist potentials of the novel, which were uncritically acclaimed in the 1970s and which were later questioned from postcolonial perspectives, emphasising the importance of Spivak's text and of the critical responses it had provoked. Looking closely at the arguments proposed by a number of critics, Buikema shows how "every particular framework produces new signs of exclusion and implies other signs of inclusion in the interpretation of *Jane Eyre*" (Buikema 1999, 47), thus demonstrating that "the readings do not exclude each other. On the contrary, every new reading adds to a deeper understanding of the gendered white middle-class identity" (ibid.).

CONCLUSIONS: THE MANY USES OF CLOSE READING FOR FEMINIST RESEARCH

The examples above illustrate that close reading relies heavily on a larger interpretive framework. It cannot exclude the context, nor a number of specific problems that are related to the position of the reader. Each one of these feminist critics closely reads the text from her own socio-critical standpoint, be it the concern with women's literary tradition and the liberation of tabooed sexuality in the 1970s; the oppression of imperialism in the 1980s; or integrative approaches to race, class and gender in the 1990s. Their similar use of close reading as method for interpretation proves that not only can close reading help to establish the grounds for oppositional readings but it can also bridge the gap between multifarious models of reading.[4] Furthermore, we can conclude with Jane Gallop that close reading is

> a widely applicable skill, of value not just to scholars in other disciplines but to a wide range of students with many different futures. Students trained in close reading have been known to apply it to diverse sorts of texts—newspaper articles, textbooks in other disciplines, political speeches—and thus to discover things they would not otherwise have noticed. (Gallop 2007, 183)

NOTES

1. For a discussion on how diverse research methodologies can lead to very different insights into the same material see Griffin (chapter 6, this volume).
2. Showalter revisits the issue several times in later works such as *The Female Malady: Women, Madness and Culture* (1985) or *Hystories* (1997).
3. On Pierre Macherey's Marxist theory of literature and his understanding of absent structure and lack in the text as the source of meanings, see Macherey (1978).
4. See Pető and Waaldijk (chapter 5, this volume) where the study of fiction is proposed as a useful tool for historical research, showing how research methods and interpretative practices are not discipline specific.

REFERENCES

Ahmed, S. 1998. *Differences that Matter: Feminist Theory and Postmodernism.* Cambridge: Cambridge University Press.

Armstrong, I. 1992. *New Feminist Discourses: Critical Essays on Theories and Texts*. London: Routledge.

Belsey, C. 2002. *Critical Practice*. London: Routledge.

Belsey, C., and J. Moore, eds. 1997. *The Feminist Reader: Essays in Gender and the Politics of Literary Criticism*. Oxford: Blackwell

Benstock, S., S. Ferriss and S. Woods. 2002. *A Handbook of Literary Feminisms*. New York: Oxford University Press.

Brontë, C. 1847. *Jane Eyre*. London: Smith, Elder and Co.

Buikema, R. 1999. From Literary Criticism to Cultural Studies: Configurations of Gender, Class, and Ethnicity in Charlotte Brontë's *Jane Eyre*. In *Differenzen ins Geschlechterdifferenz/Differences within Gender Studies: Aktuelle Perspektiven der Geschlechterfotschung*, ed. K. Röttger and H. Paul, 34 48. Berlin: Erich Schmidt Verlag.

DuBois, A. 2003. Introduction. In *Close Reading: The Reader*, ed. F. Lentricchia and A. DuBois, 1–40. Durham, NC: Duke University Press.

———. 2007. Ethics, Critics, Close Reading. *University of Toronto Quarterly: A Canadian Journal of the Humanities* 76 (3): 926–36.

Eagleton, M. 1991. *Feminist Literary Criticism*. London: Longman.

Gallop, J. 2007. The Historicization of Literary Studies and the Fate of Close Reading. In *Profession*, 181–86. New York: MLA.

Gilbert, S. M. 1979. A Dialogue of Self and Soul: Plain Jane's Progress. In *Jane Eyre: A Norton Critical Edition*, ed. R. J. Dunn, 483–90. New York and London: W.W. Norton.

———.1998. Jane Eyre and the Secrets of Furious Lovemaking. *Novel: A Forum on Fiction* 31 (3): 351–72.

Gilbert, S. M., and S. Gubar. 1979. *The Madwoman in the Attic: The Woman Writer and the Nineteenth-century Literary Imagination*. New Haven, CT: Yale University Press.

Humm, M. 1986. *Feminist Criticism: Women as Contemporary Critics*. London: Harvester Wheatsheaf.

Kamuf, P. 1980. Writing Like a Woman. In *Women and Language in Literature and Society*, ed. R. B. Mc.Connell-Ginet and N. Furman, 284–99. New York: Praeger Publishers.

Lentricchia, F., and A. DuBois, eds. 2003. *Close Reading: The Reader*. Durham, NC: Duke University Press.

Les Lettres Portugaises [Portuguese letters]. 1669. Paris: Claude Barbin.

Macherey, P. 1978. *A Theory of Literary Production*. Trans. G. Wall. London: Routledge.

Marxist-feminist Literature Collective. 1978. Women's Writing: Jane Eyre. In *A Practical Reader in Contemporary Literary Theory*, ed. P. Brooker and P. Widdowson, 112–20. London: Harvester Wheatsheaf; New York: Prentice Hall.

Meyer, S. 1996. "Indian Ink": Colonialism and the Figurative Strategy of Jane Eyre. In *Imperialism at Home: Race and Vitcorian Women's Fiction*, 60–95. Ithaca, NY: Cornell University Press.

Mills, S. 1992. Knowing your Place: A Marxist Stylistic Analysis. In *Language, Text and Context: Essays in Stylistics*, ed. M. Toolan, 182–207. London: Routledge.

———. 1995. *Feminist Stylistics*. London: Routledge.

Moi, T. 2002. *Sexual/Textual Politics: Feminist Literary Theory*. London: Routledge.

Quayson, A. 2005. Incessant Particularities: *Callibrations* as Close Reading. *Research in African Literatures* 36 (2): 122–31.

Rich, A. 1979. Jane Eyre: The Temptations of a Motherless Woman. In *Jane Eyre: A Norton Critical Edition*, ed. R. J. Dunn, 469–82. New York: W.W. Norton.

Rooney, E. 2007. Foreword: An Aesthetics of Bad Object. In *Reading in Detail*, by N. Schor, xiii–xxxv. New York and London: Routledge.

Schor, N. 2007. *Reading in Detail*. New York and London: Routledge.

Showalter, E. 1985. *The Female Malady: Women, Madness, and English Culture, 1830–1980*. New York: Pantheon Books.

———. 1995. (c. 1977). *A Literature of Their Own*. London: Virago Press.

———. 1997. *Hystories: Hysterical Epidemics and Modern Culture*. New York: Columbia University Press.

Spivak, G. C. 1993 (c. 1985). Three Women's Texts and a Critique of Imperialism. In *Feminisms: An Anthology of Literary Theory and Criticism*, ed. R. Warhol and D. P. Herndl, 789–814. New Brunswick, NJ: Rutgers University Press.

Warhol, R. 2003. *Having a Good Cry: Effeminate Feelings and Pop-Culture Forms*. Columbus: Ohio State University Press.

8 Visual Cultures

Feminist Perspectives

Rosemarie Buikema and Marta Zarzycka

The relentless increase of reproducible images often gives rise to complaints that we are being 'bombarded' with them. This quasi-military vocabulary echoes the alleged aggressiveness of the visual culture that is enforcing itself upon us (Sturken and Cartwright 2001). Since the 1970s, feminist art critics and scholars in particular have problematised the omnipresence of sexualised, and yet mythologised, female bodies both in the media and in artistic practice, claiming that the tradition of meaning assigned to gender, race and ethnicity is not given, but constructed, and that these constructions take specific visual forms (Nochlin 1970; Parker and Pollock 1981). The underlying conviction of feminist theory has always been that to be able to change the lives and material circumstances of women, we need an alternative imagery with which to identify, as well as alternative modes of making, seeing and interpreting visual culture and its institutions (Pollock 1999; Reckitt 2001). Today, the training in gender sensitive readings of images in general and of images representing women in particular constitutes a broad field of feminist practices. While feminist cultural theorists aimed at deconstructing the idealist concept of representation as an unmediated, transparent practice, postcolonial scholars argued forcefully against the Eurocentrism that pervades many discussions of the visual (Shohat and Stam 1994). Together they challenge traditional ways of seeing as well as the hegemonic character of dominant patriarchal and colonial canons.

Yet in an image-overloaded era, certain visual conventions have become self-evident, unquestioned and easily consumed. To be able to look at them more consciously, we need to think about the visual traditions as well as the social practices and power relations in which they are embedded. That is to say, we need to place them in the broader context of their cultural, historical and geopolitical significance. Therefore the kind of visual literacy we aim at here is not concerned with exposing images as 'false' or 'untrue,' hence engaging in a "reductive iconoclasm" (Mitchell 2005, 175), but rather with developing an understanding of the way in which images came into being and how they work on their audiences. An essential aspect of visual literacy in general, and scholarly work on images in particular, is making the visual communicable, developing the language that stretches beyond unreflective metaphors and clichés. Feminist visual literacy, for its part, sheds light upon the often untransparent relationships of gender, race and ethnicity present in the image.

In this chapter, we map out the main concerns of feminist visual analysis, the fields of interest it covers and the methods it deploys. In order to demonstrate how gender-sensitive analysis can be practiced, we shall consider two distinct images, not coincidentally representing women. Although women are prevalent in the visual sphere, patterns of traditional gender divisions and hierarchies are still inscribed upon the female body. Both of our examples tackle the problem of the female body being simultaneously overly visible and marginalised in visual culture. The first example builds on the tensions between the portrayals of the female body in the traditional discipline of art history and in feminist art critique, while addressing the concept of the gaze. The second one comes from contemporary press photography, a field relatively new to feminist critique, and opens the question concerning a particular tradition within this genre, i.e., that of the representation of women as universal symbols of oppression in (military) conflict. Both artefacts will appear to overturn the visual traditions from which they stem.

Building upon the academic tradition of formal, semiotic, psychoanalytic and intertextual analysis, we will point out what feminist theory has brought to visual studies and the visual sphere in general. Similarly to other chapters in this part, we introduce here the range of methods that can be used to interpret images and provide literature references to develop those methods further. While we suggest various criteria for a critical approach to visual materials, we attend to certain concepts more than others, depending on their relevance to the content and context of the images at hand.

OLIMPIA: RECLAIMING THE GAZE

The scene of Katarzyna Kozyra's *Olimpia* (1996; three large-scale photographs and a video) almost literally copies Edouard Manet's painting *Olympia*, first exhibited in Paris in 1865. However, a more detailed inspection of the photographs reveals various imperfections of that restaging. Whereas Manet shows us the black servant with flowers, the chaise longue covered with an expensive cloth, the black cat and the sensual nude woman, Kozyra puts herself in the scene, thus interrupting its traditional narrative. The artist's face is drawn and tense rather than seductive, despite the velvet ribbon tied around the neck in exactly the same way as in the canvas. The hairless body (the artist was undergoing treatment for cancer at the time) is thin and withered, the skin a pale yellow. The odd assemblage of bodies and objects has none of the intimacy of Manet's interior. The cat is obviously stuffed, emphasising the quasi-grotesque, artificial character of the arrangement. Manet's painting coming being undone.

But what exactly are the transformative aspects of Kozyra's disquieting photograph, and how can a gender-sensitive way of looking contribute to its reception? We will address these questions by delineating two concepts

Figure 8.1 Katarzyna Kozyra, *Olimpia*, 1996, courtesy of the artist.[1]

and two methodological tools to analyse this image: the concept of the gaze and its tradition in psychoanalytic feminist theory, and the concept of nudity/nakedness and the meanings it generates as a semiotic sign.

Let us first locate our analysis in the fields of traditional art history, visual culture studies and feminist theory, paying particular attention to the concept of the gaze. John Berger (1972), in his oft-cited book *Ways of Seeing*, states that in Western visual culture—whether in the art of painting or advertising—it is men who do the acting while women just make a passive appearance. In other words, men look and women are being looked at. The most important function of the female body in visual culture is its to-be-looked-at-ness. The feminist concern with visual analysis therefore is first and foremost aimed at exposing and differentiating this representational tradition. It was Laura Mulvey who, in writing her influential essay 'Visual Pleasure and Narrative Cinema (1975),' created insight into the gender specific practice in film and other image genres. Feminist research into images has often been based on Mulvey's analysis of Hollywood cinema, but can be enormously significant for the analysis of still images too. Mulvey's vocabulary is drawn from psychoanalysis and semiotics. That is to say, in thinking about the fascination involved in looking at images, she draws a connection between the medium's formal aspects, narrative concerns and processes of identity construction on the part of spectators. A first step in a gender-sensitive reading of images is thus to examine whether men and women are systematically portrayed in different manners. The second step involves examining the meaning of those differences: watching a film, that is, the classic situation of looking at projections on screen while sitting in darkness in a theatre has, from the start, carried connotations of scopophilia and voyeurism—the latter being linked with the desire to receive or possess something or somebody. Mulvey goes on to emphasise that in the classic cinematic tradition, the camera position inevitably enforces the spectator to gaze along with the male character towards the objectified female body that is reduced to passive spectacle. Gaze, perspective and the film's editing thus determine who can look, or whose perspective is being deployed, and what can be seen; which worlds are revealed, which concealed; which identification possibilities are within reach, which are marginalised. The male gaze embodies in fact a form of defining power. Within Mulvey's analysis of classic representation history, the female body functions as indicator of sexual difference, of the other, the deviant, the passive. If, however, women actively return the gaze or in another way threaten to become the owner of gaze or agency, then women—inevitably—until the early 1990s at least, pay for this singularity through death, as for example in Alfred Hitchcock's *Vertigo* (Smelik 1998).

Mulvey's essay has been enormously influential on both feminist film theory and art criticism. However, the institutionalisation of the universal, impartial, incorporeal male gaze was widely questioned by feminist scholarship in various frameworks. Jackie Stacey (1992, 1994) demonstrated that film produces a range of gendered spectator positions, and therefore different responses to the visual pleasures offered by them. Similarly, Kaja Silverman (1996) argued that the eye can 'read against the grain' and look beyond the normative aspects of the cultural image-repertoire: the male is not always the controlling subject nor is the female always the passive object. Mary Ann Doane (1991) used Joan Riviere's (1996) concept of the masquerade (i.e., presenting womanliness as something that can be assumed and worn as a mask) to question the concept of essential femininity subjected to the masculine view. Finally, Teresa de Lauretis (1994) criticised Mulvey for not allowing the possibility of women themselves looking at women and thus erasing the specificity of lesbian desire.

We will now show how the different strands of the feminist debate concerning the concept of the gaze converge in Kozyra's photograph, which makes a harsh departure from scopophilic practices and replaces these by a visual assault of the eye/I. The deliberately disturbed pleasure of watching is the main theme of *Olimpia*. In the face of an ongoing traumatisation caused by a life-threatening disease, the viewer is confronted with an uneasy feeling of sameness and difference, the blurring of boundaries between normativity and its crisis. That blurriness defies the position of the masculine, penetrative gaze about which Mulvey writes. The refusal to cede the act of viewing entirely to others constitutes *Olimpia* as both object *and* subject of the gaze.[2] The artist meets the viewer's gaze, reversing it, forcing him/her to rethink and verify the settled order of values by drawing attention to the crisis of the sick, malfunctioning body. In doing so, she safeguards her self-image. In this respect, Kozyra's conscious self-display seems to reclaim the primary narcissism which according to Irigaray was taken away from women by the representational tradition of Western culture (Irigaray 1985). Primary narcissism, the presymbolical sense of belonging, the sense of feeling one with oneself, is lost when little girls grow up and have to inscribe themselves in the heteronormative symbolic order. That order is characterised by a lack of adequate articulations for women and a lack of acknowledgement of the differences between them (which are also race-, ethnicity- and class- related).

As mentioned earlier, the artist's body, although immediately recognised within the iconographical trope, is troubling and disconcerting. Consequently, the language we might use to describe it involves certain ruptures. Whereas the body in Manet's painting could still be called a *nude* body (coded as the educated, balanced, prosperous body clothed in art, containing all that was seen as threatening and uncontrolled in women),[4] Kozyra's Olimpia becomes a *naked* body: vulnerable, intimate, deprived of clothes and self-revealing (Nead 1992). The concept of the nude, both as a body and as a genre of painting, stems from a semiotic tradition that is centrally concerned with the construction of social differences through signs, ideological complexes and dominant codes, in relation to a broader system of meanings (Bal and Bryson 1991; Rose 2007). Posing for *Olimpia*, Kozyra has written herself into a traditional economy of art—the exploitation of the desirable female body. She replicates the iconographic theme of *Venus pudica*: the gesture that both covers the female genitals, but also directs the (male) gaze to them (Broude and Garrard 1994, 2005).[5] *Venus pudica* has for centuries figured as a symbol of Western art in general. It functions as a Barthesian myth (1973): a structure not defined by the object of its message, but by the way in which it conveys meanings broadly naturalised in Western culture, legitimising social inequalities. We can challenge the concept of the nude with that of 'nakedness.' This split in language might be a process of what Bal (1996) calls 'double exposure'—not only exposing the sign itself, but also displaying the interpretations of/around it that recall the societal rules and regulations inscribed on the body of an individual (Foucault 1978). While Manet's *Olympia* was indebted to Titian's *Venus of Urbino* (1538) and Goya's *The Nude Maja* (1800), both showing the same pose, it was also influenced by nineteenth-century erotic photography. In this way, Kozyra's restaging of the theme through the photographic medium recalls its predecessor's sources, yet shifts it from pornographic consumption to aesthetic confusion.

The naked/nude body in *Olimpia* is accompanied by another sign that reveals the constructions of social differences: the figure of a black servant. Staging the white mistress next to a black servant is part of a long tradition of representing the black female body as both serviceable and sexual. Sander L. Gilman (2003) points out that the linkage of two visual conventions of femininity—the woman of colour and the prostitute—in nineteenth-century iconography resulted in the sexuality of the black body becoming an icon of deviant sexuality and female sexuality in general (see also Moore and Wekker, this volume).[6] Yet, whereas Gilman sees the black female in Manet's painting as the emblem of syphilis brought to Europe by sailors travelling beyond the continent, Kozyra stresses the staged, proplike character of the servant, the equivalent of the stuffed cat. Race and gender become the masquerade, a play that reveals their societal and ideological constructions.

What we have pointed out so far, using the example of *Olimpia*, is that a feminist literacy in reading and rereading images regardless of their generic, spatial and temporal locations, involves various signposts:

1) an awareness of visual codes and traditions in general (such as nudity in Western art history)
2) knowledge of the gendered structures of those codes and traditions (such as the gaze)
3) attentiveness to the gendered and racialised issues in the process of (self) representation (the self-portrait, the black servant).

These signposts are present not only within the image, but also in its discursive relations with other images. Kozyra's photograph, repeating a painting, calls for an approach that acknowledges its intertextual or intermedial character (Kristeva 1980). Media refer to other media, and images to other images. Images derive both their meaning and the effect they have from this play with the visual tradition. Such play however is no arbitrary exchange of signs but deadly serious, because it is the only means of approaching reality: through images and texts, that is, through the iconographic and discursive traditions which are at our disposal. The reality of existing images can change their meaning if new images arrive on the scene; new images inevitably bring along the echoes of tradition. Kozyra's deliberate intermediality signals a shift from the Western art history tradition of the nude to the confrontational nakedness of the photographed sick body. It demonstrates that the dialogue within the visual field is ongoing and never ending. Seeing Kozyra's *Olimpia* means that Manet's painting will never be the same again, and vice versa.

MADONNA OF WARFARE: CHALLENGING THE TROPE

Our second case again involves a photograph of a woman. The photo we choose to present here belongs to the genre of press photography, and thus the claims and pretensions it has are different from those of Kozyra's self-critical artistic project. Nevertheless, as we will point out, press photography is indebted to the same gender/ethnicity/race constructions as art history. The gender-sensitive approach for this genre is a new branch on the tree of feminist visual analysis that needs to be developed further as, despite the multifarious presence of women in press photography, gender and photography have mostly been kept apart in the theoretical discourses. Photography, its history and its philosophy belong to the study of visual culture, media or art history, while gender, particularly in the context of war, has been at the heart of political theory, sociology or jurisprudence (Azoulay 2008). With the exception of several iconic photographs, such as *Migrant Mother* (1936), *Napalm Girl* (1972), *Afghan Girl* (1985), and finally soldier Lynndie England in the Abu Ghraib photos (2004), the debates on gender in the context of humanitarian photographic practices have been virtually absent (Lutz and Collins 1993). With the help of our next example we will point out the relevance of gender sensitive analysis in the genre of war coverage, and we will do so by focusing on the intermediality of certain representations of femininity. That is to say, in order to understand the effect of a particular photograph, we will focus on the interconnectedness of the different media that depend on and refer to each other, both explicitly and implicitly, constructing a wider cultural environment (Ellestrom 2010). We will address this intermediality at three different levels: the dynamic between aesthetic and political powers in the photograph, the relation between the image and the accompanying caption and the incorporation of art tradition into digital photography practice.

The photograph, taken by Luiz Vasconcelos, shows a Brazilian woman desperately trying to stop a wall of policemen from evicting her from her land. It won the recognition of the jury and the first prize in the *General News* category in the 2008 World Press Photo contest.[7] A formal analysis of the image reveals the layered presence of colours, shapes, lines and dynamic forces. Although the photograph is still, there is a strong suggestion of movement; it is obvious that the crowd of men is progressing and the woman about to fall over. The parallel lines of shields, skyline, policemen's legs and the ground constitute a set of horizontal levels, the monotony of which is disturbed by the woman's body. There is a gap in the wall of shields, through which a stick comes, ready to fall (again?) upon the woman's head, or that of the baby she is holding. Her face is contorted in physical effort and in crying out, while the baby's body is vulnerable in its nakedness. The faces and upper bodies of the policemen are invisible, their legs covered in dark uniforms and black boots, in striking contrast to the woman's colourful clothes (her orange skirt might be seen as a *punctum* of the photograph, screaming against the monotonous greyness of the background).[8] The dramatic event described here is entwined with its picturesque rendition.

What are the dynamics between the disturbing content and the engaging formal composition of the image? The 'painterly' character of this photograph (increased further when highly enlarged and presented to the audience in gallery spaces or in visually elaborate coffee-table books) might result in looking at it as a bold, colourful, aesthetically pleasing *tableau vivant* rather than a testimony of social injustice. This very photograph occupies the space between historical event and fictional emotion condensed

Figure 8.2   Luiz Vasconcelos, Brazil, 2008. ©Luiz Vasconcelos/A Crítica/AE/ZUMA.

into the moment of visual eloquence, where our indignation is frequently transformed into the admiration of the sublime spectacle (Boltanski 1999). Rather than engaging with a 'beautiful suffering' (Reinhardt, Edwards and Duganne 2007) and this image's aesthetic values (Barthes 1981; Sontag 1989; Baudrillard 1998), gender-sensitive analysis is concerned with the way this photograph is pivotal to the production of notions about power relations, citizenship and sovereignty (Azoulay 2008).

For that, one needs to examine the discursive context in which the photograph situates itself. While the image catches us in the aesthetics of the spectacle, the caption threatens to flatten out the factual events that originated it, as it delegitimises certain social and political actions: "A woman tries to resist police eviction of squatters on private land near the city of Manaus, in the state of Amazonas in Brazil. Eviction notices had been served on families living on the land some days earlier. The squatters, who were protesting against lack of housing in Manaus, were evicted after a clash that lasted two hours."[9] The woman is a nameless representative of the 'squatters,' the single bearer of gendered, ethnicised and classed identity. No perpetrators are designated, no accusations of social injustice made. By critically analysing the dynamics between image and caption, we can discern that while the central point of the image is the woman herself, she is structurally withdrawn from the narrative. Image and caption are trapped in a complex, dynamic relationship with one another. Somewhere between the cryptic text and a disturbing content lies this image's power to affect us (Zarzycka, forthcoming).

Our analysis now is geared to coming to grips with the question of why precisely this particular photograph should evoke such strong response; again we will look for answers by considering the way this image relates to other images of women in our visual culture. We argue here that the meaning and strong impact of Vasconcelos's photograph are correlated to the meaning and impact carried by certain visual conventions within the Western tradition, their wide circulation and mainstream recognition.

In order to attain a critical view on this picture, its intermedial character should be further analysed and mapped. Like many iconic images, this photograph comprises two tropes (rhetorical devices used in a figurative or non-literal sense; Bal 2002) which for centuries have been flourishing in the visual sphere. Those two tropes are highly gendered. One concerns the trope of the Madonna holding a child, a powerful representation of the nurturing, virgin-like mother (Warner 1976), whose body is a place of conflicting desires: the threshold of love; *the sacrum* and *the profanum* (Kristeva 1986); the locus of (future) pain, suffering, sacrifice, and redemption. Viewing the photograph, we immediately enter the appealing and easily consumed narrative of the primal mother defending her child and her domestic territory. Our sympathy lies with this universal mother, our concern is for her. The other iconographic trope concerns the contrast of femininity with the military (Marilyn Monroe singing to the soldiers, American mothers protesting against the war in Iraq) based on the traditional reproduction of social orders and gender roles. In photography and art, this trope often takes the form of the civilian woman facing soldiers. A famous example could be the photograph by Marc Riboud showing a young girl protesting against the Vietnam War in Washington (in 1967; Hariman and Lucaites 2007). Youth, femininity and flowers form a direct opposition to uniforms, masculinity and weapons, thus guiding our sympathy towards peace-oriented action.

Now that we have mapped the two prevalent tropes in Vasconcelos's photograph, we can deepen our understanding of this picture by trying to challenge what we have found so far: both aforementioned tropes undergo a certain shift within the picture. The settler woman is not immobile and static like the Madonna. Moving us in her enormous but fruitless effort to resist the aggressors, the woman in the photograph undermines the classic representation of the docile, graceful, contained body in Renaissance paintings. One could argue that she oscillates between the positions of two 'mothers of culture' (Bronfen 1992, 66), Mary and Eve. The transition from the pure, almost disembodied figure of the Virgin Mary, the role model of Christian de-sexualised motherhood, towards the deceptive figure of Eve, who bears children and questions the existing order, strongly negotiates female agency and its liberation from patriarchal constraints. Moreover, the biblical character of the scene is reinforced by the image of a palm tree in the background, a veritable paradise lost, like the one denied to Eve. After the act of expulsion, innocence will be destroyed; the nakedness of a child will become shameful and will have to be covered. The denial of serenity and docile motherhood changes our view of the nature of femininity represented here.

As to the second trope, the woman in the picture is neither an advocate for peace nor the supporter of brave troops; she is clearly part of the conflict. She does not mourn, granting forgiveness or absolution of guilt, nor does she advocate peace, both emotional labours traditionally ascribed to women. At first glance, one might argue that the photograph is one of the infrequent examples of the actual empowerment of women in contemporary visual culture: rather than representing the settler as the consumable object of domesticity and nurturance, she is shown as being engaged in the armed conflict. As a result, the category of 'woman,' rather than being an unproblematised homogenous concept, intersects with other axes of social difference such as ethnicity, class or positioning in the (armed) conflict. The key learning point here is how the intermedial negotiations between this and other images can change the spectator's view on femininity under war.

As we have demonstrated, a gender-sensitive reading:

1) remains critical of the purely aesthetical approach which depoliticises and consequently universalises/marginalises
2) examines the context the image is placed in, acknowledging that visual culture at large is dependent on institutional practices (i.e., the newspaper's profile, political discourse)
3) brings (back) the awareness that images help to form and in turn are formed by dominant and alternative understandings of intermedial conventions and tropes persistent in the visual sphere.

To recapitulate, the impact of this photograph relies on its recognisability and on its simultaneous challenge to established visual tropes. Cross-fertilisation of these tropes is a way of mapping the picture's intermediality. By capturing the woman in an attempt (however pointless it might be) to secure some kind of agency, by tracing its iconographical roots, this photograph produces space for negotiation of the gender binaries and simultaneously lays bare how photojournalism with its implicit goals of straightforwardness and democracy often borrows from arbitrary, asymmetrical relations of power pertaining to the visual sphere. In order to exercise feminist visual literacy, one needs to acknowledge this photograph's relation to the context in which it is embedded, as well as to many other photographs of war and conflict and paintings from centuries ago. Simultaneously, one needs to confront the discrepancy between them on all levels: cultural, ethnic, religious, linguistic and aesthetic. Because the (over) visibility of female bodies (especially of women who are culturally, racially and spatially foreign) is often characterised by the narrow margin of recurrent motifs (Mohanty 2003), we need to look at them as a part of the larger system where social relations and systems of knowledge are shaped, thus moving beyond the image's aesthetical appeal.

CONCLUSION

Using the examples of semiotic, psychoanalytic and discursive tools in this chapter, as well as a number of concepts and tropes travelling across media and genres, such as the gaze, the nude and the naked body and the woman under war, we have pointed out that in order to develop a feminist reading that works towards productive social change, it is necessary to understand representation as a political issue. The female body—be it exposed, seductive, vulnerable, self-revealing or oppressed, fighting back, marginalised—is a space where women's agency, governance and civil status are negotiated. We have demonstrated that, in order to challenge the traditional disciplines and institutions prone to replicate phallocentric structures, such as art practice and global reporting, we need first and foremost to cut through the proliferating representations of women in art and media and to realise that the universal character they assume frequently makes us relapse into forms of essentialism and homogeneity. To develop the language for talking about images, we contextualised them according to their historical, social, geopolitical and genre-related positioning and examined the relations and dependencies they create with other images and texts.

While Western culture is permeated with images, as they (digitally) circulate faster and faster, as their initial contexts are being left behind and new interconnections are being created, scholarly writing about/with/ across images necessarily needs to deal with not only the methods of visual analysis but also with the fluctuations of their meanings. The power of a single image always exceeds our ability to interpret it (Mitchell 2005); issues of representation are forever subject to intermedial applications and understandings. Each image may distort our habitual ways of seeing, and it may do so for a variety of purposes, bringing forth the questions of finding one's way in their constant flow and frequent slippage.

To redress this imbalance, various contexts for study are needed, which in turn call for a range of different approaches. As we have shown, these approaches can be concerned not only with the aesthetic power of images but also with the power relations that are produced and articulated by the different ways of seeing and imaging, as well as with the larger scope of knowledge production. Only then can we secure a potential for feminist visual studies and overcome the allocation of speaking positions from which we as viewers and academics engage in a conversation over the silent women to be viewed. And only then can images speak back.

NOTES

1. Our thanks to Katarzyna Kozyra for providing the image and copyright. Katarzyna Kozyra (born 1963) is one of the most controversial contemporary

Polish artists to date. Her performances and videos examine issues such as gender, aging, illness and religion and their social impact.

2. Self-portraiture is a technique frequently used by women artists to grant them the control over the act of showing—to counter the process of symbolic and social 'othering.' In her book *The Art of Reflection: Women Artists' Self-Portraiture in the XX Century* (1996), Marsha Meskimmon shows how lesbian, heterosexual, maternal and disabled bodies come under scrutiny in women's self-portraits and how these images are used to challenge common representational myths.

3. For feminists, discovering that women artists were structurally omitted from the discipline of art history meant that they began to question how art history had been written, exposing its hierarchies, silences and prejudices (Parker and Pollock 1981). However, in her famous text 'Why Have There Been No Great Women Artists?' (1971) Linda Nochlin rightly points out that attempts to try to answer that question have only reinforced its negative implications of feminine creativity: writing women artists back into the discipline only reinforces its boundaries and is not at all equal to the production of a feminist art history (Pollock 1988; Korsmeyer 1998).

4. Manet's painting, presenting a famous Parisian courtesan rather than an ancient goddess, is in fact seen as one of the first to begin problematising the term 'nudity' (Nead 1992).

5. Another project by Kozyra, a video called *Bathhouse* (1997), is inspired by the rituals of a communal bathhouse in Budapest and makes reference to Ingres' *The Turkish Bath* (1862) and Rembrandt's *Susannah Surprised by the Elders* (1645).

6. The exhibition in 1810 of an African woman named Saartjie Baartman, known as the *Hottentot Venus* (referring to her protruding buttocks and pronounced genitalia) further reinforced the conflation of a non-European female with the monstrous, the animal-like, and the abnormal. Baartman's body parts were exhibited posthumously also at the Musée de l'Homme in Paris until 2002 and was later buried in Cape Town (Gilman 2003; Buikema 2009).

7. World Press Photo, founded in 1955, is known for organising a prestigious annual press photography contest for professional photographers from all over the world. Each year, the pictures are awarded in eleven categories, such as Spot News, General News, Contemporary Issues and so on.

8. Roland Barthes (1981) saw *punctum* as an emotive, affect-inducing, often incommunicable 'piercing' or 'bruising' of the subject viewing a photograph.

9. World Press Photo, http://www.worldpressphoto.com (accessed August 18, 2010).

REFERENCES

Azoulay, A. 2008. *The Civil Contract of Photography*. New York: Zone Books.
Bal, M. 1996. *Double Exposures: The Subject of Cultural Analysis*. New York: Routledge.
———. 2002. *Travelling Concepts in the Humanities: A Rough Guide*. Toronto: University of Toronto Press.
Bal, M., and N. Bryson. 1991. Semiotics and Art History. *The Art Bulletin* 73 (2): 174–298.
Barthes, R. 1973. *Mythologies*. New York: Hill and Wang.
———. 1981. *Camera Lucida: Reflections on Photography*. New York: Hill and Wang.

Baer, S. 1999. Interdisziplinierung oder Interdisziplinarität—eine freundliche Provokation [Interdiscipline or Interdisciplinarity—a Friendly Provocation] *ZiF-Bulletin* (*Zentrum für interdisziplinäre Frauenforschung Berlin*) 19: 77–82.

———. 2001. Inklusion und Exklusion: Perspektiven der Geschlechterforschung in der Rechtswissenschaft. [Inclusion and Exclusion: Perspectives of Gender Studies in Law] In *Recht Richtung Frauen: Beiträge zur feministischen Rechtswissenschaft*, ed. Verein ProFri, 33–58. Bern: Verein ProFri.

———. 2005. Geschlechterstudien/Gender Studies: Transdisziplinäre Kompetenals Schlüsselqualifikation in Wissensgesellschaften. [Gender Studies: Transdisciplinary Competence as a Key Qualification in Knowledge Societies] In *Quer denken—Strukturen verändern: Gender Studies zwischen Disziplinen*, ed. H. Kahlert, B. Thiessen and I. Weller, 143–62. Wiesbaden: VS Verlag.

———. 2005a. Perspektiven der Gleichstellungspolitik—kritische und selbstkritische Fragen. [Perspectives of Equality Policies—Critical and Self-critical Questions] *STREIT* 3: 91–99.

———. 2008. Ungleichheit der Gleichheiten? Zur Hierarchisierung von Diskriminierungsverboten [The Inequality of Equalities? On the Hierarchization of Non-discrimination Rules]. In *Universalität—Schutzmechanismen—Diskriminierungsverbote*, ed. E. Klein and C. Menke, 421–50. Berlin: Berliner Wissenschaftsverlag.

———. 2009. Equal Opportunities and Gender in Research: Germany's Science Needs a Promotion of Quality. In *Science Education Unlimited: Approaches to Equal Opportunities in Learning Science*, ed. T. Tajmel and K. Starl, 103–10. Münster: Waxmann.

Baudrillard, J. 1998. *Selected Writings*. Cambridge: Polity Press.

Becher, T., and P. R. Towler. 2001. *Academic Tribes and Territories*. 2nd ed. Philadelphia: Open University Press.

Berger, J. 1972. *Ways of Seeing*. Harmondsworth: Penguin.

Boltanski, L. 1999. *Distant Suffering: Politics, Morality and the Media*. Cambridge: Cambridge University Press.

Braun, C. von, and I. Stephan. 2000. *Gender Studien: Eine Einführung*. [Gender Studies: An Introduction.]Stuttgart: Metzler.

Bronfen, E. 1992. *Over Her Dead Body: Death, Femininity and the Aesthetic*. Manchester: Manchester University Press.

Brooks, A., and A. Mackinnon, eds. 2001. *Gender and the Restructured University*. Philadelphia: Open University Press.

Broude, N., and M. D. Garrard, eds. 1994. *The Power of Feminist Art: The American Movement of the 1970s, History and Impact*. New York: Harry N. Abrams.

———, eds. 2005. *Reclaiming Female Agency: Feminist Art History after Postmodernism*. Berkeley and Los Angeles: University of California Press.

Bußmann, H., and R. Hof, eds. 2005. *Genus: Geschlechterforschung/Gender Studies in den Kultur- und Sozialwissenschaften*. [Genus: Gender Studies in Cultural and Social Sciences] Stuttgart: Kröner.

Buikema, R., and I. Van der Tuin, eds. 2009. *Doing Gender in Media, Art and Culture*. London: Routledge.

Casale, R., and B. Rendtorff, eds. 2008. *Was kommt nach der Genderforschung? Zur Zukunft der feministischen Theoriebildung*. [What comes after Gender Research? On the Future of Feminist Theory Formation] Bielefeld: transcript Verlag.

Deuber-Mankowsky, A. 2008. Gender ein epistemisches Ding? Zur Geschichtlichkeit des Verhältnisses von Natur, Kultur, Technik und Geschlecht. [Gender an Epistemic Thing? On the Historicity of the Relationship between Nature, Culture, Technology and Gender.] In *Was kommt nach der Genderforschung? Zur Zukunft der feministischen Theorienbildung*, ed. R. Casale and B. Rendtdorff, 169–90. Bielefeld: transcript Verlag.

Doane, M. A. 1991. *Femmes Fatales: Feminism, Film Theory, Psychoanalysis.* New York: Routledge.

Ellestrom, L. 2010. *Media Borders, Multimodality and Intermediality.* London: Palgrave Macmillan.

European Commission. 2006. *Women and Science: Statistics and Indicators—She Figures 2006.* Brussels.

———. 2008. *Mapping the Maze: Getting More Women to the Top of Research.* Brussels.

Foucault, M. 1978. *The History of Sexuality.* Vol. 1. New York: Pantheon Books.

Fuchs S., J. von Stebut and J. Allmendinger. 2001. Gender, Science, and Scientific Organizations in Germany. *Minerva* 39 (2): 175–201.

Gilman, S. L. 2003. Black Bodies, White Bodies: Toward an Iconography of Female Sexuality in Late Nineteenth-Century Art, Medicine and Literature. In *The Feminism and Visual Culture Reader*, ed. A. Jones, 136–50. London: Routledge.

Hariman, R., and J. N. Lucaites. 2007. *No Caption Needed: Iconic Photographs, Public Culture, and Liberal Democracy.* Chicago: University of Chicago Press.

Hark, S. 2005. *Dissidente Partizipation: Eine Diskursgeschichte des Feminismus.* [Dissident Participation: A Discourse History of Feminism] Frankfurt am Main: Suhrkamp.

Helduser, U., D. Marx, T. Paulitz and K.Pühl, eds. 2004. *Under Construction? Konstruktivistische Perspektiven in feministischer Theorie und Forschungspraxis.* [Under Construction? Constructive Perspectives in Feminist Theory and Research Practices.]Frankfurt am Main: Campus.

Hornscheidt, A. 1999. Sprache und Gender in den Gender Studies—nicht der Rede wert? Die Einlösung des Anspruchs an Interdisziplinarität im Magistrastudiengang Gender Studies an der Humboldt-Universität zu Berlin aus linguistischer Sicht. [Language and Gender in Gender Studies—Not Worth Mentioning? The Redemption of the Claim of Interdisciplinarity in the Magistra Study Course Gender Studies at Humboldt University in Berlin from a Linguistic Overview.] *ZIF-Bulletin (Zentrum für interdisziplinäre Frauenforschung Berlin)* 19: 94–109.

———. 2005. Sprache/Semiotik. [Language/Semiotics.] In *Gender@Wissen: Ein Handbuch der Gender-Theorien,* ed. C. v. Braun and I. Stephan, 219–37. Köln: Böhlau.

———. 2006. *Die sprachliche Benennung von Personen aus konstruktivistischer Sicht. Genderspezifi zierung und ihre diskursive Verhandlung im heutigen Schwedisch.* [The Linguistic Designation of Individuals from a Constructivist View. Gender Specification and Its Discursive Negotiation in Today's Swedish.] Berlin: de Gruyter.

———. 2007. Sprachliche Kategorisierung als Grundlage und Problem des Redens über Interdependenzen: Aspekte sprachlicher Normalisierung und Privil egierung. [Linguistic Categorization as a Basis and Problem of Talking about Interdependencies: Aspects of Linguistic Normalization and Privileges.] In *Gender als interdependente Kategorie: Neue Perspektiven auf Intersektionalität, Diversität und Heterogenität,* ed. K. Walgenbach, G. Dietze, A. Hornscheidt and K. Palm, 65–105. Opladen: Budrich.

———. 2009. Intersectional Challenges to Gender Studies: Gender Studies as a Challenge to Intersectionality. In *Gender Delight: Science, Knowledge, Culture and Writing . . . for Nina Lykke,* ed. C. Åsberg, K. Harrison, B. Pernrud and M. Gustavson, 33–46. Linköping: Linköping University Press.

Irigaray, L. 1985. *This Sex Which Is Not One.* Ithaca, NY: Cornell University Press.

Kahlert, H. 2001. Transdisziplinarität als Programm: Frauen- und Geschlechterforschung zwischen der Sehnsucht nach Einheit und nomadischer Existenz. [Transdisciplinarity as a Program: Women's and Gender Studies between the Longing for

Unity and Nomadic Existence.] *Zeitschrift für Frauenforschung & Geschlechterstudien* 19 (3): 3–18.

Korsmeyer, C., ed. 1998. *Aesthetics: The Big Questions*. Oxford: Blackwell.

Kristeva, J. 1980. From One Identity to Another. In *Desire in Language: A Semiotic Approach to Literature and Art*, ed. L. S. Roudiez, 133–50. New York: Columbia University Press.

———. 1986. Stabat Mater. In *The Female Body in Western Culture: Contemporary Perspectives*, ed. S. Suleiman, 99–118. Cambridge, MA: Harvard University Press.

Kreutzner, G., and H. Schelhowe, eds. 2003. *Agents of Change: Virtuality, Gender and the Challenge to the Traditional University*. Opladen: Leske and Budrich.

Lauretis, T. de. 1994. *The Practice of Love: Lesbian Sexuality and Perverse Desire*. Bloomington: Indiana University Press.

Lorey, I. 2008. Kritik und Kategorie: Zur Begrenzung politischer Praxis durch neuere Theoreme der Intersektionalität, Interdependenz und Kritischen Weißseinsforschung. [Criticism and Category: On the Limitation of Political Practice through Recent Theorems of Intersectionality, Interdependence and Critical Whiteness Studies.] In *Kritik und Materialität: Reihe der Assoziation für kritische Gesellschaftsforschung*, ed. A. Demirovic, 132–48. Münster: Westfälisches Dampfboot.

Lutz, C. A., and J. L. Collins. 1993. *Reading National Geographic*. Chicago: University of Chicago Press.

Maihofer, A. 2005. Inter-, Trans- und Postdisziplinarität: Ein Plädoyer wider die Ernüchterung. [Inter-, Trans- and Postdisziplinarity: A Plea against Disillusionment.] In *Quer denken—Strukturen verändern: Gender Studies zwischen Disziplinen*, ed. H. Kahlert, B. Thiessen and I. Weller, 185–202. Wiesbaden: VS Verlag.

Meskimmon, M. 1996. *The Art of Reflection: Women Artists' Self Portraiture in the XX Century*. London: Scarlett Press.

Mitchell, W. J. T. 2005. *What do Pictures Want? The Lives and Loves of Images*. Chicago: University of Chicago Press.

Mittelstraß, J. 1989. *Glanz und Elend der Geisteswissenschaften*. [Splendor and Misery of the Humanities.] Oldenburg: BIS.

———. 1998. *Die Häuser des Wissens: Wissenschaftstheoretische Studien*. [The Houses of Knowledge: Theoretical Studies.] Frankfurt am Main: Suhrkamp.

Mohanty, C. T. 2003. *Feminism Without Borders: Decolonizing Theory, Practicing Solidarity*. Durham, NC: Duke University Press.

Mulvey, L. 1975. Visual Pleasure and Narrative Cinema. *Screen* 16 (3): 6–18.

Nduka-Agwu, A., and A. L. Hornscheidt, eds. 2010. *Rassismus auf gut deutsch: Ein kritisches Nachschlagewerk zu rassistischen Sprachhandlungen*. [Racism in Plain German: A Critical Reference Book on Racist Speech Acts.] Frankfurt am Main: Brandes and Apsel. OECD. 2006. *Women in Scientifi c Careers: Unleashing the Potential*. Paris.

Nead, L. 1992. *The Female Nude: Art, Obscenity and Sexuality*. London: Routledge.

Nochlin, L. 1970. *Women, Art and Power and Other Essays*. London: Thames and Hudson.

———. 1971. Why Have There Been No Great Women Artists? *ARTnews* 69 (1): 22–39, 67–71.

Palm, K. 2005. Lebenswissenschaften. [Life Sciences.] In *Gender@Wissen: Ein Handbuch der Gender-Theorien*, ed. C. von Braun and I. Stephan, 180–99. Köln: Böhlau.

Parker, R., and G. Pollock. 1981. *Old Mistresses: Women, Art and Ideology*. London: Routledge and Kegan Paul.

Pollock, G. 1988. *Vision and Difference: Femininity, Feminism and the Histories of Art.* London: Routledge and Kegan Paul.

———. 1999. *Differencing the Canon: Feminist Desire and the Writing of Art's Histories.* London: Routledge.

Reckitt, H. 2001. *Art and Feminism.* London: Phaidon Press.

Reinhardt, M., H. Edwards and E. Duganne, eds. 2007. *Beautiful Suffering: Photography and the Traffic in Pain.* Chicago: University of Chicago Press.

Rhoten, D., and S. Pfirman. 2007. Women in Interdisciplinary Science: Exploring Preferences and Consequences. *Research Policy* 36 (1): 56–75.

Riviere, J. 1996. Womanliness as Masquerade. In *Formations of Fantasy*, ed. V. Burgin, J. Donald and C. Kaplan, 35–45. London: Methuen.

Rose, G. 2007. *Visual Methodologies: An Introduction to the Interpretation of Visual Materials.* Los Angeles: Sage.

Shohat, E., and R. Stam. 1994. *Unthinking Eurocentrism: Multiculturalism and the Media.* London: Routledge.

Silverman, K. 1996. *The Threshold of the Visible World.* London: Routledge.

Smelik, A. *And the Mirror Cracked. Feminist Cinema and Film Theory*, London: Macmillan, 1998.

Snow, C. P. (1965). *The Two Cultures, and a Second Look.* Cambridge: Cambridge University Press.

Sontag, S. 1989. *On Photography.* New York: Anchor.

Stacey, J. 1992. Desperately Seeking Difference. In *The Sexual Subject: A Screen Reader in Sexuality*, ed. M. Merck, 244–60. London: Routledge.

———. 1994. *Star Gazing: Hollywood Cinema and Female Spectatorship.* London: Routledge.

Sturken, M., and L. Cartwright. 2001. *Practices of Looking: An Introduction to Visual Culture.* London: Oxford University Press.

Walgenbach, K., G. Dietze, A. Hornscheidt und K. Palm, eds. 2007. *Gender als interdependente Kategorie: Neue Perspektiven auf Intersektionalität, Diversität und Heterogenität.* [*Gender as an Interdependent Category: New Perspectives on Intersectionality, Diversity and Heterogeneity.*] Opladen: Budrich.

Warner, M. 1976. *Alone of All Her Sex, The Myth and the Cult of the Virgin Mary.* New York: Alfred A. Knopf.

Zarzycka, M. Forthcoming. Madonnas of Warfare, Angels of Poverty. *Photographies.*

Zentrum für transdisziplinäre Geschlechterstudien, ed. 2004. *Geschlechterstudien im deutschsprachigen Raum: Studiengänge, Erfahrungen, Herausforderungen.* [Gender Studies in German-speaking Regions: Courses, Experiences, Challenges.] Berlin: Trafo.

Part IV

Multi-, Inter-, Trans- and Postdisciplinarity

9 This Discipline Which Is Not One

Feminist Studies as a Postdiscipline

Nina Lykke

> For those who see Women's Studies as a discipline, the formation of doctoral degree programs in Women's Studies is a logical next step and a professional necessity. For those who see Women's Studies as an interdisciplinary field that feeds off, juxtaposes, integrates, and fuses the more specialized inquiries within existing disciplines, doctoral programs in Women's Studies pose serious intellectual and pedagogical problems.
>
> (Friedman 1998, 311)

Having participated since the 1970s, at both the national and international level, in the institutionalisation of women's/gender/feminist studies (from now on referred to using the shorthand feminist studies)[1], I have often been asked to define the area. What does it mean to do feminist studies? What should the institutionalisation of the area aim at? One very heated debate revolves around the issue of disciplinarity/interdisciplinarity. The quote above presents two different positions, both articulated in a certain localised historical moment: the US around the turn of the twenty-first century. However, even though US feminist texts often figure prominently on reference lists related to the debate on disciplinarity/interdisciplinarity in feminist studies (e.g., Friedman 1998; Pryse 2000; Wiegman 2002; Zimmermann 2002), the debate is not limited to the US. Feminist studies emerged out of the feminist movement and entered academia in many countries around the world from the 1970s onwards. Subsequently, the area has been discussed and developed both as a critical perspective *within* the traditional disciplines and as an endeavour which has been carried out *in between* or *beyond* existing disciplines, and sometimes even as a new discipline ('neodiscipline'; see Iris van der Tuin's discussion, chapter 1, this volume).

Different arguments have been employed to address this complex relation to traditional disciplines and organisational structures of academia. Should feminist studies be organised as an area of its own—e.g., in the shape of a centre/unit/department for feminist studies? Or should it be integrated into existing disciplinarily organised departments? Today, it is recognised by a majority of feminist researchers that there is no point in pursuing a one-size-fits-all model. There is a widespread consensus that the strategy of making feminist studies into an area of its own can exist side by side with the strategy of integrating critical feminist perspectives into existing disciplines. Although adopting the stance that these different strategies for the institutionalisation of feminist studies are not mutually exclusive is pragmatic, it does not, however, solve all problems. It is still pertinent to ask: what does it mean to do feminist studies? How does the doing of feminist studies relate to the question of disciplinarity/interdisciplinarity? How can the umbrella term 'interdisciplinarity' be refined to grasp different modes of discipline-transgressing work?

In this chapter, I shall discuss these questions. While I sustain the pragmatics of the both/and approach, I shall also, in a more visionary vein, argue for feminist studies as a *postdiscipline*, i.e., as a mode of organising scholarly knowledge production that, on the one hand, can pass as a discipline and claim the academic authority that goes with that status but, on the other hand, which also maintains a transversal openness and a dialogic approach towards all existing disciplines, and which points beyond the traditional, monodisciplinarily organised university.

First, I shall emphasise the broad commitment of feminist scholars to the crossing of disciplinary boundaries via a discussion of the currently circulating terms multi-, inter-, trans- and postdisciplinarity in order to grasp the diversity of activities in feminist studies that take place outside of monodisciplinary frameworks. Second, I shall point out how different feminist epistemological positions will lead to different stances on the question of whether or not to 'go discipline.' Third, I shall outline my own position and argue for an interpretation of the area as a postdiscipline.

MULTI-, INTER-, TRANS-, POSTDISCIPLINARITY AS ISSUES IN FEMINIST STUDIES

Boundary work in between and across disciplinary borders is widespread in feminist studies, and the field stands out as advanced when it comes to innovative experiments with cross-disciplinarity. For example, it is significant that a seminal study of interdisciplinarity in knowledge production today uses the field as one of its key case studies to illustrate currently well-established interdisciplinary fields (Klein 1996, 115f.), the other ones being cultural studies, environmental studies, urban studies and area studies. Considering the strong push towards disciplinary transgressions, it is no wonder that feminist scholars have reflected on motivations for boundary work and discussed distinctions between different modes such as multi-, inter-, trans- and postdisciplinarity. I shall take a look at some examples of such discussions.

The genealogies of the push in feminist studies towards disciplinary boundary-crossing are often located in the field's relation to political activism. Social movements do not articulate political problems in neatly packaged forms, sorted by discipline, it is argued. For example, in *A Glossary of Feminist Theory* (Andermahr, Lovell and Wolkowitz 2000) the term 'interdisciplinarity' is defined as follows:

> The academic study of women and gender typically transgresses disciplinary boundaries, even where these studies began as course units within disciplinary degrees. This characteristic process of reaching beyond established disciplines is partly a function of the questions asked, which arose initially out of the political concerns of a radical social movement, and not out of the paradigm of any discipline. (Andermahr, Lovell and Wolkowitz 2000, 135–36)

As in other areas of discipline-transgressing research, such as cultural studies or environmental studies, the term 'interdisciplinarity' is, however, often used as an umbrella term covering different ways of transgressing disciplinary boundaries. When these different kinds of transgressions are specified, it is common, as in *A Glossary of Feminist Theory*, to distinguish between a 'multidisciplinary' mode of working, which "draws upon more than one discipline" (Andermahr, Lovell and Wolkowitz 2000, 135) and 'interdisciplinarity' in a more restricted and specific sense than the umbrella term. In this more specific sense, 'interdisciplinarity' is, among other things, defined as a scholarly endeavour that "goes beyond" multidisciplinarity, "carving out an area of study whose organizing theoretical and methodological frame is constructed from cross-disciplinary sources, so that a new synthetic field of study is created over time" (ibid.). Against this backdrop, discussions of whether or not to create a new discipline have surfaced within feminist studies—as they have in other interdisciplinary areas too; for example, Cary Nelson talks about cultural studies as a "ghostly discipline with shifting borders and unstable contents" (1996, 277).

Besides multi- and interdisciplinarity, two more terms have entered into circulation as part of efforts to come to terms conceptually with scholarly endeavours to transgress disciplinary boundaries: transdisciplinarity and postdisciplinarity. Like the first two terms, these are part of general scholarly debates but have also been adopted and given specific meanings by feminist scholars.

The concept of 'transdisciplinarity' was brought into the international scholarly debate without specific reference to feminist studies. Gibbons et al. (1994) and Nowotny, Scott and Gibbons (2001) discussed the current conditions of knowledge production and how research is becoming increasingly driven by applications for external funding and focused on problem solving rather than on theory development for its own sake. These authors pointed out how this leads towards a 'transdisciplinary' mode of research (so-called mode 2 research), characterised by blurred boundaries between basic and applied research, as well as between disciplines and academic specialities.

The concept of 'postdisciplinarity' has been discussed within sociology and social theory. Some sociologists, such as Mark J. Smith (1998) and Andrew Sayer (2001), have called for a postdisciplinary framework that could follow connections in the study of social problems without letting the research endeavour be restricted by disciplinary boundaries and that could fight "disciplinary parochialism/imperialism" (Sayer 2001, 83). The term 'postdisciplinary' has also been used as part of critical transnationalist studies and related to a critique of methodological nationalism, i.e., that the horizon of one nation-state is taken as the exclusive horizon of research (e.g., Favell 2007).

In this sense, the concepts 'trans-' and 'postdisciplinary' have rather distinct reference points, but they are also used differently in different contexts. Now I shall take a look at some feminist definitions.

In their sophisticated discussion of *transdisciplinarity* in chapter 11 (this volume), Antje Lann Hornscheidt and Susanne Baer define transdisciplinary feminist studies as a reflexive mode of interdisciplinarity. They understand transdisciplinarity in gender research as the ways in which feminist researchers involved in interdisciplinary integration of knowledge, theories and methodologies from different disciplines reflect upon how they contribute to a complex analysis of a research problem, such as discrimination, for example. The critical, transdisciplinary reflections for which Hornscheidt and Baer argue should be used to consciously assess and, if necessary, change research designs and readjust procedures and outlooks taken for granted within disciplines. In the understanding of Hornscheidt and Baer, transdisciplinary modes of doing feminist studies go beyond, and radically challenge and change, the disciplines from a critical gender perspective. However, the existing disciplines are also a prerequisite for these transdisciplinary, gender-critical endeavours. Hornscheidt and Baer argue for a dynamic interplay between inter- and transdisciplinary approaches.

In contrast to such a concept of transdisciplinary feminist studies that both transgresses and builds on disciplinarity, the notion of *postdisciplinarity* may add yet another dimension to the discussion of the transformative dynamics of feminist studies. To make my point, I shall refer to US-based feminist scholar Sue-Ellen Case who defines 'postdisciplinary' feminist studies as an alternative to 'interdisciplinary' feminist studies. In contrast to the latter, which Case understands as 'a unified field' which has emerged from an activist past and which is embedded in identity politics and the project of making women visible, she argues that:

> The term 'post-disciplinary', now in current usage, announces a different relationship to fields of study than the earlier term 'interdisciplinary' might connote. We can imagine 'interdisciplinary' as a term that signals a sense of a unified field, produced through the historical convergence of subcultures, social structures, and training practices. . . . 'Post-disciplinary' retains nothing of the notion of a shared

consciousness, or of a shared objective that brings together a broad range of discrete studies. Instead, it suggests that the organizing structures of disciplines themselves will not hold. (Case 2001, 150)

So, unlike the transdisciplinary approach of Hornscheidt and Baer, which maintains existing disciplines as a prerequisite for transdisciplinary reflections, and unlike the above-mentioned endeavours to create a new discipline—i.e., a new 'synthetic' (Andermahr, Lovell and Wolkowitz 2000, 135) or 'unified' (Case 2001, 150) field[2]—Case wants to question the very existence of the disciplinary organisation of knowledge production. She suggests that the more activist-related part of feminist research is already in the process of turning its back on the disciplines.

MULTI-, INTER-, TRANS-, POSTDISCIPLINARITY: A PLEA FOR A COMBINED APPROACH

The landscape of feminist positions on cross-disciplinarity is diverse, and the above-mentioned references represent only a few examples. What I have argued for in more detail elsewhere (Lykke 2010) is an approach that makes it possible to further unfold the rich potential embedded in multi-, inter-, trans- and postdisciplinarity. In this sense, I agree with Hornscheidt and Baer (chapter 11, this volume) as well as with Mia Liinason (chapter 10, this volume), who argue for multi-, inter- and transdisciplinarity as different aspects that can work productively together. However, I shall include the notion of postdisciplinarity, as discussed by Case (2001), in this debate.

In order to make my case for the inclusion of all four aspects as useful thinking technologies, I need to make myself accountable for my definitions of multi-, inter- and transdisciplinarity before I enter into the discussion of the role of postdisciplinarity, and let me also emphasise that I shall pay attention to somewhat different aspects of these modes of working than the ones quoted above.

First, I shall suggest a definition of the term 'interdisciplinary' that differs from the one referred to by both Andermahr, Lovell and Wolkowitz (2000) and Case (2001). I do not think it does justice to the diversity of different ways of performing 'interdisciplinarity' in feminist research to restrict the definition of the term to a quest, informed by standpoint feminist identity politics, for a field defined as 'synthetic' (Andermahr, Lovell and Wolkowitz 2000) or 'unified' (Case 2001). In line with Liinason (chapter 10, this volume) and Hornscheidt and Baer (chapter 11, this volume), I would instead like to keep the term 'interdisciplinarity' as part of the toolbox that makes it possible to specify different modes of working transversally across disciplines independent of epistemological stance. In addition to the standpoint feminist quest for syntheses, the term should also be able to include modes of working that can refer to disciplinary boundary transgressions in research informed by postmodern feminisms who seek neither syntheses nor unification.

Second, I shall approach 'transdisciplinarity' more in line with Liinason's definition, i.e., as a space for the unfolding of research questions that are unrelated to disciplines rather than as a site for critical reflections on disciplines (the stance of Hornscheidt and Baer). However, I should also mention that I see the two slightly different definitions of 'transdisciplinarity' as nonexclusive supplements to each other.

So how do I define multi-, inter- and transdisciplinarity? As described in more detail elsewhere (Lykke 2010), I define *'multidisciplinarity'* as a collaboration between different disciplines around a shared research problem that maintains a strict division of labour between the disciplinary canons and modes of working. In contrast, and much in line with Hornscheidt and Baer, I suggest a definition of *'interdisciplinarity'* as a mode of working that generates transversal dialogues between different disciplinary approaches and, in so doing, creates an experimental space for the emergence of unexpected synergies between heterogeneous perspectives. 'Interdisciplinarity' is here to be understood as a bricolage of different disciplinary perspectives. Through open, experimental dialogues, interdisciplinary modes of working may generate methodological and/or theoretical innovations, but this does not automatically lead to unification and unilaterality in the sense of identity politics (as implied by Andermahr, Lovell and Wolkowitz 2000; and Case 2001).

Within this frame of interpretation, the term 'interdisciplinarity' differs from 'multidisciplinarity,' because it allows boundary work and boundary transgressions to take place between different disciplinary modes of working. Moreover, 'interdisciplinarity' also differs from *'transdisciplinarity.'* I define the latter as yet another mode of working that, contrary to the interdisciplinary mode, goes beyond the boundaries of existing disciplines. In the transdisciplinary mode research problems and thinking technologies are articulated in ways that are not 'owned' by any specific disciplines.

I shall exemplify the different working modes with reference to a key issue in feminist studies: how do we analyse gender/sex? Against the background of my definitions, gender/sex is being analysed as a multidisciplinary problem when, for example, a sociological account of gender as a social relationship is combined with a biological/medical analysis of sex differences. An interdisciplinary approach to gender/sex will, by contrast, allow sociological and biological approaches to blend and mix, questioning clear-cut boundaries between social and bodily-material aspects.

A transdisciplinary approach will be different again in the sense that, for example, it will take a questioning of the clear-cut boundaries between social and material aspects as a starting point for the theorising of gender and sex as inextricably interwoven in a dynamic, nondeterminist and nonessentialising way. Following this definition, I interpret the rich field of feminist theorisings of gender/sex as an example of the development of new thinking technologies that takes place in a space beyond the existing disciplines. No existing discipline can claim to 'own' the issue. Feminist gender/sex theories constitute a thinking technology that is generated at a site beyond existing disciplines. It may lead back to a reflexive critique of the disciplines, as suggested by Hornscheidt and Baer (chapter 11, this volume), but it may also lead towards further reflections beyond the disciplines.

Finally, what about '*postdisciplinarity*'? Whereas multi-, inter- and transdisciplinarity are concepts that can be used to describe different *modes of working* across and in between disciplinary boundaries, I prefer, in line with Case, to define 'postdisciplinarity' as a term that can aptly refer to *modes of organising* academic knowledge production—and more precisely to a removal of the traditional disciplinary structures. I agree with Case that disciplines have often performed as hegemonic structures that create obstacles to the creation of open, transversal dialogues across disciplinary borders and the kind of free boundary-crossing that is often the basis for the emergence of unexpected synergies. In my opinion, disciplinary boundary-crossing is one of the dynamics that has made feminist studies innovative, and this is to me an important reason for not wanting to let the push towards establishing a site for a discipline-like knowledge production end up in an endeavour to simply organise a new discipline. Here I agree with Iris van der Tuin (chapter 1, this volume). Such a discipline would very easily cut itself off from the strong potential for innovative research that a relentless multi-, inter- and transdisciplinary mode of working creates. However, I also think that relatively stable sites for in-depth reflections of transdisciplinary issues and for further elaboration of transdisciplinary thinking technologies are much needed. So I argue for a mode of organising that takes into account the needs for *both* transversal openness *and* stable sites for transdisciplinary reflections. Against this background, I suggest that feminist studies be considered a *postdisciplinary discipline (shorthand: postdiscipline)*. I shall define what I mean by this in the ensuing sections (see also Lykke 2004, 2010).

TO DISCIPLINE OR NOT TO DISCIPLINE?

To define what I mean by a postdiscipline, I shall take a detour to consider a mapping of the ways in which the question of disciplining looks from the point of view of different feminist epistemological positions. I shall use Sandra Harding's classic, but still much used, distinction between *feminist empiricist epistemologies*, *feminist standpoint epistemologies*, and *feminist postmodern epistemologies* (Harding 1986) to describe different dimensions of the dilemmas occurring on the trajectory that has given impetus to the question of whether or not to discipline. I shall also elaborate on Harding's distinction and insert a fourth position, which elsewhere I have termed *feminist postconstructionist epistemologies* (Lykke 2010). I shall define this position and discuss how it may make it possible to argue for a coherent platform for the unfolding of feminist studies as postdiscipline, i.e., as a disciplinelike structure that keeps up a transversal multi-, inter- and transdisciplinary openness and sustains moves towards a postdisciplinary university.

Let me first consider the problem of disciplining from a *feminist empiricist epistemological* position. For this branch of feminist theorists the question of constructing a new discipline is a nonissue. From a feminist empiricist perspective, there is no need to establish a space beyond existing disciplines. Feminist empiricists believe that science should be carried out as usual, while taking the positivist rules of neutral and unbiased observation more rigorously into account to prevent gender bias from occurring. Against this backdrop, there is no incentive to create alternative spaces beyond the disciplines. Quite the contrary. The feminist empiricist answer would be to stay within the disciplines and better consolidate their foundations, i.e., make them take seriously positivist ideals of eliminating bias.

From a *feminist standpoint epistemological* viewpoint, things look different. Seen from this position, the traditional disciplines distort the analysis of women's perspectives. As a consequence, it would seem logical to construct a new unified field of study, a new 'successor-discipline' (Harding 1986, 142), which reconstructs the world from the standpoint of women, i.e., from what is seen as a nonbiased and nondistorted outlook. It is obvious that the term women's studies in its classic sense is discursively linked to this kind of theorising. The women's studies centres, as they were defined in the US in the 1970s and 'imported' into various European universities from the late 1970s onwards, were defined as meeting places for people from different disciplines who shared common ground in their wish to make the standpoint of women a foundation for their research and teaching, i.e., who wanted to do research for, by, with and about women. A logical endpoint of this trajectory is, as theorised by Harding (1986), a kind of 'successor-discipline,' which would make up a platform for studying the 'authentic' interests of women and for analysing the world from their point of view.

However, to follow a standpoint feminist trajectory to this conclusion, and actually institutionally pursue such a new discipline, would also be problematic in the eyes of many standpoint thinkers. Seen from a standpoint feminist perspective, it would perhaps create a platform for developing an 'authentic' analysis, but it would miss out on the establishment of an important critical feedback link to the disciplines. The new discipline would establish itself outside and beyond these, and the 'old' disciplines would be free to continue with business as usual, marginalising women and analytically distorting their interests and outlooks, without being challenged from within. Moreover, the movement that Harding (1986) so aptly theorised, from the question of women in science to the science question in feminism, to a comprehensive, feminist critique of the epistemological and methodological foundations of science, including its disciplinary structure, could not unfold in a ghetto outside of the disciplines. This, too, would be a problem seen from the point of view of many standpoint feminists. The establishment of a critical feedback link to the structure of science and the disciplines is in line with the fundamental and radical science critique of feminist standpoint thinkers and motivates a standpoint feminist hesitancy about embracing a trajectory that leads towards disciplining. In this way, standpoint feminists can become caught in a dilemma between the wish for a successor-discipline on the one hand and for radical transformations of the disciplines on the other.

When I consider the dilemmas of positioning feminist studies from a *postmodern epistemological position*, the perspectives shift again—and some dilemmas become even more pressing. For postmodern feminists, the push towards disciplinary transgressions would not lead to the wish for a new discipline in any traditional sense: such a discipline would not be attractive to postmodern feminists because it would have to be built on an identity politics that would look highly problematic from a postmodern stance. Nevertheless, a joint nodal point (Laclau and Mouffe 1985, 112), a site for in-depth reflections of "temporary crystallizations in ongoing feminist negotiations of located theory making" (Lykke 2010, 49), could appear important when seen from a postmodern feminist stance. At least, I shall confess to this kind of dream myself.

However, the dilemmas become pertinent within this framework as well. Life within the solid walls of academia demands that feminist nomads (Braidotti 1994), queers (Butler 1993), cyborgs (Haraway 1991), new mestizas (Anzaldua 1987) and other boundary creatures put a plate with their name on the door, thereby indicating an identity which entitles them to recognition and resources. However, to carry out their kind of feminist theorising—which challenges the taxonomic rules of the dominant game in town, going against its demands for clear categories—the feminist nomads, queers, cyborgs and new mestizas have to fight a contradictory battle for the right to put up a plate with the name of a 'proper object' (Butler 1997). The feminist nomads, queers, cyborgs and new mestizas have to fight for a name tag, even though they would love to be able to do without such a thing. A name tag gives access to recognition and funding of their activities, but it is a slippery thing because it also goes against the grain of postmodern feminist endeavours to deconstruct, destabilise, blur boundaries and freely follow rhizomatic[3] lines of thought without taking doors with different name tags, called disciplines, into account. The feminist nomads, queers, cyborgs and new mestizas know that the purpose of the name tag on the door is to make those living behind it do what they do not want to do, namely, pin down exactly what is the core content of their doings. What is their canon? What is their main object of study? What are the appropriate theoretical and methodological approaches to this particular object of study? What exactly does 'normal' scientific activity look like within this area of research and teaching? So the dilemma for feminist nomads, queers, cyborgs and new mestizas is this: how can they defend both the name tag and the deconstructive or rhizomatic approaches that radically resist the exclusions inherent in 'proper objects' (Butler 1997), defy the stabilising foundationalism of canons, evade clear categorical distinctions, and retain space for a free and passionate flow of thoughts?

As I have elaborated it elsewhere (Lykke 2010), major trends in feminist theorising have both *moved into but also beyond postmodern thought and poststructuralism*. This has resulted in reflections on epistemology which, on the one hand, are informed by postmodern problematisations of universally fixed categories and taxonomies and, on the other, reclaim a partial and situated objectivity. I have previously defined this tendency as *postconstructionist* (Lykke 2010). Unlike both standpoint and postmodern epistemologies, postconstructionist ones can, in fact, establish a foundation for feminist studies as a postdisciplinary discipline without becoming caught up in pressing dilemmas such as the ones described above. I shall, therefore, proceed to this position.

As an illustration of the postconstructionist trend in feminist studies, I turn to the feminist scholars Donna Haraway (1991) and Karen Barad (2007). Like postmodern epistemologists, both see the knower as embedded in the world she studies: not able to stand aside and take a look from 'outside.' But in contrast to postmodern epistemologists, they also argue that the knower can establish a partial objectivity. Haraway argues that the knower must make her/himself accountable for the embodied and contextualised 'site' from which s/he observes the world and for the 'sighting' technologies (technological apparatuses/research tools, thinking technologies, bodily outfits and so on) through which s/he interprets her research 'objects' (Haraway 1991). Combining quantum physicist Niels Bohr's interpretation of light as both waves and particles with feminist poststructuralist theory, Barad defines partial objectivity as based on what she calls constructed or 'agential' cuts between knower and known (Barad 2003, 815). Contrary to the universal 'cut' of Cartesian philosophy and positivism, which positions the human knower 'outside' of the world to be studied, the knower in quantum physicist Niels Bohr's epistemology is always part of the experimental apparatus. If the knower chooses one kind of apparatus/research tool, light will appear as waves, while the choice of another will construct it as particles. The knower is in this sense the one who makes the 'cut,' i.e., sets up the particular apparatus that produces a certain result. But this does not imply that the experiment ends up in total relativism. The feminist stance that Barad deduces from Bohr's reflections on quantum physics is neither purely relativist/subjective nor purely objective in a universalist sense. The knowledge that results from the experiment is local, situated, partial, contextual (i.e., dependent on the specific apparatus chosen by the knower). But within this local framework it is to be understood as a reliable and objective piece of knowledge. What Barad does is to give the feminist epistemology of situated knowledge and partial objectivity, as theorised by

Haraway, an underpinning of quantum physics. (See also the discussions of Barad in chapters 1 and 2, this volume.)

I have discussed Barad's stance in more detail elsewhere (Lykke 2010). In this chapter, I shall apply it to the discussion of whether or not to discipline feminist studies. Barad's ontoepistemological (Barad 2007, 185) stance—her way of claiming that ontological and epistemological issues are inextricably entangled—can push further the debate on whether or not to discipline feminist studies. It may sustain an argument for a provisional and nonuniversal definition of feminist studies as a postdiscipline.[4]

With a platform in Barad's ontoepistemology, it can be argued that it is necessary to construct provisional cuts (for example, discipline-like structures) to produce new knowledge. Building on this argument, feminist postconstructionists can avoid the dilemma of *either* sustaining a process of universalisation and congealing of certain scientific structures (disciplines, 'proper' objects, canons and so on) *or* giving up the idea that feminist studies should claim the academic authority and resources that are allocated to disciplines. Within the framework of Barad's ontoepistemology and her claim that *cuts are necessary* in scholarly work, the construction of solid and discipline-like platforms can be justified in that it allows for an in-depth study of ways to theorise gender/sex and its intersections with other social power differentials and for further developing the thinking technologies of feminist studies. Informed by the *provisional* character of all cuts in Barad's theory, it is at the same time possible to argue for a transversal, dialogical approach that is open to multi-, inter- and transdisciplinary modes of working, and that in this way radically sustains a postdisciplinary critique of the monodisciplinarily organised university. To claim *both* discipline-like stability *and* postdisciplinary change in this sense requires a conscious awareness that the constructed cut (the solid, disciplinelike platform) is provisional, temporary and nonuniversal, embedded in the discursive-material flow of knowledge production, social change and cultural-natural re/generation.

CONCLUSION

In conclusion, I shall underline that I consider feminist studies to be strongly enough anchored theoretically and through worldwide research communities, educational programmes, journals, book series, conference traditions and so on to sustain the idea that the field can pass as a discipline and claim the academic authority of one. I think it is important to position the field in this way to be entitled to power and resources in current academia, where disciplinary structures still hold. *But* I do not think it is a viable option to simply 'go discipline' to obtain this goal. So in this chapter, I have argued for feminist studies as a *postdiscipline, i.e., a discipline which is not one,* to slightly reframe a quote from Luce Irigaray (1985). I have underlined the importance of a transversal—multi-, inter- and transdisciplinarily defined—openness towards all other disciplines and interdisciplines and argued for further development of platforms for postdisciplinary feminist critiques of universities based on monodisciplinary hegemonies.

A postdiscipline may sound as contradictory as having the cake and eating it too. However, I have interpellated Karen Barad's ontoepistemological framework to theoretically sustain my argument, and I shall end with the claim that organising feminist studies as a postdiscipline is feasible in certain spatiotemporal locations. As an example and to situate my position, I shall refer to the interdisciplinary feminist studies unit where I am employed as professor at Linköping University, Sweden. We are, in fact, organised as a postdisciplinary discipline in the sense I have argued for here. Institutionally, our activities are defined as *thematic* feminist studies. Thematic research is officially defined at my university as an alternative to disciplinary research and organised accordingly. To be defined as a 'theme' means to have status as a unit with its own transdisciplinary team of professors, PhD students, educational programmes and so on. In addition to a thematic unit for gender studies, my university runs parallel ones for 'themes' such as studies of ethnicity, children, water and environment, technology and social change. It is enriching for feminist studies to be organised as a thematic postdiscipline, and at the same time to form part of an environment with many other postdisciplines. This opens up a lot of possibilities for cross-cutting collaboration.

With this local reference I want to situate my position but also to stress that the discipline-based university is in a process of change. It is obvious that a plurality of feminist strategies are being developed against this backdrop, and in line with the diversity which I see as one of the strengths of feminist studies, I welcome this plurality as productive.

NOTES

1. Even though I use feminist studies as shorthand, the main point of reference is the umbrella term women's/gender/feminist studies. I follow the tradition of the European feminist curriculum development network, ATHENA, and discuss the area in a nonexclusive way. But I choose 'feminist studies' as shorthand because I consider it to be the most appropriate term: it shifts the perspective from the object of study to the political and epistemological position of the subject of research, and it stresses the genealogical links to feminist activism and social movements (Lykke 2010).
2. See also Iris van der Tuin's critical discussion of gender studies as a 'neodiscipline' (chapter 1, this volume).
3. In the philosophy of Gilles Deleuze and Félix Guattari (1992), which is currently being embraced by a growing number of feminist theorists (see Edyta Just's discussion in chapter 17, this volume), the botanical image of the rhizome (underground plant stems that move horizontally in all directions) refers to knowledge production processes that follow associative 'lines of flight.' These processes are in contrast to more traditional ones which, like taproots, grow deeper into the earth along a straight and predetermined

line. Deleuze's reflections on rhizomatics are part of his redefinition of what it means to think, and some feminist theorists who share with Deleuze "a concern for the urgency, the necessity to re-define, re-figure and re-invent theoretical practice" (Braidotti 1994, 100) have strongly welcomed these endeavours "to "image" the activity of thinking differently" (ibid.).

4. For a further discussion of Barad's theoretical framework and its potentials in terms of paving a way out of feminist dilemmas as regards the un/doing of the problematic essentialising, exclusionary and universalising effects of disciplining and canons, see also Iris van der Tuin's rethinking of the wave model as a theoretical tool for feminist analyses (chapter 1, this volume).

REFERENCES

Andermahr, S., T. Lovell and C. Wolkowitz. 2000. *A Glossary of Feminist Theory.* London: Hodder Arnold.

Anzaldua, G. 1987. *Borderlands/La Frontera: The New Mestiza.* San Francisco: Aunt Lute Books.

Barad, K. 2003. Posthumanist Performativity: Toward an Understanding of How Matter Comes to Matter. *Signs: Journal of Women in Culture and Society* 28 (3): 801–31.

———. 2007. *Meeting the Universe Halfway: Quantum Physics and the Entanglement of Matter and Meaning.* Durham, NC: Duke University Press.

Braidotti, R. 1994. *Nomadic Subjects: Embodiment and Sexual Difference in Contemporary Feminist Theory.* New York: Columbia University Press.

Butler, J. 1993. *Bodies that Matter: On the Discursive Limits of "Sex."* London: Routledge.

———. 1997. Against Proper Objects. In *Feminism Meets Queer Theory,* ed. E. Weed and N. Schor, 1–31. Bloomington: Indiana University Press.

Case, S. 2001. Feminism and Performance: A Post-Disciplinary Couple. *Theatre Research International* 26 (2): 145–52.

Deleuze, G., and F. Guattari. 1992. *A Thousand Plateaus: Capitalism and Schizophrenia.* Trans. Brian Massumi. London: Continuum.

Favell, A. 2007. Rebooting Migration Theory: Interdisciplinarity, Globality and Post-disciplinarity in Migration Studies. In *Migration Theory: Talking Across Disciplines,* ed. C. Brettell and J. Hollifield, 259–78. 2nd ed. New York: Routledge.

Friedman, S. S. 1998. (Inter)Disciplinarity and the Question of the Women's Studies Ph.D. Established and Proposed Women's Studies Ph.D. Programs in North America. *Feminist Studies* 24 (2): 301–25.

Gibbons, M., C. Limoges, H. Nowotny, S. Schwartzman, P. Scott and M. Trow. 1994. *The New Production of Knowledge: The Dynamics of Science and Research in Contemporary Societies.* London: Sage.

Haraway, D. 1991. Situated Knowledges: The Science Question in Feminism and the Privilege of Partial Perspective. In *Simians, Cyborgs and Women: The Reinvention of Nature,* 183–201. London: Free Association Books.

Harding, S. 1986. *The Science Question in Feminism.* Ithaca, NY: Cornell University Press.

Irigaray, L. 1985. *This Sex Which Is Not One.* Trans. Catherine Porter and Carolyn Burke. Ithaca, NY: Cornell University Press.

Klein, J. T. 1996. *Crossing Boundaries: Knowledge, Disciplinarities, and Interdisciplinarities.* Charlottesville: University Press of Virginia.

Laclau, E., and C. Mouffe. 1985. *Hegemony and Socialist Strategy: Towards a Radical Democratic Politics.* London: Verso.

Lykke, N. 2004. Women's/Gender/Feminist Studies—A Post-disciplinary Discipline? In *The Making of European Women's Studies*, ed. R. Braidotti, E. Just and M. Mensink, 91–102. Utrecht: ATHENA.

———. 2010. *Feminist Studies: A Guide to Intersectional Theory, Methodology and Writing*. New York: Routledge.

Nelson, C. 1996. Always Already Cultural Studies: Academic Conferences and a Manifesto. In *What is Cultural Studies? A Reader*, ed. J. Storey, 273–87. London: Arnold.

Nowotny, H., P. Scott and M. Gibbons. 2001. *Re-Thinking Science: Knowledge and the Public in an Age of Uncertainty*. Cambridge: Polity.

Pryse, M. 2000. Trans/Feminist Methodology: Bridges to Interdisciplinary Thinking. *NWSA Journal* 12 (2): 105–18.

Sayer, A. 2001. For Postdisciplinary Studies: Sociology and the Curse of Disciplinary Parochialism/Imperialism. In *For Sociology, Legacies and Prospects*, ed. J. Eldridge, J. MacInnes, S. Scott, C. Warhurst and A.Witz, 83–91. Durham, NC: Sociology Press.

Smith, M. J. 1998. *Social Science In Question: Towards A Postdisciplinary Framework*. London: Sage.

Wiegman, R. 2002. *Women's Studies on its Own*. Durham, NC: Duke University Press.

Zimmermann, B. 2002. Women's Studies, NWSA, and the Future of the (Inter) Discipline. *NWSA Journal* 14 (1): viii–xviii.

10 Why Interdisciplinarity?
Interdisciplinarity and Women's/ Gender Studies in Europe

Mia Liinason

Some years ago, I was asked to be a junior researcher in a European research project about interdisciplinarity. I was delighted, of course, and excited about the opportunity to explore the problems and possibilities of interdisciplinarity. On the afternoon of the same day, I had a meeting with two experienced academics. I told them I had been invited to take part in a research project and both enthusiastically congratulated me on my luck. They were eager to know about my collaborators, and following that, they wanted to know about the research topic. When I told them that I was supposed to investigate possibilities and obstacles for interdisciplinarity, they both sighed. "It's a dead end," one of them said. The other one fell silent. At the time, I thought their reactions simply reflected their personalities, but when I recall this conversation now, I can see that their reactions are actually indicative of the kind of everyday life in the academy to which all scholars can relate.

One important aspect of the story is the enthusiastic response to the news that I had been given a research project—independent of the content of the project. This reflects the continuous lack of funding or research time amongst scholars in general, and often for interdisciplinary scholars in particular. Another interesting aspect of the conversation is the order of my fellow academics' questions. To these scholars, it was more important to know with whom I was supposed to work than the topic of the project. To be sure, the social dimension of research is a seldom mentioned but nevertheless crucial aspect of research. We academics influence each other intellectually when we decide what to develop further or avoid in a collaborative project. Finally, their resigned reaction to interdisciplinarity is thought provoking: "It's a dead end." This puzzled me at the time and has since. On the one hand, it would be easy to read this response as boredom or plain ignorance. However, on the other hand, I find it more intriguing to read it as an attempt to interrupt the current widespread promotion, and accompanying criticism, of interdisciplinarity, which does little to further uses of the term.

At a time when interdisciplinarity has become both widely embraced *and* criticised by European research policies in general, and in women's/gender

studies in particular, this laconic comment made me think about the importance of deconstructing the binary effects of the disciplinary/interdisciplin-
ary divide. The mention of interdisciplinarity can cause the re/production of
a stereotypical figure of disciplinarity as a 'rigid entity' with 'policed boundaries' and a 'firm core.' Likewise, simple justifications of disciplinarity re/
produce a stereotypical figure of interdisciplinarity as 'superficial' and 'eclec-
tic.' Accordingly, I find it helpful to keep in mind that the division between
disciplinarity and interdisciplinarity is an historical construction.

Thus, before I present interdisciplinarity in women's/gender studies—
which is the aim of this chapter—I want to emphasise that *all varieties* of
disciplinary boundary-crossing challenge the extreme specialisation of the
established disciplines, as well as the arbitrariness of disciplinarity in itself
(Holm and Liinason 2005b, 7). It is this action of "challenging what would
otherwise be taken for granted as the proper organization, content, methodology, or purpose of research that creates and defines interdisciplinarity,"
suggest Liora Salter and Alison Hearn (1996, 43). This is true regardless
of the character of border crossing, whether it is more or less theoretically
driven, and more or less bound to some specific body of knowledge. Interdisciplinary modes of working can thus in different ways develop, enhance
or transgress conventional disciplinary approaches, as also stressed in
chapter 11 of this volume. Here, Antje Lann Hornscheidt and Susanne Baer
give an in-depth description of three possible ways in which inter/disciplin-
ary working models engage with disciplines: integrated in the disciplines;
working across disciplinary boundaries; or moving beyond disciplinary
boundaries 'towards an integration of different forms of knowledge.' However, the emerging women's/gender studies as a subject in its own right
also raises new challenges to these issues. In chapter 1 of this volume, Iris
van der Tuin reflects on these challenges for women's/gender studies as a
neodiscipline and gives examples of useful conceptual and methodological
tools that, from a neodisciplinary perspective, offer a reassessment and a
transgression of disciplinary modes of working.

In the following discussion on interdisciplinarity in women's/gender
studies, I align myself with the definitions of the terms multi-, inter- and
transdisciplinarity that Nina Lykke offers in chapter 9 of this volume. Here,
Lykke also introduces postdisciplinarity as a mode of *organising* knowledge production different to multi-, inter- and transdisciplinarity, which
she understands as modes of *working across* disciplinary boundaries.
Notably, even though a discipline in practice, academic life is always also
both intellectual and institutional; the term 'discipline' refers to cognitive
divisions in research and university communities (Klein 1996; Salter and
Hearn 1996, 38). Several disciplines that are perceived as quite stable today
are actually rather new and perhaps not that static after all. For instance,
in Sweden, political science, statistics and geography escaped from history,
their 'original discipline,' as late as the early twentieth century. At Uppsala University, sociology emerged from practical philosophy around 1947

(Svensson 1980, 112, 119). Today, individual interdisciplinary scholars, ministries and funding bodies criticise rigid disciplinarity, which—due to a high level of specialisation—has led to its isolation from and lack of importance to social and other pressing issues in the complex societies of today (Latour 1993, 8). Furthermore, disciplinary borders and the fragmentation of knowledge into specialised areas has been compared with nation building and criticised for representing relations of power as much as any rational cut in the body of knowledge (Boxer 2000, 122; Lykke 2004, 94).

IS INTERDISCIPLINARITY ONLY A BUZZWORD?

Interdisciplinarity is clearly a buzzword in the current higher education (HE) policies of the EU. The Bologna Process, with its decentralisation of the decision-making process and harmonisation of HE, is but one expression of the ambition to produce a more flexible system of HE both in the EU as a whole and in the different European national contexts. The increasing demand for intellectual exchanges and theoretical collaboration is perceived as, among other things, a reaction to a disciplinary fragmentation that has produced research results which nobody but the research team itself can use. Thus, interdisciplinarity is promoted because of a need for knowledge that can deal with the disparate questions of today's complex societies (Latour 1993, 8; European Commission 1995; Holm and Liinason 2005b). Moreover, according to the European Commission the "severe lack of flexibility" in HE and research training is one of the four handicaps Europe has to face when competing with the US and Japan in particular (European Commission 1995, 25, 27). In effect, interdisciplinarity is promoted as a form of applied or problem-oriented research designed to develop international competition (between European countries or between Europe and other parts of the world). Clearly, the EU wants to meet societal needs by counteracting disciplinary fragmentation and the lack of flexibility through an increasing amount of externally funded research. Funding bodies in various European national contexts, as well as the European Union itself have made this clear (Holm and Liinason 2005b; Keskinen and Silius 2006).

When interdisciplinarity, flexibility and harmonisation are emphasised in order to increase competitiveness, prestige and financial resources, and when the endeavours to reach those goals lead to a closer relationship between private enterprises and universities, alert intellectuals criticise this commodification of knowledge and invent labels such as "academic supermarkets" (Puig de la Bellacasa 2001, 106). The increasingly market-driven nature of HE and research is already an established fact. In the UK, for instance, market demands are described as the "over-riding criterion for establishing new courses," which means that new courses can be established while others are closed down, depending on interest from students (Griffin, Medhurst and Green 2005, 62). In today's neoliberal European university system which sees economic profit and the benefit of society as the main aims for scholars and students, interdisciplinarity is deployed as the primary mode of working, to be realised through flexibility for scholars, teachers and students and their mobility across various kinds of borders, both disciplinary and also national, regional, cultural and linguistic ones. Ministries and educational policies treat interdisciplinarity as a way of delivering/selling commoditised knowledge to students, the labour market and society (Hark 2007). This poses a particular challenge for scholars who wish to employ interdisciplinarity as a critical concept:

> Inter- and transdisciplinarity thus seem to be able to both fit into models of neoliberal market- and management-oriented reforms of HE and at the same time figure as foundations of the radical and transformative potential of Women's Studies, Gender Studies, Queer Studies, Gay and Lesbian Studies or Postcolonial Studies. Hence, one could indeed argue that inter- and transdisciplinarity function like magical signs (Katie King 1994), that is, as empty signifiers meaning whatever their users want them to mean. (Hark 2007, 12, 13)

At this point, some readers might ask why some feminist scholars still choose to stick to interdisciplinarity. Indeed, neither interdisciplinarity as a market commodity, nor interdisciplinarity as a means of making education more responsive to institutional or economic demands, are akin to the notion of interdisciplinarity as it used in feminist scholarship. However, it is not interdisciplinarity as such that creates the difficulties, rather the problem is created by the neoliberal system of HE. Consequently, interdisciplinarity may run the risk of losing its meaning when, as is the case today, it is predominantly promoted and supported as a form of applied or problem-oriented research. I would therefore in this chapter like to advocate a careful use of interdisciplinarity in feminist scholarship by focusing on some of the key reasons why feminist scholars still use interdisciplinarity, in spite of the mismatch with its use as a means of fulfilling the neoliberal ideologies of the present system of HE. Indeed, those feminist scholars who favour interdisciplinarity use it as a tool and critical concept for a range of different epistemological, political, institutional and practical reasons, included among which is the ambition to challenge disciplinary boundaries and extend possible meanings and knowledge practices (Hemmings and Kaloski-Naylor 2006, 63).

ACADEMIC FEMINISM AND INTERDISCIPLINARITY

In the late 1960s and early 1970s, the lack of research on women awakened the need for an extension of the empirical knowledge of women's lives. Women's studies scholars thus identified the social, material and political lives and experiences of women as the primary object of research (Göransson 1983; Borderias 2002; Braidotti 2002; Griffin and Braidotti 2002). The explicit wish for a holistic perspective on research objects, and the ambition to integrate 'women's perspectives' in every disciplinary branch of study, led to arguments for a thematic mode of working where the object of investigation, e.g., 'gender', 'ethnocentrism,' 'heterosexism,' was the preferred point of departure for the design of the study rather than a disciplinary base, such as literature, medicine or history. The critique of objectivity—a key issue in feminist scholarly work—was expressed in terms of a critique of mainstream scholarly language, methods, attitudes and values as androcentric and biased (Westman-Berg 1979, 187; Grosz 1993). When successful, the critique of mainstream research led to thematic modes of working. Here, the emphasis in mainstream research on a departure point located in the method of study was questioned, while the research question was presented as the preferred starting point for a scholarly investigation (Esseveld and Davies 1989, 17). Focusing on a wish to change or a desire to transform, feminist work in the academy has been described as motivated by a feminist political imperative, instead of being motivated by a 'disciplinary aim' such as knowledge accumulation (Hemmings 2008). In effect, interdisciplinary work among academic feminists is chosen for both epistemological and political reasons.

The institutional status of women's/gender studies is another element in discussions about the interdisciplinary character of the field. The problems of its organisation within the academy are often described as a significant feature of the politics of women's/gender studies. In this discussion, academic feminists debated if scholarship focused on women/gender/sexualities/ethnicities should be interdisciplinarily organised in autonomous units/departments or integrated into already existing disciplines (Lykke 2010, chapter 2). With explicit attention to the concomitant risks of autonomy—i.e., isolation—and integration into the established disciplines—i.e., ignorance—both varieties came to be promoted in European countries such as the UK, the Netherlands, Sweden and Finland (Göransson 1983; Griffin and Braidotti 2002; Hemmings 2006). The subject field has developed differently in different European national contexts due to financial support and organisational structures in the academy, demands from students and engagement from individual teachers. The possibilities for interdisciplinary research and education are to a large extent dependent on the HE structures in each national context. Compared to a strictly state-controlled HE system, where most interdisciplinary initiatives are hampered, an autonomously governed university sector is understood as more profitable for scholars who wish to develop cross-disciplinary collaborations (Griffin, Medhurst and Green 2005; Le Feuvre and Metso 2005). However, in much of Europe today a successful academic institutionalisation of several units/departments of women's/gender studies, complete with full-time professors, BA and MA programs, PhD training and so on has taken place. This raises the paradoxical question whether or not this interdisciplinary subject field ought to be regarded as an actual discipline. The notion of women's/gender studies as a subject field in its own right has also been criticised by scholars who have found it difficult to identify with the proper object or the depth of knowledge in this inter-disciplinary field (Lykke, chapter 9, this volume; and Lykke 2010, chapter 3). Here, arguments have been raised around the intellectual and theo-retical limitations of the field. Wendy Brown argues, for example, that women's studies has lost its object, core and aim of investigation after the poststructuralist critique of the category women (Brown 1997, 84), and Danish gender studies scholar Bente Rosenbeck asks if the interdisciplin-ary character of women's/gender studies is inevitably condemned to 'light versions' of 'ordinary disciplines': philosophy light, literature light and so on (Rosenbeck 1999). Brown and Rosenbeck raise important questions for scholars working in the field of women's/gender studies as a subject of its own. However, their arguments provocatively relate gender studies to the notion of the disciplinary either/or, creating boundaries for the pres-ervation of certain pieces of knowledge, objects, methods and theoretical frameworks. They also assume that training and research which do not travel along formerly approved routes cannot reach the same depths as canonised forms of knowledge.

Finally, the interdisciplinary working mode is also chosen by women's/ gender studies scholars for practical reasons. In the early years of wom-en's/gender studies, the need to find collaborative partners and establish networks was basically a question of finding partners in conversation (Griffin and Braidotti 2002). The first meeting of Nordic women's/gender scholars in 1973 was followed by more and other collaborations arranged by women's/gender scholars. Societal changes, globalisation and the transformation of HE policies in Europe also established a wider space for conversations among feminist scholars, which has been described as significant for the establishment of meeting points as well as a further institutionalisation of women's/gender studies centres in various national contexts (Calloni 2001, 50, 58; Saarikangas 2005, 204). This is visible in today's vivid transnational collaborations between women's/gender stud-ies scholars across Europe with the ATHENA network that gave rise to the transnational collaboration which engendered this volume, serving as a case in point. ATHENA is a collaborative network across different disciplines, institutions and national borders (Griffin and Braidotti 2002, 2).[1] The network serves a range of purposes, from offering a common platform for women's/gender studies in Europe to creating meeting points for women's/gender studies scholars and providing infrastructural possi-bilities for education and research in women's/gender studies. Organised into different working groups, the ATHENA network is well suited for scholars who wish to find collaborative partners from different national and academic contexts.

HOW TO REACH INTERDISCIPLINARITY

Interdisciplinarity is, thus, promoted at different levels of HE in Europe, from the EU as a whole to the different European national contexts. In spite of this strong promotion of interdisciplinarity, it is noteworthy that in the European context the possibilities for interdisciplinarity in education before masters or PhD level are more infrequent. Pre-university and undergraduate education is first and foremost characterised by disciplinarity (Griffin, Medhurst and Green 2005; Liinason and Holm 2006, 26). This can be understood as the result of notions of interdisciplinarity as an instrumental rather than a cognitive activity by policy makers at transnational, national and local levels. As applied science, instrumental interdisciplinarity is perceived as one way of developing international competitiveness in the institutions for HE of the European Union *in toto*, and in countries like France, Norway, Spain and Sweden (Holm and Liinason 2005a; Le Feuvre and Metso 2005; Widerberg, Braaten and Hjelde 2005; Carrera Suárez and Viñuela Suárez 2006).

Disciplinary specialisation becomes a necessary condition for different forms of interdisciplinary collaboration when interdisciplinarity is perceived as a problem-solving activity and not as a way to push ideas further. Indeed, the interdisciplinary perspective of women's/gender studies has also been described as a training in mental flexibility, where scholars and students with different disciplinary orientations learn each other's language(s). One of those scholars is Marjorie Pryse, who suggests that the 'cross-cultural and critical interdisciplinary' knowledge seeking in women's/gender studies can constitute a methodology of the field (Pryse 1998, 17; Pryse 2000, 109). Often, however, it is difficult to reach such a level of integration, so that the research project really results in synergetic effects on methods, interpretative and/or theoretical frameworks. Accordingly, in what follows, I will focus on three important elements of interdisciplinarity in practice.

First, the possibilities for developing productive, theoretical and methodological explorative interdisciplinary collaborations, and not only multidisciplinary collaborations that are more limited in scope (for a discussion of the distinction between multi- and interdisciplinarity, see chapter 9, this volume) are largely the result of the researchers' willingness to challenge their own intellectual habits (Griffin, Medhurst and Green 2006, 39). Studies describing these interdisciplinary research projects found that the members had an openness and willingness to rethink aspects of their work throughout the entire working process. Research projects in which the research process as such was not discussed but taken for granted resulted in "partners withdrawing into their disciplinary shells, and working in parallel rather than together" (Griffin, Medhurst and Green 2006, 39; Le Feuvre and Metso 2005). Thus, the transformation of one's own conceptual habits and intellectual routes is an important but often neglected consequence of the embrace of interdisciplinary research projects (Griffin, Medhurst and Green 2006, 43).

Second, given the fact that the discussions about concepts, methods and working processes are time consuming, *time and money* are key to the development of synergies and transformative intellectual work. Complaints about a lack of time and money among interdisciplinary scholars are not only about poor conditions in the academy in general. These complaints are also an important clue as to the reasons why interdisciplinary scholars resign and revert to more individual work than originally planned (Carrera Suárez and Viñuela Suárez 2006, 17; Keskinen and Silius 2006, 59; Liinason, Alnebratt and Holm 2006). Finally, the inter- or transdisciplinary researcher often has a multi-institutional affiliation, i.e., connections with several departments/institutions, which highlights the *social aspect* in research. Notably, explorations of interdisciplinary collaboration have emphasised the importance of collaborative research networks where "intellectual and emotional affinities" are described as "critical in long-term research networks" (Griffin, Medhurst and Green 2006, 36). In the following, I present two case studies of interdisciplinary research, with the ambition to examine the particular problems and possibilities of interdisciplinary research. The first project presented is an 'interdisciplinary' research project where interdisciplinarity was not reached; the second project presented is understood as a project where new synergies emerged. I gathered the material for these case studies through semistructured interviews with the coordinator/researcher of the respective projects. I also interviewed the chair of the research council responsible for the funding of these two projects.[2] The interviews each took between one hour and one and a half hours.[3] In the following descriptions of the research projects, I give a brief presentation of the frames of the project. Then, I explain the coordinator's/researcher's description of each research process and finally provide an analysis of the project, in which I account for my own conclusions.

CASE STUDY 1

Presentation of the Project

This research project was coordinated by a scholar from a department of religion. Two researchers were appointed to the project and the project was planned, designed and performed within the field of science of religion. The aim of the project was to study social and cultural constructions within, as well as through, divination (the art of prophecy) in Celtic, Old Norse, Greek-Roman and Indian cultures. The scholars wanted to visualise connections between traditions of divination and the construction and reconstruction of gender in connection to practices of divination. The study used several methods including textual analysis, field studies, interviews, participatory observation and oral history to gain information about myths, histories, rituals and legends.

Research Process

From the start this project was divided into three subprojects, which the coordinator described as creating certain boundaries within the frames of the larger project. Due to this, the scholars avoided the process of problematising and questioning their own routes of working and intellectual habits together with the other partners in the project. Even though they still had meetings and discussions of general overlaps, the scope and depth of the discussion was significantly diminished.

Despite the division in subprojects, the research group continued to have common discussions around significant elements in the research process, for example, the methods used and the understanding of key concepts. Notably, the research group had different understandings of central concepts used in the project, such as *gender*, for instance. These disagreements became, according to the coordinator, decisive for the outcome of the research project and for the collaborative process, which she describes as a 'failure.'

Moreover, the collaborative process in the research project became more difficult because of a lack of time. During the project, the project coordinator became a professor, which she describes as an advancement that required much work. Consequently, the research team came to the conclusion that everyone should write her/his own part. When the project coordinator subsequently had to step down from the role as coordinator in the project due to the demands of her job, the project was left without a coordinator because none of the other members in the group could take on the task of coordinating the project. Over time, deep controversies between the researchers and the department arose, which the project coordinator explains as resulting from the low amount of funding for the project. However, this also led to collaboration difficulties within the research team. In line with the growing conflicts, the research team met less and less frequently, despite an initial agreement about regular meetings and the importance of discussing key issues in the project. After the project time ran out, the coordinator states that they did not bring the project to an end.

Discussion

This was a project with internal difficulties. Much time and effort was absorbed by the conflict, and towards the end of the project, they had not reached any formal conclusion, collaborative publication or joint paper presentation. Also, towards the end of the project, this project suffered from a severe lack of cooperation because of the lack of coordinator, epistemological disagreements and little time and money.

As the coordinator describes, the scholars' avoidance of probing discussions around concepts and methods was one major reason for the 'failure' of the project. I understand the difficulties around concepts and methods partly as the result of closed minds and partly as the result of the lack of time and money. Discussing assumptions and developing one's own ontological and epistemological reasoning is a key aspect in interdisciplinary work (Griffin, Medhurst and Green 2006, 43). Consequently, in this project, the research team's inability to reach a common understanding of key concepts such as gender points to one of the challenges of interdisciplinary work: realising the potential of interdisciplinarity in order to push our conceptions further. In effect, this shows that interdisciplinarity is not only a question of combining working methods but also about intellectual habits and a curious openness.

As discussions around concepts, methods and working process take a lot of time, sufficient time and money is key to the development of synergies and transformative intellectual work. Therefore, if interdisciplinary scholars complain about lack of time and money, this should not simply be understood as the usual complaints over bad conditions in the academy in general. Particularly if the scholars live in different cities or different countries, funding for travel and accommodation is a basic need for the team of scholars to be able to meet regularly.

CASE STUDY 2

Presentation of the Project

This research project was conducted by a single researcher. In this project, the scholar investigated the incompatible moral and structural outlooks that drive competing notions of men within a strategic alliance around fatherhood. Through examinations of the sexual politics and complex gendered implications of the alliance, the scholar traced the ways in which masculinisation and heteronormativity are reinforced within fatherhood politics, describing how this alliance differentiates 'masculinity' from women and gay men by placing the control of innately promiscuous male heterosexuality at the centre of the social and moral order. Among other things, she examined how sport and religion function as unifying and contested homosocial arenas. The study was empirically based and explored multiple dimensions and voices through interviews as well as participant observation. This study reveals the racial and sexual politics of fatherhood and illuminates ties between fatherhood politics, the marriage movement and the Promise Keepers.[4]

Research Process

As described by this scholar, the advantages of inter- or transdisciplinary research are the wide scope of possibilities offered when the research question and not the researcher's specialisation is in focus. Inter- or transdisciplinary work offers not only a greater intellectual but also an institutional freedom when one is not restricted to people at the 'home' department in the search for collaborative partners. However, there are also disadvantages with this independence, such as the risk of becoming isolated.

One of the reasons mentioned by this scholar for the choice to work interdisciplinarily is funding. In the interview, she explains that her 'home department' had given her little financial support, a sign both of the bad financial situation of the home department and of the fact that it did not want to support research that was produced along other tracks than the conventionally disciplinary ones. Therefore, it would have been more difficult for this scholar to stay within the framework of her discipline than to work interdisciplinarily. Another reason she gives for the decision to work interdisciplinarily was her wish to focus on contrasting arguments and rhetorics surrounding masculinity and conceptions of family, race and gender. To do so she needed to go beyond the canons of the existing disciplines and embark on a transdisciplinary way of working.

Discussion

Through research questions which are not rooted in a specific discipline, a transdisciplinary working mode is presented in this research project, where the ontological and epistemological points of departure in the research move beyond disciplinary borders and engage with the ways in which cultural, social and political aspects are intertwined.

The description of this research project, moreover, shed light upon the social aspect in inter- or transdisciplinary research. Often, the inter- or transdisciplinary researcher has a multi-institutional affiliation, i.e., connections with several departments/institutions. This implies, however, that the researcher is not really 'at home' in any department. In this case study, the scholar describes the lack of an institutional base both as an advantage and a disadvantage: without an official position at a department she is offered independence but simultaneously exposed to the risk of isolation. This consequently put a pressure on the importance to find a social and intellectual community from which it is possible to establish networks and to produce collaborative research.

CONCLUDING NOTE

The inter- and transdisciplinary way of working in women's/gender studies has as its departure point theoretical and epistemological questions, while methods are chosen on the basis of problem area and scientific framework. As an interdisciplinary subject field, women's/gender studies challenges the predominant knowledge-structure by advocating a mixture of alternative methods and research strategies.

Keeping in mind that challenging my own intellectual points of departure is the result of training, together with a willingness to discuss with others and to push one's own intellectual capacities, I was recently inspired by Cynthia Enloe's writings about curiosity as a cognitive occupation which is able to push the limits of our understanding and our methodological habits: "I've come to think," Enloe writes, "that making and keeping us uncurious must serve somebody's political purpose. I have also become convinced that I am deeply complicit in my own lack of curiosity. Uncuriosity is dangerously comfortable if it can be dressed up in the sophisticated attire of reasonableness and intellectual efficiency: 'we can't be investigating everything!'" (Enloe 2004, 3). While admitting our need for decent working conditions, this quotation from Enloe is a useful reminder about the unruly sense of joy often to be found in feminist scholarship. Indeed, when I allow myself to challenge the secure foundations and easy routes, things always turn out to be much more complex and intellectually tempting than they first seemed to be.

NOTES

1. The Advanced Thematic Network in European Women's Studies (ATHENA) was founded in 1999. The network "brings together 80 institutes in the interdisciplinary field of Women's and Gender Studies. Our aim is to unite scholars, teachers and stakeholders from civil society and public institutions in the field of gender and diversity" (ATHENA Web site, http://www.athena3.org/).
2. The research council was discontinued in 2000, but between the early 1980s and 2000 it was the principal funding body for the support of collaborative interdisciplinary research in Sweden.
3. The interview for the first case study was a face-to-face interview at the office of the coordinator of the project on October 7, 2005. The interview for the second case study was conducted over the telephone October 10, 2005. The interview with the chair of the research council was conducted over telephone on October 12, 2005.
4. The Promise Keepers is an international ultraconservative Christian organisation for men (Promise Keepers website, http://www.promisekeepers.org/about).

REFERENCES

Borderias, C. 2002. Grace Report: Feminist Studies and Research in Spain 1989. In *The Making of European Women's Studies*. Vol. 4, ed. R. Braidotti, J. Nieboer and S. Hirs, 204–9. Utrecht: ATHENA.

Boxer, M. 2000. Unruly Knowledge: Women's Studies and the Problem of Disciplinarity. *NWSA Journal* 2 (2): 119–129.

Braidotti, R. 2002. The Uses and Abuses of the Sex/Gender Distinction in European Feminist Practices. In *Thinking Differently*, ed. G. Griffin and R. Braidotti, 285–307. London: Zed Books.

Brown, W. 1997.The Impossibility of Women's Studies. *differences* 9 (3): 79–101.

Calloni, M. 2001. Albanian Women after Socialism and the Balkan War. In *The Making of European Women's Studies*. Vol. 3, ed. R. Braidotti, I. Lazaroms and E. Vonk, 49–60. Utrecht: ATHENA.

Carrera Suárez, I., and L. Viñuela Suárez. 2006. Interdisciplinarity, Research Policies and Practises: Two Case Studies in Spain. *Research Integration*. http://www.hull.ac.uk/researchintegration (accessed August 22, 2005).

Enloe, C. 2004. *The Curious Feminist: Searching for Women in a New Age of Empire*. Berkeley: University of California Press.

Esseveld, J., and K. Davies. 1989. *Kvalitativ kvinnoforskning* [Qualitative women's studies research]. Stockholm: Arbetslivscentrum.

European Commission. 1995. Green Paper on Innovation. http://europa.eu/documents/comm/green_papers/index_en.htm (accessed June 1, 2008).

Gavanas, Anna. Postdoctoral, Leeds University (researcher). Interview with author 2005-10-10.

Griffin, G., and R. Braidotti. 2002. Introduction: Configuring European Women's Studies. In *Thinking Differently: A Reader in European Women's Studies*, ed. G. Griffin and R. Braidotti, 1–28. London: Zed Books.

Griffin, G., with P. Medhurst and T. Green. 2005. Disciplinary Boundaries between the Social Sciences and Humanities: National Report on the UK. *Research Integration*. http://www.hull.ac.uk/researchintegration (accessed January 24, 2005).

Griffin, G., P. Medhurst and T. Green. 2006. Interdisciplinarity in Interdisciplinary Research Programmes in the UK. *Research Integration*. http://www.hull.ac.uk/researchintegration (accessed August 22, 2005).

Grosz, E. 1993. Bodies and Knowledges: Feminism and the Crisis of Reason. In *Feminist Epistemologies*, ed. L. Alcoff and E. Potter, 187–216. New York: Routledge.

Göransson, A. 1983. Om den svenska kvinnoforskningens läge och villkor [About the situation and conditions for women's studies in Sweden]. *Kvinnovetenskaplig tidskrift* 3: 17–31.

Hark, S. 2007. Magical Sign: On the Politics of Inter- and Transdisciplinarity. *Graduate Journal of Social Science* 2 (4): 11–33.

Hemmings, C. 2006. The Life and Times of Academic Feminism. In *Handbook of Gender and Women's Studies*, ed. K. Davies, M. Evans and J. Lorber, 13–34. London: Sage.

———. 2008. Interdisciplinarity and Feminist Theory. Lecture from Practising Interdisciplinarity in European Gender Studies, June 24, Radboud University, Nijmegen, the Netherlands.

Hemmings, C., and A. Kaloski-Naylor, eds. 2006. *Practising Interdisciplinarity in Gender Studies*. York: Raw Nerve Books.

Holm, U. M., and M. Liinason. 2005a. Disciplinary Boundaries between the Social Sciences and Humanities: National Report on Sweden. *Research Integration*. http://www.hull.ac.uk/researchintegration (accessed May 31, 2006).

———. 2005b. Disciplinary Boundaries between the Social Sciences and Humanities: Comparative Report on Interdisciplinarity. *Research Integration*. http://www.hull.ac.uk/researchintegration (accessed August 22, 2005).

Keskinen, S., and H. Silius. 2006. Interdisciplinarity, Research Policies and Practises: Two Case Studies from Finland. *Research Integration*. http://www.hull.ac.uk/researchintegration (accessed December 28, 2006).

Klein, J. T. 1996. *Crossing Boundaries: Knowledge, Disciplinarities, and Interdisciplinarities*. London: University Press of Virginia.

Latour, B. 1993. *We Have Never Been Modern*. New York: Harvester Wheat-sheaf.

Le Feuvre, N., and M. Metso. 2005. Disciplinary Barriers between the Social Sciences and Humanities: National Report on France. *Research Integration*. http://www.hull.ac.uk/researchintegration (accessed January 1, 2005).

Liinason, M., K. Alnebratt and U. M. Holm. 2006. Interdisciplinarity, Research Policies and Practices: Two Case Studies from Sweden. *Research Integration*. http://www.hull.ac.uk/researchintegration (accessed December 1, 2007).

Liinason, M. and U. M. Holm. 2006. PhD's, Women's/Gender Studies and Inter-disciplinarity. *NORA*—Nordic Journal of Women's Studies 14 (2): 115–30.

Lykke, N. 2004. Women's/Gender/Feminist Studies—A Post-disciplinary Dis-cipline? In *The Making of the European Women's Studies*. Vol. 5, ed. R. Braidotti, E. Just and M. Mensink, 91–101. Utrecht: ATHENA.

———. 2010. *Feminist Studies: A Guide to Intersectional Theory, Methodology and Writing*. New York: Routledge.

Näsström, Britt Mari. Professor, Göteborg University (project coordinator). Inter-view with author 2005-20-07.

Pryse, M. 1998. Critical Interdisciplinarity, Women's Studies, and Cross-Cul-tural Insight. *NWSA Journal* 10 (1):1–24.

———. 2000. Trans/Feminist Methodology: Bridges to Interdisciplinary Think-ing. *NWSA Journal* 12 (2): 105–118.

Puig de la Bellacasa, M. 2001. Flexible Girls: A Position Paper on Academic Genderational Politics. In *The Making of European Women's Studies*. Vol. 3, ed. R. Braidotti, I. Lazaroms and E. Vonk, 95–111. Utrecht: ATHENA.

Rosenbeck, B. 1999. Tvär-, mång- eller intervetenskap: Har tværfagligheten noget på sig? Eller hvad har den så på? [Cross-, multi- or interscience: Does interdisciplinarity have any clothes on? or what, then, does it wear?]. In *Undervisning i kvinno- och könsforskning i Norden: rapport från symposium i Stockholm 28–29 september 1998. Conference proceeding from Lessons and learning—Nordic symposium on leading in women's and sex research (Stockholm 1998)*, ed. E. Lundgren, 27–31. Oslo: Skriftserie från Centrum för kvinnoforskning vid Stockholms universitet, NIKK.

Saarikangas, K. 2005. SIGMA National Report: Women's and Gender Studies in Finland, 1995. In *The Making of European Women's Studies*. Vol. 6, ed. R. Braidotti and A. van Baren, 194–216. Utrecht: ATHENA.

Salter, L. and A. Hearn. 1996. *Outside the lines: Issues in Interdisciplinary Research*. Montreal and Kingston: McGill-Queens University Press.

Svedin, Uno. Chair of the Forskningsrådsnämnden (Swedish Council for Planning and Coordination of Research). Interview with author 2005-10-12.

Svensson, L. 1980. *Från bildning till utbildning: Universitetens omvandling från 1870-talet till 1970-talet (From learning to teaching: The transformation of the universities from the 1870s to the 1970s)*. Gothenburg: Sociologiska institutionen, no. 21.

Westman-Berg, K. 1979. Gråt *inte—forska! Kvinnovetenskapliga studier sam-lade av Karin Westman-Berg (Don't cry—research! Studies in Women's Studies collected by Karin Westman-Berg)*. Stockholm, Prisma.

Widerberg, K., E. S. Braaten and I. Hjelde. 2005. Norway—National Report on Disciplinary Barriers between the Social Sciences and the Humanities. *Research Integration*. http://www.hull.ac.uk/researchintegration (accessed January 24, 2005).

11 Transdisciplinary Gender Studies
Conceptual and Institutional Challenges

Antje Lann Hornscheidt and Susanne Baer

Doing transdisciplinary gender studies is challenging. We propose discussing some of the challenges involved, and in particular we shall focus on gender studies grounded in a feminist perspective. More precisely, we will discuss gender studies in light of understandings of disciplines and related formations of knowledge, and we shall conceptualise transdisciplinary gender studies based on a critical assessment of conceptual and institutional aspects which shape the field. We also suggest understanding transdisciplinarity as a reflexive way of dealing with disciplines, rather than a move against or beyond them. In the first part of the chapter, we introduce our concept of transdisciplinarity in gender studies, in the context of ten years' experience of a study programme in transdisciplinary gender studies at Humboldt University in Berlin (HU). We offer a discussion of the concept of disciplinarity in and for gender studies, as well as of the concept of inter-disciplinarity and, eventually, transdisciplinarity.

We do not address what some may call postdisciplinarity in gender studies in this chapter, as we are interested in the effects of interactions between and across disciplines and argue that there is no productive move beyond them. Moreover, we do not discuss multidisciplinarity, which is often the name of a form of interdisciplinary work, i.e., interaction between disciplinary approaches that do not aim at mutual transformations and synergies between theories and methodologies. As will become clear from our arguments about interdisciplinarity, we consider multidisciplinarity as a concept which is more relevant to mainstream research than to critical gender studies. For an elaborate discussion of the concepts of post- and multidisciplinarity and their relation to inter- and transdisciplinarity, we shall refer readers to chapter 9 in this volume.

The concepts of disciplinarity, inter- and transdisciplinarity that we shall concentrate on here determine orders of academic knowledge, and they impact upon feminist attempts to challenge them, too. However, they have been and are still used very differently, depending on discipline, academic culture, field of research, questions asked and methods used to answer them, usages in a community and goals pursued in institutions. We do not pretend to cover all of these. We shall rather focus on the application of these terms in certain academic feminist debates, which in some way follows up on the discussion of these debates in chapters 9 and 10 in this volume. In particular, we aim at exploring a variety of inter- and transdisciplinary gender studies practices in light of their disciplinary effects. Although the questions we ask here are asked in many academic contexts, we will analyse and discuss a number of challenges specific to gender studies. We hope to contribute to the development of transdisciplinary gender studies both as a field of fascinating research and teaching, as well as a cooperative and, at least in this sense, feminist academic practice.

TRANSDISCIPLINARITY IN GENDER STUDIES

Transdisciplinarity seems to be a key term in several contexts of European gender studies. Like other key terms, this also means that it serves as a 'black box' in that its precise meaning is rather unclear. The term is understood differently by different agents in the academic field around and within gender studies. To approach our definition of the term transdisciplinarity, we will first discuss the concepts of disciplinarity and interdisciplinarity and then turn to the definition of transdisciplinarity.

We propose an understanding of inter- and transdisciplinarity as concepts that are strongly built upon the existence of disciplines. Disciplines are fragile but long-living artefacts which, in turn, have a strong impact on how knowledge production is organised and understood. They are powerful tools for, as well as products of, hegemonic knowledge production in that they also—albeit implicitly—define what knowledge *is* more generally. This includes defining accepted and financed as well as 'excellent' research and its aims. Hence, disciplines and their ensuing institutionalisation in universities and research institutions have powerful effects on what can be asked and investigated, and on what can be *known*.

With that said, power is not all there is to disciplines. Disciplines allow for orientation in complex worlds and for fast consensus, based on shared understanding and accepted standards. As such, disciplines are also contingent and subject to change; they are defined by their scientific interests, methods and their reach. The younger the discipline, the more transparent its definition, and the older a field, the more it is taken for granted. Disciplines also always reflect a division of labour, hence subdivisions in science and research and a separation of issues, subjects and material. This amounts to culturally specific assumptions of relevant distinctions, be they between what is still believed to consist of 'two cultures' (humanities and sciences; Snow 1965) or between currently defined areas of scholarly knowledge such as arts/humanities; the social sciences; natural, medical and technical sciences and so on. These distinctions are intertwined with cultural constructions of divisions between nature and culture, brain and body, soft and hard and so forth, and they represent—unsurprisingly—a deeply gendered way of looking at, or of gendering, the world in general and knowledge production in particular.

On the one hand, gender as a category and/or object can be integrated into different disciplines and therefore into a mainstream, institutionally established structure of an academic field. On the other hand, gender studies also reflects upon the disciplines: their points of departure, scientific presuppositions, topics chosen and (maybe more importantly) topics rejected, methods applied and norms re/produced. As a consequence, gender studies has not only added to knowledge within disciplines but has also engendered a thorough reflection on how knowledge is produced and subdivided, and on how academic knowledge production is organised in terms of its gendered and political effects. Thus, gender studies is not only an addition to but also an intervention into disciplinary canons. Viewed in this way, it becomes clear that gender studies requires and produces various re/actions and changes on different levels.

In Germany today, and in light of the general developments of orderings of knowledge production in academic fields, there are at least three different reactions to, or varieties of, gender studies. These may be called disciplinary, interdisciplinary and transdisciplinary effects, in our understanding of the terms. We suggest that such a subdivision into disciplinary, inter- and transdisciplinary effects can help to illustrate how gender studies impact on academic knowledge production in different ways.

NEW ISSUES AND QUESTIONS IN THE
DISCIPLINES: DISCIPLINARY ENHANCEMENT

Research on gender has a long tradition of posing new questions about old issues, and in challenging established norms and presuppositions. Classic questions include: who or what is the (universalised) object of research? What kind of assumptions about gender are at play in the field? Is the method biased in some way so as to establish a generic male or stereotypical female? Also, more broadly, how is this kind of knowledge production gendered? Such questions, when permitted and taken seriously, contribute to enlarging and enriching research perspectives in many academic fields. This has been a challenge to disciplinary canons, which have then been (partly) revised (Von Braun and Stephan 2000; Kahlert 2001; Bußmann and Hof 2005; Hark 2005; Maihofer 2005). Researchers focused on gender have often questioned the underlying norms within their disciplines by asking what role gender could and should play and by questioning the absence of gender in the knowledge production of their respective disciplines. This is what we call disciplinary enhancement.

Disciplinary enhancement has its benefits. Working within a discipline enables researchers to maintain a strong disciplinary identification—despite the changes caused by the addition of a gender perspective—and to focus on gender in many different ways. It qualifies the discipline but does not leave its broader frame. This pays in an academic world which cherishes disciplines, and it shares quick orientation and fast consensus which constitute the discipline itself.

However, this is not all there is to accepted and often 'excellent' research, nor to gender studies. Disciplinary enhancement may also be a trap, at least for feminists. Depending on how gender is conceptualised, work on gender within a discipline may very well challenge the heart of the discipline in question rather than just enhance some aspect of it. It may (and we think it should) require a continuous re/orientation of methods and material, approaches and concepts and a re/positioning of people working within this frame. Consequently, there is an inherently critical effect of gender studies, which may even amount to the challenge of transdisciplinarity that will be discussed later in this chapter. It is also noteworthy that such radical investigations into gender as a dimension of knowledge production have led to the marginalisation of researchers and of the topics, methodologies, theories and methods which are particularly suitable for research around gender within disciplinary orders of knowledge. Attempts to enhance may very well amount to exclusion (Fuchs, Von Stebut and Allmendinger 2001). This seems to be one reason why gender researchers are very often positioned at the (often extremely creative) margins of 'home' disciplines. To avoid dealing with the implications for the discipline as such, it is an easy way out for the guardians of 'true' disciplinary content, of 'real' science, to define critical gender research as an optional (rather than long-awaited) addition to a discipline's research agenda, an agenda which through this move ultimately remains ungendered or free from considerations of gender. Research on gender is, in other words, often made a side issue in the disciplines. Then, gender researchers very often simultaneously become and see themselves as marginalised even within their 'home' disciplines.

It is important to understand the ways in which this marginalisation impacts on the specific understandings of disciplines as well as of interdisciplinarity and transdisciplinarity. When gender researchers are located on the margins of their home disciplines, positioned as dissidents to a traditional disciplinary knowledge, inter- and transdisciplinarity carry a specific meaning and location for them and for others. One might suggest considering whether a radical challenge to the disciplines becomes gendered itself, feminised, while disciplinarity stays strong, 'masculine.' This marginalisation however stands in stark contrast to more general trends around disciplines, where we find several calls for broadening perspectives, cooperation and eliminating bias. Research is contantly on the move. Such calls, however, do not necessarily encompass the elimination of gender bias—neither on the level of researchers' gender categorisations nor on the level of questions and issues in research.

NEW QUESTIONS BEYOND TRADITIONAL FIELDS OF KNOWLEDGE: INTERDISCIPLINARY PERSPECTIVES

There are a variety of ways to study gender. Some enhance the disciplines, but many also work across disciplines, as in interdisciplinary research. For example, in gender studies at HU, which is committed to transcinarity, collaboration among researchers is in fact often framed as interdisciplinary—albeit as embodying interdiciplinarity at its best, rather than collecting diverse points of view. Here, interdisciplinarity is understood as a way to conduct collaborative research between two or more disciplines, combining their respective hypotheses, assumptions, methodologies and findings. In mainstream research interdisciplinarity is often just an exchange of findings (i.e., it equals what, according to chapter 9 of this volume, can also be defined as 'multidisciplinary' research, a mode of working that is to be understood as distinct from interdisciplinary research in which potential synergies between theories and methodologies are explored and findings not just added to each other). In gender studies, interdisciplinarity usually means that researchers from two or more disciplines define a similar research interest, discuss and combine methodological approaches and enhance findings, on whatever dimension of gender.

Let us give an example: research on discrimination. This may be pursued as an interdisciplinary collaboration. One could start by discussing a shared curiosity, e.g., in norms which underlie concepts of discrimination. Then, one formulates sets of different questions relevant to each discipline, in accordance with such shared interest. Legal studies may ask about regulations of discrimination, legal practices around it and the effects of such practices, while linguistics may ask about the impact and role of language use in these contexts. If legal studies and linguistics are combined in an interdisciplinary collaboration, several new questions may arise: Is a certain language use a form of discrimination and subject to law? Does intent or effect matter, for example, in a case of sexist discrimination? The linguist may foreground the former, and the researcher from legal studies may foreground the latter. The collaboration will create not just a fruitful discussion of both perspectives; rather, it will change the very questions we ask: does law care about linguistic aspects, and can linguistics enhance understandings of discrimination in areas of legal practice, such as courts? This kind of interdisciplinary cooperation could enhance and complicate our knowledge of discrimination by using important contributions made by the two disciplines involved.

If interdisciplinarity is such an expansion of information, it will certainly improve research, and often the knowledge produced will travel back to the disciplines or shape new subdisciplines. If we move beyond this and such findings are put to further use, other things may also change, however. Questions may arise which are situated beyond single disciplines. In these cases, it becomes clear that interdisciplinarity means more than just an addition of different types of knowledge.

This kind of interdisciplinary research is, as a commitment if not a practice, widely established within German gender studies on the level of research projects and study programmes. Within most gender research milieux it is acknowledged that it will require different disciplinary contributions to take gender—conceptualised as an historically and culturally contingent phenomenon of varying shape which is closely connected to other such categorisations (see also the discussion of 'intersectionality' in chapter 3, this volume)—as a starting point.

However, from outside of the field of gender studies, things look differently: it is not the dominant perception that gender studies is based on different disciplinary contributions. In the broader German theoretical and methodological discussion on interdisciplinarity, gender studies experiences and publications are also still rarely perceived or taken up (i.e., for example, by Mittelstraß 1989, 1998). Although many institutions call for and some actively support interdisciplinary research, most institutions do not recognise gender studies as having experience with such an approach (Baer 2005). Thus, we can observe a kind of double exclusion: not only is knowledge on gender still marginalised in many academic settings (with the possible exception of the social sciences, which profit from the longest tradition of feminist interventions in the German academic context), but knowledge and experience of inter- and transdisciplinarity developed within gender studies is also widely ignored. It is also noteworthy that there are currently additional hegemonic strategies in use for handling gender knowledge. Gender issues are, for example, included only on the surface level of study programmes and agendas, or gender is used solely as a keyword in new BA and MA study programme guides. This is similar to the surface integration of feminist issues in mainstream politics in Germany and Northern Europe in which politicians call themselves 'feminist' but fail to engage deeply with feminist issues (Baer 2005a; Hornscheidt 2006).

To summarise, it is important to stress that interdisciplinary work, at least in gender studies, means more than adding and in a simple sense combining knowledge. By elucidating approaches chosen within disciplines and articulating their limitations, a sharp awareness of the disciplines' varying ways to produce knowledge can be developed, including a critical assessment of the questions posed, the theories applied and the methods used, as well as the disciplinary genre conventions governing how research is re/presented. Such knowledge is fundamental in learning how to learn in alternative ways.

REFLECTING UPON TRADITIONAL ORDERS OF KNOWLEDGE: TRANSDISCIPLINARY CHALLENGES

What happens if we move beyond collaboration, as in the case of the interdisciplinarity we have just described? Transdisciplinary understandings of gender and knowledge production promise to go one more step further—beyond comparing different disciplines and even beyond reframing each disciplinary question, towards an integration of different forms of knowledge. Transdisciplinarity is based upon a systematically critical reflection on all disciplines, their agenda, methodology and established findings. Although all good research should do this, research realities are different. What we call transdisciplinary work is, first and foremost, *explicitly* reflexive research.

In our understanding, transdisciplinary work not only aims at the integration of different types of knowledge. Rather, it also calls for a critical, theoretical reflection based on a shared interest in gender that cuts across and challenges the involved disciplines on several levels. To be sure, interdisciplinary cooperation in research can—and does—have transdisciplinary effects if different disciplinary backgrounds and norms are questioned and reflected upon. But these norms often remain implicit and may be buried under boundary work to re/stabilise disciplines themselves (Becher and Towler 2001). Instead, if the collaborating disciplines actively and explicitly reflect on their own positions, presuppositions, possibilities and limitations in the process of their (interdisciplinary) collaboration, we would call this a transdisciplinary project.

To return to our example of research on discrimination, both the topic and the approaches taken are subject to scrutiny in a transdisciplinary project. In legal studies, this allows us to understand different sets of norms, the legal pluralism which underlies concepts and regulatory regimes of discrimination. It forces us to challenge the very notion of normativity itself. In addition, the practices and effects both of legal language and the language practices the law addresses can only be understood if the limitations of the legal concepts of and methodological assumptions surrounding language are understood and additional information on the uses of language are included. In linguistics, the cooperation with legal studies challenges notions of agency and the ways in which normative constructions of subjectivity are produced from various perspectives. It forces us to challenge assumptions of language. Then, different concepts of norms (social, individual, formal and informal) and underlying legal as well as linguistic perceptions and definitions, not least of discrimination, can be considered. Against this background, both the scope of interest of linguistic and of legal studies can be defined more precisely.

Transdisciplinarity, in our understanding, is thus not a farewell to disciplines but rather a strong commitment to quality in disciplines. It is in no way their dissolution; in reflecting the presuppositions of a discipline, its strengths can often be formulated more clearly, beyond avoidance of bias. At the same time, transdisciplinary collaboration helps to understand when and how it can be productive to work together with other disciplines, how disciplines are themselves constructions based on complex decisions, inclusions and exclusions, with strengths and limitations.

As such, we argue transdisciplinarity is not just an optional choice for gender studies. Rather, it is a necessity if gender studies intends to remain feminist. Feminist theory allows us to understand the politics of knowledge, and feminist gender studies have to engage with such politics. This is why feminist gender studies should be committed to working within and across disciplines (Maihofer 2005). Understood this way, transdisciplinarity is an extension of a feminist heuristic. Gender studies, in our understanding, therefore has to be transdisciplinary to be feminist gender studies;

otherwise, it may be interesting research but is more likely to enhance rather than transform academic disciplines.

The gender study programmes at HU are built upon this concept of transdisciplinarity. They focus on cross-sectional topics, *knowledge, interdependencies, transformations, representations, normativities and interventions*. This indicates that transdisciplinarity, as a research programme, changes ways of asking questions within and beyond disciplines. With regard to interdependencies (or intersectionalities; see chapter 3, this volume), we pose questions like: what is the connection between gender and other categorisations such as 'race' (recently; Nduka-Agwu and Hornscheidt 2010), class, ethnicity, religion and belief, dis/ability and age? What constitutes categories, what do they have in common, and how and why do they differ (Helduser et al. 2004; Hornscheidt 2007)? Are there hierarchisations? Which intersections occur when, and how, and which do not? And not least: can we address their interrelatedness as interdependency, intersectionality, diversity, interlocking systems or in some other way? Here, gender studies aims to react to processes and structures of discrimination in a socially relevant way. (See also the introduction to the concept of 'intersectionality' in chapter 3, this volume, where it is more elaborately discussed how it has become a key term in contemporary gender studies.)

CHALLENGES TO THE CHALLENGE: TRANSDISCIPLINARY WORK IN GENDER STUDIES

Gender studies, we dare to suggest, are at the forefront of developments in the world of academic knowledge production, in a world of knowledge societies (Brooks and Mackinnon 2001; Kreutzner and Schelhowe 2003). Driven by an interest in disciplinary limitations, and partly due to discrimination by the guardians of the disciplines, gender researchers have developed styles and ways of cooperation which allow for working around these limits. A US study indicates that women and others othered, i.e., those traditionally excluded from the worlds of science, tend to populate emerging academic fields (Rhoten and Pfirman 2007). However, since such sea changes affect many structures, they do not come without challenges (European Commission 2006; OECD 2006; European Commission 2008). Such challenges may be understood in light of conceptual, institutional, teaching and career aspects. We shall look at the conceptual challenges here.

One effect of thinking about and working with transdisciplinarity in gender studies is the blurring of distinctions between disciplines: it sometimes becomes entirely unclear how disciplines are constituted. On the one hand, in transdisciplinary studies, differences encountered between disciplines include epistemological backgrounds, theoretical directions, methods, research questions, concepts and even questions about the ways in which the different steps in the research process should be organised and named. Differences in terminology and traditions very often lead to communication problems, which may be solved, however, by a careful inspection into the vocabularies used. Transdisciplinary collaboration thus can promote understanding of the type, meaning and dynamics of concepts and terminologies. It also emphasises the importance of reading texts or material within the context of respective disciplinary traditions. On the other hand, it can also be the case that researchers from different disciplines (but with a shared interest in gender) have more in common in their research projects than a gender researcher has with her/his colleague from the same discipline.

Taken further, this observation raises an important question about transdisciplinarity: is it really and necessarily based on different traditional disciplines as its central criterion? In fact, it also may be that researchers with one disciplinary background work together in a transdisciplinary way. This happens if they start from different epistemological perspectives, if they understand the very concept of knowledge in different ways or if they apply different methodologies.

Transdisciplinarity often seems to be one way to 'understand' disciplinary limits and norms, thus becoming a self-fulfilling prophecy. Transdisciplinary collaboration, however, is also one instance in which we are forced to identify with and define our 'own' discipline, which sometimes has reductive and stereotyping effects. Thus, transdisciplinary gender studies require a thorough engagement with the 'other' and oneself. This presupposes a distinct reflection on the very nature of one's work, in light of the weight of disciplinary boundaries and with a lucid assessment of power.

This has several implications. *First*, we must consider whether and how the knowledge production of different agents in one disciplinary field effects different statuses. Work on the disciplinary presuppositions and norms may lead to enhancement, but also to exclusion from a discipline to some extent. Even if transdisciplinary collaboration is meant to have positive and reflective effects, these can—somewhat paradoxically—be ignored and excluded. Therefore, transdisciplinary work requires a precise reflection upon what a discipline means and demands, and how people and work is situated in relation to it. More precisely, we need to understand that researchers often do not simply represent 'their' disciplines if they engage in gender studies. Rather, transdisciplinarity becomes an exercise in defining (a) one's 'home' discipline, (b) a set of gender studies related to the 'home' discipline, (c) another discipline (with which one engages within the framework of an interdisciplinary project as discussed above), (d) a different set of gender studies (related to the discipline with which cooperative relations has been established) and so on. This way of conceptualising transdisciplinarity challenges the assumption that transdisciplinarity means to move beyond disciplines or to combine them in a simple sense. Two gender researchers from different disciplines, when they meet for transdisciplinary collaboration, may not identify with or work within their 'home' disciplines as such. If gender studies are critical, research with some focus on gender is always already beyond the mainstream of a disciplinary canon. More often, gender research moves in the margins of the disciplines, and many researchers invent new directions beyond the discipline itself.

Second, gender studies researchers are mostly more or less ignored in mainstream academic debates on inter- and transdisciplinarity, due to their marginalisation within their 'home' disciplines. It is the feminist version of transdisciplinarity which is often rejected by proponents of transdisciplinarity. In Germany, for example, we have seen the institutionalisation of interdisciplinary life sciences at many universities, without the slightest interest in the work done in gender studies on this topic (Palm 2005; Deuber-Mankowsky 2008). Gendered aspects of life then continue to be ignored, either through superficial assumptions about gender or its complete absence, although it is hard to imagine how gender can be ignored in research on reproductive technologies and genetics. There, interdisciplinarity as a new and innovative concept is celebrated while simultaneously gendered knowledge is excluded. By labelling an approach as inter- or transdisciplinary nonetheless, this deficit becomes more or less invisible.

Third, the 'home' disciplines of collaborative, transdisciplinary gender researchers are often perceived in very traditional ways, maybe with the exception, again, of the social sciences. Whether through enhancing a researcher's own understanding of her/his 'home' discipline' or through others ascribing certain qualities to a researcher on the basis of her/his perceived 'home' discipline, collaboration can cause gender researchers to be reduced to 'their' discipline in limiting ways. Again, this may be a political move, it may result from lack of knowledge, or it may indeed be interesting. For example, legal gender studies are often perceived as studies of equality law, but in fact they cover a wide range of legal, social, political, economic and cultural reflections on norms, including law. Similarly, linguistics may be reduced to studies of language, whereas it in fact addresses a variety of concepts way beyond words.

Fourth, there is a tendency to hierarchise disciplinary gender knowledge within the transdisciplinary gender studies context (Baer 1999; Hornscheidt 2009). This causes a double marginalisation of research positions. The perception of disciplines is so strong and long lasting that even gender researchers reproduce traditional disciplinary norms, even if they themselves are speaking from other positions. This may be due to the fact that gender researchers today have had a traditional disciplinary education in almost all cases. For example, legal studies are often mystified, whereas cultural studies are taken to be more accessible; or gender studies in medicine are taken as bioaffirmative, whereas political science is seen as critical per se. Or, linguistics is seen as a field of structural and generativist theories and research on formal aspects of grammar, yet it is a broad field also interested in language use and language as a tool to construct realities (Hornscheidt 2005). Based on this reductive perspective, a discipline can easily be classified as less or more important for gender studies as a whole.

This raises a *fifth* question: what is the status of different forms of disciplinary knowledge productions in a transdisciplinary approach to gender studies? Historically, gender studies have seen a variety of prime research interests, which also drive different disciplines. For example, German gender studies have long focused on social relations and educational aspects; issues around cultural modes of representation came later, and issues of interest in other disciplines have not even emerged because they are rather untouched by prevailing systematic accounts of gender in the German-speaking area. Gender studies is a discipline which challenges hierarchical orderings of knowledge, yet one's own practices of hierarchisation may be hard to address, which then amount to subtle or implicit dominance (Baer 1999; Hornscheidt 1999). Such dominance occurs in gender studies which, indeed, is not always acting as a field of equals among equals. Hierarchies of knowledge production (what kind of knowledge is most central to gender studies?) are to be found on many different levels. One level is the politics of appointments. Another is the curriculum in study programmes. Both are selective, through either exclusion or preference, because resources are extremely limited for gender studies. Selection, however, is also based on substantial programmatic preferences or strategic interest. All of them contribute to increasing competition as conceptual and institutional aspects are interwoven (Hark 2005).

The *sixth* issue to consider is the status of disciplines and disciplinary 'origins' of researchers. This is an effect of more than a decade of gender studies programmes in Germany, located within the field characterised by strong differences and diverging ideas of the future. These differences include disciplinary divides; different heuristic starting points independent of disciplinary origins; and the effects of biographies which include experiences of privilege or marginalisation, one's politics and the like. Sometimes, it is not clear which perspective trumps which alternative approach. Here, findings on transdisciplinarity should inform academic politics. On the one hand, we need to reflect critically on the different gender concepts underlying different research projects (Baer 2009). On the other hand, we need to accept and respect different concepts and their existence and uses, as well as to reflect on their limitations in the respective contexts.

Finally, it is the category of gender itself which is formative in transdisciplinary gender studies. The HU brochure states that "the category gender is always investigated in its complex interplay with other categories such as *sexuality, 'race', class, age, citizenship, disability* and *faith* and *beliefs*, thus continuously opening further perspectives, questions and fields of knowledge" (2004, 1). When gender studies was founded at HU, critical interests in race, class and sexuality were on the agenda, but the positioning of gender as the central focus of research was not yet subject to complex conceptual considerations or to outright political challenges. As time went by, 'differences' rather than difference, 'inequalities' rather than inequality, and multiple or moving subjects beyond fixed identities rather than identity and roles became more important. Today, the question of how to handle different categories or categorisations and their complex interplay has become central for research and teaching of gender studies. In light of these developments, should gender cease to be the primary category, a starting point and/or a focus of/in analysis?

The HU brochure states that "the field of Gender Studies at HU today also includes Queer Studies, critical racism research, Post-Colonial Studies, and other critical approaches in [and across and between] different disciplines" (2004, 1). However, HU does not substitute gender with anything else, as distinct to other institutions that move to potentially equalising and dehierarchising diversity studies, a move which also risks assuming problematic analogies. If gender as a category needs to be understood as interdependent with a large number of other, socially constructed categorisations and aspects (Walgenbach et al. 2007), it may seem logical to decentralise gender as a category in research and teaching as well.

This certainly raises the question what lies at 'the heart' of gender studies. Is it discrimination, identity formations, the functioning of different and complex categorisations, 'diversity' or the like—or is it still the functioning of gender as a central category for identity construction, and for analysis as well? Rather than defending a particular response, we need to understand such questions are a result of the continuous, inherently critical and systematic self-reflection in gender studies. They are a strength of our work, yet challenge its very basis. Therefore, there is a strong need to address them.

OUTLOOK

We have argued that gender studies includes a transdisciplinary practice, but transdisciplinarity is also a challenge to gender studies both on the level of ideas as well as in practical terms. It is our impression that there is a need to ask more questions around the issue, and to answer them, too, rather than emphasise ambiguity or ambivalence, complexity and contingency:

1) Is gender studies *really* a new discipline or a new transdiscipline, and what should this mean, exactly? There is a danger of gender studies becoming the resort of many 'dissident' disciplinary researchers, who are thus (easily) excluded from their disciplines, in turn.

2) If gender studies maintains the principles of transdisciplinarity, how far will they stretch? Are there disciplines which simply do not fit? And are there disciplines which are especially well equipped to further the causes of gender studies, rather than implicit dominance? There is a hierarchisation of different disciplinary knowledges contributing to gender studies in different contexts, which often results in the acknowledgement of only a rather small number of active key disciplines. But how do we want the field to work in the future?

3) Or does gender studies enhance the disciplines, and will it slowly submerge back into them and some other newly emerging fields, like life sciences? Are we subject to a disciplinary drift, a specialisation and profiling? And will transdisciplinarity become normalised as a form of disciplinary competence?

4) If gender studies do not simply evaporate, will—and should—gender studies remain gender studies or change into another field (Casale and Rendtorff 2008)? The popular concept of intersectionality challenges the status of the category of gender as the lead concern of gender studies (see chapter 3, this volume). The concept of 'interdependency' requires us to analyse any category (or categorisation) as interdependent with others per se (Walgenbach et al. 2007). But meanwhile, others do diversity studies, affirming such categories as differences, and yet others have suggested 'difference studies' or 'discrimination studies' as alternatives.

To suggest a direction, we believe there is more to learn and gain than often thought if gender studies re/orients itself towards feminist epistemologies. This implies focusing again on the category of gender or, as we prefer, on gender categorising, but in new and different ways. The recent discussion on intersectional perspectives, or interdependency, can lead to a new discussion of the status of categories, and the dynamics of inclusion and exclusion may gain revived attention (Baer 2001; Hornscheidt 2007; Lorey 2008). In addition, gender studies also poses an ongoing challenge to our production of knowledge, our understanding of research and our positioning in institutions. This challenge is productive. It leads to new ideas and concepts of knowledge and understanding. It would be an important asset to the world of science, and we indeed dare to think to the world in general. Transdisciplinarity, understood properly, may serve as a valid basis for gender studies in the future.

REFERENCES

Baer, S. 1999. Interdisziplinierung oder Interdisziplinarität—eine freundliche Provokation. *ZiF-Bulletin* (*Zentrum für interdisziplinäre Frauenforschung Berlin*) 19: 77–82.

———. 2001. Inklusion und Exklusion: Perspektiven der Geschlechterforschung in der Rechtswissenschaft. In *Recht Richtung Frauen: Beiträge zur feministischen Rechtswissenschaft*, ed. Verein ProFri, 33–58. Bern: Verein ProFri.

———. 2005. Geschlechterstudien/Gender Studies: Transdisziplinäre Kompetenz als Schlüsselqualifikation in Wissensgesellschaften. In *Quer denken—Strukturen verändern: Gender Studies zwischen Disziplinen*, ed. H. Kahlert, B. Thiessen and I. Weller, 143–62. Wiesbaden: VS Verlag.

———. 2005a. Perspektiven der Gleichstellungspolitik—kritische und selbstkritische Fragen. *STREIT* 3: 91–99.

———. 2008. Ungleichheit der Gleichheiten? Zur Hierarchisierung von Diskriminierungsverboten. In *Universalität—Schutzmechanismen—Diskriminierungsverbote*, ed. E. Klein and C. Menke, 421–50. Berlin: Berliner Wissenschaftsverlag.

————. 2009. Equal Opportunities and Gender in Research: Germany's Science Needs a Promotion of Quality. In *Science Education Unlimited: Approaches to Equal Opportunities in Learning Science*, ed. T. Tajmel and K. Starl, 103–10. Münster: Waxmann.

Becher, T., and P. R. Towler. 2001. *Academic Tribes and Territories*. 2nd ed. Philadelphia: Open University Press.

Braun, C. von, and I. Stephan. 2000. *Gender Studien: Eine Einführung*. Stuttgart: Metzler.

Brooks, A., and A. Mackinnon, eds. 2001. *Gender and the Restructured University*. Philadelphia: Open University Press.

Bußmann, H., and R. Hof, eds. 2005. *Genus: Geschlechterforschung/Gender Studies in den Kultur- und Sozialwissenschaften*. Stuttgart: Kröner.

Casale, R., and B. Rendtorff, eds. 2008. *Was kommt nach der Genderforschung? Zur Zukunft der feministischen Theoriebildung*. Bielefeld: transcript Verlag.

Deuber-Mankowsky, A. 2008. Gender ein epistemisches Ding? Zur Geschichtlichkeit des Verhältnisses von Natur, Kultur, Technik und Geschlecht. In *Was kommt nach der Genderforschung? Zur Zukunft der feministischen Theorienbildung*, ed. R. Casale and B. Rendtdorff, 169–90. Bielefeld: transcript Verlag.

European Commission. 2006. *Women and Science: Statistics and Indicators—She Figures 2006*. Brussels.

————. 2008. *Mapping the Maze: Getting More Women to the Top of Research*. Brussels.

Fuchs S., J. von Stebut and J. Allmendinger. 2001. Gender, Science, and Scientific Organizations in Germany. *Minerva* 39 (2): 175–201.

Hark, S. 2005. *Dissidente Partizipation: Eine Diskursgeschichte des Feminismus*. Frankfurt am Main: Suhrkamp.

Helduser, U., D. Marx, T. Paulitz and K.Pühl, eds. 2004. *Under Construction? Konstruktivistische Perspektiven in feministischer Theorie und Forschungspraxis*. Frankfurt am Main: Campus.

Hornscheidt, A. 1999. Sprache und Gender in den Gender Studies—nicht der Rede wert? Die Einlösung des Anspruchs an Interdisziplinarität im Magistrastudiengang Gender Studies an der Humboldt-Universität zu Berlin aus linguistischer Sicht. *ZIF-Bulletin (Zentrum für interdisziplinäre Frauenforschung Berlin)* 19: 94–109.

————. 2005. Sprache/Semiotik. In *Gender@Wissen: Ein Handbuch der Gender-Theorien*, ed. C. v. Braun and I. Stephan, 219–37. Köln: Böhlau.

————. 2006. *Die sprachliche Benennung von Personen aus konstruktivistischer Sicht. Genderspezifizierung und ihre diskursive Verhandlung im heutigen Schwedisch*. Berlin: de Gruyter.

————. 2007. Sprachliche Kategorisierung als Grundlage und Problem des Redens über Interdependenzen: Aspekte sprachlicher Normalisierung und Privilegierung. In *Gender als interdependente Kategorie: Neue Perspektiven auf Intersektionalität, Diversität und Heterogenität*, ed. K. Walgenbach, G. Dietze, A. Hornscheidt and K. Palm, 65–105. Opladen: Budrich.

————. 2009. Intersectional Challenges to Gender Studies: Gender Studies as a Challenge to Intersectionality. In *Gender Delight: Science, Knowledge, Culture and Writing . . . for Nina Lykke*, ed. C. Åsberg, K. Harrison, B. Pernrud and M. Gustavson, 33–46. Linköping: Linköping University Press.

Kahlert, H. 2001. Transdisziplinarität als Programm: Frauen- und Geschlechterforschung zwischen der Sehnsucht nach Einheit und nomadischer Existenz. *Zeitschrift für Frauenforschung & Geschlechterstudien* 19 (3): 3–18.

Kreutzner, G., and H. Schelhowe, eds. 2003. *Agents of Change: Virtuality, Gender and the Challenge to the Traditional University*. Opladen: Leske and Budrich.

Lorey, I. 2008. Kritik und Kategorie: Zur Begrenzung politischer Praxis durch neuere Theoreme der Intersektionalität, Interdependenz und Kritischen Weißseinsforschung. In *Kritik und Materialität: Reihe der Assoziation für kritische Gesellschaftsforschung*, ed. A. Demirovic, 132–48. Münster: Westfälisches Dampfboot.

Maihofer, A. 2005. Inter-, Trans- und Postdisziplinarität: Ein Plädoyer wider die Ernüchterung. In *Quer denken—Strukturen verändern: Gender Studies zwischen Disziplinen*, ed. H. Kahlert, B. Thiessen and I. Weller, 185–202. Wiesbaden: VS Verlag.

Mittelstraß, J. 1989. *Glanz und Elend der Geisteswissenschaften*. Oldenburg: BIS.

———. 1998. *Die Häuser des Wissens: Wissenschaftstheoretische Studien*. Frankfurt am Main: Suhrkamp.

Nduka-Agwu, A., and A. L. Hornscheidt, eds. 2010. *Rassismus auf gut deutsch: Ein kritisches Nachschlagewerk in rassistische Sprachhandlungen*. Frankfurt am Main: Brandes and Apsel.

OECD. 2006. *Women in Scientific Careers: Unleashing the Potential*. Paris.

Palm, K. 2005. Lebenswissenschaften. In *Gender@Wissen: Ein Handbuch der Gender-Theorien*, ed. C. von Braun and I. Stephan, 180–99. Köln: Böhlau.

Rhoten, D., and S. Pfirman. 2007. Women in Interdisciplinary Science: Exploring Preferences and Consequences. *Research Policy* 36 (1): 56–75.

Snow, C. P. (1965). *The Two Cultures, and a Second Look*. Cambridge: Cambridge University Press.

Walgenbach, K., G. Dietze, A. Hornscheidt and K. Palm, eds. 2007. *Gender als interdependente Kategorie: Neue Perspektiven auf Intersektionalität, Diversität und Heterogenität*. Opladen: Budrich.

Zentrum für transdisziplinäre Geschlechterstudien, ed. 2004. *Geschlechterstudien im deutschsprachigen Raum: Studiengänge, Erfahrungen, Herausforderungen*. Berlin: Trafo.

WEB SITES

Zentrum für transdisziplinäre Geschlechterstudien. http://www.gender.hu-berlin. de (accessed July 20, 2008).

Part V
Professionalisation

12 The Professionalisation of Feminist Researchers
The Nordic Case

Harriet Silius

Women's/gender studies as a field of study, knowledge and research has been professionalised throughout Europe in the course of the last few decades. In some parts of Europe this development has occurred slowly and in others more rapidly (see chapters 13 and 14 in this volume for the Spanish and German cases, respectively). While Europe in general seems to have had an uneven institutionalisation (Griffin 2005a), developments in the Nordic[1] countries are assumed to look similar. Unsurprisingly, the Nordic countries are often believed to be emblematic of a smooth and successful professionalisation. Is this the case? Can one talk about one pan-Nordic development, implying the same patterns in every Nordic country? In addition to the professionalisation of women's/gender studies in Denmark, Iceland, Finland, Norway and Sweden, is there also a regional Nordic development? These are some of the questions that I will explore in greater detail in this chapter through the following themes:

1) disciplinisation
2) institutionalisation
3) by assessing the degree of professionalisation.

FROM ACTIVIST BEGINNINGS TO INFLUENTIAL RESEARCH

In the late 1960s and early 1970s, the women's movement was strong in the Nordic countries (Bergman 2002). Many activists were university teachers/researchers or civil servants holding an academic degree. In Finland the movement had in the very early days a strong emphasis on equality between women and men. In contrast, the Danish and Swedish movements were more radical, focusing on emancipation. The movement professionalised mainly in two directions in the Nordic region: academia and what was to be called the equality or the equal opportunities sector. The development within the Finnish equality sector, for example, was described in the project Employment and Women's Studies (EWSI) (Tuori and Silius 2002).[2]

Nordic gender equality has been the object of several studies. At first, Nordic researchers presented Nordic gender equality as a success story (Haavio-Mannila et al. 1985; Bergqvist et al. 1999). Then they moved to questioning the success as well as the notion of the Nordic (von der Fehr, Jónasdóttir and Rosenbeck 1998). Recent critical research approaches question, criticise and trouble the very foundations of Nordic equality (Magnusson, Rönnblom and Silius 2008). Meanwhile, political support for gender equality measures is losing legitimacy to diversity policies, and discursive equality is considered politically correct.

In the following description of the professionalisation of women's/gender studies in the Nordic university sector I draw on the EWSI project mentioned above, Nordic sources and assessment experiences. The EWSI study identified three phases of institutionalisation of women's/gender studies training in universities: the activist phase, the establishment phase and the professionalisation phase (Silius 2002, 513). Gabriele Griffin (2005b, 89–90) further elaborated on these three phases, adding the integration, the disciplinisation and the autonomy phases into the original model (see also chapter 14, this volume).

During the activist phase, the women's movement was strongest in Denmark[3] and weakest in Finland (Bergman 2002), leaving Iceland, Norway and Sweden in between. Whereas Denmark, Norway and Sweden experienced strong autonomous grassroots movements in the 1970s, Iceland's activists saw their heyday in the 1980s with the presence of a Feminist Party in parliament (Dominelli and Jonsdottir 1988). No other Nordic country has reached this achievement, despite the Swedish attempt (the 'Feminist Initiative,' a Feminist Party coalition that ran for Parliament in 2006). During the activist phase, individual optional women's studies modules began to appear within traditional disciplines, although most women's studies-related work was carried out outside academia (Griffin 2005b, 89).

The establishment phase was quite similar in all Nordic countries. Research, and often training too, was institutionalised through the establishment of interdisciplinary centres in the universities from the 1980s onward (Lykke et al. 2004); both generic and thematic, (typically) multidisciplinary women's studies modules were introduced in Nordic universities. Cooperation across the Nordic countries had started in the 1970s (Rosenbeck 1998; Bergman 2000) but was institutionalised more thoroughly in the 1990s with the establishment of the Nordic Institute for Women's Studies and Gender Research (NIKK) in 1995. The third phase, the professionalisation of gender studies, is still in progress.

The result of the last three decades of feminist activities in the Nordic universities has been the establishment and development of feminist research in all five countries, including the emergence of researchers who, for decades, have worked with both theoretical and empirical questions in gender research. Gender research is established as a field of knowledge, both as an independent strand of thought and as an elaboration of different disciplines. Three decades is not a long period of time in academia.

Consequently, most gender researchers have been or are pioneers in their field of work. They have claimed a field of their own, established, elaborated and enlarged it. Coming from different disciplines, many wanted more or better knowledge than was offered in their 'mother disciplines.' They have worked as pioneers, tokens and battering rams, creating their field of knowledge and sharing their experiences with colleagues and students. They were not mainstream students or scholars of their 'mother discipline' but rather those who were prepared to risk not succeeding, being marginalised and perhaps not returning to the mainstream. Many succeeded in their endeavours. These are some of the reasons why one can argue that what was created was influential. However, if a new field of knowledge emerges, to what extent does it 'count' as a full-fledged discipline? Is that discipline institutionalised in the same way as other comparable fields of knowledge? (Lykke, chapter 9, this volume). And finally, have women's/gender studies scholars created a labour market for themselves in the universities?

INDICATORS OF DISCIPLINISATION

Although the concepts of disciplinisation and institutionalisation do not mean the same, they are interconnected. To put it simply: a field of knowledge becomes a discipline when it is institutionalised into the scientific field, into scholarship and research. How this happens, which processes occur and which features impact on the results are questions investigated in the field of sociology of science (Keskinen and Silius 2005; Krebs and Wenk 2005). Scholars usually count the following as indicators of disciplinisation: the existence of professorships, scientific conferences, journals and a system to assure continuation of the field, i.e., PhD training. Disciplinisation involves the creation of academic subjects and training programmes. How academic subjects arise is a complicated and, above all, haphazard or unsystematic process, partly due to national and institutional educational policies. The establishment of training programmes as a marker of institutionalisation primarily concerns PhD training. By PhD training as part of disciplinisation I mean that senior scholars in the field supervise junior ones, either in a master-apprentice relationship or in more collective forms. Drawing on Griffin's work (2005b, 90–91), six indicators of disciplinisation of women's/gender studies in the Nordic countries may be analytically distinguished:

1. The Existence of (Autonomous or Faculty-based) Women's/Gender Studies Centres or Departments

In all Nordic countries and at trans-Nordic level, centre-like units were established to gather gender scholars together for cooperation and inter-disciplinary activities such as seminars, lectures, documentation, information and dissemination, joint research projects and so forth. This happened over a ten-year period in the 1980s. The first Danish centre started in Odense in 1981, followed by centres at the universities of Aalborg, Aarhus, Copenhagen and Roskilde in 1982. Denmark used to be a country with women's studies centres in all universities.

The centres at the older universities in Norway and throughout Sweden were also founded in the 1980s. In Finland the first centre at Åbo Akademi University started in 1986. The Icelandic Centre for Women's and Gender Studies, 'an independent research institute' at the University of Iceland (RIKK 2008), was founded in 1991. It is worth noting that almost all (autonomous, independent) Danish centres disappeared in the 2000s: some no longer exist, and others were amalgamated into bigger, integrated centres or departments. Compared to the other four Nordic countries, the Danish situation is quite different, although there may be similar cases in some continental European countries. The Nordic exception is thus Denmark. It does not, however, necessarily imply that Danish gender scholarship is less disciplinised, rather that its position seems to be less stable.

By 2010 almost all centres in the Nordic countries were faculty-based units, although many of them started as multidisciplinary centres outside the faculty structure. The degree of autonomy depends above all on how much autonomy a subject or discipline has within a specific university or university system. Belonging to a faculty, department or group of departments may therefore be both a sign of disciplinisation and of mainstreaming and integration into other disciplines.

At the Nordic level, NIKK's main tasks involved networking among researchers, information and dissemination, and also initiation of Nordic research projects, PhD training and research-policy related activities. The two Ks in NIKK used to stand for 'women and gender' in Norwegian (*kvinner og kjönn*). Since 2008 this has become 'knowledge about gender' (*kunnskap om kjönn*). The change of name was part of a new contract with the Nordic Council of Ministers (a joint Nordic governmental body consisting of the Ministers for Equality). As a result NIKK changed its name in English to Nordic Gender Institute. The observant reader will note that in the English version the words 'women's studies' and 'research' were avoided. In Norwegian the word 'women' was skipped. Whereas the original version of NIKK's name very much referred to academia, the later one refers to units for equal opportunities (the English version), documentation and information centres (the Scandinavian version). Although names mould our discursive practices and images, one should not draw hasty conclusions about the consequences of the change of names without taking into consideration the performed activities.

2. The Existence of (Annual) Scientific Conferences

In the typical example of a discipline, a learned society or professional association organises a conference for scholars in its field of knowledge. This usually takes place annually because positions in associations have to be filled and accounts approved once a year. If no association exists, university centres or departments may organise research conferences, or scholars might do this themselves. This used to be the case in Sweden, because the Association of Gender Studies Scholars in Sweden was only founded relatively recently. Swedish Gender Studies scholars argued for a long time that a professional association was a type of unwanted bureaucracy leading to a loss of autonomy. In contrast, the Danish Association for Gender Studies was started in 1990 and has since then organised annual conferences attended by large numbers of Danish gender researchers.

Nordic conferences on women's/gender studies have been organised since the 1980s, but not annually. In addition to generic Nordic conferences, Nordic gender historians for example have organised conferences every third year since 1983.

3. The Existence of Scientific, Preferably Refereed, Journals

All countries except Iceland have a generic women's/gender studies journal, of which some twenty volumes have appeared. The Swedish journal (formerly *Kvinnovetenskaplig tidskrift*, now *Tidskrift för genusvetenskap*) is the oldest; it started in 1980 as a Nordic journal. The Finnish journal *Naistutkimus/Kvinnoforskning* [Women's studies] has been a refereed journal for more than twenty years, the Danish equivalent has been refereed since the mid-1990s, and the journals in Norway and Sweden have more recently moved into this phase. There are three Nordic journals: the English *NORA* (started in 1993), *Lambda Nordica* (1989, on gay and lesbian studies) and *Norma* (2007, on masculinity studies). All are refereed.

4. The Number of (Endowed) Named Chairs, Professorships

In the mid-1980s, eight permanent associate professorships were allocated to the Danish women's studies centres. These associate professorships were integrated into disciplines or broader institutions, however, during a backlash in the 1990s (Lykke 2004, 35–36). Full professorships in gender studies did not occur in Denmark until the 2000s. By 2010 there were three Danish professorships with a gender studies component (at the Danish School of Education at Aarhus University and at the universities of Aalborg and Copenhagen). Iceland has no named professorships (and only one lectureship). In Finland eight professorships in women's studies were established in the late 1990s, in addition to one that already existed. Later, some of them were abolished and some not filled. In Norway professorships exist at the gender studies centres of Oslo, Bergen and Trondheim. Most of the Norwegian professorships are not named as being within gender studies but rather include gender studies in a traditional discipline (history, political science, psychology and so on). They are, however, affiliated to and located at a gender studies centre. In addition, some professors have recently been appointed at university colleges. In the mid-1990s in Sweden, Mr. Tham, Minister of Education, earmarked government funding for thirty-one new professorships for women with the aim of promoting female researchers in Swedish academia. In addition, nine professorships were earmarked for gender studies, of which six were intended to strengthen gender research in traditional disciplines. The other three were designed to set up a new interdisciplinary department at Linköping University with its own PhD programme in gender studies. Since then Swedish universities have gradually established professorships in gender studies as well as in traditional disciplines with a named gender component. In 2010 there are altogether more than twenty of these professorships in Sweden (about half of them are in gender studies and linked directly to gender studies centres/units/departments, and the other half are located within the disciplines but defined by a named gender studies component). This is by far the highest number of gender studies professorships in the Nordic countries. In the context of the number of gender studies centres, however, the amount of professorships in gender studies is not that impressive. For quite a long period gender studies centres in Sweden did not lobby for professorships because they did not want staff at different hierarchical levels, but instead cherished the flat organisation of the 1970s. Today, the process of establishing new professorships continues in Sweden and to a certain degree in Norway, but has stopped in Finland.

5. The Existence and Range of PhD Training

PhD training depends everywhere on professors. In the twentieth century PhD training in the humanities and the social sciences in the Nordic countries did not require specific courses but rested solely on writing a thesis under the supervision of a professor. In 1995 the Finnish Research School in Women's and Gender Studies started working in four-year periods (equivalent to the time of a PhD programme). This gender studies PhD training programme offers fewer than ten salaried positions, and the students of the programme are affiliated to women's studies at their respective universities. Meanwhile, gender studies scholars in Denmark and Norway organised a few courses per year. A doctoral programme similar to the Finnish one will start in Norway in 2011. In 2010 seven universities in Sweden offered a PhD programme in gender studies. In addition, a nationwide PhD programme (InterGender) with international partners started in 2008 with funding from the research council. Between 2004 and 2009 there was a Nordic PhD programme called the Nordic Research School in Interdisciplinary Gender Studies, directed by Prof. Nina Lykke, Linköping University. The school offered a number of PhD training modules annually for students from the Nordic countries, the Baltic countries and Northwest Russia.

6. Recognition of the Field by Various Important Actors Such as Research Councils and Assessing Bodies

The recognition of a discipline by various key decision-making bodies relevant to higher education in a given country such as ministries, higher-education funding authorities and so forth is of importance both symbolically and practically. I shall here primarily discuss competition-based earmarked money at research council level. The Danish research council funded major gender research programmes in the 1980s and 1990s. In Finland the recognition from the research council has been more marginal, whereas Iceland has a centre of excellence. For more than a decade, the Norwegian and Swedish research councils have offered specific programmes on gender research, and in Sweden a nationwide teaching assessment exercise was completed in 2007. Furthermore, in Sweden three Centres of Gender Excellence were established for a five-year period (Gendering Excellence, GEXcel) at Linköping and Örebro Universities, Challenging Gender at Umeå University and GenNa at Uppsala University, a sign of high recognition (see chapter 14, this volume, for the German case).

In summary, there are considerable differences between the five Nordic countries. Although it might appear as if gender studies is not a full-fledged discipline in Denmark, this is a matter of opinion. It is clear that government support and the interest of university leaders are minimal, but with its long history, one may argue that gender studies in Denmark is well integrated into traditional disciplines.

The results that were discussed above are also summarised in table 12.1.

INDICATORS OF INSTITUTIONALISATION

Disciplinisation and institutionalisation go hand in hand as part of the academic professionalisation process of women's/gender studies. By

Table 12.1 Disciplinisation of Women's/Gender Studies in the Nordic Countries in 2010

	GS centres	Annual Conference	Referee Journal	Professor-ships	PhD training	Recognition of research council
Denmark	No	Yes	Yes	Three	Some	Some
Finland	Yes	Yes	Yes	Six/Seven	Yes	Some
Iceland	Yes	Yes	No	None	No	Yes
Norway	Yes	Yes	Yes	Nine	Some	Yes
Sweden	Yes	Yes	Yes	More than 20	Yes	Yes
Nordic	Yes	Some	Yes	n/a	Yes	n/a

institutionalisation in this context I mean the development of feminist research and teaching activities into continuous, stable, normalised practice, in contrast to *ad hoc* activities. This is also the definition used in Silius (2002) and Griffin (2005b). In total, Griffin has identified eight indicators to measure the degree of institutionalisation of women's studies. As I have dealt with some of them in relation to disciplinisation, in the following I apply the remainder of Griffin's indicators to the Nordic scene:

1. The Existence of Women's/Gender Studies Centres or Departments

The existence of a women's/gender studies centre is not a prerequisite for institutionalised training activities, although a departmental type of structure is how universities in Europe normally organise their teaching activities. For administrative reasons (with efficiency or saving as the aim) disciplines and departments have recently amalgamated into groups of disciplines in several universities in the Nordic countries, which may imply loss of autonomy. In these cases, sometimes the situation of women's/ gender studies improves because of better gateways to influential actors. Sometimes, however, it deteriorates because of complicated bureaucracy (*Utvärdering* 2007, 35–37). In spite of these structural reforms towards bigger units, a department may be characterised as a unit that plans, coordinates, develops and facilitates training programmes. Usually there is also a named person who is responsible for the subject/discipline. Without a centre, department or similar network of women's/gender studies teachers, training depends on the initiative of single teachers. The same applies to research, although research activities are carried out not only by single researchers, but in very various kinds of projects.

2. The Existence of Lectureships or Other Senior (Postdoctoral) Positions in the Field or the Academic Standing of the Staff Involved

There are two major ways to hire staff to teach women's/gender studies. One can either appoint lecturers at women's/gender studies units or teachers in senior positions within traditional disciplines who teach women's/gender studies modules either at their own department or jointly at a women's/gender studies centre. On the one hand, the existence of lectureships and other postdoctoral positions in the Nordic countries is generally very limited. Sweden, however, has a more considerable number of postdoctoral positions in gender studies, and several Swedish universities have more than one lectureship in gender studies. On the other hand, most programmes in the other countries are taught by professors, readers or equivalent senior staff. The level of academic seniority of the staff involved is thus often higher than in other disciplines. This has proved to be the case in Sweden (*Utvärdering* 2007).

3. The Existence of a Training Programme in Women's/Gender Studies on Different Levels (Undergraduate, Postgraduate, PhD)

The existence and range of degree-awarding under- and postgraduate programmes varies in the Nordic countries. In addition to BA, MA and PhD programmes in women's/gender studies, i.e., as a degree-awarding major, women's/gender studies may exist as a minor. In principle, minors can be part of both BAs and MAs, more rarely of PhD programmes. From occasional modules—usually called courses in the Nordic countries—as optional specialisations within a traditional discipline, women's/gender studies has unevenly institutionalised into programmes. Simply put: institutionalisation in Finland and Sweden is high, but in Denmark, Iceland and Norway it is low. In Denmark most training takes place in the traditional disciplines (*Køn i undervisning* 2008), due to the integration of gender studies into the disciplines and the abolishment of women's studies centres in the 1990s. The situation in Norway is different. For decades, centres in Norway used to be research centres only, without teaching. Occasionally they organised optional modules, often at PhD level. Only in relation to the Bologna Process have some BA and MA programmes been introduced (KILDEN 2008). Iceland is a country that lacks full programmes because of its small size and more recent trends towards disciplinisation. Swedish training in gender studies started as a minor and developed throughout the 1990s to degree-awarding programmes at BA and MA level. Taught PhD programmes are a phenomenon of the twenty-first century and are now available at seven Swedish universities. In Finland, Bologna-type MA programmes in women's studies started in 2005. The Finnish PhD programme that started in 1995 became a full degree-awarding programme in women's studies in 2002, with the affiliated universities also offering an MA programme.

4. The Amount and Kind of Funding (Temporary or Structural) Available

This is an important indicator which will not be considered here. Funding systems vary and are not very transparent which is why a representative picture is out of the scope of this chapter. A general observation would be that what used to be permanent at Nordic universities is in the process of change. For example, permanent positions are changing into fixed-term ones, and the status of civil servant has been abolished in Finland.[4] New rules imply that universities are now much freer to change their priorities. This may sometimes be desirable for women's/gender studies if positions are stabilised, resources increased or more competent staff hired and sometimes the reverse when centres are closed or activities downsized. In this chapter I have related disciplinisation predominantly to research, and institutionalisation to training. As shown above they are interrelated, and teaching at university level is based on research. Although all Nordic countries are occupied with research, significant differences exist concerning training. The differences in institutionalisation are summarised in table 12.2.

INDICATORS OF PROFESSIONALISATION

Earlier research on professionalisation has been criticised because of its dominant Anglo-American context and male centredness. Many studies in the sociology of professions used to start by trying to establish a divide between the professions and other occupations.[5] Some of the most common indicators were: academic education based on a highly specified field of knowledge; monopoly in a labour market; prestige and professional ethos; and a certain autonomy, for example in the form of a self-regulating body of professionals (Jarausch 1990; Silius 1992; Schmidbaur 2002). On the European continent this division is less clear-cut, mainly because many professionals are or used to be civil servants. The relationship between the professions, the state, the educational system and the market also varies across countries due to different societal contexts in Europe (Torstendahl and Burrage 1990). Because of the importance of the context, some scholars have even avoided the concept of professionalisation (Benoit 1994; Freidson 2001; Evetts 2003).

Feminist scholars have revealed both the gendered construct of earlier notions of profession as well as the specificities of female professional projects (Crompton 1987; Silius 1992; Witz 1992; Davies 1996). Others have criticised the ideological implications of traditional theories of professions concerning gender, class and race (Allen 1987). Instead of asking, 'Is this a profession?' critical research on professions asks, 'How are professions created and organised?' (Abbott 1988; Henriksson and Wrede 2004). If you ask, 'Is gender studies a profession?' the answer is no; there is no occupation including gender comparable to the physician's, lawyer's or university professor's profession. In the EWSI project (see Silius 2005) past women's

Table 12.2 Institutionalisation of Women's/Gender Studies in the Nordic Universities in 2010

	Centre	Post-docs incl. professors	Minor	BA	MA	PhD modules	PhD programme
Denmark	No	< 5	Yes	No	A few	Yes	No
Iceland	Yes	< 5	Yes	No	No	No	No
Finland	Yes	> 10	Yes	Yes	Yes	Yes	Yes
Norway	Yes	> 10	No	A few	A few	Yes	No
Sweden	Yes	> 40	Yes	Yes	Yes	Yes	Yes

studies students in nine European countries were interviewed about their jobs. It turned out that the most frequent job among them was the academic profession, i.e., they worked as university teachers and researchers. At the time, I did not regard these jobs as one single profession, nor did I see the positions as homogeneous. These university teachers and researchers have, however, to a very important extent created their own jobs and in addition, the content of their work, the use of scientific as well as tacit knowledge and developed new knowledge. In this sense they are highly professionalised and their expertise can be seen as a very specific form of professionalism.

Through the creation of new fields of knowledge such as women's/gender studies, new borders, hierarchies and specialisms emerge in academia (see chapters 9 and 11, this volume). This process (Witz 1992; Silius 2002, 509) can certainly be regarded as a typical women's professional project. To conclude, women's/gender studies scholars have created a labour market of their own in Nordic universities as teachers and researchers. In addition to the academic profession, according to the EWSI study, women's studies graduates have professionalised their expertise in several other fields (see chapters 13 and 14, this volume).

To summarise, by the professionalisation of gender studies I mean the process through which occupations arise where knowledge of gender research is a prerequisite for successful practice. These occupations are mainly found in academia, but also *extra muros*. In contrast to the analysis of occupations held by former women's studies students, which was the focus of the EWSI project (Silius and Tuori 2004; Silius 2005), in this last section I shall try to assess to what degree jobs exist in the Nordic countries where women's/gender studies expertise is required. Through the disciplinisation and institutionalisation of women's/gender studies as an academic subject, university programme or discipline, such jobs occur mostly in academia. In addition, extramural jobs such as senior-level researcher jobs at independent research institutes are an important sector in Norway, although this sector is predicted to shrink in the future (Jordheim Larsen and Widerberg 2006).

Professions such as law or medicine have, to some degree, a monopoly in a labour market, but this is not the case with women's/gender studies graduates. Nor does the discipline have the same prestige as, for example, law or medicine. However, one may argue that women's/gender studies has developed a professional ethos found in specific teaching practices at universities (Griffin and Hanmer 2005) and in how women's/gender studies graduates deal with their workplace culture (Silius and Tuori 2004). The autonomy of a profession is usually measured by identifying some form of a self-regulating body of professionals, i.e., a professional association from which one can be expelled in the case of misconduct. Although professional associations for women's/gender studies students and scholars exist in the Nordic countries and also at joint Nordic level, they work in the same manner as associations for historians, sociologists or philosophers, more like scientific societies than like a professional association for practising lawyers (advocates). The degree of professionalisation of women's/gender studies in the Nordic countries is summarised in table 12.3.

CONCLUSION

In this chapter I set out to determine whether one can talk about a single 'Nordic' development, implying the same pattern of professionalisation of women's/gender studies in every Nordic country. The answer to this question is no; there are considerable differences. *Iceland* differs because of its small size (gender studies takes place only at the University of Iceland). One may also see *Denmark* as different because the disciplinisation and institutionalisation that were developed there from the early 1980s to the beginning of the 1990s suddenly took a step backwards. Instead of independence or autonomy, most gender scholars in Denmark seem to prefer an affiliation with other disciplines and research groups. Gender studies could be said to have been merged, integrated or mainstreamed in Danish academe without much fuss. In contrast, in *Finland* one can see a straightforward process of both disciplinisation and quite recent institutionalisation. In my opinion, however, this result represents only a middle degree of professionalisation. *Norway*, in its turn, is distinctive due to the long lack of training opportunities, or put more positively, Norway has a strong focus on research activities and a resolute strategy of integration. Finally, *Sweden* differs because nowhere else have disciplinisation, institutionalisation or professionalisation reached the same level. In contrast to Norway, Swedish gender studies scholars have consciously aimed at developing gender studies into an autonomous inter- or transdisciplinary field of knowledge in addition to integration into other disciplines.

I also asked if professionalisation of women's/gender studies in the Nordic countries has been smooth and successful. The answer to this question is the same as to the question above; it depends on which country one considers. It was not smooth anywhere, but in some environments it has happened more easily than in others. Finally, I asked if there was also a regional Nordic

Table 12.3   The Degree of Professionalisation of Women's/Gender Studies in the Nordic Countries in 2010

	Jobs in academia	Senior jobs in research institutes	GS jobs in equal opps or equivalent	Degree of professionalisation
Denmark	Few	No	Few	Low
Iceland	Few	n/a	Few	Low
Finland	Some	A few	Few	Middle
Norway	Some	Some	Yes	Middle
Sweden	Several	Some	Yes	High

development in addition to professionalisation of women's/gender studies in specific countries. My answer is still yes, due to NIKK, the Nordic Gender Institute and the aforementioned journals and conferences. Furthermore, future PhD and MA programmes offer opportunities to build on existing research cooperation and networking. The assessment of the degree to which women's/gender studies is professionalised in the Nordic countries is a conclusion based on the arguments in this chapter. Two countries were identified as having a low degree of professionalisation (Denmark and Iceland), two to have a medium degree (Finland and Norway) and only one to have reached a higher degree of professionalism (Sweden). This result indicates that the process of professionalisation of women's/gender studies has not yet come to an end in any of the Nordic countries.

NOTES

1. The term Nordic refers to a specific geographical region, and also to a cultural space or social community. This more or less imagined community is linked together by historical ties, lifestyles and cultural norms.
2. The EWSI project was a major EU funded research project titled *Employment and Women's Studies: The Impact of Women's Studies Training on Women's Employment in Europe* (Griffin 2002, 2004, 2005a). It is the first cross-national analysis of professional outlets of women's/gender studies in Europe. The aim of the EWSI project was to study the impact of women's studies-training on women's employment in nine European countries (see also chapters 13 and 14, this volume).
3. Drude Dahlerup (1998) has extensively analysed the Danish feminist movement of the 1970s called the Redstockings.
4. University teachers have lost some privileges (and duties) that were connected to the status of civil servant.
5. 'Professionalisation' is understood here as meaning how a group of specialists or university educated people create an occupation of their own. 'Professions' are thus those occupations that require a specialist training, usually at university, and 'professionals' are people who work in a profession.

REFERENCES

Abbott, A. 1988. *The System of Professions: An Essay on the Division of Expert Labor*. Chicago: University of Chicago Press.

Allen, D. 1987. Professionalism, Occupational Segregation by Gender and Control of Nursing. In *The Politics of Professionalism, Opportunity, Employment, and Gender*, ed. S. Slavin, 1–24. New York: Haworth Press.

Benoit, C. 1994. Paradigm Conflict in the Sociology of the Professions. *Canadian Journal of Sociology* 19 (3): 303–29.

Bergman, S. 2000. Women's Studies in the Nordic Countries—Organisation, Strategies and Resources. In *The Making of European Women's Studies*. Vol. 2, ed. R. Braidotti, E. Vonk and S. van Wichelen, 51–64. Utrecht: ATHENA.

Bergman, S. 2002. *The Politics of Feminism: Autonomous Feminist Movements in Finland and West Germany from the 1960s to the 1980s*. Åbo: Åbo Akademi University Press.

Bergqvist, C., A. Borchorst , A.-D. Christensen, V. Ramstedt-Silén, N. C. Raaum and A. Styrkársdóttir, eds. 1999. *Equal Democracies? Gender and Politics in the Nordic Countries*. Oslo: Scandinavian University Press.

Crompton, R. 1987. Gender, Status and Professionalism. *Sociology* 21 (3): 413–28.

Dahlerup, D. 1998. *Rødstrømperne: Den danske Rødstrømpebevægelses udvikling, nytænkning og gennemslag, 1970–1985* [The Redstockings: The development, new thinking and breakthrough of the Danish Redstocking movement, 1970–1985]. Kopenhagen: Gyldendal.

Davies, C. 1996. The Sociology of Professions and the Sociology of Gender. *Sociology* 30 (4): 661–68.

Dominelli, L., and G. Jonsdottir. 1988. Feminist Political Organization in Iceland: Some Reflections on the Experience of Kwenna Frambothid. *Feminist Review* 30: 36–60.

Evetts, J. 2003. The Sociological Analysis of Professionalism: Occupational Change in the Modern World. *International Sociology* 18 (2): 395–415.

Fehr, D. von der, A. Jónasdóttir and B. Rosenbeck, eds. 1998. *Is There a Nordic Feminism? Nordic Feminist Thought on Culture and Society*. London: UCL Press.

Freidson, E. 2001. *Professionalism: The Third Logic*. Cambridge: Polity Press.

Griffin, G., ed. 2002. *Women's Employment, Women's Studies, and Equal Opportunities 1945–2001: Reports from Nine European Countries*. Hull: University of Hull Press.

———, ed. 2004. *Employment, Equal Opportunities and Women's Studies: Women's Experiences in Seven European Countries*. Frankfurt am Main: Ulrike Helmer Verlag.

———, ed. 2005a. *Doing Women's Studies: Employment Opportunities, Personal Impacts and Social Consequences*. London: Zed Books.

———. 2005b. The Institutionalization of Women's Studies in Europe. In *Doing Women's Studies: Employment Opportunities, Personal Impacts and Social Consequences—Women's Experiences in Seven European Countries*, ed. G. Griffin, 89–110. London: Zed Books.

Griffin, G., and J. Hanmer. 2005. The Impact of Women's Studies on Its Students' Relationships and Everyday Practices. In *Doing Women's Studies: Employment Opportunities, Personal Impacts and Social Consequences—Women's Experiences in Seven European Countries*, ed. G. Griffin, 141–94. London: Zed Books.

Haavio-Mannila, E., D. Dahlerup, M. Eduards, E. Gudmundsdottir, B. Halsaa, H. M. Hernes, E. Hänninen-Salmelin, B. Sigmundsdottir, S. Sinkkonen and T. Skard, eds. 1985. *Unfinished Democracy: Women in Nordic Politics*. Oxford: Pergamon Press.

Henriksson, L., and S. Wrede, eds. 2004. *Hyvinvointityön ammatit* [The professions of welfare work]. Helsinki: Gaudeamus.

Jarausch, K. 1990. *The Unfree Professions: German Lawyers, Teachers, and Engineers, 1900–1850*. New York: Oxford University Press.

Jordheim Larsen, C., and K. Widerberg. 2006. Interdisciplinarity, Research Policies and Practices: Two Case Studies in Norway. *Research Integration*. http://www.york.ac.uk/res/researchintegration/ (accessed April 6, 2008).

Keskinen, S., and H. Silius. 2005 The Moving Boundaries of Research Structures and Funding. *Research Integration*. http://www.york.ac.uk/res/researchintegration/ (accessed April 6, 2008).

Krebs, R., and S. Wenk. 2005. Current Debates about the Construction of Knowledge in the Social Sciences and Humanities and the Impact of these on Disciplinization in Eight European Countries. *Research Integration*. http://www.york.ac.uk/res/researchintegration/ (accessed April 6, 2008).

Køn i undervisning–undervisning i køn [Gender in training–training in gender]. 2008. En kortlægning af kønsperspektivet i dansk universitetsundervisning. Copenhagen: Koordinationen for kønsforskning.

Lykke, N., A. Lundberg, S. Knudsen and L. Strandberg. 2004. *Women's/Gender/Feminist Studies: PhD Training in the Nordic Regions of Europe.* Nordic Research School in Interdisciplinary Gender Studies, Publications no. 1. Linköping: Tema Genus Report no. 3.

Magnusson, E., M. Rönnblom and H. Silius, eds. 2008. *Critical Studies of Gender Equalities: Nordic Dislocations, Dilemmas and Contradictions.* Gothenberg: Makadam.

Centre for Women's and Gender Studies at the University of Iceland (RIKK). 2008. http://www.rikk.hi.is (accessed April 6, 2008).

Rosenbeck, B. 1998. Nordic Women's Studies and Gender Research. In *Is There a Nordic Feminism? Nordic Feminist Thought on Culture and Society*, ed. D. von der Fehr, A. Jónasdóttir and B. Rosenbeck, 344–57. London: UCL Press.

Schmidbaur, M. 2002. *Vom 'Lazaruskreuz' zu 'Pflege aktuell': Professionalisierungsdiskurse in der deutschen Krankenpflege 1903–2000* [From Lazarus Cross to Current Care: Discourses of Professionalisation in the German Medical Care 1903–2000]. Königstein: Ulrike Helmer Verlag.

Silius, H. 1992. *Den kringgärdade kvinnligheten: Att vara kvinnlig jurist i Finland* [Contracted Femininity: The Case of Women Lawyers in Finland]. Åbo: Åbo Akademi University Press.

———. 2002. Comparative Summary. In *Women's Employment, Women's Studies and Equal Opportunities 1945–2001*, ed. G. Griffin, 470–514. Hull: University of Hull.

———. 2005. The Professionalization of Women's Studies Students in Europe: Expectations and Experiences. In *Doing Women's Studies: Employment Opportunities, Personal Impacts and Social Consequences*, ed. G. Griffin, 111–40. London: Zed Books.

Silius, H., and S. Tuori. 2004. Gender-neutral Finland? Women's Studies Students as Gender Experts in Finland. In *Employment, Equal Opportunities and Women's Studies*, ed. G. Griffin, 163–86. Königstein: Ulrike Helmer Verlag.

Torstendahl, R., and M. Burrage, eds. 1990. *The Formation of Professions: Knowledge, State and Strategy.* London: Sage.

Tuori, S., and H. Silius. 2002. Finland. In *Women's Employment, Women's Studies and Equal Opportunities 1945–2001*, ed. G. Griffin, 69–121. Hull: University of Hull.

Utvärdering av ämnet genusvetenskap vid svenska universitet och högskolor. Stockholm: Högskoleverket, Rapport 2007:17 R.

Witz, A. 1992. *Professions and Patriarchy.* London: Routledge.

WEB SITES

Finnish Research School in Women's and Gender Studies. http://www.naistutkimuksentohtorikoulu.fi/english (accessed August 19, 2010).

GEXcel. http://www.genderexcel.org (accessed August 19, 2010).

GenNa. http://www.genna.gender.uu.se (accessed August 19, 2010).

InterGender: Research School in Interdisciplinary Gender Studies. http://www.intergender.net (accessed August 19, 2010).

KILDEN, *Studietilbud i kjønnsforskning i Norge.* http://kilden.forskningsradet.no/c17274/artikkel/vis.html (accessed April 6, 2008).

Umeå Centre for Gender Studies. http://www.ucgs.umu.se (accessed August 19, 2010).

13 The Professionalisation of Feminist Researchers
The Spanish Case

Isabel Carrera Suárez

In a study carried out between 2001 and 2003, within a EU-funded project on employment and women's studies (EWSI; results published in Griffin 2002, 2004, 2005; see also this volume, chapters 12 and 14), we analysed the impact of women's studies training on employment in Spain as perceived and experienced at that particular moment, by means of questionnaires and interviews with women's studies students.[1] Our background report and final publications (Carrera Suárez and Viñuela Suárez 2002, 2004), like other related analyses of the history of women's studies in Spain (Birriel Salcedo 2002; Casado Aparicio 2002), foregrounded the rapid developments after Franco's death in 1975, and the consequences of this growth of the field in a semi-institutionalised setting. Such consequences included a certain degree of freedom in organising curricula, but also a tendency for women's studies to exist in optional courses or postgraduate studies only and, given the somewhat dubious recognition of the field, to constitute a double shift and a career hindrance for the academics involved. We also found that most full programmes tended to exist as PhD programmes, primarily geared towards academic learning and research or, less frequently, as specialised professional degrees in the form of *Títulos propios*, a postgraduate category which lacked official status and therefore national and professional validity. Data on courses were not easy to locate, given their positioning outside regular degrees, and the level of institutionalisation of women's studies and related employment opportunities was very moderate.

Although some of the structural obstacles for these studies (and for related academic careers) remain firmly in place today, a number of things have changed quite dramatically in the intervening years due to two factors: first, political change and the driving force of a socialist government which, since its election in 2004, has been foregrounding equality in legislation and practices; and second, the major revision of the higher-education system through the Bologna Process. Despite social resistance and material difficulties (recently increased by the international economic crisis), these two factors have combined to create an unpredicted opportunity for increased recognition of women's studies, both in the academic and professional worlds.

The following pages offer a brief overview of the Spanish higher-education system and the historical development of women's studies within it, followed by a discussion of the new developments in academic structures and their relationship to professional opportunities for women's studies students.

HIGHER EDUCATION AND THE DEVELOPMENT OF WOMEN'S STUDIES IN SPAIN

The Spanish higher-education system is traditionally very centralised, uniform and state dependent. It is mostly public (state run) and ruled by national regulations, although in the past decades a varying degree of decentralisation has taken place, with regional government and universities gaining partial control. The main actors at national level are the Ministry of Education and the new Ministry of Science and Innovation which was created in 2008 to focus on research. The restructuring of higher education in Spain began with the consolidation of democracy, when the first socialist government introduced a major reform of the obsolete structures, in 1983, through the Ley de Reforma Universitaria (University Reform Act, or LRU). This act emphasised research and reorganised staff and resources into discipline-based departments, versus the previous education-based and more fragmented structure of schools. It also introduced the national registry of disciplines, still in place today, with few variations, and proclaimed the theoretical 'autonomy' of universities, reinforced in 1996 when the transfer of educational funds to regional governments was completed and academics became employees of the universities rather than of the ministry.

The importance of political intervention in higher education in Spain was confirmed as recently as 2001, in the upheaval created by the Ley Orgánica de Universidades (LOU), passed by Aznar's conservative government in an attempt to effect yet another major transformation in the university system. Private universities were favoured, external governing bodies and controls were reinforced and staff recruitment was returned to a centralised national selection system, a so-called *habilitación*. The evident failure of the latter made it one of the priorities for change in the agenda of the socialist government elected in 2004, and reforms have already taken place. Political shifts notwithstanding, two things remain constant in the Spanish system:

1) major decisions on education are made at a national level, usually in the Ministry of Education.
2) a rigid disciplinary structure governs teaching, research and promotion.

A relatively recent and influential development is the National Quality Assurance and Accreditation Agency (ANECA), which evaluates degrees, universities and individual academics; ANECA (like its regional counterparts) is also very rigidly discipline oriented and was created by the ministry, although works independently.

Universities depend mostly on state funding, together with student fees, European funds, local institutions and an emerging contribution from the private sector. Despite recent efforts to increase private involvement, research is promoted primarily by the state and by regional governments, with public universities and their associated institutes as major actors, together with the Centro Superior de Investigaciones Científicas (CSIC), a public body with sites across the country and an extended staff devoted exclusively to research in priority areas.

This context conditions the development of women's studies within the academe, and as Elena Casado Aparicio (2002) has argued, examining the historical specificities of the creation of these studies may also help to understand their strengths and their limitations. As is true of other countries, women's studies did not originate inside the academic community but in the social movement on which it is based—feminism—which in the Spain of the 1970s grew in parallel to the struggle against Franco's dictatorship and the campaign for full democratic rights. This context has influenced the prominence of a rights- and equality-based feminism within Spanish academe, at times obscuring work carried out in less state-oriented areas of feminism which have nevertheless developed steadily through the decades. The final years of the 1970s saw the establishment of the first seminars and courses in women's studies, developed by feminist academics whose personal commitment created centres in specific universities by the beginning of the following decade.

The 1980s, under socialist rule, were a period of unprecedented political and legal support for equality: the creation in 1982 of the Instituto de la Mujer (Institute for Women's Issues), a government-dependent institution located in Madrid (in the Ministry of Social Affairs), was to play a crucial role in promotion and funding as well as in the triennial Plans for Equal Opportunities. This timely support came as universities entered the era of the LRU, with its emphasis on research and competitive projects. The context thus allowed for a rapid dissemination of women's studies, and the final years of the decade saw the establishment of regional equal-opportunities bodies and the entrance of Spain into the EU, bringing political models for equity and further opportunities for networking. Women's studies thus gained a high degree of (semi)institutionalisation in a very short period, and feminist research and publications acquired an important presence in universities, although specialists could not escape the double shift, moving between their official discipline and the extra (and contested) work in women's studies.

By 1995 there were thirty-one seminars/institutes for women's studies in Spain and two important national networks: the Women's Studies University Association (AUDEM) and the Spanish Association of Historical Research on Women (AEIHM), both created in 1991 and holding annual conferences to this day. In this decade several of the women's studies seminars were also turned into research institutes, an improvement in academic recognition, while the dissemination of feminist knowledge in publications, conferences and seminars became widespread.

Much of this early research was enabled by the inclusion, in 1996, of a specific Programme for Gender and Women's Studies in the National Research and Development (R&D) Plan, which not only promoted research in the field but also helped to normalise the scientific status of women's studies, much devalued by traditional academics and governing bodies. Once again, this was achieved through the pressure of the feminist movement in academe, channelled through the Institute for Women's Issues, which signed an agreement with the National Commission of Technology and Science, responsible for assessing and funding projects. Such steps often received political impetus from the equality bodies in the government, rather than from the universities or higher-education governing bodies themselves, which were entrenched in traditional and male-dominated structures.

Gabriele Griffin (2006) has defined three key characteristics which may account for the difficulties that women's studies encounters in achieving institutional recognition:

> 1) [I]t is a single-sex subject which promotes women in predominantly secular, co-educational cultures that do not practise very overt forms of gender segregation; 2) it is an overtly political discipline with a transformative agenda focused on gender relations, in cultures and institutions dominated at the managerial and decision-making levels by men and by the notion of objective uninvested knowledge; 3) it is an interdisciplinary subject in educational structures that are still, for the most part . . . very rigidly monodisciplinary. (Griffin 2006, 88–89)

Griffin suggests that these characteristics represent a challenge to the institutions into which women's studies has inserted itself, resulting in the precarious position it continues to occupy despite three decades of existence (ibid., 89). This model accurately describes the situation in Spain, aggravated by the extreme rigidity of discipline-based structures in the higher-education system, which strictly govern access to posts, assignment of staff to departments, assessment of merit and of research projects and teaching and organisation of study programmes, among other crucial matters. The stability and promotion of women's studies specialists can sometimes be seriously compromised by these powerful structures, despite the obvious commitment of its practitioners and the relative success story of women's and gender studies in the academic world. In the struggle for recognition, women's studies specialists are therefore torn between dismantling these structures (and enabling transdisciplinarity), bypassing them (strategically handling assessment, accreditation, curricula and so on) or joining them by demanding the creation of a formal discipline (*area de conocimiento*) of women's studies. Such strategic and reflexive dilemmas are not unique to the Spanish context (see particularly Hornscheidt and Baer, chapter 11, this volume).

WOMEN'S STUDIES IN 2010: A WORLD IN MOVEMENT

In the 2001–2003 EWSI study we found that the expectations of women's studies students regarding employment were very low, often nonexistent, and that they generally chose to enrol for personal reasons and to further their education and their specific knowledge. Those who held jobs did report having applied their education in their work, and all students wanted to enter paid employment, but most expected to apply their knowledge after the job had been secured (for instance, having become civil servants or obtained a permanent job for which gender expertise was not required or even acknowledged). Given that many were PhD students, a high number desired to become academics but perceived their training in women's studies as a hindrance because no jobs were available in this field, and their only option was to apply through a particular discipline (usually that of their undergraduate studies), where women's studies training was, at best, underrated (Carrera Suárez and Viñuela Suárez 2004). Despite this pessimistic outlook, the results also showed that their real possibilities of obtaining jobs were above their expectations, a situation supported by the experiences of past students despite their recourse to the discourse of "sheer luck and pure chance" (Silius 2005). Overall, the results demonstrated that:

1) they developed relevant and transferable skills
2) they were risk takers and committed to paid work
3) the networking, mentoring and peer support did aid them in their search for employment, despite strong resistance from employers inside and outside the academy.

In general, the students interviewed critiqued the lack of career orientation while doing women's studies and the lack of recognition of their expertise by employers afterwards, even in the area of equal opportunities. Among our specific recommendations at the end of the project were better career orientation and better channels of communication between university and employers.

The results described above were obtained by interviewing students whose experience of women's studies had taken place in one of three categories: PhD programmes in women's studies, courses included within other studies (often as options) or postgraduate *Títulos propios* in women's studies (specific and professional, but not recognised as official degrees). These were the options available, as MA courses were not yet an official academic category. Less than a decade later, the map has changed considerably, partly because the Spanish Ministry of Education decided to implement the Bologna Process by transforming postgraduate studies, an opening which many feminist academics seized upon and used to establish official MA degrees in gender and women's studies. While other disciplines debated the relationship between their undergraduate and graduate degrees, with a rather paralysing effect, women's studies for once found an advantage in the lack of undergraduate degrees, saw the chance to occupy its space in an employment-oriented market and transformed its PhD programmes and *Títulos propios* into the newly defined *Programas Oficiales de Postgrado* which included official MA degrees and, in some cases, related PhD programmes. Some of the enabling factors for the relative success story[2] were related to the nature of the studies themselves and to their established history: a few of the existing PhD programmes already held the quality-assessed *Mención de Calidad* from the Ministry, all could claim equivalent degrees in other European countries (particularly northern European), many had international networks and exchanges in place, all could demonstrate social and employment orientation and some had already established work placements. Crucially, they did not duplicate undergraduate studies and offered a new career path to students. All of these factors were part of the criteria for approval of new degrees by ANECA and by regional governments. Some of these criteria had also governed the awarding of the prestigious *Mención de Calidad* for PhD programmes, which reinforced the academic status of the women's or gender studies programmes that held them.[3]

The first group of official MAs (*Programas Oficiales de Postgrado*) were assessed and approved in 2005/6 and taught the following year. The first generation of women's studies students with an official MA considered valid at national level had therefore emerged by the end of 2007. Soon other institutions followed in the wake of these pioneering 'Bologna' programmes: Catalan universities (Barcelona, Autónoma de Barcelona, Girona, Rovira i Virgili, Lleida, Politécnica de Cataluña, Vic) jointly offered an MA in women's studies, gender and citizenship; Granada officialised its Erasmus Mundus MA programme in gender and women's studies, as did Universidad Complutense de Madrid (two, one in social sciences, another in health), Universidad del País Vasco, Universidad Internacional Menéndez Pelayo, Deusto and the European University of Madrid. Across all registered degree programmes today, most titles use the term 'gender' rather than 'women' and have some focus on equality, partly showing the influence of state policies, which govern funding and employment prospects. There have been relatively minor changes in the general regulations (Royal Decree RD1393/2007, which among other things more clearly separates MA and PhD programmes) and a more substantial transformation will take place through the pending national regulation of doctorate studies (*RD de Doctorado*) to be passed in 2010, but the adapted Bologna structure insists firmly on the professional side of MA studies. This has resulted in many employment-oriented MAs in women's/gender studies. In 2010, the national register of degrees (RUCT, Ministry of Education) lists twenty-four official MA programmes in gender or women's studies and thirteen PhD programmes in the same specific area (see table 13.2). The gain in recognition at postgraduate level, like the improved visibility for employment, is evident. However, inside the academy, the disciplinary regime is still firmly in place, and no permanent positions can be officially advertised in the field.

Table 13.1   Official Postgraduate Programmes in Women's Studies at Spanish Universities 2007–8

University	Title	Area
Autónoma de Madrid	Interdisciplinary Gender Studies	Social Sciences and Humanities
Cádiz Huelva	Gender, Identity and Citizenship	Social Sciences and Humanities
Granada	Women's and Gender Studies GEMMA	Humanities
Jaume I Miguel Hernández (Elche)	Equality and Gender in Public and Private Environments	Humanities and Social Sciences
Oviedo	Gender and Diversity / Women's and Gender Studies GEMMA	Humanities
Santiago de Compostela	Education, Gender and Equality.	Education
Valencia	Gender Studies	Social Sciences and Law
Vigo	Gender Studies	Humanities and Education
Zaragoza	Gender Relations	Social Sciences and Law

Source: Based on the official list of national postgraduate programmes, approved by the University Coordination Council and published in the Official Bulletin of the State (*Resolución de 17 de mayo de 2007 de la Secretaría General del Consejo de Coordinación Universitaria, por la que se publica la relación de los programas oficiales de posgrado*) (Boletín Oficial del Estado, 14 de junio de 2007, Núm. 142; author's translation [ICS]).

European networks have played an important role in the process of institutionalisation. EU funding for programmes and exchanges such as WISE, ATHENA, ERASMUS, SIGMA or, more recently, ERASMUS MUNDUS, were crucial in providing external referents for women's studies and in reinforcing their claims. Although certain groups of feminists were very oriented towards national and equality issues, others had firm international links, and multidisciplinarity also meant joining feminists in areas such as English studies, where internationalisation had occurred naturally and transnational agreements were long established. The importance of European backing for status was shown in the establishment of the first ERASMUS MUNDUS MA programme in women's/gender studies (GEMMA, approved by the European Commission in 2006) in which two Spanish universities are taking part, Granada as coordinator and Oviedo as a partner. Although both had long-established traditions of women's studies, in the case of Oviedo enhanced by a *Mención de Calidad* in its PhD programme, acknowledgement by the EU conferred unprecedented authority to both programmes in their respective universities.

Table 13.2 PhD Programmes in Gender or Women's Studies at Spanish Universities Adapted to European Higher Education Area (EHEA) 2010

University	Title	Verification	
U. Autónoma de Madrid U. Salamanca	Interdisciplinary Gender Studies	2005	2007
U. Complutense de Madrid	Women and Health	—	2007
U. Cádiz U. Huelva	Gender, Identity and Citizenship	2005	
U. Granada	Women's and Gender Studies	2005	
U. Internacional Menéndez Pelayo (UIMP)	Studies for Gender Equality: Human, Social and Legal Sciences.	2005	2007
U. Jaume I U. Miguel Hernández (Elche)	Equality and Gender in Public and Private Environments	2005	
U. Oviedo	Gender and Diversity	2005	2007
U. País Vasco /EHU	Feminism, Gender and Equality	2005	
U. Rey Juan Carlos	Gender and Health	—	2007
U. Santiago de Compostela	Education, Gender and Equality.	2005	
U. Sevilla	Women and Writing	—	2007
U. Valencia	Gender Studies	2005	
U. Vigo	Gender Studies	2005	

Source: RUCT. Registro de universidades, centros y títulos. MEC. https://www.educacion.es/ruct/home.do (accessed August 20, 2010). The titles are originally in Spanish (author's translation). These are programmes adapted to EHEA and approved by ANECA after the first regulation (RD 56/2005), and/or in the second, stricter 'verification' process (RD1393/2007).

Since 2004, the political context has become more favourable to the development of women's studies and feminist research. The socialist government brought in direct legislation promoting equality, and for the first time, higher education was specifically targeted. The first reference to universities was made in the Act Against Gender Violence, which established that: "Universities will include and promote . . . training, teaching and research in gender equality and non-discrimination" (I.I.4.7) and legislates the lifelong training of staff in equality, aiming at the transfer of knowledge and skills to develop a nonsexist and egalitarian education. This was followed in 2007 by the Equality Act, which devotes a full article to the promotion of women in higher education (II.II.25), stating that public administrations will "promote teaching and research on the meaning and reach of equality between men and women" through three specific actions:

1) inclusion of courses on equality in the curricula
2) the creation of specific postgraduate programmes
3) specialised research and studies in the area.

Other articles in this act deal with teaching women's presence in history (II.II.24), sex segregated statistics (II.I. 20), the use of nonsexist language (II.I.11), and the creation of Equality Units in all Ministries (VIII.77); several deal with equal representation in decision-making bodies.

A few weeks after the Equality Act was passed, specific legislation on equality within higher education was also passed in the form of the LOM-LOU or "Modification Act of the LOU (University Act)" (*Ley Orgánica 4/2007, de 12 de abril, por la que se modifica la Ley Orgánica 6/2001, de 21 de diciembre, de Universidades, LOMLOU*), an amendment of the 2001 LOU. The preamble defines the role of universities and research as conveyors of particular values in the context of "the challenge of contemporary society to achieve a tolerant and egalitarian society in which fundamental rights and freedom, as well as equality between men and women are respected" and is specific about its goals:

> This Act promotes the response of universities to this challenge, not only through the integration of such values as goals . . . but also through the establishment of mechanisms which will allow the achievement of parity in representation bodies and a higher participation of women in research groups. (LOMLOU 4/2007: Preamble)

The most important specific measures, introduced by the act as mandatory for all universities, are:

1) the creation of Equality Units in all universities
2) the production of periodic reports on the application of the principle of gender equality
3) the balanced representation of women and men (60 per cent/40 per cent) on all boards for elections, promotion and peer evaluation.

Such legislation should benefit women's studies through reinforcement of the discipline and creation of job opportunities for specialists, but implementation of this has met with resistance or passivity in many quarters. On reelection in March 2008, equality for women was one of the three main points of action stated by President Rodríguez Zapatero, together with economic growth supported by the knowledge society and sustainable development. A new Ministry of Equality was created and a paritary government (six women) introduced for the first time in Spanish history. The moment seemed propitious for positive developments in women's studies;

the close relationship between government and higher education in Spain might, on this occasion, provide opportunities for recognition and funding. However, the results of that legislation were only beginning to flourish when the economic crisis brought cuts to all public spending and fuelled conservative attacks on the Ministry of Equality and related laws already fiercely contested by conservative sectors.[4]

Many of the measures just described were the result of pressure from and direct dialogues with feminists, NGOs and women working in the fields affected. The work of the Institute for Women's Issues as mediator between government and women's groups and the action taken by associations and NGOs led the way. In the academic world, women's studies specialists demanded the creation of an undergraduate degree and the mainstreaming of gender courses, together with recognition and financial support for existing postgraduate studies and general support for research. Meetings and conferences, such as those organised by AUDEM between 2000 and 2004, resulted in tentative mappings of curricula adapted to the Bologna Process, and the signing of a manifesto in 2004 by more than 1,000 university lecturers demanding a nationally recognised undergraduate degree in women's studies, although the degree has not yet been established. Major conferences brought together important actors in women's studies to discuss the possibilities of graduate and postgraduate degrees adapted to the European Higher Education Area (Pedregal 2007), and the demands of coordinators of postgraduate programmes in women's studies brought about much-needed financial support for administration contracts and student grants, offered by the Institute for Women's Issues since 2007.[5]

WOMEN'S STUDIES AND ACADEMIC PROFESSIONALISATION

In general terms, women in Spanish academe suffer from the presence of a glass ceiling more than the European average (European Commission 2008). Data segregated by sex show a quantitative and qualitative deficit of women in the academy, which grows in the higher categories, producing the usual 'scissors diagram' for the statistics: women enter HE in higher numbers and there are more women graduates; but when it comes to employment in academia the trend is inverted, and the deficit grows with status (see table 13.3).

The tendency to attribute this difference to a history of late access of women into universities, a process that will amend itself with time, is proved wrong by comparing relevant statistics in the 1960s and today (Unidad de Mujeres y Ciencia 2007). A study on women and science in Spain, commissioned by the Fundación Española para la Ciencia y la Tecnología (Spanish Foundation for Science and Technology; FECYT 2005, 17) and coordinated by Eulalia Pérez Sedeño and M. J. Santemases, reached three (somewhat unsurprising) conclusions:

Table 13.3   Percentage of Men and Women at Spanish (State) Universities

2005-2006	Students	Graduates	Junior lecturers	Senior lecturers	Professors
Women	54,5	60,3	37,9	36,2	13,9
Men	45,4	39,6	62	63,7	86

Source: Unidad de Mujeres y Ciencia (UMYC). 2007 Académicas en cifras 2007. Madrid: Ministerio de Educación y Ciencia.

1) There are no differences between the scientific production by men and women from the same professional level, thus any hierarchical discrimination is unjustified in a system which considers itself meritocratic.

2) Nevertheless, there are important differences between the number of men and women accessing positions with the highest salaries and professional value, which suggests that the decisions do not have a meritocratic base, but a sexist one.

3) The slow growth in the number of women in the professional categories of teaching and research does not match the speed and achievement of women graduates and doctors.

The study also concludes that peer review is open to (gender-)biased judgements. Seeking to mitigate this imbalance, one of fifty-four measures to promote equality approved by the Cabinet (March 4, 2005) was the creation of the Women and Science Unit (UMYC) which aimed to work with decision-making bodies to remove obstacles and increase the presence of women in research (Vicepresidencia Primera del Gobierno y Ministerio de la Presidencia 2005).

Women who aspire to enter the academic profession through women's studies in Spain still face discrimination, particularly since there are no positions specifically for the field, and they must enter through another discipline. Although there are institutes of women's studies within universities, and these can offer PhD programmes, there are no departments (the decisive staff units in the system) and no posts exist with such a denomination because women's studies is not a nationally registered discipline. Women's studies academics who hold university positions have secured them through other areas, usually in the humanities and social sciences, mainly history, philology (languages and literatures), sociology, philosophy and education, although women's studies experts are found in almost any field. Despite this evident obstacle, women's studies PhD students do access the academic world, and the official support (scholarships and funding for research projects among them), together with tutoring, peer support, mentoring and growing networks facilitate their integration, particularly as some of the older experts begin to occupy positions of responsibility and decision making, especially around quality assessment and hiring committees.

NONACADEMIC PROFESSIONALISATION

The new postgraduate structure, particularly the professional MA programmes, combined with the recent equality legislation described earlier, is producing a more extended labour market for women's studies experts. The MA programmes have a clear employment-oriented line and include work placements in public administration, NGOs or the private sector. This is a crucial change from the situation explored in 2003 in the EWSI project, when students pointed out the need precisely for such placements and for career orientation. Students in the first generations of the MA in Oviedo, for instance, now report finding jobs for which their expertise was awarded specific value.

The intake of students into women's studies programmes has also changed due to an important academic factor related to the Bologna Process: easier access for students from shorter degrees (*Diplomaturas*) who were previously excluded from PhD programmes. This has attracted students from labour-oriented studies, particularly in fields such as social work or nursing, whose career expectations are different from former PhD students. Thus, official women's studies programmes in Spain are joining the group of degrees directly relevant to employment and career prospects.

The Bologna Process has thus effected a change from the prevalent Humboldtian concept of learning towards a more applied, employment-oriented concept which was relatively alien to the previous Spanish system. Although women's studies should be careful not to lose its theoretical grounding, which is very highly valued by students (Griffin 2002, 2004; Carrera Suárez and Viñuela Suárez 2004) and essential for feminism, the results for employment are expected to be positive in the long run. The interaction between theory and practice, which students interviewed for the EWSI project vindicated, and which is the very basis of women's studies, seems to happen more readily in the new context. So far, much of the employment made available by these changes tends to be casual, as it often depends on short-term funding for specific projects, NGOs or even equal-opportunity actions. This is not ideal, and in a country like Spain, where becoming a civil servant is favoured as a secure option, the social and family pressure to seek a permanent job is very strong. However, of the five sectors of employment for women's studies students identified by Harriet Silius (2005, 118)—research and education, equal opportunities, civil society, journalism and information, and the social and health sector—those which offer stability do not require, or even reward, gender expertise for access, although most of them do supply women's studies courses with mature students who intend to apply the acquired education to their jobs. Some of these students also find in women's studies programmes an opportunity to further their careers, as the new official structure favours this option through more flexible access.

CONCLUSION AND PROSPECTS

Spain has experienced two periods of very rapid change, the first serving to establish research and the foundations of women's studies programmes in universities (1980s, following democratisation and the political activist period) and a second in the last decade (particularly between 2004 and 2010), in which the combined effect of the Bologna Process and progressive government measures favoured the professionalisation of women's studies inside and outside the academic context. However, the obstacles of discipline-based structures and resistance to the field remain powerful in the academic world, and recognition of the professional skills of women's studies training by employers outside universities also leaves room for improvement.

Most of the indicators of disciplinisation and institutionalisation discussed by Silius in chapter 12 of this volume could now be assessed quite favourably in Spain were it not for the extreme rigidity of the discipline system, which prevents professorships or Departments from being designated Women's Studies, since no such discipline exists in the national register. However, there are research institutes with improved recognition after recent university laws, there is a growing number of professors and lecturers who are specialists, and the high number of nationally recognised postgraduate degrees is a hopeful sign. Annual conferences in the field, specialist journals and PhD training have multiplied and provide strong networks for mutual support, while funding has increased specifically for gender MA programmes and R&D projects. Career prospects have also clearly improved in the field of equal opportunities, with a new need for specialists created by recent legislation. Furthermore, it remains mostly true, as the 2003 EWSI project confirmed, that women's studies programmes provide a supportive environment for publishing, research, teamwork and international collaboration, all of which help to open academic doors. Whereas in 2003 (EWSI project) we insisted on the lack of means to enforce equality, the recent Equality Law (and the subsequent regional laws) could now provide the necessary instruments for change. Some of this change seems already to be taking place, and working in favour of the professionalisation of women's studies. Students begin to report on their expertise being valued for jobs in administration, NGOs, political counselling, social work; some have even taken the initiative to establish private gender-consultancy firms. It is a world in transition, which would look more hopeful had the world crisis not hit so suddenly, threatening regression to conservatism and disregard for social issues.

NOTES

1. I would like to acknowledge the work of Laura Viñuela Suárez in the two EU projects from which this chapter draws, and also Espora Consultoría de Género—directed by Laura and by Gloria Rodríguez Hevia, former students

from the women's studies PhD programme in Oviedo—for the data provided for the 2008 update.

2. Nine specific programmes were approved in the first year by ANECA, and nineteen universities offered studies with gender or women's studies content within more general programmes. Many of them turned into independent MA programmes in subsequent years.

3. The history of the naming of 'women's studies' (*Estudios de la mujer/de las mujeres*), 'feminist studies' and 'gender studies' in the Spanish context is discussed by Birriel (2002, 218) and Casado Aparicio (2002, 233). This history reflects both changes in feminist thought and complex negotiations with local and national authorities, but neither standpoint nor curricular content differ substantially. I use these different terms in the text to reflect the variety of names encountered.

4. In the period between writing and publication, the Ministry of Equality was suppressed, thus confirming fears of conservative pressure: Cabinet changes produced in October 2010 demoted the equality body and moved it to the Ministry of Health, Social Affairs and Equality.

5. The list of programmes funded by the Instituto de la Mujer in 2009 (BOE 11–01–2010, http://www.boe.es/boe/dias/2010/01/11/index.php) may also offer a map which includes unofficial degrees and courses, often quite professionally specific.

REFERENCES

Act Against Gender Violence. 2004. (Ley Orgánica 1/2004, de 28 de diciembre, de medidas de protección integral contra la violencia de género. BOE n° 313 29/12/2004) http://www.boe.es/aeboe/consultas/bases_datos/doc.php?id=BOE-A-2004–21760 (accessed August 12, 2010).

Birriel Salcedo, M. 2002. SIGMA Women's Studies Report: Spain, 1995. In *The Making of European Women's Studies*. Vol. 4, ed. R. Braidotti, J. Nieboer and S. Hirs, 210–29. Utrecht: ATHENA.

Boletín Oficial del Estado. 14 de junio de 2007, Núm. 142. http://www.boe.es/boe/dias/2007/06/14/index.php (accessed August 20, 2010).

Carrera Suárez, I. and L. Viñuela Suárez. 2002. Spain. In *Women's Employment, Women's Studies, and Equal Opportunities 1945–2001: Reports from Nine European Countries*, ed. G. Griffin, 427–69. Hull: University of Hull Press.

———. 2004. The Impact of Women's Studies Training on Its Students in Spain. In *Employment, Equal Opportunities and Women's Studies: Women's Experiences in Seven European Countries*, ed. G. Griffin, 187–211. Frankfurt am Main: Ulrike Helmer Verlag.

Carrera Suárez, I., L. Viñuela Suárez and C. Rodríguez González. 2005. Disciplinary Barriers between the Social Sciences and Humanities: Spain. *Research Integration*. http://www.york.ac.uk/res/researchintegration/National_reports.htm (accessed April 16 2008).

Casado Aparicio, E. 2002. Women's Studies in Spain: An Update. In *The Making of European Women's Studies*. Vol. 4, ed. R. Braidotti, J. Nieboer and S. Hirs, 230–42. Utrecht: ATHENA.

Equality Act. 2007. (Ley Orgánica 3/2007, de 22 de marzo, para la igualdad efectiva de mujeres y hombres. BOE no. 71 de 23/3/2007, p. 12611–12645). http://www.boe.es/aeboe/consultas/bases_datos/doc.php?id=BOE-A-2007–6115. (accessed August 12, 2010).

European Commission. 2008. Mapping the Maze: Getting More Women to the Top in Research. http://ec.europa.eu/research/science-society/index. cfm?fuseaction=public.topic&id=1541 (accessed April 16, 2008).

FECYT (Fundación Española para la Ciencia y la Tecnología). 2005. *Mujer y Ciencia: La situación de las mujeres investigadoras en el sistema español de ciencia y tecnología.* (Spanish Foundation for Science and Technology. Women researchers' situation in the Spanish System of Science and Technology). http://www.ifs.csic.es/mujeres/documentos.htm (accessed April 16, 2008).

Griffin, G., ed. 2002. *Women's Employment, Women's Studies, and Equal Opportunities 1945–2001: Reports from Nine European Countries.* Hull: University of Hull Press.

———, ed. 2004. *Employment, Equal Opportunities and Women's Studies: Women's Experiences in Seven European Countries.* Frankfurt am Main: Ulrike Helmer Verlag.

———, ed. 2005. *Doing Women's Studies: Employment Opportunities, Personal Impacts and Social Consequences.* London: Zed Books.

———. 2006. Women's Studies, Professionalization and the Bologna Process: Cross-European Reflections. *NORA—Nordic Journal of Women's Studies* 2 (14): 87–102.

Instituto de la Mujer. *Mujeres en cifras.* http://www.inmujer.migualdad.es/mujer/ (accessed August 20, 2010).

Instituto de la Mujer. Programmes funded in 2009 (BOE 11–01–2010). http://www.boe.es/boe/dias/2010/01/11/index.php (accessed August 20, 2010).

LOMLOU. 2007. (Ley Orgánica 4/2007, de 12 de abril, por la que se modifica la Ley Orgánica 6/2001, de 21 de diciembre, de Universidades. BOE 13/04/2007). http://www.boe.es/boe/dias/2007/04/13/ (accessed August 20, 2010).

LOU. 2001. (Ley Orgánica 6/2001, de 21 de diciembre, de Universidades. BOE 24/12/2001). http://www.boe.es/boe/dias/2001/12/24/index.php (accessed August 12, 2010).

Pedregal, A. 2007a. Propuesta de declaración por la plena integración de los Estudios de las Mujeres, feministas y de género en el Espacio Europeo de Educación Superior. ("Proposal of declaration for the full integration of women's, feminist and gender studies in the Spanish EHEA") In *Los feminismos como herramienta de cambio social, II: De la violencia contra las mujeres a la construcción del pensamiento feminist,* ed. V. Ferrer and E. Bosch. 371–78. Palma de Mallorca: SP UIB.

——— 2007b. "La Historia de las Mujeres en la Antigüedad: Realidades y expectativas ante el Espacio Europeo de Educación Superior" ("Women's History in Antiquity: Realities and Expectations for the EHEA").

RUCT. (Registro de universidades, centros y títulos / Register of universities, centres and degrees) MEC. https://www.educacion.es/ruct/home.do (accessed August 20, 2010).

Silius, H. 2005. The Professionalization of Women's Studies Students in Europe: Expectations and Experiences. In *Doing Women's Studies: Employment Opportunities, Personal Impacts and Social Consequences,* ed. G. Griffin, 111–40. London: Zed Books.

Unidad de Mujeres y Ciencia (UMYC). 2007. (Women and Science Unit. Academics in numbers 2007). *Académicas en cifras 2007.* Madrid: Ministerio de Educación y Ciencia.

Vicepresidencia Primera del Gobierno y Ministerio de la Presidencia. 2005. *Informe de implementación de las 54 medidas para favorecer la igualdad entre mujeres y hombres aprobadas por el Consejo de Ministros el 4 de Marzo de 2005 (Orden de PRE 525/2005, de 7 de Marzo) B.O.E. no. 57 del 08/03/2005.* http://www.boe.es/boe/dias/2005/03/08/index.php (accessed August 20, 2010).

14 The Professionalisation of Feminist Researchers
The German Case

Marianne Schmidbaur and Ulla Wischermann[1]

Until now German women's and gender studies has successfully held its ground in the midst of ongoing restructuring and reorientation at German universities. Potentials and pitfalls of the current university formation can be characterised as follows:

1) reorganisation of the courses of studies in the context of the Bologna Process
2) focus on excellent research and international competitiveness
3) professionalisation and promotion of equal opportunity politics, powerfully strengthened by EU equal opportunities legislation
4) a steadily growing split between equal-opportunities politics and women's and gender studies.

In our chapter we give an overview of the situation in Germany on the basis of topical data and the findings of the study Employment and Women's Studies. The Impact of Women's Studies Training on Women's Employment in Europe (EWSI; see also chapters 12 and 13, this volume). Above all, we would like to offer an introduction to studying and teaching women's/gender studies in Germany.

UNIVERSITY STRUCTURES AND RESEARCH FUNDING IN GERMANY

Higher education in Germany can still be described as a dual system—even though this system is changing in the context of internationalisation. On the one hand, teaching, research and training the next generation of professors takes place under the aegis of universities and equivalent institutions. On the other hand, vocationally oriented academies exist, the universities of applied sciences (*Fachhochschulen*). Professors at universities are engaged in research and carry out research projects sponsored not directly by their departments but by the state, ministries or foundations, so-called *Drittmittel,* or third-party funding. The most important institutions promoting research in Germany are the German Research Association (Deutsche Forschungsgemeinschaft), the German Academic Exchange Service (DAAD) and German ministries on federal and on state level, followed by numerous foundations (e.g., Volkswagenstiftung, Hans-Boeckler-Stiftung, German National Academic Foundation [Studienstiftung des deutschen Volkes], Friedrich-Ebert-Stiftung, Konrad-Adenauer-Stiftung, Friedrich-Nauman-Stiftung) and industry.

Given that women can be found in only a fraction of postdoctoral and professorial positions, increasing their numbers among PhD candidates and professors is an important dimension of calls for affirmative action. The Programme to Support Equal Opportunity for Women in Research and Education (2001–2006) supported women's efforts to improve their qualifications, promoted development of women's/gender studies and supported women's participation in the natural sciences and engineering. As a result, nearly all universities witnessed the founding of centres for women's/gender studies, including mentoring programmes for women in science and technology. In 2007, the states (*Laender*) and the federal government agreed a programme which, over a five-year period, will create two hundred new professorships earmarked for women at German universities. Universities, universities of applied sciences and institutions of higher education in music, theatre and art can apply for funding based on a report on their affirmative action plans. The programme started in March 2008.

There are, however, strong disparities in status across various academic levels. Although the number of women among full professors has consistently risen and now is nearly at 50 per cent, the proportion of female faculty has not yet reached 20 per cent (figure 14.1).

Academic careers in German universities usually start after graduation with the doctorate (see figure 14.2). Traditionally, the doctorate includes an independent research project as well as final examinations. Since 1998, more structured forms of doctoral programmes (*Graduiertenkollegs*, graduate schools) have increasingly appeared in which additional training—for instance, on disciplinary methodology or key competencies—is part of the doctoral programme. Before the recent university reforms, career tracks in German universities were highly standardised, encompassing a sequence of three qualifications and hence formal degrees: university graduation and a master's degree or diploma; the doctorate; and finally the 'habilitation,' the second exam after the doctorate which is required for a tenured position or professorship. In 2000 the so-called junior professorship was introduced. The position of a nontenured 'junior professor,' modelled after the American 'assistant professor,' entitles a young academic to become a legitimate member of the faculty without having passed the habilitation exam (Sekretariat der ständigen Konferenz der Kultusminister der Länder in der Bundesrepublik Deutschland 2007; Zimmer, Krimmer and Stallmann 2007).

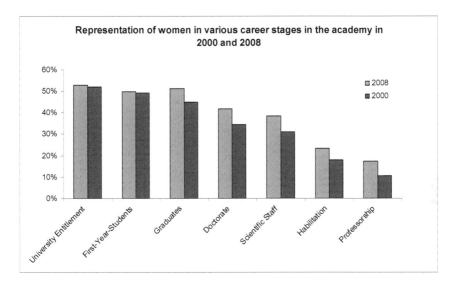

Figure 14.1 Representation of women in various career stages in the German academy in 2008. *Source:* Statistisches Bundesamt (2009, 25).

WOMEN'S/GENDER STUDIES

Women's/gender studies in West Germany arose in the context of the new women's movement in the 1970s. The field has always been politically oriented and emancipatory, aiming to contribute to women's liberation by means of analysing inequalities and differences. In East Germany, women's/gender studies developed in the 1980s and gained foothold in many universities after 1989. A significant milestone was the establishment of the Center for Interdisciplinary Feminist Research at the Humboldt University in Berlin, which today is called Center for Transdisciplinary Gender Studies (Hornscheidt and Baer, chapter 11, this volume).

Women's Studies, Gender Studies, Feminist Studies

In the beginning, the key issues for women's studies in Germany were experience and autonomy. Women's studies emphasised the importance of sisterhood, linking the personal and the political. It censured the false separation between private and public spheres and focused on diversity with regard to 'race,' ethnicity, class, age and so forth while analysing and criticising the oppression of women as a group. Women's studies also looked at women's historical and contemporary experience as well as the meaning of a feminist consciousness. In the thirty years since the field was founded, numerous feminist discourses have been developed and superseded: for example,

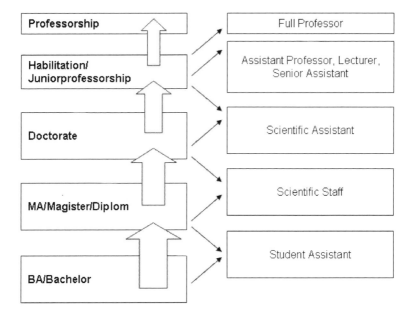

Figure 14.2   Career paths at German universities.
Source: Adapted from Majcher (2001). Women in German Higher Education. http://csn.
uni-muenster.de/women-eu/download/MajcherTP01_05.pdf (accessed July 14 2010.)

debates about feminism of equality or difference, or about the structural categories of woman/gender or the distinction between gender and sex. In Germany, as elsewhere, the focus of women's studies has shifted to the category of gender and an analysis of gender relationships.

Identifying a "symbolic system of heteronormativity" (*System der Zweigeschlechtlichkeit*; Hagemann-White 1984), the 1980s explored the subjective component in human behaviour called 'doing gender': "Gender isn't something we 'have' or 'are' but something we do" (Hagemann-White 1993, 68). The conditions and social basis for contradictions in women's lives were brought together in the concept of 'twofold socialisation' (*doppelte Vergesellschaftung*; Becker-Schmidt 1987). This theory of gender as a social category looks at the patriarchal and economic structure of domination, focusing in particular on the division of labour in the work-force and the family. Then, in the early 1990s, the gender debate set out on quite a different track. This was started by Judith Butler's *Gender Trouble* (1990), which provoked heated controversy. Should the category of gender be dissolved? The suggestion that we cannot really distinguish between sex and gender, and the idea that the material body can be declared a fiction configured as meaningful and called into existence by discourse itself, encountered significant opposition but also proved to be extraordinarily productive, causing a paradigm shift in research and teaching in women's/ gender studies which has left many traces (Wischermann 2002).

In the last few years, in Germany as elsewhere, scholars have broadened horizons to include additional social categories. Approaches such as intersectionality include other 'axes of difference': ethnicity, class, age, sexual orientation and so forth (Knapp and Wetterer 2003; Knapp 2005; Lutz 2010; see also Staunæs and Søndergaard, chapter 3, this volume). Moreover, in the light of worldwide transformations in the labour market and migration, questions of social justice and inequality are increasingly coming to the fore (Klinger et al. 2007).

Feminist studies (Lykke, chapter 9, this volume) as a political project always existed within women's/gender studies as well as a separate approach focused on the political impact. Today there is a strong plea for re-visioning research in terms of critical social theory and feminist approaches. On the other hand, gaining ground in the academy also resulted in demands for the depolitisation of women's/gender studies. One example of this depolitisation is the so-called research in gender differentiation (*Geschlechterdifferenzierungsforschung*).

In Germany, gender topics are embedded in traditional disciplines, but trans- and interdisciplinary approaches are important (Hornscheidt and Baer, chapter 11, this volume; Liinason, chapter 10, this volume; Lykke, chapter 9, this volume), as are trans- and international perspectives. Especially fruitful in all disciplines, including women's/gender studies, are those doctoral programmes and research projects that cross rigid disciplinary boundaries. The increasingly strong institutionalisation of women's studies in German universities has brought with it a canon of knowledge evident in an increasingly strong publication record. A report on women's/gender studies textbooks from 2002 noted that the anchoring of the field in specific disciplines had probably resulted in the absence of any general readers in feminist theory (Brouns et al. 2000). Today this is no longer the case. In fact, all significant publishing houses offer a spectrum of readers and handbooks in the field (Bock 2005; Gerhard et al. 2008; Lenz 2008).

The Institutionalisation of Women's/Gender Studies

Together with the development of women's/gender studies there has been a continuing effort to anchor its results, theories and methodologies in university research and teaching.

Research on women and women's studies experienced a spontaneous birth in the universities towards the end of the 1970s. In Germany shortly thereafter the first attempts were made to institutionalise these initiatives: one important step towards recognition was the founding of regional working groups for feminist academics at various universities and the setting-up of committees to coordinate course offerings within the disciplines. The creation of women's studies professorships and the launch of interdisciplinary centres gradually led to an institutionalisation of women's/gender studies within German universities. This more than thirty-year history has been characterised by its initial culture of opposition which soon became interventionist (Kirsch-Auwärter 1996; Müller 1997) and as a move from women's studies to gender studies (Braun 1995). There are four phases in this development:

1) the initial phase, intimately connected to the women's movement and tending to remain more or less outside the institution
2) the phase of invasion into and anchoring within the university, marked by discussions about autonomy versus institutionalisation
3) the professionalisation phase in which women's/gender studies have been increasingly coordinated and stabilised by means of the first generation of active women's studies professorships (Hagemann-White 1995, 23–41)
4) the so-called institutionalisation phase (Bock 1998, 106), in which women's studies majors and certificate programmes were set up beginning in about the mid-1990s (Mazari et al. 2002, 407ff).

The advantage of this institutionalisation lies in making women's/gender studies visible. In the best of cases, supportive networks within the university have been built and, at the same time, they have positive political effects outside the academy. Nonetheless—and this is frequently discussed in Germany—separation into departments as a quasi discipline risks marginalising and ghettoising the field since traditional disciplines can then feel 'relieved' of their responsibility to integrate women's/gender studies.

Today the institutionalisation of women's/gender studies in Germany is based on three pillars. First, there are approximately twenty-three interdisciplinary research groups or research centres like the Cornelia Goethe Centre for Women's and Gender Studies at the Goethe-University Frankfurt am Main or the Center for Transdisciplinary Gender Studies at the Humboldt University, Berlin. Second, about 101 chairs dedicated to women's/gender studies exist. Third, there are networks of feminist scientists such as the Women's Research Network North-Rhine Westphalia. Centres, professorships and networks are the driving forces behind mainstreaming women's/gender studies in established disciplines and majors. In addition, increasingly free-standing courses at BA and MA level, certificate programmes and structured PhD programmes have been launched.

CAREER PATHS AND PROFESSIONAL INTERESTS OF WOMEN'S/GENDER STUDIES GRADUATES

To date the largest examination of professional development and careers entered by women's/gender studies graduates (male and female) in Germany took place in 2001 and 2002 within the framework of the EWSI research project (Griffin 2002, 2004, 2005). At that time, sixty-nine current students and fifty-six graduates from five universities and one joint venture programme were asked about their experiences. From this we gained initial data about the first jobs of graduates who studied women's/gender studies in Germany.

Fields of Employment

Most of the graduates in the EWSI study either continued working at universities as researchers and as teachers; went into education more generally; worked with women's projects or organisations including as volunteers; or entered public and private sector jobs dealing with affirmative action, political consulting or social work. Some became journalists or health professionals (Gerhard et al. 2004; Schmidbaur 2004a, 2005). In addition, a broader spectrum of individual careers was named. These included a variety of people-oriented fields, social services, social work and care-giving professions. A good number entered communication fields as public relations specialists, journalists or publishers. Work in libraries and archives was also mentioned. A few became architects or urban planners. Finally, translators and attorneys were also represented.

The EWSI study revealed that women's/gender studies graduates identify to a large extent with the content and aims of their courses, and this finding was independent of whether or not the individuals majored in women's/gender studies or had integrated women's/gender studies courses into other fields such as social sciences, cultural studies or humanities. Their studies had equipped them with a profound knowledge of feminist approaches within their individual disciplines, including an awareness of the social, cultural and historical dimensions of gender hierarchy. They were also able to develop further as a result of exposure to theories and methodologies in women's/gender studies, achieving key academic and professional qualifications such as thinking in terms of inter- and transdisciplinarity, problem solving and communication skills. Their 'scientifically informed employability' (*wissenschaftlich basierte Beschäftigungsfähigkeit*), as the German Science and Humanities Council calls skills like this (Wissenschaftsrat 2000, 21), opened a broad spectrum of professions and jobs for women's/gender studies graduates. In summary, hiring opportunities are good, and in fact, significantly better than the students had expected when they started higher education. This is true especially for the German EWSI sample but for most of the partner countries involved, too (figure 14.3).

Above all, training in women's/gender studies affected job opportunities in two ways. First, it influenced choice of profession. Graduates were most keen to enter the following fields: academia (including research); education; the administration of women's projects or NGOs; and journalism, public relations or the civil service in affirmative action positions. In addition, a background in women's/gender studies helped determine the agenda in all professions.

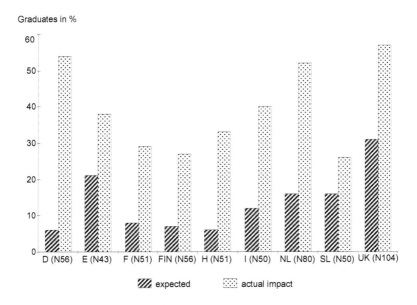

Figure 14.3   Women's studies graduates' expected and actual impact on employment opportunities.
Source: EWSI. Abbreviations: D=Germany, E=Spain, F=France, FIN=Finland, H=Hungary, I=Italy, NL=Netherlands, SL=Slovenia, UK=United Kingdom, N=number of interviews.

In general, graduates in women's/gender studies could be found in all lines of endeavour in which other social scientist and humanities graduates work. Like sociologists, they are distributed across a variety of careers and their CVs reveal unique individual trajectories (Zacharias 2003). Prognoses for career development are also similar to those for graduates in sociology and the humanities. Social scientists as well as women's/gender studies graduates share a fate (or a chance) of entering new fields of employment (Berendt et al. 2002, 190). They have to create their jobs, as one EWSI interviewee put it.

Beyond teaching and research, female social scientists in Germany, like women's/gender studies graduates, tend to find employment in social work, administration or media and in charitable organisations to a greater degree than their male counterparts, and they work more often in the public sector than the private one (Einarsdóttir 2002; Teichler 2002). Yet professions with a distinct gender component are gaining prominence. Analyses of career paths and information for students in the social sciences have already begun to name 'women,' 'affirmative action' or 'women's issues' as specific professional choices (Von Alemann 1995; Gernand and Zinn

2000). The growing interest of male students in the field also suggests the extent to which it has gained in importance in the world of work.

The EWSI study showed that graduates in women's/gender studies exhibited a special interest in remaining in academia as researchers and teachers. Yet such university positions offer ambivalent compensations; job satisfaction and identification with the subject matter are offset by precarious working conditions and career advancement.

As in other countries, the doctorate is a precondition for entry into academia. During the three to five years it takes to complete a degree, the PhD candidate can occupy an assistantship whose duties include academic committee work, research and teaching. It is also possible with the help of a grant to concentrate fully on doctoral research. Grants are provided by universities, numerous foundations or graduate schools supported by the German Research Foundation (*Deutsche Forschungsgemeinschaft*). Since 1992 eleven doctoral programmes in women's/gender studies including study programmes as well as grants have been set up.

PROFESSIONALISATION: WORK IN PROGRESS

Postmaterialistic Values

For students and graduates in women's/gender studies, personal and political interests are in the foreground. Career plans tend to be vague (see Gerhard, Schmidbaur and Wischermann 2004; Silius and Tuori 2004). This holds true for the social sciences and humanities equally (Agreiter and Schindler 2002; Jahr et al. 2002). For both male and female women's/gender studies graduates, career concepts emphasise social values and the nature of the work rather than extrinsic material aims and motives (a secure position, income, promotion).

Respondents in the EWSI study generally stressed a subjective approach to professional employment. Their descriptions of work were positive and enthusiastic. They want to be employed, preferably in areas where they can apply what they have learned as students. As one graduate put it:

> [I]t's not like, okay, I've written a dissertation so I know I can do it and can stop now. No. Instead I have this extreme, massive desire to find satisfying, fulfilling work. And that's really very important, more important than my private life. I want to enter a good profession that I'll enjoy. Frankly, that's the most important thing. (DP17)[2]

Those graduates who hold managerial positions in various fields have embarked on their careers at a later age. Only one named 'money' and 'power' as important. Engagement, the feeling of doing something worthwhile for women, recognition and self-approval were their central aims.

Gender Knowledge, Gender Competence

When asked to evaluate their gender expertise, students and graduates in the EWSI survey named a range of themes requiring specific knowledge and comprehensive theoretical awareness. They listed various topics of concern to them in their different majors and job categories. Generally speaking, the knowledge they mentioned resulted from a combination of various disciplines and was often tailored to a precise, highly qualified specification. When asked in what areas she considered herself an expert one lecturer in union-related education gave a highly enthusiastic answer:

> [O]n the labour market and whatever touches on neoliberalism and globalisation, areas concerned with double contradictions in state socialism, theory concerning human capital, approaches derived from so-called classical women's studies, for instance what women's history has contributed to our thinking that has been complemented by a broadened gender approach generally applicable in the sociology of labour. That's where I'm fit. (DP16)

In the opinion of our respondents, women's/gender studies as a whole increased the options open to them. Our graduates experienced women's/gender studies as 'empowerment.' Their courses helped them to 'become conscious of their interests' and to concentrate on certain careers. In answer to the question whether her education had opened doors and increased opportunities, one graduate employed in a women's project said, "In the quest for my own interests, my studies were generally empowering" (DP11). One graduate who had already had professional training and is today an educator in union-sponsored programmes explained, "My courses certainly reinforced my self-confidence" (DP6).

When asked what meaningful skills and knowledge they had acquired as students and whether they considered themselves experts in women's/gender studies, our respondents mentioned a variety of abilities, skills and knowledge. Transferable skills were described with phrases such as "a specific way of dealing with things," an "other perspective," the ability to "recognise structures" and to "analyse contextual relationships." An historian, for instance, when asked about the kind of expert knowledge she derived from her studies explained: "Regarding history I would say it's a certain approach or a specific way of looking at society and seeing clearly that gender always plays a role in historical situations" (DP19). The social scientists emphasised growing awareness of structures. One graduate presently working in adult education observed:

> Yes, I would characterise it as expertise because it seems to me, as a female academic concerned with gender issues, you gain insight into social structure that then allows you to approach and analyse problems in a

more detailed, differentiated way. So from that perspective it's a matter of expert knowledge or expert women's knowledge that you learned. (DP9)

Our respondents emphasised that they improved their "communication skills" and were better able to work in teams. One graduate employed today in municipal politics describes these skills as the most important result of her studies applied to her professional life:

> Yes, simply to observe, also to analyse, how things work and then to reflect on the consequences to be drawn from it. Where can you expect change to start? And what will result from those changes, how will they affect the group, its goal and individual goals? So I would say that this skill in particular, to step back, to observe and to analyse, helps a great deal. (DP1)

The gender competencies sketched above can be called 'key qualifications,' defined as long-term competencies in a fast-changing professional landscape. Such competencies include social skills (attitude, orientation, talents and communication skills), methods and practical skills (languages, ability to work with media and continuing professional education) and citizenship competencies (for instance, a sense of justice in terms of sensitivity to right and wrong; Schmidbaur 2004b).

Key qualifications in women's/gender studies emerge from a basic knowledge of social structures differentiated by gender; knowledge of gender relations as hierarchical and constructed; and exposure to gender epistemologies, the study of processes governing behaviour among individuals, group dynamics, conflict resolution in labour relations and so forth as well as detailed knowledge of various specific contexts. As the EWSI project shows, gender competence can be mutually influential vis-a-vis experience and interests, thereby becoming key to biographical development, personal talents and social engagement. Applying knowledge and competencies to analysis of, and efforts to transform, hierarchical gender relations empowers students in women's/gender studies. Scholars are challenged to surpass their own individual aims, develop self-confidence and agency. Gender competence becomes key at the level of personal and social abilities, the level of method and practical applications and, above all, at the level of citizenship (Schmidbaur 2004b).

Career Planning

Among the students interviewed there was only one following a clear career plan, initially not in the area of gender issues. Only after attending a particular lecture did she begin to consider women's/gender studies. Until that point the steps to reach her professional aim had been clearly laid out: career-relevant courses in her major leading to her degree, followed by perfecting her foreign language skills and searching for an internship in her career field. She was the only student we questioned who, as an addendum to the official interview, called for stronger ties between the academy and vocational training. All other students conveyed more of a vague, indecisive impression. They wanted 'somehow' to remain in a field where gender issues would be relevant but it was unclear precisely where this desire would lead them.

Graduates described their career plans in a similar fashion. They had "no set aim" (DP1). It was "coincidence" that they had landed in their present jobs (DP7). "Career development was unclear"; it had never been "planned exactly to go into academia," one graduate who now works at a university explained (DP12). No special orientation had guided her studies, and she had therefore not been expecting anything in particular, declared another who worked in an similar academic setting (DP13). In a typical manner one graduate employed in a comparatively secure position in her dream field described it this way:

> I'm not a planner, absolutely not. I just let life wash over me (laughs). I've never planned. Well, of course I planned to graduate and then I did it. And then before I charged into my final essays I thought I'd really enjoy doing a doctorate. So I finished and only then did I know my next goal, to write a dissertation. How I was going to pay for it, whether I was going to work or apply for a fellowship, I hadn't thought about that at all. Well, and when the job offer came to work on a research project, I grabbed it, logically. And when it ended after three years I realised I wanted to finish writing the dissertation. What comes next . . . I mean, it's always difficult, and it wasn't easy for me either to live with so much indecision. (DP19)

This description shows what appears as "lack of planning" and "coincidence." Many of our interviewees created the impression of having simply drifted, not knowing where they were going. However, they also jumped at opportunities to work in those areas that interested them, and often they were themselves surprised to be in the right place at the right time, as the following example aptly demonstrates. When asked what she did after completing her studies one graduate said:

> [T]his legal aid job in an attorney's office, this secretarial thing, it was simply a stop-gap for me. I just wanted to find any kind of job that allowed me to use my education. And it just so happened that this position was free and I applied. And it worked. And I'm thinking, in any case, this is an area where I can apply what I learned at university. Because for us, a major emphasis is on gender specific seminars, gender equality teaching, that is, we sharpen our vision and want to make other people sensitive, too. (DP6)

When asked if she had planned to follow this career path, she responded, "Well, it wasn't actually mapped out, but it was something I wanted, a dream I had, to someday earn my living doing what I had been busy with in addition to my studies, union-related education. Yes, that had been a dream of mine. And then it just happened more like a coincidence that a job opened up." Only when reminded that she had in fact taken steps that could lead to this conclusion did she admit, "Yes, okay. So it didn't just fall into my lap. I had to apply and take extra courses to qualify. And I always kept in touch" (DP6).

Networking

In many respects, graduates continued to benefit from the networks they set up during their studies. One of the graduates we interviewed, for instance, was planning to work with her network of academics on a project concerning labour conditions for women who clean public buildings. After graduation, another interviewee, a freelance academic, had maintained her network of contacts which funnelled contracts her way. She was invited, for instance, to report on the situation of women academics and students or plan and manage a study of women graduates. How useful such contacts are to professional women is described by a forty-six-year-old educator employed in adult education:

> Well, in my first job I could completely apply everything I learned. Because I developed a course for women. So I planned and taught it. And if there was an aspect I hadn't mastered myself, I could call on a good network stemming from my university years. I know a lot of women so I could quickly invite guest speakers. (DP5)

A thirty-two-year-old graduate confirmed the significance of networks for her personal career and advanced study:

> There's simply a flow of information I wouldn't otherwise enjoy. And of course that means the opportunity to hear if any posts are free, what possibilities there are or to think about whether to go for a doctorate or not. That's something I haven't yet made up my mind about. It's something I mull over a lot but isn't yet concrete. And I think, here my network is helpful. (DP6)

In many of the sixteen German states women's/gender studies associations exist. Most prominent are the networks Women's Studies North Rhine-Westphalia and the Association of Women's and Gender Studies Centres and Institutions of Higher Education in the State of Hesse (KONZEN). Since 2003, centres for women's/gender studies in Germany, Austria and Switzerland have been participating in exchanges. The first workshop 'Gender Studies in the German-Speaking Areas: Experience and Challenges' was organised in 2003 by the Center for Transdisciplinary Gender Studies at Humboldt University. Since then, annual meetings have taken place, each with a different thematic focus. These conferences offer networking opportunities among members and discussions of higher education policies, as well as opportunities to exchange experience and problems in the field. In 2010 the scientific Gender Studies Association Germany was founded, which aims at networking and promoting women's/gender studies in Germany.

CONCLUDING PROSPECTS

In recent years, German universities have undergone significant change. Triggered by the Bologna Process and its required BAs and MAs, new curricula have been developed and programmes more thoroughly structured. These developments will inevitably affect the career plans of women's/gender studies graduates. Thus, we can expect coincidence to play an increasingly smaller role than was the case during the EWSI research period.

The importance of career goals for younger academics is expressed in the numerous mentoring programmes at German universities that support this aim. For instance, at the University of Frankfurt a mentoring programme was first developed and then anchored in all five Hessian universities. These programmes include advice on all levels of certification: the Women Mentors' Network (*MentorinnenNetzwerk*) guides students in science and technology; in 'SciMento' you find science and technology postdoctorals; and in the programme 'ProProfessur' clients from the natural sciences, the social sciences and humanities receive tips on how to secure professorial qualifications. A second important factor in higher-educational reform is a focus on international networking. It is becoming increasingly expected of younger academics that they gather experience abroad, and this is financially supported by international doctoral programmes or DAAD grants for study in foreign countries.

German women's/gender studies is on the move. It is too early to draw conclusions as to whether these reforms in higher education will lead to an increase or decrease in women's/gender studies or what the effects of the Bologna Process, excellence initiatives and entrepreneurial universities will be. Women's/gender studies has pioneered their path into German universities. It seems crucial how the critique it provides will be assessed for the development of future academy: as impediment or as innovation. There remains a lot of work to be done. But it is worth the trouble.

NOTES

1. Chapter and interview material translated by Tobe Levin.
2. The abbreviation DP17 means D=Germany, P=past student, 17=interview number.

REFERENCES

Agreiter, M., and G. Schindler. 2002. Geistes- und Sozialwissenschaftler für die europäische Wirtschaft. *Sozialwissenschaften und Berufspraxis* 25 (1/2): 117–38.

Alemann, H. von 1995. Die disparaten Berufsfelder von Soziologen: Fachliche Identitätsbildung in der außeruniversitären Soziologie. *Sozialwissenschaften und Berufspraxis* 18 (1): 4–20.

Becker-Schmidt, R. 1987. Die doppelte Vergesellschaftung—die doppelte Unterdrückung: Besonderheiten in der Frauenforschung in den Sozialwissenschaften. In *Die andere Hälfte der Gesellschaft*, ed. L. Unterkircher and I. Wagner, 10&25. Wien: Verl. d. Österreich. Gewerkschaftsbundes

Berendt, E., H. Kallweit, and H. Kromrey. 2002. Primat der Theorie? Arbeitsmarkt, Qualifikationen und das Image der Soziologie. In *Soziologie im Wandel: Universitäre Ausbildung und Arbeitsmarktchancen in Deutschland*, ed. R.Stockmann, W. Meyer, T. Knoll, 187–97. Opladen: Leske and Budrich.

Bock, U. 1998. Am Ausgang des Jahrhunderts: Zum Stand der Institutionalisierung von Frauenstudien an deutschen Universitäten. *Feministische Studien* 2 (16): 103–17.

Bock, U. 2005. Überblick und Bestandsaufnahme: Lexika, Glossare und Handbücher zur Frauen- und Geschlechterforschung. http://www.querelles-net.de/forum/forum15-1.shtml (accessed July 9, 2010).

Braun, K.1995. Frauenforschung, Geschlechterforschung und feministische Politik. *Feministische Studien* 2 (13): 107–17.

Brouns, M., B. Waaldijk, M. Birriel, E. Oleksy, V. Sunnari and U. Wischermann. 2000. Towards an Evaluation of Women's Studies Teaching Manuals in Europe. In *The Making of European Women's Studies: A Work in Progress Report on Curriculum Development and Related Issues*, ed. R. Braidotti and E. Vonk, 36–49. Utrecht: Utrecht University.

Butler, J. 1990. *Gender Trouble: Feminism and the Subversion of Identity*. New York and London: Routledge.

———. 1991. *Das Unbehagen der Geschlechter*. Frankfurt: Suhrkamp.

Einarsdóttir, T. 2002. European Graduates: Cross-country Diversity and Gender Disparity. *European Journal of Education* 37 (4): 333–46.

Gerhard, U., M. Schmidbaurand and U. Wischermann. 2004. 'A Little Bit Wiser': The Impact of Women's Studies on Its Students' Experiences and Expectations in Germany. In *Employment, Equal Opportunities and Women's Studies: Women's Experiences in Seven European Countries*, ed. G. Griffin, 52–76. Königstein: Ulrike Helmer Verlag.

Gerhard, U., P. Pommerenke and U. Wischermann, eds. 2008. *Klassikerinnen feministischer Theorie: Grundlagentexte*. Königstein: Ulrike Helmer Verlag.

Gernand, D., and J. Zinn. 2000. Soziologie als Beruf: Tips und Infos zu Studium und Berufsfindung für StudienanfängerInnen. www.bds-soz.de/Soziologie%20als%20Beruf.pdf (accessed July 14, 2010).

Griffin, G., ed. 2002. *Women's Employment, Women's Studies, and Equal Opportunities 1945–2001*. Hull: University of Hull.

———, ed. 2004. *Employment, Equal Opportunities and Women's Studies: Women's Experiences in Seven European Countries*. Königstein: Ulrike Helmer Verlag

———, ed. 2005. *Doing Women's Studies: Employment Opportunities, Personal Impacts and Social Consequences*. London: Zed Books.

Hagemann-White, C. 1984. *Sozialisation: weiblich—männlich?* Opladen: Leske and Budrich

———. 1993. Die Konstrukteure des Geschlechts auf frischer Tat ertappen? Methodische Konsequenzen einer theoretischen Einsicht. *Feministische Studien* 2 (11): 68–78.

———. 1995. *Frauenforschung—ein Weg in die Institution*. Bielefeld: Kleine.

228   Marianne Schmidbaur and Ulla Wischermann

Jahr, V., D. Frechenhäuser, T. Büchner and T. Galgon. 2002. Marburger Politolog-Innen auf dem Arbeitsmarkt revisited: Die Jahrgänge 1993–2000. http://www.uni-marburg.de/fb03/politikwissenschaft/studium/berufschancen/absolventenbefragung2000 (accessed July 14, 2010).

Kirsch-Auwärter, E. 1996. Anerkennung durch Dissidenz: Anmerkungen zur Kultur der Marginalität. In Kultur in Bewegung. Beharrliche Ermächtigungen, ed. E. Kirsch-Auwärter and I. Modelmog, 25–47. Freiburg: Core.

Klinger, C., G.-A. Knapp and B. Sauer, eds. 2007. Achsen der Ungleichheit: Zum Verhältnis von Klasse, Geschlecht und Ethnizität. Frankfurt am Main: Campus-Verlag.

Knapp, G.-A. 2005. "Intersectionality"—ein neues Paradigma feministischer Theorie? Zur transatlantischen Reise von "Race, Class, Gender." Feministische Studien 23 (1): 68–81.

Knapp, G.-A., and A. Wetterer, eds. 2003. Achsen der Differenz: Gesellschaftstheorie und feministische Kritik. Münster: Westfälisches Dampfboot.

Lenz, I., ed. 2008. Die neue Frauenbewegung in Deutschland: Abschied vom kleinen Unterschied; Eine Quellensammlung. Wiesbaden: VS Verl. für Sozialwiss.

Lutz, H., ed. 2010. Fokus Intersektionalität: Bewegungen und Verortungen eines vielschichtigen Konzepts. Wiesbaden: VS Verl. für Sozialwiss.

Majcher, A. 2001. Women in German Higher Education. http://csn.uni-muenster.de/women-eu/download/MajcherTP01_05.pdf (accessed July 14, 2010).

Mazari, S., U. Gerhard and U. Wischermann. 2002. Germany. In Women's Employment, Women's Studies, and Equal Opportunities 1945–2001, ed. G. Griffin, 394–426. Hull: University of Hull.

Müller, U. 1997. Von der Gegen- zur Interventionskultur: 'Frauenforschung' als institutionalisierte Sozialwissenschaft. In Frauen-Universitäten: Initiativen und Reformprojekte im internationalen Vergleich, ed. S. Metz-Göckel and F. Steck, 157–77. Opladen: Leske and Budrich.

Schmidbaur, M. 2004a. Frauen- und Geschlechterstudien in Europa: Das europäische Forschungsprojekt Employment and Women's Studies. Feministische Studien 22 (1): 94–106.

———. 2004b. Schlüsselqualifikationen durch Gender Studies—Ergebnisse der Studie: Employment and Women's Studies. In Geschlechterstudien im deutschsprachigen Raum. Studiengänge, Erfahrungen, Herausforderungen, ed. Zentrum für transdisziplinäre Geschlechterstudien an der Humboldt-Universität zu, 121–27. Berlin: trafo.

———. 2005. Gender Studies und Professionalisierung: Beschäftigungsfähigkeit und Beschäftigungsaussichten von Studierenden und AbsolventInnen der Frauen- und Geschlechterstudien/Gender Studies. In Quer denken—Strukturen verändern: Gender Studies zwischen Disziplinen, ed. H. Kahlert, B. Thiessen and I. Welled, 275–300. Wiesbaden: VS Verl. für Sozialwiss.

Sekretariat der ständigen Konferenz der Kultusminister der Länder in der Bundesrepublik Deutschland (KMK). 2007. The Education System in the Federal Republic of Germany 2005: A Description of the Responsibilities, Structures and Developments in Education Policy for the Exchange of Information in Europe. Bonn: Secretariat of the Standing Conference of the Ministers of Education and Cultural Affairs of the Länder in the Federal Republic of Germany. http://www.kmk.org/dossier/dossier_en_ebook.pdf (accessed April 4, 2008).

Silius, H., and S. Tuori. 2004. Gender-neutral Finland? Women's Studies Students as Gender Experts in Finland. In Employment, Equal Opportunities And Women's Studies: Women's Experiences in Seven European Countries, ed. G. Griffin, 163–86. Königstein: Ulrike Helmer Verlag.

Statistisches Bundesamt. 2009. Hochschulstandort Deutschland 2009. http://www. destatis.de/jetspeed/portal/cms/Sites/destatis/Internet/DE/Presse/pk/2009/ Hochschulstandort/begleitmaterial,property=file.pdf (accessed July 14, 2010).

Teichler, U. 2002. Potentiale und Erträge von Absolventenstudien. *Sozialwissenschaften und Berufspraxis* 25 (1/2): 9–32.

Wischermann, U. 2002. The Pedagogic Dimension of Women's and Gender Studies. In *Gender Studies in Europe*, ed. L. Passerini, D. Lyon and L. Borghi, 147–57. Florence: European University Institute.

Wissenschaftsrat. 2000. Empfehlungen zur Einführung neuer Studienstrukturen und -abschlüsse (Bakkalaureus/Bachelor—Magister/Master) in Deutschland. http://www.wissenschaftsrat.de/download/archiv/4418-00.pdf (accessed July 14, 2010).

Zacharias, G. 2003. *Studienführer Sozialwissenschaften. Soziologie, Politikwissenschaft.* Würzburg: Lexika-Verlag.

Zimmer, A., H. Krimmer and F. Stallmann. 2007. Women at German Universities. In *Gendered Career Trajectories in Academia in Cross-National Perspective*, ed. R. Simieńska and A. Zimmer, 209–40. Warsaw: Wydwnictwo Naukowe Scholar.

WEB SITES

Professorship programme. http://www.bmbf.de/de/494.php (accessed July 14, 2010).

Cornelia Goethe Centre for Women's and Gender Studies at the Goethe-University Frankfurt am Main. http://www.cgc.uni-frankfurt.de/ (accessed July 14, 2010).

Center for Transdisciplinary Gender Studies at the Humboldt University, Berlin. http://www.gender.hu-berlin.de/zentrum/ (accessed August 11, 2010).

Doctoral programmes in women's/gender studies. http://www.fu-berlin.de/ zefrauen/datensammlung/graduiertenkollegs/Auflistung.html (accessed July 14, 2010).

List of chairs dedicated to women's/gender studies http://www.fu-berlin.de/zefrauen/ datensammlung/genderprofessuren/index.html (accessed July 14, 2010).

Women's Research Network North-Rhine Westphalia. http://www.netzwerk-frauenforschung.de/ (accessed July 14, 2010).

EXAMPLES OF ADDITIONAL FREE-STANDING COURSES

http://www.zefg.fu-berlin.de/datensammlung/studiengaenge/chronologisch.html (accessed July 14, 2010).

http://www.uni-marburg.de/genderzukunft/studium/studienfuehrer-gender/studienfuehrergenderstudies/index_html (accessed July 14, 2010).

http://www.zefg.fu-berlin.de/datensammlung/graduiertenkollegs/Auflistung.html (accessed July 14, 2010).

KONZEN. http://www.konzen-hessen.de/ (accessed July 14, 2010).

Gender Studies Association Germany. http://www.fg-gender.de (accessed July 14, 2010).

Part VI

The Choice of Topic and Research Questions

Some Examples

15 My Dissertation Photo Album
Snapshots from a Writing Tour

Doro Wiese

A photo album is a way to reconstruct personal history (Schade 1993). Although photographs are supposed to show only instants in time, their compilation creates a different way of viewing. Photos put together tempt their viewers to construct a story line between them that is not displayed in the photographs themselves. The border of a snapshot in a photo album is therefore the starting point for the construction of a story; it is the interface between the reality displayed in the photograph and the engagement of the viewer. Taking up this notion, I want to display different snapshots made of words that I took while writing my dissertation. Although these snapshots are taken from different angles, show diverse places and people and display different genres of writing, all of them are concerned with change. What is changing? And how can we ourselves change in a constructive way? Somewhat predictably perhaps, I diagnose our times as rapidly changing. A pervasive turbo-capitalism is unfolding that sweeps away many traditions in its sway, but do we have to give in to these developments? Is there a way to imagine a political and economic order that escapes these tendencies? Can we "wrest tradition away from the conformism that is working to overpower it" (Benjamin 2006, 391)?

In this chapter, I aim to carve out some possibilities for 'resisting' the pervasive grasp of a capitalism that is mostly seeking a potential economic surplus value. Dissertation writing, which is the genre I deal with, is also susceptible to this economic motivation. Being a necessary step to climb the academic latter (Just, chapter 17, this volume) it is prone to be reduced solely to the aim of getting ahead in academia. Although I do not want to advocate abandoning this aspect of dissertation writing, I want to bring to the fore another mechanism that I believe will inevitably happen when writing a dissertation: giving in to the process of learning. Writing and reading—key practices in the humanities—are media in the full sense of the word: they are far from being transparent practices but are intermediate or intervening substances (Chun 2006, 3). Paper used to be considered as a medium of circulation (as was money; ibid.), but in our postmodern turn to the 'new,' this fact constantly slips our minds.[1] Nevertheless, this forgetfulness does not make it impossible to ask anew: What kind of forces emerge when writing and reading? What work do they do? As reading and writing are far from disappearing, I think it is worthwhile to ask these questions, especially as the branch of learning I belong to—the humanities—constantly engages in these mediating practices.

What then do reading and writing mediate? Following Gayatri Chakravorty Spivak's suggestions in *Death of a Discipline* (2003), I want to argue here that both activities are techniques for deconstructing notions of a self-present and self-possessing subjectivity. Furthermore, writing and reading potentially *suspend certainties*, and thus create a time and a place from which to question knowledges we presumably 'have.' Mediating other times, peoples and worlds, reading and writing are precisely those practices that allow us *to be othered*, to be haunted by difference in and for itself. To exemplify this claim, I want to delve into my own experiences of writing a dissertation, which allowed me to engage in the creative act of 'postmemory,' a term introduced into cultural theory by Marianne Hirsch (1997, 1999). Hirsch argues that postmemory entails "conceiving oneself as multiply interconnected with others of the same, of previous, and of subsequent generations, of the same and of other—proximate or distant—cultures and subcultures" (Hirsch 1999, 9). In her view, postmemory involves "projection, investment, and creation" (ibid., 8) that children of survivors of cultural or collective trauma generate to approach a 'hole of memory': a term which psychoanalyst Nadine Fresco (1984) used to diagnose the specific relation that children of Holocaust survivors have to the distorted or untold memories of their parents. Different from memory through generational distance and from history by personal connection, "postmemory is a powerful and very particular form of memory precisely because its connection to its object of source is mediated not through recollection but through an imaginative investment and creation" (Hirsch 1997, 22). In this essay, I want to show how reading Jonathan Safran Foer's novel *Everything Is Illuminated* (2003) facilitated a postmemory that helped me to bridge a gap to other traumatic histories—genocide, the Shoah, racial apartheid—that are haunted by the inability to adequately represent them: because they are too painful to relate to, because there is no possible account for the lives that are lost, because there is no one who will listen to the witnesses or because the testimonies are repressed by the dominant forms of historical representation. Yet the literaricity of *Everything Is Illuminated*—that is, the use of vocabulary, syntax, character, narration, plot, the whole configuration of a chronotopic world (Bakhtin 1981)—allowed me to get in touch with precisely this inability to represent one's history: through the gaps, the fissures, the silences, the mysteries of the text of the novel, the effects it describes, the language it uses, the concepts of time and space it employs and its self-reflexive turn towards its own limitations. While on the one hand the novel stages the inability to render one's history, on the other hand it engages with it. Thus, *Everything Is Illuminated* is connected with the cathexis that drove me to choose a dissertation topic dealing precisely with these issues.

In other words: one of the texts I had chosen established a dynamic with me that made me able to understand the reasons for my selection as other, but related, stories folded in on me. While I would like to meander through fragmentary bits and pieces of impressions that encircle the notion of (my) dissertation writing and what it does to me, I hope that some of these story lines serve as an interface and prompt readers to carry them further, into their own dissertation's photo album.

SNAPSHOT 1: OF BEING IN THE HUMANITIES

When I look out of the window, I see a wide, grey sky arching over a copse of trees. Straining my ears, I hear the engine noises of passing ships. Occasionally, they emit a warning signal when another ship has infringed the navigation regulations, and repair work from the docks is audible from time to time. All these sensations are quite typical for my former home, Hamburg, which I am visiting while I write this chapter, staying in a flat close to the waterside. Like many of my Hamburgian compatriots, I have a certain nostalgia for its industrial harbour. Although I still remember a time when neither port nor docks but the Lake Alster in the centre was the emblem of the city's bourgeoisie, nowadays its docklands are the focus of attention. This turn to the waterside—that Hamburg shares with maritime European counterparts such as London, Marseille, Barcelona—costs the city enormous sums. Since 1998, the city has spent 360.61 million Euro on expertise and infrastructure for a newly planned city district ('Harbour-City') in former harbour arsenals.[2] The planned subway line alone will cost 298 million Euro. Less well known is the investment of the city in new buildings on the former harbour terrain, including constructing a 'living bridge' (370 million Euro); situating a philharmonic orchestra in one of the old warehouses (40 million Euro); and establishing a maritime museum (30 million Euro) for a private collector called Peter Tamm, a former Sunday paper colleague of the former senator of culture Dana Horakova. As the third-richest region in Europe,[3] one should assume the City of Hamburg can afford these luxuries when presenting itself as 'the doorway to the world'[4] to every visitor setting foot on Hamburgian grounds.

Yet the spendthrift attitude with which the City Council approaches the conversion of its harbour arsenals is in no way reflected in its expenditures for higher education. In 2007, the faculties of the University of Hamburg received in total 122.24 million Euro, which is one-third of the costs of a 'living bridge,' and the humanities in particular will suffer severe cutbacks in the coming years. By 2012, if all goes to plan, the number of students will be reduced to 60 per cent of current levels and academic staff will be halved (Stegemann 2007). This is a continuation of an already alarming overall German trend: in the period between 1995 and 2005, 1,451 academic positions were eliminated, 663 of them connected to the humanities

(Stegemann 2007). This trend, summarised by Spivak as capitalist imperialism's "effort to win the world for calculation" (Spivak 2003, 54), is reflected in the agreement made between Hamburg's Ministry of Research and Technology and the University of Hamburg regarding objectives and cash rewards. The preface of the agreement acknowledges the university's importance for Hamburg's growth: the university is a global player in Hamburg's competition with other cities as a location of industry and services. However, growth is only measured economically and, in this light, the humanities appears quite unprofitable and can accordingly be cut back to an absolute minimum.

SNAPSHOT 2: TRAFFIC WITH LANGUAGE IS RISKY BUSINESS

Despite this tendency to economise learning, I want to argue here for a quite different approach. Following Spivak's suggestions in *Death of a Discipline* (2003), I would like to privilege "an institutional calculus recording or instrumentalizing undecidability" (Spivak 2003, 49) and acknowledge the educative power of two of the humanities' key practices: reading and writing. Like Spivak, I argue against trivialising reading and writing "as the allegory of knowing and doing" (Spivak 2003, 28) and, like Edyta Just (chapter 17, this volume), I want to understand writing as a more intricate undertaking. Here, I want to appreciate reading and writing's ability to *suspend certainties*, an ability that Spivak (2003) also stresses. Traffic with language is always risky business, yet this traffic is potentialised in reading and writing as it deconstructs from the start any notion of self-presence—a notion that Derrida criticised thoroughly for its phallogocentric tendency to assume a distinct and authoritative subject-position (Derrida 1976, 12), and that Just undermines in chapter 17 of this volume by introducing Deleuze's and Guattari's, as well as Lacan's, concepts of desire. Not only might the reader be absent from the scene of writing and vice versa (Derrida 1988), one could also understand reading and writing as techniques for losing notions and experiences of self-presence and self-possession. If we see, as David L. Clark suggests, writing as "a sending whose origins, like its addressees, are enigmatic," and reading as "a chance encounter rather than an act of cognitive certainty" (Clark 2007, 303), we are getting close to the kind of learning called for by Spivak when she writes, "let literature teach us that there are no certainties, that the process is open, and that it may be altogether salutary that it is so" (2003, 26).

Although these self-deconstructive encounters in reading and writing seem fragile and far from profitable, I want to argue here for their political necessity. They permit the emergence of an incommensurable difference that is precisely respected through an understanding of its uncontainability and ungraspability, and thus propose an ethical approach to alterity that seems necessary for any democratic proceedings. Furthermore they engage us, readers and writers alike, into a process of imagining beyond the limits of the already known, a process also stressed by Petö and Waaldijk (chapter 5, this volume). Spivak calls this imaginative function 'teleopoiesis' (2003), in which projecting our imaginings into a space far away and into a future perfect is also a feminist undertaking directed at the collective of women yet to come. The difficulties of forming a feminist transnational collective that Spivak mentions in her text—by supplementing Derrida's *Politics of Friendship* through a reading of Virginia Woolf's *A Room of One's Own* with the question of gender—can only be faced when the imagination is used for "giving in, without guarantees, to the teleopoietic gaze of others" (Spivak 2003, 45).

Shakespeare's imagined sister, whom Virginia Woolf so powerfully evokes in her essay, is to Spivak the figure of the 'Third-World Woman.' To let ourselves be encountered by her, we must work for her, as Virginia Woolf has predicted for Shakespeare's sister: "As for her coming without that preparation, without that effort on our part, without that determination that when she is born again she shall find it possible to live and write her poetry, that we cannot expect, for that would be impossible. But I maintain that she would come if we worked for her, and that so to work, even in poverty and obscurity, is worth while" (Woolf 2005, 633). The benefits of this work are clear: not only will Shakespeare's sister come, but the contact with reality that Woolf claims as a necessary component of her coming is also working for a future and a past, the creation of a timeline that exceeds our very being. Writing and reading are tools to figure this contact and are therefore media in the full sense of the word: they are mediators between different times, peoples and worlds so that these 'others,' the transnational feminist collective yet to come, can haunt our present. These others are called forth by the close attention paid to language and the surrender to it that reading and writing implies.

SNAPSHOT 3: AN UNCALCULATED ENCOUNTER WITH 'THE OTHER SCENE OF WRITING'

The last sentences prompt me to come to the most important point I want to put forward in this chapter. So far, I have outlined the present conditions of academic writing in the German context and it should furthermore be noted that, at present, only 13.6 per cent of professors are women, although 40 per cent of dissertations are written by them (Wissenschaftsrat 2007, Drs 803–7). However, I have also indicated that in the key practices of the humanities—reading and writing—something else happens that escapes the economising tendencies of our late-capitalism's globe. Despite all the economic pressures that one can find in the academy—standardising time, work and the lives of everyone in its machine—I want to propose that we hold this 'other scene of writing' in high regard. Furthermore, I want to suggest that the 'othering' of oneself that we experience through language *always* takes place—even, also and especially in such writings as a dissertation which is generally perceived as work one undertakes to get a step further on the academic career ladder. Whether one wants to or not, writing and reading as *mediating* practices *always* contain the chance of learning, of stretching beyond the limits of the already known, by letting the subject be haunted by virtual others in time and place, a decentring that propels readers and writers alike into a future they will have helped to imagine in a teleopoetic way. Here, I want to theorise this 'scene of writing' so urgently needed in a society that increasingly aims at profitability—although one might argue that to make her come, the generalisable Shakespeare's sister, one must also be able to put this orientation aside and to consider working in "poverty and obscurity" (Woolf 2005, 633). Furthermore, one should note that Woolf does not say that to work means being poor and obscure, but rather that one should work in an *uncalculating* manner, without naming a prize, solely with the aim that she comes into being. It is thus a quite different economy that Woolf conjures as being "worth while"—an economy in which our present working is indispensible for a future to come, but which has no other exchange value than her coming and the possibilisation of her writing. Yet, one should also note that Woolf, after a lengthy lecture about women writers' poor working conditions making it virtually impossible for them to write unless they are economically independent and have a room of their own, formulates an aporia by proclaiming that the imaginative investment in Shakespeare's sister's coming will also make it possible for other women to work in "poverty and obscurity." In other words, the transcription of 'worth' and 'investment' into a different economy is *another* condition of writing, alongside all the economic and spatial necessities that one might have. This investment should make it 'worth while' not only to fight for the possibilisation of her writing, which includes having money and a room of one's own, but also to work uncalculatingly for her coming. What can we get from this investment? I believe that one, quite simply, could learn. To work 'in an uncalculating manner' might be one of the preconditions for the arrival of the unexpected guest, the never and not-thought-of.

SNAPSHOT 4: A FAMILY PICTURE

What I am alluding to here is associated with my long-standing engagement with Deleuze and Guattari's philosophical conceptualisations, specifically of writing, thinking and time. Yet I also owe my affective and passionate cathexis to some experiences that were solely made possible through the mediating practices of reading and writing. When I chose to write about Jonathan Safran Foer's novel *Everything Is Illuminated*, I knew that the novel deeply touched me. It tells the story of a Jewish-American writer in search of the woman who saved his grandfather's life from the Nazis in the Ukraine. Being of German origin, reading such a novel always means to confront an important part of one's country's history, and not only in an abstract way. I grew up with people who fought as soldiers in World War II and with the absence of people who never came back from it. In the German context, this might mean growing up with people who sustained fascism, who were or effected being a Nazi. Men who were drafted had at least encountered and caused innumerable deaths—if not through participation in war atrocities, then more likely than not in the crusade to Eastern Europe [Ostfeldzug].[5] However, members of my father's side of the family were communists and, as such, one of the first targets of Hitler's criminal regime. As early as 1933, men from this side of the family were sent to 'work camps' in the north of Germany, where they underwent forced labour in peat bogs under horrible working conditions, deprived of sleep, food and—according to the few descriptions that were passed on in my family—sometimes serving as shooting targets for the commanding officers. I believe these stories could be true, as the work camps where the men were imprisoned—Börgermoor, later Esterwegen—go down in history as 'the hell on the skirts of the woods,' due to reports of massive harassment and numerous murder cases.[6] Yet not all the men from my father's side of the family died in the work camps. Those closest to my father's family, my 'adopted' grandfather[7] and my Uncle August, left the work camp in 1938, only to be denounced by people living in the same village for reengagement in communist activities. Accordingly, they were first sent back to prison and then forcefully 'drafted' to a punishment battalion[8] going to the eastern front. During the last days of the war, in May 1945, my 'adopted' grandfather was captured by the Russian army and died of exhaustion shortly after. Meanwhile, my Uncle August survived, but he never spoke about the time between 1933 and 1945.

To return to the point I wish to make by putting this family history into the context of reading and writing about *Everything Is Illuminated*, when I chose to write about a topic that deals with a massive collective trauma like the Shoah, I knew perfectly well that my family history had influenced my choice. Although the men's deaths were hardly ever addressed directly (only close to dying did my 'adopted' grandmother begin to confide parts of their and her story to me), I knew from certain edgy behaviour on the part of the surviving women that they were mourned and missed. Yet, being part of the family, I was used to this edginess and accepted it without further questions. Only bits and pieces uttered here and there, and the concern of my father for his adopted mother, Hilde, let fragments of the puzzle to be pieced together. Later it occurred to me that the anticommunist attitude, predominant in Western Germany, most probably contributed to the prevalent silence of the women who were being harassed and isolated during Nazi times; their house frequently searched by the Gestapo, unable to get employment and therefore money, faced with the Nazism of the villagers meant that anticommunism prolonged their silence as a mode of resistance. Yet, when reading *Everything Is Illuminated*, I was aware of these issues and even saw them as one of the sources of my political and intellectual engagement. However, I was unconscious of the effects these stories had caused within me.

When I wanted to start writing about *Everything Is Illuminated*, I was faced with an enormous resistance on my part. Delaying writing and feeling exhausted were some of my initial responses to the task of examining this book in depth. Only when a good friend, Heiko Stoff, asked me about the book's content and I burst into tears when describing how one protagonist—the grandfather—was forced to betray his best friend to the Nazis, did it occur to me that here lay the key to one of the biggest traumas in my family: my grandfather was denounced by someone who must have known him, and this person was among the people we knew and with whom we lived. The sadness of having a loss and a crime *that* close to home, the immense abyss it created, was at first overwhelming. Yet it also made it possible for me to trace some of the despair that must have driven the women of my family into silence.

SNAPSHOT 5: CALLING FORTH THE WOMEN

In what way did *Everything Is Illuminated* facilitate this insight? As I mentioned earlier, the story of a betrayal partly triggered a realisation about the source of an enormous grief running through the veins of my family. Yet the story line in itself did not play the most important role in this coming to terms. Rather, the plot of the novel and the use of language *in addition* to the story line created this—to me—most astonishing effect. As an epistolary novel, it is mainly composed of letters written by two main characters, Alex and Jonathan. Yet through their choice of words and rhetorical devices both narrative strands create a world that is "one galaxy removed on planet Auschwitz" (Sicher 2000, 66). Jonathan's 'letters' are rather a manuscript in which he tells the story of a Jewish shtetl extinguished by a Nazi raid in the most fantastic and therefore 'incredible' way. Alex, who was his translator during his visit to the Ukraine, uses in his letters such a distorted version of English that his language makes it necessary for the readers to become his translators while he retells, at Jonathan's request, what happened during their unguided tour through the atrocities of Nazism. This deprivation of an 'original' description of an event—the reader supplementing the translator Alex, the translator Alex supplementing his translation belatedly, the rendering of the grandfather's story through these multiplying twists and folds of a supplemented supplementing, while the 'history' of the Shtetl is withdrawn from knowledge and must be invented—creates exactly the ethical position of postmemory. That is to say, indebted to the memories of the Shoah without claiming them, knowing about the unspeakability of its trauma, but still engaging with it.

This ethical position is enabled by the metaleptic narrative form of *Everything Is Illuminated* that, as Gérard Genette has so convincingly argued, changes the implicit contract between a work of fiction and its reader: the 'voluntary suspension of disbelief' is replaced by a 'playful simulation of believability,' such that the reader becomes directly engaged in the 'fictional' action (Genette 2004, 23–25; translation mine). Through the engagement of the reader as Alex's translator and receiver of their entire correspondence, s/he becomes directly involved in the production of meaning, and any attempt to 'speak authentically' is lost from the start. Assuming the position of the translator generally means to transpose an 'original' text, such that "the translator can never do what the original text did. Any translation is always second in relation to the original, and the translator as such is lost from the very beginning" (de Man 1986, 80), as Paul de Man shows in his rereading of Walter Benjamin's *The Task of the Translator*. This notion is inherent in the latter's original German title, *Die Aufgabe des Übersetzers*, since *die Aufgabe* means not only 'task,' but 'being defeated' or 'giving up.'[9] In the context of *Everything Is Illuminated*, I would like to argue that this giving up is not necessarily a defeat, but rather a surrender to the "reading of and in love" (Spivak 1992, 178) that translating entails. As Spivak argues in *The Politics of Translation* (1992), we cannot access the translator's position without becoming "the most intimate reader" of a text (Spivak 1992, 181) and, as such, we have to accept how it points to "the limits of language," the "silence," and "the absolute fraying of language" (ibid.) when, through our agency as translators, logic and rhetoric are split up.[10] This is an effect of translation warded off by the original text (ibid.) that comes into being when we surrender to the experience of the 'other' in language.

Assuming the position of a translator can show us how "a world is made for the agent" (Spivak 1992, 179) since the splitting up of language makes accessible a threefold notion of it as rhetoric, logic and silence. If we stage this notion—which is, in Spivak's eyes, the task of the translator, to give Paul de Man's intervention another twist—we assume an ethical position that Spivak sees as a facilitation of "love between the original and its shadow" (ibid., 178): a love that not only stages a yearning to close that abyss between being and language—an abyss that shows itself exactly in the fraying of language split up by logic and rhetoric—but that also allows the exchange between "the original and its shadow." However, this exchange is only possible if one accepts the fundamental difference between the two positions while being infected by the structure of its staging. The literaricity of the text allows, in other words, a "heteropathic identification'" described by Hirsch as "'[i]t could have been me; it was me, also' and, at the same time, 'but it was not me'" (Hirsch 1997, 9), and that becomes the vehicle for a heteropathic memory that spans different times in its "teleopoietic gaze" (Spivak 2003, 45) through which we are othered to ourselves. Through its literaricity, *Everything Is Illuminated* thus sustains an ethical position that embraces alterity lovingly, that accepts a fundamental difference while engaging with it: an ethical position that allows for a different economy of learning, an economy that I believe should be seen as worthwhile in the humanities. For me, it created a position that allows me to call forth my grandmother,[11] so that I can figure all that I miss of her and that has remained silenced all her life: "but I maintain that she would come if we worked for her, and that so to work, even in poverty and obscurity, is worth while" (Woolf 2005, 633).

NOTES

1. If anything, 'newness' is used to erase the existence of previous media ("a case in point the 'discovery' of the 'new world'"; Chun 2006, 3), while the purportedly new is constantly categorised, described and proscribed. These obscuring tendencies make it necessary, as Wendy Hui Kyong Chun has so convincingly argued, to interrogate "the forces behind any emergence, the importance of shifting from 'what is new' to analyzing what work the new does" (ibid.). Here, I would argue that this necessary archaeology of media should also include the 'old' media that are far from disappearing.
2. See parliamentary printed matter DS 18/6227 (15.07.10), 7–8.
3. Hamburg (FRG), with its gross domestic product (GDP) at 200 per cent of the EU-27-average and its purchasing power standard (PPS) at 47,200 PPS, is the third-richest region of Europe, only surpassed by Inner London at 337 per cent (79,400 PPS) and Brussels at 233 per cent (55,100 PPS). In comparison, the poorest region, North East Romania, has 25 per cent (5,800 PPS) EU-27-average per inhabitant. PPS is a conversion tool used in the EU to compare the purchasing power of average inhabitants between countries with different currencies. Recent statistical data can be found in the Eurostat Regional Yearbook 2009 of the European Commission.
4. Since Medieval times, Hamburg has called itself by this name.
5. The Hamburg Institute for Social Research has constructed a widely debated but scientifically well-grounded exhibition titled 'Crimes of the German Wehrmacht: Dimensions on a War of Annihilation 1941–1944.' An outline of the exhibition can be found on their Web site.
6. See the homepage of the Esterwegen memorial, http://www.gedenkstaette-esterwegen.de/ (accessed July 15, 2010).
7. He is not my 'real' grandfather, but the husband of one of my grandmother's sisters: the family in which my father grew up, since my grandmother died at his birth. As this sister and her daughter were part of our family, I call him 'adopted' because he is, by social relation but not by blood, something like a 'grandfather.'
8. Punishment battalions were battalions in which soldiers were commonly used as 'cannon fodder,' a scheme which was secretly fought by some ex-prisoners by organising resistance in the army (Burckhardt and Erxleben 1965; Burckhardt, Erxleben and Nettball 1986; Klausch 1987).
9. *Aufgabe* means 'task' in English, but also 'give up' when it derives from the verb *aufgeben*.
10. The splitting up of logic and rhetoric is exploited in Derrida's *Monolingualism of the Other* when he states, "I have only one language, it is not mine" (Derrida 1998, 1). Logically, this sentence cannot make sense because one cannot

have something that is not one's own. Yet its rhetoricity, played out through its antinomy, helps to question what *kind* of ownership language implies, and if its 'ownership' and the 'belonging' it promises might be permeated with its history and power location. Derrida here uses his monolingualism to show how his being other—an Algerian Jew speaking French, a language experienced as being spoken 'elsewhere'—already infects his sense of the French language, such that a geo/political location has an important influence on access to language which, in the example of Derrida, can be experienced as splitting up. In the context of my argumentation, I see this as a painful, yet interconnected experience.

11. To call forth an imagined person could be regarded as one of the desires which sustain writing, as Just describes in her chapter in this volume.

REFERENCES

Bakhtin, M. M. 1981. Forms of Time and Chronotope in the Novel. In *The Dialogic Imagination*, ed. M. Holquist, trans. C. Emerson and M. Holquist, 84–258. Austin: University Press of Texas.

Benjamin, W. 2006. On the Concept of History. In *Selected Writing*. Vol. 4, *1938–1940*, ed. M. W. Jennings and H. Eiland, 389–401. Cambridge, MA: Harvard University Press.

Burckhardt, H., and G. Erxleben. 1965. *Strafdivision 999 [Punishment Division 999]*. Berlin: Deutscher Militärverlag.

Burckhardt, H., G. Erxleben, and K. Nettball. 1986. *Die mit dem blauen Schein: Über den antifaschistischen Widerstand in den 999er Formationen der faschistischen deutschen Wehrmacht (1942–1945)* [Unworthy to Bear Arms. The Anti-Fascist Resistance of 999-Devisions in the Armed Forces of Fascist Germany, 1942–1945]. Berlin: Deutscher Militärverlag.

Chun, W. H. K. 2006. Introduction: Did Somebody Say New Media? In *New Media, Old Media. A History and Theory Reader*, ed. W. H. K. Chun and T. Keenan, 1–11. London: Routledge.

Clark, D. L. 2007. Bereft: Derrida's Memory and the Spirit of Friendship. *South Atlantic Quarterly* 106 (2): 291–325.

Derrida, J. 1976. *Of Grammatology*. Baltimore: Johns Hopkins University Press.

———. 1988. *Limited Inc*. Evanston, IL: Northwestern University Press.

———. 1998. *Monolingualism of the Other; or, The Prosthesis of Origin*. Palo Alto, CA: Stanford University Press.

Eurostat: Eurostat Regional Yearbook 2009. http://epp.eurostat.ec.europa.eu/cache/ITY_OFFPUB/KS-HA-09–001/EN/KS-HA-09–001-EN.PDF (accessed July 15, 2010).

Foer, J. S. 2003. *Everything Is Illuminated*. London: Penguin.

Fresco, N. 1984. Remembering the Unknown. *International Review of Psycho-Analysis* 11 (4): 417–27.

Genette, G. 2004. *Métalepse: de la figure à la fiction*. Paris: Seuil.

Hamburgische Bürgerschaft. [City Parliament of Hamburg]. 2007. Parlamentsdrucksache DS 18/6227. [Parliamentary Paper 18/6227] http://www.hamburgische-buergerschaft.de/cms_de.php?templ=info_sta.tpl&sub1=387&sub2=405&cont=415 (accessed July 15, 2010).

Hamburg Institute for Social Research. Crimes of the German Wehrmacht: Dimensions on a War of Annihilation 1941–1944. http://www.verbrechen-der-wehrmacht.de/docs/home_e.htm (accessed July 15, 2010).

Hirsch, M. 1997. *Family Frames: Photography, Narrative, and Postmemory*. Cambridge, MA: Harvard University Press.

————. 1999. Projected Memory. In *Acts of Memory: Cultural Recall in the Past*, ed. M. Bal, J. Crewe and L. Spitzer, 3–24. Hanover: University Press of New England.

Klausch, H.-P. 1987. *Die Geschichte der Bewährungsbataillone 999 unter besonderer Berücksichtigung des antifaschistischen Widerstandes*. [The History of the Probation Units 999 with Due Regard to their Anti-Fascist Resistance]. Köln: Pahl-Rugenstein.

Man, P. de. 1986. 'Conclusions': Walter Benjamin's 'The Task of the Translator.' In *The Resistance to Theory*, 73–106. Minneapolis: University of Minnesota Press.

Schade, S. 1993. Der Schnappschuß als Familiengrab. [The Snapshot as a Family Tomb]. In *Zeitreise: Bilder/Maschinen/Strategien/Rätsel*, [Time Travel. Images / Machines / Strategies / Enigmas], eds. M. Heller, M. Scholl and G. C. Tholen, 287–301. Basel: Stroemfeld/Roter Stern.

Sicher, E. 2000. The Future of the Past: Countermemory and Postmemory in Contemporary American Post-Holocaust Narratives. *History & Memory* 12 (2): 56–91.

Spivak, G. C. 1992. The Politics of Translation. In *Destabilizing Theory: Contemporary Feminist Debates*, ed. M. Barrett and A. Phillips, 177–200. Palo Alto, CA: Stanford University Press.

————. 2003. *Death of A Discipline*. New York: Columbia University Press.

Stegemann, T. 2007. Universitäten: Qualitätsoffensive ohne Personal. [Universities. Quality-Offensive without Staff]. http://www.heise.de/tp/r4/artikel/26/26010/1. html (accessed July 15, 2010).

Wissenschaftsrat [Science Council]: Empfehlungen zur Chancengleichheit von Wissenschaftlerinnen und Wissenschaftlern. [Recommendations for Equal Job Opportunities of Male and Female Scholars] http://www.wissenschaftsrat.de/texte/8036–07.pdf (accessed July 15, 2010).

Woolf, V. 2005. A Room of One's Own. In *Selected Works of Virginia Woolf*, 561–635. London: Wordsworth Edition.

16 Intimate Truths about Subjectivity and Sexuality

A Psychoanalytical and a Postcolonial Approach

Henrietta L. Moore and Gloria D. Wekker

In this chapter we, two feminist anthropologists, are in constructive conversation about a little-known, tantalisingly short Dutch psychoanalytical case study from 1917, in which three apparently white and upper-class Dutch women claim to possess 'Hottentot nymphae.' This is the coded contemporary term used to refer to the supposed morphology of black women's genitalia, i.e., the three women are implying that they possess overdeveloped labia minora. We pose somewhat different sets of questions to the case study. While Wekker argues that with the term Hottentot nymphae, the women are implicitly making meaningful statements about gender, race, sexuality and subjectivity, Moore claims that we simply do not have enough information to understand really what is happening with these women, and instead focuses on the racial and gendered images circulating in the analytic context and cultural production. Using psychoanalytic, postcolonial and intersectional approaches, in each of our readings we lay out the content, significance and context of the case study. Through close reading and analysis of this case study we hope to show, first and foremost, the different and complementary contributions these various approaches offer to the analysis of subjectivity, sexuality, gender and race. Our analyses jointly serve to illustrate our key insight that the concepts of self and other that came into being in Western modernity were dependent on the politics of colonial relations. Thus, as we will claim, it does not make sense to understand white female subjectivity in abstraction from gender and race.

With this conversation and our two different sets of questions and approaches to the analysis of the case study, we place ourselves within long-standing debates in the humanities and the social sciences about the nature of subjectivity, the self, the 'I': how is it possible and what does it mean to enunciate an 'I'? From antiquity to our own times, this question has preoccupied many theorists, not least among whom are Descartes, Freud and Foucault. Unsurprisingly, however, none of these theorists paid adequate attention to how processes of subjectification are interlaced and intertwined with gender, race and other axes of signification. Thus, a second goal of the article is to bring to the fore—rather concisely—how a version of psychoanalysis can be developed that fundamentally takes gender and race into account, as is evident in Moore's reformulations (Moore 2007).

CASE STUDY: THE MASCULINITY COMPLEX IN WOMEN

At the second meeting of de Nederlandsche Vereeniging voor Psycho-Analyse (the Dutch Society for Psycho-Analysis), on June 23, 1917, in Amsterdam, the psychiatrist J. H. W. van Ophuijsen delivered a talk entitled 'Casuistische Bijdrage tot de kennis van het mannelijkheidscomplex bij de vrouw (Casuistic contribution to the knowledge of the masculinity complex in women).' According to the minutes of the meeting in the *Nederlands Tijdschrift voor Geneeskunde* (The Dutch Journal for Medicine), May 18, 1918, the gist of Van Ophuijsen's talk was the following: Freud found, and others have confirmed, that there is an unconscious complex which has as its core the infantile imagination of the possibility that the woman would also possess male genitals. Van Ophuijsen calls this complex 'the masculinity complex' and Freud later acknowledges his intellectual debt to Van Ophuijsen in his 1919 paper 'A Child Is Being Beaten.' According to the summary of the lecture, the complex expresses itself in different ways:

> [E]mbitterment not to have been born as a man, the tense expectation on the part of the woman that she will at some point in the future still obtain the male organ, depression, as if the male genital, whether by her own fault or not, has been lost (castration complex etc.). With those women who have this complex to a strong degree, one seldom finds masculinity in behaviour and appearance, they seldom also manifest homosexuality, but one does find a kind of competitiveness with men, in intellectual and artistic respects and in relation to their own gender. On the basis of fragments of a number of cases and analyses, Van Ophuijsen tries to argue that the masculinity complex is correlated with that part of infantile sexuality which is tied to the functions of clitoris and bladder, and the lust feelings that are connected to them. (*Nederlands Tijdschrift voor Geneeskunde* 1918, 1428; contributor's translation)

In the later published version Van Ophuijsen (1924) explains the difference between the masculinity and the castration complexes, which closely resemble each other. In the latter, women experience a feeling of guilt because the loss, the damage of the genital organ is supposed to be the result of wrongdoing, the punishment for a sexual lapse. In the former, 'the wish to be a boy' engenders a feeling of having been ill treated and thus of bitterness. Van Ophuijsen's case study consists of five women who are in analysis with him, all of whom have a strong memory of having observed the male organ of their father or brother in their youth. Furthermore, several of them behave as if they had male genitals, i.e., they urinate while standing up or they sit like men, with their legs spread, "as if they want to prevent their genitals from being crushed." Van Ophuijsen diagnoses them as suffering from psychastenia with obsessions, otherwise called "obsessional neurosis" (Van Ophuijsen 1924, 62).

We do not learn much about these women. Of one, the patient H., it is mentioned that she is a composer and a piano player; but no information is given on the activities or occupations of the other patients. There is one passage in the article, however, that is of key importance for our endeavour:

> It might perhaps be not without significance that three of the five patients informed me of their own accord that they possessed 'Hottentot nymphae': this fact, which they had already noticed very early in their lives, led them to the conviction that they were different from other women . . . I would rather define the attitude present as one of rivalry with men in the intellectual and artistic spheres. (Van Ophuijsen 1924, 41)

Van Ophuijsen also claims that the patient H. had the expectation that an organ would grow out from within, based on her Hottentot nymphae (Van Ophuijsen 1924, 47), the overdeveloped labia attributed to black women. While the women call on Hottentot nymphae, thus on 'race,' to make a statement about themselves and on what is 'wrong' with them, Van Ophuijsen does not pay any attention to it and substitutes gender for race: their neurosis is that they are suffering from rivalry with men. How are we to read the significance and the meaning of this case study?

PSYCHOANALYSIS AND RACE: WOMEN WHO GROW PENISES (MOORE)

The birth of psychoanalysis coincides with a period of high colonialism and nationalist conflict in Europe, as well as with a distinctive separation of the human and natural sciences that bore the marks of increasing professionalism based on the findings of nineteenth-century science. This is the context in which Van Ophuijsen addresses the Dutch Society for Psycho-Analysis in June 1917. His ostensible subject is the newly created problem of the 'masculinity complex,' a strange term that links object choice to sexual morphology and competition with males. The complex is evidenced by a fantasy of masculinity which is said to lead to women behaving as though they possessed male genitals. This strange situation is made more puzzling when Van Ophuijsen notes: "I did not find to any great extent in any of these cases what is called a masculine disposition; nor indeed a masculine appearance and expression, a contempt for men, or a predilection for masculine activities." What we do learn is that three of the five patients informed him "of their own accord" that they possessed "Hottentot nymphae," which led them to the conviction that they were different

from other women (Van Ophuijsen 1924, 41). We do not in this short article have enough information to understand really what is happening with
any of these women, but what we can recognise is a clear application of
Freud's ideas regarding the relationship of female sexuality to the Oedipus
complex, the successful resolution of the complex and the move from clitoral to vaginal satisfaction. Underpinning all this is the long-standing idea
that women interested in phalluses must be lesbian or that lesbians desire
to have phalluses (see De Lauretis 1994). As it happens, Van Ophuijsen's
article gives little indication of any lesbian sexual practices and only minimal evidence of lesbian fantasies.

Let us turn then to the symbolic fulcrum of the paper—the thing that
Van Ophuijsen drops into his text so casually and inexplicably never
returns to—the fact of Hottentot nymphae. In his manner of presentation,
Van Ophuijsen suggests that the women used this term to refer to themselves. I am unsure about this. It is true that since the eighteenth century
and the great voyages of European discovery there had been a fascination
with the classification of specimens, including humans as well as plants
and animals, and the result was a large literature on both racial and sexual
differences (Schiebinger 1990, 388–89). Science in its quest for knowledge
about humankind became another means through which the question of
otherness and origins was explored, and in this process there was a sutur-
ing of race and sex which focused on visible differences. Throughout the
nineteenth century, the focus was increasingly on the genitalia of women,
as the terrible story of Sarah Bartmann makes so unnervingly plain;[1] and
by the twentieth century, sexual degeneracy was not only linked with
disease and prostitution but with race and with sexual perversion. There
was often a thin line between science and pornography in this regard, and
early psychoanalytic writing very blatantly displays this unwholesome set
of connections. In this context, it might be more accurate to contemplate
the possibility that it was not the women themselves who used this racialised terminology but, rather, that the discourse which allowed them to link
physical differences between genitals to excessive sexuality, and possible
sexual 'dysfunction' in the form of homosexuality, was one that inevitably
drew on the analyst's associations with race.[2] Racial fantasies thus circulate
within the analytic context, allowing forms of difference to overdetermine
each other. They are fantasies that are constructed in analysis rather than
revealed by them, and this might also be true of the lesbian phallic fantasies
that fill the picture painted by Van Ophuijsen.

It is important here to take a step back briefly and enquire more fully
into the relationships between fantasy, processes of subjectification and
the roles that race and gender play in these formations. Ultimately, all psychoanalytic theories link the formation of the subject to desire and fantasy and to the way in which external worlds and social relations impinge
upon them. However, within the different theoretical traditions, there
are different ideas about how the child's earliest fantasies link to what

happens later in life, how the ego is formed and exactly how we should envisage the relationship of fantasy and identification to dominant social and cultural representations. There are thus differing accounts of the relationship of the imaginary to the symbolic. What they agree on is that separation from the mother and identification with oneself, with others and with the world are the conditions of subjecthood (Moore 2007, 64). Psychoanalysis has always maintained that representation and symbolism are the interface that allows for the emergence of an embodied, thinking agent who is also tied psychically and culturally to values and forms of difference through sensations, emotions, drives and desires. This being so, subjectivities (gender identities) must always be tied to sexual difference, to what is made historically and individually of an anatomy that is engaged with a world already subject to the workings of gender difference. However, I propose we recognise that this understanding of sexual difference is not something immutable, something that is everywhere and always the same, something that is subject to an unchanging symbolic law, but is rather something that is open to cross-cultural variation and social change over time and is always constituted in and through its relations to other forms of difference (Moore 2007, 123).

It is the process of the formation of the body ego via the medium of representation that makes this possible because it ties that process to social and cultural valuations and understandings, most specifically as they are inflected by power and difference. This being so, we now have a comprehensible link between the unconscious and the discursive, between the imaginary and the symbolic. The capacity for making representations is essential for the formation of the body ego. Culture and history do not come to the individual from outside but are part of its evolving constitution and continuing relation to the world. Fantasies of the embodied self are linked to fantasies of relations and identifications with others. The earliest representations of significant others are caught up with forms of gender difference that have no realisable expression outside their relations with other forms of difference, such as race, class and ethnicity. I argue that gender is the ground for the emergence of sexual difference, but it can never be a neutral, uninflected set of categories and relations. Feminist scholars writing on the relationship between race and psychoanalysis make this evident when they point out that "'whiteness'" is a racial category . . . and that no theory of the acquisition of gendered subjectivity can proceed on an unexamined assumption of neutrality'" (Moore 2007, 123, 124).

Our earliest representations and fantasies about our bodies and the bodies of others develop at the same time as our neurological competences. As each child develops both neurologically and physically, it acquires the capacity to recognise objects (including other people), to understand that it is separate from the bodies of others, to distinguish its internal world from the external world. As these competencies develop, the earliest fantasies are relinquished; they are repressed and become part of the unconscious. If this did not happen, we would be caught in our own fantasised internal world (Moore 2007, 7).

Fantasies are always both individual and social; they emerge in a social context, as part of an embodied psychosomatic process that encourages the child to reach towards the world. This process combines fear and excitement, pain and pleasure. It establishes boundaries, both as separation and as connection. It is the social history of fantasy that ensures that no one is the sole author of their fantasies, and as such they remain both intrinsic to the individual and irredeemably other. Fantasy scenarios thus display common elements across cultures: who am I for the other; what does this or that body part signify; where do I come from? Race, like sexual difference, is a regime of bodily visibility and as such appears natural. It is also, like sexual difference, not only an embodied attribute but a feature of social institutions, ideologies and distributions of power and resource. It is involved in the earliest fantasies and representations through which the body-ego emerges. Race and sexual difference are mutually imbricated so it does not make sense to ask which is more foundational, but equally it is a mistake to collapse them into each other, to imagine that as forms of difference they are always elaborated to the same degree and in the same way. These fantasies are part of us and can be brought into play most noticeably through encounters with the fantasies of others which may replicate the disturbing, frightening and exciting enigmas of our earliest encounters with the meanings of others (Laplanche 1999, 221–33).

The reference to 'Hottentot nymphae' in the case study is particularly interesting because it gives material substance to a long running fantasy that the morphology of the genitals might reveal the nature of sexuality, that the enigma of sexuality might be revealed through a closer examination of the body. Jennifer Terry discusses a contemporary study conducted in New York in the 1930s in which a group of lesbians were examined by experts, in order to identify, treat and prevent homosexuality; the traits that were said to distinguish them from other women included larger than average vulvas, longer labia minora, wrinkled or thickened labia minora and large and erect clitorises (Terry 1990, 332–33). Of note is the idea that desire and the practices it engenders somehow physically alter the genitals, but equally curious is the notion that a minute examination of the body will tell us something about differences in desire. There are, of course, many forms of genital modification around the world. Elongation of the labia minora, usually for the purposes of enhancing sexual pleasure, is reported from Africa and the Americas. Among the Bushmen/Hottentot, the elongated labia are considered a congenital feature, but elsewhere elongation is a desired outcome of particular practices and is sometimes done by girls themselves, by other girls or by men. The corresponding belief systems are variable, as are the ideas about sexuality, pleasure and desire with which they are associated. In general, modification of the genitals operates along the axes of sameness and difference, so that many groups that practise circumcision speak of removing the male parts of women and creating the differences between women and men; while others who practice labial elongation may refer to or imply a connection between these organs and the penis.

The idea that women have penises has been part of psychoanalytic discussions from the earliest days. Theorists argue that children of both sexes initially believe their mother possesses a penis, and at later stages they think that although she is castrated she retains the paternal penis inside her. The various debates about female castration, the nonresolution of the Oedipus complex and penis envy need not detain us here, but what is of interest is that the penis in fantasy is a detachable object that is neither female nor male. Many societies work over these fantasies in myth, narrative and ritual, and a common story from many parts of the world is that women originally had penises before they were stolen from them by men. Many such accounts fuse the fantasies of bodies and body parts to understandings of physical and social reproduction. This process can be seen at work in the curious emergence of racial and sexual researches in the nineteenth century where the quest for knowledge focuses on what difference signifies, who these others are for me, where they come from, how they reproduce. Such research, as the bizarre depiction of a scientist looking at Sarah Bartmann's genitalia through a telescope reveals, was often blatantly eroticised (Gilman 1985, 218–20). Freud linked sexuality to knowledge through what he called the 'sexual researches of children.' These researches concern such things as the origin of babies, the nature of the parental relationship and the differences between the sexes (Moore 2004, 736). Freud wrote, "although they go astray in a grotesque fashion, yet each one of them contains a fragment of real truth; and in this they are analogous to the attempts of adults, which are looked at as strokes of genius, at solving the problems of the universe which are too hard for human comprehension" (1977, 193). I am not arguing here that all scientific research is motivated by or reducible to childhood fantasies. What I am suggesting is that such fantasies circulate within cultural productions—art, literature, film, medicine, science—and that race and sexual difference are involved in fantasised relations to the bodies and body parts of others, including carers, and by extension certainly doctors and psychoanalysts. These differences while not reducible to each other are mutually invoked through regimes of visibility and difference, and our inevitably fantasised relation to them.

THE CODED LANGUAGE OF HOTTENTOT NYMPHAE (WEKKER)[3]

Given the Dutch demographical structure in 1917, I am assuming the women in this case study were white and, given the costs attached to psychoanalytical treatment, were from a middle- or upper-class background. Initially for the sake of the argument, but beyond that for the sake of the production of inclusive knowledge about the Netherlands and about race as an equally important grammar of difference as gender, let us entertain the thought that it actually *was* these women themselves who used the term Hottentot nymphae. I am arguing that the term is neither meaningless nor coincidental, but that the women are implicitly making statements with it about gender, race, sexuality and subjectivity. Against the backdrop of a still dominant historical discourse in the Netherlands that maintains that colonialism was something that took place overseas and therefore hardly left any traces in the metropolis itself, a so-called colonialism of the exterior, I am interested in reading this case study as telling us something meaningful about the ways the bodies of these white upper-class female analysands were requisitioned and interpellated by black female bodies, as well as about the resulting psychic economies of these women and, finally, about what Van Ophuijsen's substitution of gender for race meant.

My most central assumption is thus that they actually used the literal term 'Hottentot nymphae.' This is underscored by the fact that Van Ophuijsen uses inverted commas around 'Hottentot nymphae.' It is noteworthy that Van Ophuijsen does not explain what he means by the term, thus making it seem plausible that his audience, which is a professional audience of doctors and psychiatrists, is familiar with it (see n2). There are, moreover, ample reasons to assume that by the 1910s and 1920s, psychoanalytical insights had reached a more general, educated audience in Dutch society (Bulhof 1983). Ultimately, it is hard to understand why the term figures at all in Van Ophuijsen's article, if the women did not use it. Since Van Ophuijsen clearly is not inclined to accept their definition of the situation—after all, he dismisses their opinion which deploys race and proffers his own reading in terms of gender—why would he bring the word up at all, if they did not use it? It might be the case, as Moore suggests, that the sudden appearance of the term 'Hottentot nymphae' is an expression of the racial fantasies free-floating in the analytic context, thus emanating from Van Ophuijsen himself. We are confronted then with a complicated situation of disavowal, the simultaneous affirmation (when it emanates from himself) and denial (when it is suggested by the women) of a thought. Caught in this untenable situation, Van Ophuijsen dissociates, as I claim below in my third question. However, more importantly, as I will also show, there were ample other everyday sites in society where the women would have been exposed to racial imagery and representations.

I will ask four questions about this case study, but first I want to stress the rare and possibly unique glimpse the case study offers us of white female upper-class subjectivities which were produced in Dutch Diaspora space (Brah 1996) in the 1910s and the role race played in those psychic economies. I adopt a postcolonial framework to read this case study, coupled with the notion of a cultural archive (Said 1993) and an intersectional perspective. With the cultural archive, Edward Said refers to "a particular [nineteenth-century] knowledge . . . structures of attitude and reference . . . and structures of feeling" that subject races should be ruled (1993, 52). Ultimately, I am interested in the widespread but unexplored/underexplored ways in which race nestled itself in the Dutch cultural archive, in the forcefulness, passion and even aggression which race in the Netherlands elicits, while at the same time elusiveness and denial reign supreme (Wekker, forthcoming). Underlying my proposal is the attempt to read metropolis and colonies as one analytic field, as Frantz Fanon already urged decades ago (Fanon 1967), seeking to find insights into how knowledge was produced along paths that went from metropolis to colony and the other way around (Stoler 1995, 2007). In this particular case, the most burning issue is: how is it that these white women could make use of a racial discourse to make statements about their sexual subjectivity? And what is at stake when they enunciate an 'I' that adopts features that are commonly ascribed to a racialised and vilified group?

My questions are as follows: first, what are the sites in Dutch society in which these white, female patients would acquire 'knowledge' about black women's sexuality? After all, dominant common sense has it that with Dutch 'colonialism of the exterior,' until the middle of the twentieth century race had pertinence only in the colonies, not in the metropolis. Race, in the sense in which it was (and sometimes unfortunately still is) understood, i.e., as 'blackness,' was something that played out 'over there,' not here. Race was blackness and seemed to have nothing to do with the 'civilised' white human subject (Walton 1997). It is, then, striking that three of the five women in this era had access to a discourse of race to talk about their gender and sexuality. Sander Gilman has pointed out that by the 1920s, it would have become commonplace to associate sexuality, and in particular a sexuality that exceeded or contradicted a clearly heterocentric model (as in the case of the prostitute, the lesbian or the hysteric), with the image of the 'Hottentot,' the stereotype of black female sexuality (Gilman 1985). To which conventions and in which domains would these women have been exposed with regard to race? There are four possibilities.

First, there is the figure of the black servant which is ubiquitous in *European art* of the nineteenth and early twentieth centuries, whose main function is to sexualise the society in which s/he is found and to mark illicit sexual activity (Gilman 1985). Another, second site would have been the *world exhibitions*, sites where blacks—in all shapes and forms—could be gazed at. Throughout the nineteenth and the beginning of the twentieth centuries, African women were exhibited in Europe as examples of a primitive sexuality (Buikema 2009). Between 1825 and 1913, there were thirty-four exhibitions of 'exotic people' in the Netherlands (Grever and Waaldijk 1998; Sliggers 2009). Photographic postcards in which black and Middle Eastern women were displayed in erotic poses were a variation on this theme. Various exotic populations had their own stereotypes, which were repeated again and again: the inhabitants of Africa were long associated with savagery, barbarism, cannibalism and immorality. The *popularisation of medical and anthropological 'research' in magazines*, prominently featuring the Hottentot apron or enlarged labia would form a third site of 'knowledge.' A fourth site would be *commerce*, whereby on the covers of products from the colonies (soap, tea, coffee, cocoa and sugar) images of blacks were displayed (Nederveen Pieterse 1990). It thus seems fair to conclude that the three 'patients' would have been exposed to images, ideas, ideologies and representations of 'race' and black women in everyday life. Thus, apart from the analytic situation, there would have been ample sites in everyday life where these women would have been exposed to images and representations of blackness. The different sites I have just outlined also illustrate the fruitfulness of considering metropolis and colonies in one analytical field, showing the mutual imbrication of cultural productions here and there.

My second question is, what is at stake in these white women's adoption of the coded language of 'Hottentot nymphae'? It would seem that it is impossible for these women to speak directly about their own gender and especially about their active sexuality, geared as it supposedly is toward clitoral and urethral pleasures, because doing so would place them, in psychoanalytical understandings to which they might very well have been privy, in the unfavourable category of possessing an immature, inappropriate sexuality: not passive, not receptive, not focused on the vagina. Thus, they need to displace those feelings onto black women who, after all, had been identified with excessive sexuality since the Middle Ages (Gilman 1985). At the same time, however, they are also displacing themselves in the colonial, gendered, racialised and heterosexualised order of things; they seem to be embracing a racial grammar that has assigned a particular, fixed place to particular actors; specifically they have embraced a more intense libido and affective states that are the domain of black women (Stoler 2007), thus shunning the normative sexuality that is assigned to white women.

Jean Walton, in her brilliant article 'Re-Placing Race in (White) Psycnoanalytic Discourse: Founding Narratives of Feminism' (1997), in which she rereads a number of (more or less) well-known psychoanalytic case studies in which women analysands have racialised fantasies, argues along the same lines:

> Since it had become probable by the 1910s that defiance of the feminine role would inevitably be 'diagnosed' as a 'masculinity complex' (that is, if you do not wish to be 'feminine', you must wish to be 'masculine'), these women would seem to have sought an alternative means of asserting a gendered identity that both was and was not officially 'feminine.' (Walton 1997: 233)

Although their identification with black women might, on the one hand, be read as a transgressive gesture, on the other, it leaves the supposed purity and putative passivity of white female sexuality intact and thus reinstates the binary nature of the sexualities ascribed to black and white women. Thus, in the Dutch cultural archive of the era, a strong libido is racialised as black and feminine.

My third question is concerned with why Van Ophuijsen discards the women's own racialised understandings of their situation and prefers to frame their predicament in terms of gender. What is that substitution about? Contextually, it is important to keep in mind that in Western Europe, this was a time of huge social change, especially in terms of gender relations, and gender and sexuality were foremost on people's minds, both among the general public and among medical professionals. Drawing on research about American 'medical opinion' about homosexuality in the period between 1903 and 1925, Karin Martin suggests there was a keen interest in female homosexuality as a response and (in part) as resistance to the suffrage and early women's movement. Female 'inverts' disobeyed gender norms—being attracted to other women, not wearing dresses, having short hair, wanting to be on top—and their behaviour was deemed deeply undesirable. Doctors thought that lesbianism would lead to masturbation, nymphomania, feeling superior to men or being a suffragist (Martin 1993, 248). All of this, of course, is implicitly about white women.

Against this background, it would seem reasonable that Van Ophuijsen was more exercised by the grammar of gender than by that of race. Coupled with the fact that race as a category pertaining to whites was evacuated and that thinking both categories simultaneously was unthinkable, he does not pay any attention to what his patients are telling him. Given the chain of associations set in motion by the identification with black women's sexuality—its lasciviousness, its excessiveness, the overdevelopment of the clitoris which may very well lead to those excesses which are called 'lesbian love,' the 'unhealthy attention' to the clitoris to the expense of the vagina, and a generally too-active sexuality—it stands to reason that Van Ophuijsen has to dissociate and "cannot acknowledge that these white women are enacting a specifically cross-racial, rather than cross-gendered, identification" (Walton 1997, 234).

Michel Foucault has been highly influential in the past decades with his conceptualisation of three processes by which, in Western culture under modernity, human beings are made into subjects: dividing practices, scientific classification and 'subjectification' (Dreyfus and Rabinow 1982, 208). Were one inclined to make a Foucauldian analysis of this case study, or in light of the lack of attention he affords race and gender a Stolerian or McClintockian analysis (McClintock 1995; Stoler 1995, 2007), certainly the processes of scientific classification and subjectification would have to come into full, intersectional view. With processes of 'subjectification' Foucault refers to the processes of self-formation in which the person is active (as opposed to the dividing and classificatory practices). It would be exceedingly interesting, though given the scarcity of data it seems hardly feasible, to follow the "operations on [people's] own bodies, on their own souls, on their own thoughts, on their own conduct, characteristically entailing a process of self-understanding, which is mediated by an external authority figure" (Rabinow 1984, 11), in this case the psychoanalyst.

Finally, my fourth and most overarching question: what is the significance of this case study for psychoanalysis and, more generally, for the study of subjectivity and the exploration of the place of race in the Dutch cultural archive? Although actual black people were largely an absent presence in the Netherlands at the time, the case study shows that "racial difference forms the *content* of the fantasy life of these white female subjects, yet it is not a constitutive component of the psychoanalytic interpretation of the analyst" (Walton 1997, 228). In other words, the explicit discourse on gender and sexuality of the period was informed by implicit assumptions about racial difference, which have so far hardly been acknowledged. A rereading of this case study along intersectional lines throws new light on the presence of race in the Dutch cultural archive at a time when it has been largely deemed to be absent, and also on the formations of female metropolitan selves. Thus, the concepts of self and other that came into being in Western modernity were dependent on the politics of colonial relations, and a postcolonial approach to the study of subjectivity has to take that into account. It does not make sense to understand white female subjectivity in abstraction from gender and 'race.' And more generally, the analysis of this case study again shows how the still dominant practice in the Dutch academy of keeping metropolis and colonies apart in separate analytical fields (see also Legêne 2010) results in the maintenance of significant racial blinders about practically all things, but significantly about (sexual) subjectivity.

NOTES

1. Sarah Bartmann was known as the Hottentot Venus. She was a Khoisan woman from South Africa and lived from 1789 to 1815. She was a slave and was sent to Europe to be exhibited to the European public. This display of her 'unusual' bodily form—large buttocks and elongated labia—was considered a form of entertainment (see Gilman 1985).
2. 'Hottentot nymphae' (*Hottentottenschürze*), moreover, appears to be a standard term of medical sexual pathology at the time describing what was considered to be 'malformed' female genitals. The psychoanalysts who for most part were medical doctors were informed by and took part in that discourse. See for example Hirschfeld (1920, 200).
3. Part of this research was made possible by a visiting scholarship grant at the Centre of Gender Excellence, GEXcel, located at Gender Studies, Linköping University and Örebro University, Sweden, and funded by the Swedish Research Council.

REFERENCES

Brah, A. 1996. *Cartographies of Diaspora: Contesting Identities (Gender, Racism, Ethnicity)*. London: Routledge.

Buikema, R. 2009.The Arena of Imaginings: Sarah Baartman and the Ethics of Representation. In *Doing Gender in Media, Art and Culture*, ed. R. Buikema and I. van der Tuin, 78–93. New York: Routledge.

Bulhof, I. N. 1983. *Freud en Nederland: De Interpretatie en Invloed van zijn Ideeën*. Baarn: Uitgeverij Ambo.

Dreyfus, H., and P. Rabinow. 1982. *Michel Foucault: Beyond Structuralism and Hermeneutics*. Chicago: University of Chicago Press.

Fanon, F. 1967. *Black Skin, White Masks*. Trans. C. L. Markmann. New York: Grove Press.

Freud, S. 1977. On the Sexual Theories of Children. In *On Sexuality*, Vol. 7. Harmondsworth: Penguin.

Gilman, S. 1985. Black Bodies, White Bodies: Toward an Iconography of Female Sexuality in Late Nineteenth-century Art, Medicine and Literature. *Critical Inquiry* 12 (1): 204–42.

Grever, M., and B. Waaldijk. 1998. *Feministische Openbaarheid: De Nationale Tentoonstelling van Vrouwenarbeid in 1898*. Amsterdam: IISG/IIAV.

Hirschfeld, M. 1920. Sexualpathologie: Ein Lehrbuch für Ärtzte und Studierende. Bonn: A. Marcus and E. Weber Verlag.

Laplanche, J. 1999. *Essays on Otherness*. London: Routledge.

Lauretis, T. de. 1994. *The Practice of Love: Lesbian Sexuality and Perverse Desire*. Bloomington: Indiana University Press.

Legêne, S. 2010. *Spiegelreflex: Culturele Sporen van de koloniale Ervaring*. Amsterdam: Uitgeverij Prometheus, Bert Bakker.

McClintock, A. 1995. *Imperial Leather: Race, Gender and Sexuality in the Colonial Contest*. New York: Routledge.

Martin, K. 1993. Gender and Sexuality: Medical Opinion on Homosexuality 1900–1950. *Gender and Society* 7 (2): 246–60.

Moore, H. L. 2004. On Being Young. *Anthropological Quarterly* 77 (4): 735–46.

———. 2007. *The Subject of Anthropology*. Cambridge: Polity Press.

Nederlands Tijdschrift voor Geneeskunde, no. 20 (May 18, 1918): 1428.

Nederveen Pieterse, J. 1990. *Wit over Zwart: Beelden van Afrika en Zwarten in de Westerse Populaire Cultuur*. Amsterdam: KIT en Stichting Cosmic Illusion Productions.

Ophuijsen, J. H. W. van. 1924. Contributions to the Masculinity Complex in Women. *International Journal of Psycho-Analysis* 5 (1924): 39–49.

Rabinow, P., ed. 1984. *The Foucault Reader*. New York: Vintage Books.

Said, E. 1993. *Culture and Imperialism*. New York: Vintage Books.

Schiebinger, L. 1990. The Anatomy of Difference: Race and Sex in Eighteenth-Century Science. *Eighteenth-Century Studies* 23 (4): 387–405.

Sliggers, B. 2009. *De Exotische Mens: Andere Culturen als Amusement*. Tiel: Lannoo.

Stoler, A. L. 1995. *Race and the Education of Desire: Foucault's History of Sexuality and the Colonial Order of Things*. Durham, NC: Duke University Press.

———, ed. 2007. *Haunted by Empire: Geographies of Intimacy in North American History*. Durham, NC: Duke University Press.

Terry, J. 1990. Lesbians under the Medical Gaze: Scientists Search for Remarkable Differences. *Journal of Sex Research* 27 (3): 317–39.

Walton, J. 1997. Re-Placing Race in (White) Psychoanalytic Discourse: Founding Narratives of Feminism. Abel, E. et al, eds. *Female Subjects in Black and White. Race, Psychoanalysis, Feminism*. Berkeley, Los Angeles, London: University of California Press: 223–251.

Wekker, G. Forthcoming. Diving into the Wreck: Intersections of Gender, Race, Sexuality and Class in the Dutch Cultural Archive. In *Dutch Racism*, ed. P. Essed and I. Hoving. Amsterdam: Rodopi.

Part VII

Coda
The Desires of Writing

17 If Writing Has to do With Desire, What 'Kind' of Desire Is That?

Between Jacques Lacan and Gilles Deleuze

Edyta Just

Climbing the stairs to the top of the scholarly world one must pass through many levels. Three of these levels can be easily distinguished: bachelor, master and doctoral. To move from one to the other a kind of 'passport' is needed. These are, respectively, a bachelor's, master's and doctoral degree. This 'passport' is a measurement of one's involvement, perseverance, determination, skills, abilities and potential. The 'passport' thus marks the efforts undertaken. It takes a significant period of one's life to make it across the borders. In all cases, however, what is required is a written text: a paper, a thesis, is a *sine qua non* of being finally granted the 'passport.' Not to diminish the importance of the bachelor's and the master's phases, the doctoral one—commonly referred to as a PhD phase—requires, in my opinion, special attention.

Undoubtedly, a PhD student or a PhD candidate represents a specific kind of 'warrior.' First, because in most of the cases, it is a real challenge to launch oneself into and then survive the long PhD 'journey.' Obtaining a PhD position, surviving financially, having a private life and remaining relatively sane are only a few of the issues one must face and deal with throughout the process. Second, because a PhD student is expected to produce a 'block,' or rather a 'three-dimensional solid,' which is generally referred to as 'a book,' or preferably 'the book.' The well-structured, well-written and well-argued 'block' which is expected to materialize at the end of the process is already 'present' at the beginning. The virtual presence of the final result of the PhD phase may be rather intimidating, if not to a certain degree paralysing, for the one who stands on the 'start line.' To conquer the fear of not delivering what is required one has to become a 'warrior.' Certainly, one knows that without writing, the book cannot appear. However, especially at the beginning, feeling a direct link between these two states is not an easy exercise. Despite these anxieties, at a certain point, the writing process becomes inevitable and engages everyone without exception. Four years of writing a dissertation—a number that for some may shrink and for some expand considerably—represents a period which does not go by unnoticed. To be a PhD student is to spend a significant amount of time every day writing, with breaks for sleep, nutrition and bits of a private life before returning after a short while to the writing again.

All of this has led me to certain conclusions. First, I guess it could be a real help for a PhD student to become equipped with such concepts of the writing process that can make one more confident and less fearful when it comes to the 'PhD writing exercise.' Second, it can be very useful to draw attention to the phenomenon of 'continuous' writing for the concepts it provides.

Many theories and concepts concerning writing, some of which I will briefly refer to later, have been developed and articulated (see, for example, Bataille, Derrida, Barthes, Culler). Interestingly, though, no one has focused on the fact that one may keep on writing, continue writing, get immersed in writing, dwell in writing for a meaningful amount of time, that writing can become a job and a lifetime occupation for both scholars and nonscholars. From my perspective the 'dwelling' and 'plunging' into writing for days, months and, in many cases, years, indicates that writing has 'something' do to with desire. If so, then with what 'kind' of desire is the process of writing associated? In my opinion, mapping how the writing process can be linked to the desiring process, and also defining the 'kind' of desire, may be helpful to PhD students' understanding of the writing process.

Desire has been differently approached, defined and conceptualised. In this chapter, I refer to Jacques Lacan's and Gilles Deleuze's concepts of desire because both of them approach desire as constantly 'switched on,' as a continuum. The similarity between their approaches, however, ends here. For Lacan, desire never belongs to the subject that results from entering the Symbolic order. He sees desire as linked to fantasies and to the Symbolic. Desire is situated on the side of acquisition; it is about lack; it is detached from its object, producing not real but imaginary objects. As such, desire can never be fulfilled and satisfied, and so it continues to exist (Lacan 1977). In contrast, for Deleuze, desire is a positive and constructive force. It is located on the side of production. Therefore, desire is not about lack, a lack of a real object. The object of desire is not detached and absent but situated on the plane of immanence where desiring production takes place. Consequently, desire does not function on the fantasy level and does not produce imaginary objects. Characterised by connection and production, desire continues and, more importantly, it continues to produce (Deleuze and Guattari 1983).

In this chapter, I will first briefly touch on different theories and conceptualisations of the writing process to show that, one the one hand, writing is a phenomenon that has attracted much attention while, on the other hand, the phenomenon of the 'continuous' writing has not yet been much discussed. Second, I will try to find out if writing can be linked to the desiring process by referring to concepts of desire and by answering questions such as: Why do I write? What does it mean for me to write? How does it feel when I write? What happens when I write? Following that, I will try to determine on which side of the 'desire divide' (i.e., Lacan's or Deleuze's concepts of desire) one may locate the writing process: does it stand for Lacanian lack or rather does it go 'hand in hand' with Deleuzian production? I will then outline certain concepts of the writing process while simultaneously presenting how they can be helpful to a PhD student, who stands at the 'start line' with a virtually present expected/required book yet to be actualised. In doing so, I will prove that the 'continuity' of writing is a good 'start line' when proposing useful concepts of the writing process for a PhD student.

WRITING: WHAT THE 'OTHERS' HAVE TO SAY

In the psychoanalytic tradition, the process of writing is conceptualised as the process of understanding. Writing is supposed to aid comprehension, tracking and mapping of the unconscious processes. For Georges Bataille writing constitutes a violation as one oversteps one's own boundaries when tracking the unconscious processes (Bataille 1985). Writing is then an exploration of how many boundaries can be broken. It involves the inevitable cruelty of encountering the other. Jacques Derrida, on the other hand, claims to undo the foundation of violence and advocates for writing as a productive critical mode (Derrida 1978). Meanwhile, for Roland Barthes, "the comedy of writing" is the way in which "we . . . last a bit longer than our voice," through which we "*inscribe ourselves* somewhere" (1985, 3; emphasis in original). Among other topics, Barthes asks what gets lost when the writing process takes place. He argues that in writing we lose ourselves because writing helps to

> protect ourselves [as] we keep an eye on ourselves, we censure and delete our blunders, our self-sufficiencies (or our insufficiencies), our irresolution, our errors, our complacencies, sometimes even our breakdowns . . . in short, all the watered silk of our image-repertoire, the personal play of our self. (Barthes 1985, 4)

Furthermore, Barthes also emphasizes that, in writing, many words and expressions which may appear in speech are not articulated. In this sense, writing is again about losing. Writing makes

> the sentence . . . hierarchical . . . it is developed, as in the staging of a classic drama, the difference of role and stage positions; in becoming social (since it passes to a larger and less familiar public), the message recovers a structure of order; 'ideas,' entities so difficult to delineate through interlocution, where they are constantly overwhelmed by the body, are put here in the foreground, there in the background, yet elsewhere in contrast. (Barthes 1985, 6)

As such, for Barthes "to write means in a certain manner: *I think better*, more firmly; I think less of you, I think more for the 'truth'" (1985, 6; emphasis in original). Jonathan Culler emphasises that writing has been deeply underestimated by the linguistic science. He points out that

> linguistic science . . . designates writing as a way of recording speech, a sign of a sign, which is irrelevant to the nature of language in general . . . that the writing is . . . a corruption of speech: writing is a mode of representation that can erroneously affect or infect conceptions of language, which ought to be based solely on the proper and natural form of language, speech, whose priority to writing is at once phylogenetic, ontogenetic, functional, and structural. (Culler 1988, 217)

Culler advocates developing "a linguistics of writing" that will "attend seriously to the structures, strategies, and effects of writing" and that can proceed by paying attention to the forms of writing in speech, to possible relations and patterns relegated to the margins of linguistics (1988, 226). However, there is a moment of hesitation when he considers whether a linguistic of writing should focus on

> extend[ing] linguistic to problematical but important domains, adding on description in supplementary fashion, or . . . [on] recast[ing] the enterprise by seeking to place the marginal at the center. (Culler 1988, 221)

The scholars and the theories I have referred to are a small sample of the many available. The ways in which writing has been conceptualised vary significantly, and different concepts provide different ideas about what writing is/can be 'all about.' Undoubtedly, they all contribute significantly to understanding the phenomenon, while at the same time indicating that writing is a process worthy of enquiry and understanding. This strongly articulated interest in the writing process indicates that I am on the right path, or perhaps more precisely, that I am on a not-so-unusual track in trying to write about writing. With that said, none of these theories provide any evidence to suggest that the phenomenon of 'continuous' writing, the 'immersion' in writing, has been thought about and received attention.

DOES ANYONE SENSE DESIRE?

In the introduction I pointed out that the phenomenon of 'continuous' writing may indicate that the writing process can be linked to desiring processes, as conceptualised by Lacan and Deleuze. Both Lacan and Deleuze approach desire as the force that never ceases, never stops but continues, flows and goes on endlessly. As desire is about a 'continuum,' 'continuous' writing can be perceived as both evidence and the outcome of the process of writing being a desiring one, of the fact that writing is about desire. However, I find such an explanation a little too simplistic. Desire 'proceeds' for certain 'reasons.' Therefore, in order to map out if writing is about desire, it appears important to find out why one actually writes and writes.

Lacan would have said that the human subject who 'lives in culture' does not have desires of its own, and this is because of the existence of the Symbolic order. The moment one enters the level of the Symbolic, one undergoes "subjection to the symbolic codes of culture" (Wright 1992, 43). It appears that in culture one has little chance of desiring precisely what one could have desired in an environment freed from existing cultural norms, objectives and demands. As such, one does not desire what one truly wants, but instead desires what one is told to desire. Furthermore, when existing in the Symbolic one has only fantasies left and, to borrow from Slavoj Zizek (1991), it is through them that one learns how to desire. Following this line of argument, it is easy to conclude that desires constructed through fantasies can never be satisfied and as such, they must be about a lack. One cannot obtain that which is not Real. Lacanian desire is placed on the side of acquisition, thus desire can never grasp the desired object. The object of desire always remains detached from desire. Thus, desire is endlessly doomed to miss its object, to stand for a lack. In this sense, desire is not directed at its object but rather 'immersed' in its own lack. It is this very lack that ensures the continuity of desire. Lacanian desire is not about 'grasping' but rather constantly 'reaching out for,' to be left empty-handed. Desire as seen by Lacan can only produce fantasies and imaginary objects whose 'content' is informed and fuelled by the Symbolic. As such, desires are always involved in the unceasing production of fantasies, which simultaneously designates their inability to be fulfilled and satisfied once and for all. Thus desire continues precisely because of lack. Consequently, remaining in Lacanian reality means being confined to the made-up world, complete with prescribed desires and an omnipresent lack, with few chances to flee.

Transposing this onto the experience of a PhD student, her/his required book and the process of writing it, one can say that one desires to have a book written because of the manner in which universities operate and function nowadays. As the book is a 'passport' to a higher level, the 'possible economic surplus value' which dominate academia (Wiese, chapter 15, this volume), both influence a PhD student's desire. The book also opens the barrier to the wonders and respect of academic life. Thus, if one wants to get there, one needs to prove one's worth by delivering a solid written piece. At the same time, any PhD candidate is surrounded by doctoral colleagues, professors, countless numbers of great books already written, excellent ideas explored and cum laude(s) awarded. Academia appears to be about excellence, omnipotence and infallibility. Therefore, the notion of the 'good enough' book may quite easily be superseded in the mind of a PhD candidate by the desire to produce instead something more akin to a 'best seller.' There is a desire for a book, for an excellent book, but the book is not yet there. In this moment the writing comes into play. Only the one who writes knows how exhausting and demanding the whole process may be.

When I write, the excellent and finished book is always virtually present. Yet, when I write I cannot easily sense its presence. It is at a certain point like being in the void. I write but my object of desire seems not to be there with me. At the same time it appears to me that everything I have written is not as excellent, perfect and brilliant as I have 'imagined,' as I have wanted it to be. Thus, I am writing; I come back to writing every time I take a break or have a little rest. I continue the whole process constantly changing, rearranging and rewriting what I have already enclosed in the sentences to have it perfect, to have it just the way I have 'dreamt' about. In this sense I can say that the writing process is linked to desire and to desire as conceptualised by Jacques Lacan. I write for the book, for a perfect book, that is in a way never there and that is so distant. My writing is a desiring process which has and yet lacks its object; my writing is an endless process of reaching out for but apparently not really being able to grasp the desired object. When I write I see the written books, I sense the perfection of the academia; I am fuelled by the Symbolic. Can my desire ever be satisfied? I write as I lack, I lack as I write. Trying to reach my 'fantasy' I 'dwell' in writing, I am 'immersed' in writing, I continue writing. It appears that writing does represent a desiring process, yet the lack and dissatisfaction underlying it does not leave me with a very cheerful spirit.

In contrast, Deleuze does not agree with the Lacanian conceptualisation of desire and strives for the radical redefinition of the term. He emphasises that the moment desire is placed on the side of acquisition "we make desire an idealistic (dialectical, nihilistic) conception, which causes us to look upon it as primarily a lack: a lack of object, a lack of the real object" (Deleuze and Guattari 1983, 25). He does not agree that

> the real object that desire lacks is related to an extrinsic natural or social production, whereas desire intrinsically produces an imaginary object that functions as a double of reality, as though there were a 'dreamed-of object behind every real object', or a mental production behind all real productions. (Deleuze and Guattari 1983, 26)

On the contrary, he points out that "there is no such thing as the social production of reality on the one hand, and a desiring-production that is mere fantasy on the other" (Deleuze and Guattari 1983, 28). Deleuze criticises an understanding of desire that sees it as producing only fantasies and as producing them by "detaching itself from the object" intensifying "that lack by making it absolute: an incurable insufficiency of being." For him to reduce "desiring-production to a production of fantasy" is not to see it as "a process of production" (Deleuze and Guattari 1983, 26). Deleuze stresses that what desire produces are not fantasies or imaginary landscapes but the Real. For him desire produces reality and its product is equally real. He concludes:

> [D]esire does not lack anything; it does not lack its object . . . Desire and its object are the same thing . . . Desire is a machine, and the object of desire is another machine connected to it. Hence the product is something removed or deducted from the process of producing: between the act of producing and the product, something becomes detached, thus giving the vagabond, nomad subject a residuum. The objective being of desire is the Real in and of itself. (Deleuze and Guattari 1983, 27)

Desire does not lack the object but is equal to it. Thus, to desire means to produce, to make, to invent and what gets produced/made/invented cannot be qualified as a fantasy. What gets produced is real, it does exist. Desire produces and its product is real, therefore "the real is not impossible; on the contrary, within the real everything is possible, everything becomes possible" (Deleuze and Guattari 1983, 27). In this sense, instead of desire being a lack and negative force, it becomes redefined as a productive and positive one. Referring to Deleuze and Guattari, Elizabeth Grosz emphasises the importance of redefining productive desire as that which "does not provide blueprints, models, ideals, or goals. Rather it experiments; it makes: it is fundamentally aleatory, inventive" (1995, 180). For Deleuze desire continues not because of the lack but because of the constant production.

Transposing this once again onto the experiences of a PhD student, her/his required book and the process of writing it, one may notice a close connection between the three of them. Without a PhD student, the writing process cannot take place and the required book has no chance of eventually appearing; without writing, the expected book can never be ready. The process of writing is a *sine qua non* of having the book. One writes because writing creates the possibility of holding in one's own hands one's very own thoughts embedded in a certain amount of pages and enclosed within a frame of two nice covers.

I write because the object of desire is virtually with me, although not always tangibly sensed. Whenever I write, the book is more present than ever as it undergoes its actualisation. My writing and the book are closely tied, two machines connected to one other. The connection this linkage produces and the product is a written piece. It does not matter how long the piece is. It may be of one, two or twenty pages; what truly matters is that I have it and that it has my own thoughts in it. And so I write; I 'dwell' in writing, I am 'immersed' in writing, I come back to writing as writing allows me to produce: to produce my book that becomes also my very own 'expression.' In this sense the writing process is definitely about desire, a desire that has much to do with a joyful and pure Deleuzian production.

With the above discussion I conclude that the writing is about desire. Surprisingly, however, writing appears to have as much in common with

Lacanian lack as with Deleuzian pure production, and I guess both can actually work. I can see my writing as a result of my constant dissatisfaction. My writing can be taken for an endless 'reaching out for' something that I will never 'grasp.' My writing can be approached as fuelled by lack and being all about lack. Despite this, I still do something. In a sense this very lack keeps me active. After all, lack can be seen as a force resulting in an activity. It is only this constant disappointment that still bothers me. If only I could have taken the perfect book out of my head. On the other hand, I can perceive my writing as a pure production, as a busy, noisy machine unceasingly spitting tangible sheets of paper and perceptible letters out of its restless entrails. My writing can be seen not as 'reaching out for' but rather 'nailing down,' as here and now but never later. Thus, my book stops appearing as 'somewhere out there' but rather as 'right here' and 'right now.' My book also becomes my very own 'perfect' expression which can give me a sense of empowerment and control.

Writing is definitely about desire. What remains is the important question of whether the writing-desiring process should be aligned with Lacanian or Deleuzian thinking.

AT THE WRITING DESK WITH LACAN OR DELEUZE?

Culture inevitably creates and informs one's desires. The Lacanian Symbolic is not so far away if one looks for it. The cultural codes, the prison of language, alienation, they all certainly exist. Lack evoked by a mirror lurks around all the time. Desperate search for a unity and a solid identity do take place. This is a rather scary vision, but not at all an impossible one. However, what is really terrifying is the inability to leave and escape from such 'reality': there are no chances for transformation and metamorphoses. You are doomed to live in the Imaginary informed by the Symbolic, you are doomed to lack yourself and forever 'look for' fulfilment and a sense of wholeness.

The desire to have a book written might not be one's own desire. The book image linked to the Symbolic inputs may appear unreachable. The tangible book, one's object of desire seems to exist in a different, impenetrable dimension. The desiring-book subject appears to be left with nothing or, in the best case, in a state of moderate desperation. It can also be that existential lack, which every human subject experiences according to Lacan, may eventually be conquered by the appearance of the book. This could be one's belief. In this sense the subject's position on the side of acquisition is 'double.' The subject is reaching out for the perfect yet not-quite-there book believing that, when reached, it would bring a sense of wholeness and completeness to life (that is not yet present). However, before this happens one has nothing and so the 'starting' position is about lack. In this sense the process of writing can be seen as a process of 'reaching out for,' of seeking fulfilment, of 'grasping' the ungraspable.

I write because I want something. I write because I want my book, my exquisite book. I write because it can give me satisfaction, it can fulfil my 'needs' and mend my lacking existence. It occurs quite often that when I write I have the sensation that what I have written is not good enough. When I write I fear that I will never reach the 'meta-line.' When I write I compare myself with the perfect other-writer only to feel the impossibility of reaching that level. My writing is in a sense a very sad and tiring process. It is like walking in a circle, tiptoeing in silence, swimming in messy waters, mobile-immobility, a scream expressing an inability of fulfilment. It is not an alien sensation to me to feel as if I had achieved nothing previously when I start writing again, when I am back to writing after a break. I often do not feel really satisfied, and I do not usually reckon that my existential gap/lack has been mended. My writing is the 'Lacanian desiring process' with no chance to repair the lack situated underneath my very existence.

Although one's writing is about desire placed on the side of acquisition, one might have a perfect book in mind, and so one produces imaginary objects and fantasies, that is, one also produces 'something' real. Inevitably, writing is a tangible translation of thoughts into words and sentences. Although often in slow motion, writing produces numbers of pages which are not pure fantasies but actual-real objects saved in binary codes on the computer or stored in the cupboard when printed out. Writing also produces a real 'expression' of one's own. Furthermore, one's writing-desiring production is not only a production of words or pages of one's own 'expression,' it is also a production of a space. It is a space into which many things fall. It is impossible to count them all, so I will mention only a few. The writer's body finds its place there, the computer with its technological sophistication, the keyboard, the articles read, the books browsed, the memories of the courses and seminars taken and the conferences attended, one's perfect book, one's parents/friends/colleagues' expectations, the comments of one's supervisors, one's headache, the rain behind the window, all this is there. In this space things constantly interact, intertwine with each other, merge and entangle in/with each other. Rosi Braidotti (2006) emphasises that Deleuzian desire is about pure 'plenitude.' In the similar vein, Alison Ross stresses that it is about "the construction of assemblages," it is "an experimental, productive force, but also . . . a force able to form connections" (Ross 2005, 63, 64). The space produced during the process of writing is a Deleuzian assemblage. This space is his plane of immanence where 'things' gather, bump into one other, pass through each other and cross over one another. It is a space of Deleuzian territorialisation and deterritorialisation, of stratification and destratification. Thus, it is a space where nothing remains a separate entity, a space of constant becoming. By producing and creating the space, the assemblage, the plane of immanence, writing is a desiring process precisely as Deleuze defines it. Grosz points out that desire as conceptualised by Deleuze is "the force of positive production, the action that create things, makes alliances, and forges interactions" (Grosz 1995, 179).

When I write I sense my mum being proud of me, I hear the rain or feel the sun coming through my window, I refer, quote, analyse and compare various authors, I am reminding myself of what I have heard during countless discussions at seminars and conferences. In this sense my writing is a creative practice of bringing all those things together, and then displaying them after they have being changed and transformed at the plane of immanence. My writing as the 'Deleuzian desiring process' is also a very enthusiastic and joyful exercise. First, because it gives me sensations of actually doing something and, second, because I am making connections or building arguments with various theories and concepts; I play with words and words play with me. When I write I interact with everything so there is no longer 'I' but the plenitude of the assemblage(s) I am in. When I write my borders dissolve and I become 'inhuman.' I reach the level of 'inhumanity' and I also transform myself when assembling with endless concepts, approaches and various points of view. The more I write, the more metamorphoses I undergo. Thus, my writing is also my constant Deleuzian becoming of something else, the becoming-imperceptible that can only happen when desire is at stake. Becoming-everything, getting-everywhere I experience satisfaction and the fulfilment of/by 'plenitude.' This process of becoming-everything can be compared to what Doro Wiese calls a "creative act of 'postmemory'" or of "othering of oneself," a process which leads to the increased ability of "imaging beyond the limits of the already known" (Wiese, chapter 15, this volume).

CONCEPTS, CONCEPTS

It is apparent that the writing process is a desiring one, but once again, it seems that it has as much in common with a Lacanian as with a Deleuzian understanding of the term. Writing may be perceived as being about lack and as being located on the side of acquisition. However, even when seen as a lack it can still be perceived as linked to an activity. The idea of a perfect book that cannot easily be materialised seems to indicate the 'lacking nature' of the writing process, but writing can also be seen as a creation of connections and alliances, as a constant becoming and a pure production. It can also be conceptualised as enabling one's own 'perfect' expression, thus again being about a pure production. In summary, in my opinion it can be helpful to a PhD student to conceptualise the writing process as both Lacanian and Deleuzian desiring processes.

To approach writing as a 'Lacanian desiring process' is to realise that academia significantly influences students' perceptions not only of their work but also of themselves, and notably affects one's sense of self-esteem. Such comprehension, on the other hand, helps one to understand that the perfect book carried in one's head is a kind of a construct. Therefore, it may become easier for a student to understand the reasons for her/his possible frustration and disappointment. It also becomes more feasible for a student to dismiss the anxieties and dissatisfaction she or he may experience. At the same time, if the writing process appears to be a highly tiring and exhausting exercise, one may precisely understand why and as such deal with it in an affirmative manner. Furthermore, the concept of writing as a 'Lacanian desiring process' can also make one aware that the job can be done and the product can be delivered, even if writing is hard and the perfect book appears too distant and too perfect to be reached.

To approach writing as a 'Deleuzian desiring process' is to perceive it as the creation of a highly varied and diverse assemblage. It is also to recognise that the object of desire is closely linked to the process itself. Therefore, a student can comprehend that there is no gap between writing and the expected final product. What is more, when writing is seen as resulting in delivering the 'real products' (i.e., tangible sheets of paper, one's own 'expression') the gap between the writing exercise and the 'perfect book' seems to be even more profoundly bridged. Isn't it comforting for a student to realise that whenever s/he writes, the required book is not an unreachable object? I believe that such realisation may significantly help a PhD student to overcome her/his fears of not providing what is expected from her/him and instead to enjoy the writing exercise. When the 'start line' becomes the 'meta-line,' a challenging journey no longer appears so scary. Furthermore, the assemblages formed through writing create and offer a fantastic possibility of becoming. Why do such realisations help those who write? If one comprehends that writing is about transformations, then the whole process appears to be linked to the pure enrichment of oneself—rather an alluring perspective, I would say. Furthermore, with the writing process conceptualised as becoming-everything, becoming-imperceptible, one can find out that it is not the book that brings the sense of wholeness and ultimate satisfaction. When there is no longer 'I' because 'I' dissolves in the process of becoming-everything, 'I' does not appear to 'need' this wholeness whatsoever. By becoming-everything the alienation of 'I' is overcome, and as such 'I' does not 'need' objects to become satisfied. In this sense the process of writing constitutes the finest fulfilment and satisfaction. Such recognition, in my opinion, might be very helpful when, for a variety of reasons, a doctoral student has to stop her/his PhD journey without getting the book written. The realisation that the writing process is about fulfilment prevents the sensation that one may end up with nothing.

CONCLUSION

To concentrate on the continuity of writing and to look for connections to the 'Lacanian' and/or 'Deleuzian desiring process' appears to have been a good idea after all. Writing can definitely be conceptualised as the desiring process, with both Lacan's and Deleuze's models offering ways of understanding this process. Understanding writing as both the 'Lacanian' and 'Deleuzian desiring process,' a PhD student can start and continue her or his 'journey' in a more cheerful way. The Lacanian 'writing-desire' can be used to comprehend why sometimes things are tough and why sometimes it is hard to translate one's own ideas into real words. The Deleuzian 'writing-desire' works as a good and positive force or fuel that makes things run. Writing approached as a pure production, as joy, as passion, as transformation and becoming and as pure satisfaction, fulfilment and enrichment. Without doubt, both concepts can help a PhD Icarus to keep on flying.

REFERENCES

Barthes, R. 1985. From Speech to Writing. In *The Grain of the Voice: Interviews 1962–1980*, 3–7. New York: Hill and Wang.

Bataille, B. 1985. *Literature and Evil*. London: Marion Boyars.

Braidotti, R. 2002. *Metamorphoses: Towards a Materialist Theory of Becoming*. Cambridge: Polity Press.

———. 2006. *Transpositions: On Nomadic Ethics*. Cambridge: Polity Press.

Culler, J. 1988. *Framing the Sign: Criticism and Its Instructions*. Norman: University of Oklahoma Press.

Deleuze, G. 1994. *What is Philosophy?* New York: Columbia University Press.

———. 2001. *Pure Immanence: Essays on a Life*. New York: Zone Books

Deleuze, G., and F. Guattari. 1983. *Anti-Oedipus: Capitalism and Schizophrenia*. London: Continuum.

———. 1987. *A Thousand Plateaus: Capitalism and Schizophrenia*. London: Continuum.

Derrida, J. 1978. *Writing and Difference*. Chicago: University of Chicago Press.

Grosz, E. 1995. *Space, Time, and Perversion*. New York: Routledge.

Lacan, J. 1977. *The Four Fundamental Concepts of Psychoanalysis*. London: Hogarth Press / Institute of Psycho-Analysis.

Ross, A. 2005. Desire. In *The Deleuze Dictionary*, ed. A. Parr, 63–64. Edinburgh University Press.

Wright, E. 1992. *Feminism and Psychoanalysis: A Critical Dictionary*. Oxford: Blackwell Reference.

Zizek, S. 1991. *Looking Awry: An Introduction to Jacques Lacan through Popular Culture*. Cambridge, MA: MIT Press.

Contributors

Susanne Baer is professor of public law and gender studies at the Faculty of Law at Humboldt University, Berlin, Germany, and James W. Cook Global Law Professor at the University of Michigan Law School, US. She is affiliated with the Centre for Transdisciplinary Gender Studies at Humboldt University, has directed the national German Gender Competence Centre and is involved in several international research projects on gender equality, including TARGET (Transnational Applied Research in Gender Equity Training) and QUING (Quality in Gender and Equality Policies). She has published extensively within the field of gender theory, fundamental rights, gender equality and antidiscrimination law and politics, including 'Dignity, Liberty, Equality: A Fundamental Rights Triangle of Constitutionalism,' *University of Toronto Law Journal* (2009); and coedited *Schubladen Schablonen Schema F. Stereotype als Herausforderung für Gleichstellungspolitik* (2009).

Rosemarie Buikema is professor of art, culture and diversity at Utrecht University, The Netherlands. She is head of the Department of Media and Culture Studies and chairs the Graduate Gender Programme. She is the Utrecht coordinator of GEMMA and scientific director of the Netherlands Research School of Women's Studies (NOV). She has broadly published on feminist theory, postcolonial studies and memory studies and currently works in the field of transitional justice and the arts. Her latest book is *Doing Gender in Media, Art and Culture* (coedited with Iris van der Tuin) (2009).

Isabel Carrera Suárez is professor of English at the University of Oviedo, Spain, where she is coordinator of the MA and PhD programmes in women's studies, as well as of the Erasmus Mundus MA Programme GEMMA. She has published extensively on contemporary women writers, postcoloniality and women's studies and was part of the EU-funded projects EWSI (Employment and Women's Studies) and Research Integration.

Allaine Cerwonka is professor of gender studies at Central European University, Budapest, Hungary. Her books include *Improvising Theory:*

Process and Temporality in Ethnographic Fieldwork (with Liisa Malkki) (2007) and *Native to the Nation: Disciplining Landscapes and Bodies in Australia* (2004). Other work of hers has recently appeared in *Signs: Journal of Women and Culture* (2008).

Gabriele Griffin holds the Anniversary Chair in Women's Studies at the University of York, UK. Her research interests centre on contemporary women's cultural production and on women's studies as a discipline. She is cofounding editor of the journal *Feminist Theory*. Her publications include *Thinking Differently: A Reader in European Women's Studies* (2002); *Who's Who in Lesbian and Gay Writing* (2002); *Contemporary Black and Asian Women Playwrights in Britain* (2003); *Employment, Equal Opportunities and Women's Studies: Women's Experiences in Seven European Countries* (editor and contributor) (2004); and *Doing Women's Studies: Employment Opportunities, Personal Impacts and Social Consequences* (editor and contributor) (2005).

Antje Lann Hornscheidt is professor of gender studies and linguistics at the Center for Transdisciplinary Gender Studies at Humboldt University, Berlin, Germany. Her research interests include linguistic sexisms and racisms, constructionist models of interdependent analysis of discrimination and privileging, discourse analysis, post/colonial studies and transdisciplinarity. She has published extensively within these fields, among others *Rassismus auf gut deutsch: Ein kritisches Nachschlagewerk zu rassistischen Sprachhandlungen* (together with Adibeli Nduka-Agwu) (2010); *Gender resignifiziert* (2008); and *Gender als interdependente Kategorie: Intersektionalität—Diversität—Heterogenität* (coedited with K. Walgenbach, G. Dietze and K. Palm) (2007).

Edyta Just holds a master's degree in political sciences and a PhD in gender studies. She is an affiliated researcher with gender studies at the Department of Media and Culture Studies and the Graduate Gender Programme of the Faculty of Humanities of Utrecht University, The Netherlands. Her professional profile at present can best be described as cultural studies of science and technology, with a strong interest in the epistemological and ethical implications of technologies and visualisation techniques. Furthermore, her field of expertise also includes ethics and political sciences.

Mia Liinason is a PhD student at the Department of Gender Studies, Lund University, Sweden. She was a member of the Board of the Nordic Research School in Interdisciplinary Gender Studies and chief editor of the online journal *Graduate Journal of Social Science* (GJJS) (http://www.gjss.org). She is a member of the editorial board of *NORA—Nordic Journal of Feminist and Gender Research*. Her research focuses on interdisciplinarity and epistemologies in feminist studies.

Jasmina Lukić is an associate professor and currently head of the Department of Gender Studies at the Central European University in Budapest, Hungary. Her research work is in literary and cultural studies and in Slavic studies. Her most recent publications include an edited volume, *Women and Citizenship in Central and Eastern Europe* (with Joanna Regulska and Darja Zavirsek) (2006).

Nina Lykke is professor of gender and culture and head of the Unit of Gender Studies, Linköping University, Sweden. She is director of an international Centre of Gender Excellence, GEXcel, as well as scientific leader of a Swedish-International Research School in Interdisciplinary Gender Studies. She has been scientific director of the Nordic Research School of Interdisciplinary Gender Studies, managing director of the European Feminist Studies association AOIFE and long-standing member of the European thematic network in women's studies, ATHENA. She has published extensively within the areas of feminist theory, intersectionality studies, feminist cultural studies and feminist technoscience studies, including *Between Monsters, Goddesses and Cyborgs* (coedited with R. Braidotti) (1996), *Cosmodolphins* (coauthored with M. Bryld) (2000), *Bits of Life* (coedited with A. Smelik) (2008), and *Feminist Studies: A Guide to Intersectional Theory, Methodology and Writing* (2010).

Maureen McNeil is professor of women's studies and cultural studies and works in the Centre for Gender and Women's Studies, the Centre for Economic Aspects of Genomics and the Centre for Science Studies at Lancaster University, UK. Her recent publications include *Feminist Cultural Studies of Science and Technology* (2007) and *Human Cloning in the Media: From Science Fiction to Science Practice* (with Joan Haran, Celia Kitzinger, and Kate O'Riordan) (2008).

Henrietta L. Moore is the William Wyse Chair of Social Anthropology at the University of Cambridge and the director of the Culture and Communications Programme at the Centre for the Study of Global Governance, London School of Economics (LSE), UK. She has a long-term research engagement with Africa, and her research programme has focused on gender, livelihood strategies, social transformation and symbolic systems. She is the author of *The Subject of Anthropology: Gender, Symbolism and Psychoanalysis* (2007). She is a Fellow of the British Academy, a Fellow of the Royal Society of Arts and Academician of the Learned Societies for the Social Sciences.

Andrea Petö is an associate professor at the Department of Gender Studies at the Central European University, Budapest, Hungary, where she is teaching courses on social and cultural history of Europe. Her books include *Women in Hungarian Politics 1945–1951* (2003) and *Geschlecht, Politik und Stalinismus in Ungarn: Eine Biographie von Júlia Rajk*

(2007). Presently she is working on gendered memory of World War II and political extremism.

Celia Roberts is senior lecturer in the Department of Sociology and works in the Centre for Gender and Women's Studies and the Centre for Science Studies at Lancaster University, UK. Her recent publications include *Messengers of Sex: Hormones, Biomedicine and Feminism* (2007) and *Born and Made: An Ethnography of Preimplantation Genetic Diagnosis* (with Sarah Franklin) (2006).

Adelina Sánchez Espinosa is senior lecturer in English literature at the University of Granada, Spain, and a member of the UGR Women's Studies Research Institute. She is director of two Andalusian Government Research Plan Projects: 'Reception, Genres and Gender in English Literature' Research Group and 'CURE: Rewriting Bodies—Pain and Violence in Women's Literature' Research Project of Excellence. She has served as vice president of AOIFE (Association of Institutions for Feminist Education and Research in Europe) and scientific coordinator for GEMMA, an Erasmus Mundus master's degree in women's and gender studies. Her research focuses on masculinities, body politics and the application of feminist literary and film theories to late Victorian culture. Her most recent book is *Cuerpos de Mujeres: Miradas, Representaciones e Identidades* (2007).

Marianne Schmidbaur has a PhD in the field of social care and is currently scientific manager at the Cornelia Goethe Centre for Women's and Gender Studies at the Goethe University, Frankfurt am Main, Germany. Her teaching and research interests include women's movements, higher education and social policy/care. She was a lecturer in further education and has worked on several research projects on the topic of higher education, amongst others the EU-funded project on 'Women's Employment, Women's Studies and Equal Opportunities in Europe.' At present she is researching a project on networks of care.

Harriet Silius is professor of women's studies at Åbo Akademi University, Finland. She was a member of the board for the Nordic Research School in Interdisciplinary Gender Studies. She was president of the European Feminist Studies association AOIFE, and she is now copresident of ATGender, the European Association for Gender Research, Education and Documentation. Her research interests are feminist research methods, ethnicity and migration, professionalisation, European comparative research, women's everyday life and the institutionalisation of gender studies. Her latest European project focused on changing knowledge and disciplinary boundaries through integrative research methods in the social sciences and humanities. Recent publications include 'The Professionalization of

Women's Studies Students in Europe: Expectations and Experiences,' in *Doing Women's Studies: Employment Opportunities, Personal Impacts and Social Consequences* (2005); 'Making Sense of Gender in the Study of Legal Professions,' *International Journal of the Legal Profession* (2003); and 'Women's Employment, Equal Opportunities and Women's Studies in Nine European countries—a Summary,' in *Women's Employment, Women's Studies, and Equal Opportunities 1945–2001* (2002).

Dorthe Staunæs is associate professor at the Department of Learning, DPU, University of Aarhus, Denmark. She is director of a Research Programme of Organization and Learning at the University. She has published extensively within the field of gender and ethnicity with a special focus on schools and organisations, including 'From Culturally Avant-Garde to Sexually Promiscuous: Troubling Subjectivities and Intersection in the Social Transition from Childhood into Youth,' *Feminism & Psychology* (2005); and 'Where Have All the Subjects Gone? Bringing Together the Concepts of Intersectionality and Subjectification,' *NORA— Nordic Journal of Feminist and Gender Research* (2003).

Dorte Marie Søndergaard is professor of social psychology and gender studies at the Department of Learning, DPU, University of Aarhus, Denmark. She is director of the Research Programme in Diversity and Learning and director of the interdisciplinary research team eXbus: Exploring Bullying in School. Her main writings have focused upon the constitutive processes of gendered subjectivities and of inclusion and exclusion in varying contexts such as universities, private business and schools. A substantial part of her publications addresses the development of poststructuralist theory, new materialist theory and empirically analytic methodologies, including 'Academic Desire Trajectories: Re-tooling the Concepts of Subject, Desire and Biography,' *European Journal of Women's Studies* (2005); and 'Making Sense of Gender, Age, Power and Disciplinary Position: Intersecting Discourses in the Academy,' *Feminism & Psychology* (2005).

Iris van der Tuin is assistant professor in gender studies at the Department of Media and Culture Studies and the Graduate Gender Programme of the Faculty of Humanities of Utrecht University, The Netherlands. She teaches on feminist theory, feminist classics and philosophy of science and publishes on the same topics. She is copresident of ATGender, the European Association for Gender Research, Education and Documentation. Her publications include 'Jumping Generations: On Second- and Third-Wave Feminist Epistemology,' *Australian Feminist Studies* (2009); 'Deflationary Logic: Response to Sara Ahmed's "Imaginary Prohibitions": Some Preliminary Remarks on the Founding Gestures of the "New Materialism,"' *European Journal of Women's Studies* (2008);

as well as the edited volume *Doing Gender in Media, Art and Culture* (coedited with Rosemarie Buikema) (2009).

Berteke Waaldijk is professor of language and culture studies at the Faculty of Humanities, Utrecht University, The Netherlands. Her research centers around comparative and interdisciplinary perspectives on post/colonial and social definitions of citizenship and national identity. She has published extensively within these fields, including *Teaching with Memories: Best Practices from Teaching Women's History in Europe* (coedited with Andrea Pető) (2006) and *Transforming the Public Sphere: The Dutch National Exhibition of Women's Labor in 1898* (coauthored with M. Grever) (2004). She has for several years been director of the European curriculum network, ATHENA, funded under the EU's Socrates programme. She also chairs a thematic working group, 'Work, Gender and Society,' within the EU-funded research Network of Excellence CliohRES—Creating Links and Overviews for a New History Research Agenda for the Citizens of a Growing Europe.

Gloria D. Wekker holds the Aletta Chair in Gender and Ethnicity in the Faculty of Humanities at Utrecht University, The Netherlands, and is the director of GEM, the Center of Expertise on Gender, Ethnicity and Multiculturalism in Higher Education at the same university. With a long-term research engagement in the Caribbean, her research interests include constructions of sexuality and subjectivity in the black Diaspora and gendered and ethnicised knowledge systems in the Dutch academy and society. Among her most recent book publications is *The Politics of Passion: Women's Sexual Culture in the Afro-Surinamese Diaspora* (2006), for which she was awarded the Ruth Benedict Prize of the American Anthropological Association in 2007.

Doro Wiese is a junior teacher at Utrecht University, The Netherlands, where she arrived through a Marie Curie Scholarship of the European Union. She has been working as a journalist and translator of Judith Butler and Gayatri Chakravorty Spivak (among others) and is author of several performances with debuts at the Volksbühne, Berlin, and the Deutsches Schauspielhaus, Hamburg. Among her current publications are 'Halluci-Nation: The Entanglement of Race, Gender, and Sexuality in the Varuh Meje—Guardian of the Frontier,' in *Identities: Journal for Politics, Gender, and Culture* (2008); and '"He Looked for Truth in Facts and Not in Stories": Powers of the False, Crimes of Historiography, and Forces of Fabulation in *Gould's Book of Fish* by Richard Flanagan,' in *Deleuzian Events: Writing|History*, ed. H. Berressem and L. Haferkamp (2009).

Ulla Wischermann is a senior gender researcher at Frankfurt University, Germany. She works as deputy director in the Cornelia Goethe Centre for Women's Studies and teaches in the Department of Sociology. Her main research is in gender studies, media studies, Internet communication, social movement theory and theories of public and private spheres. She is coeditor of the German feminist scientific journal *Feministische Studien* and active in several national and international research projects and European networks, including ATHENA. She has published extensively on media and history, for instance *Frauenbewegungen und Öffentlichkeiten um 1900: Netzwerke—Gegenöffentlichkeiten—Protestinszenierungen* (Women's movements and public spheres: Networks, counter-public-spheres, and resistance) (2003).

Marta Zarzycka is an assistant professor at the Gender Studies Department at Utrecht University, The Netherlands. She teaches and publishes in the field of visual studies, feminist art history and photography. In her current research she focuses on the role of war photography in shaping collective Western consciousness. She is currently coediting the volume *Carnal Aesthetics: Transgressive Imagery and Feminist Politics*.

Index

Note: Page numbers ending in "f" refer to figures. Page numbers ending in "t" refer to tables.

A

Abbott, A., 192
Abir-Am, P. G., 31
Abu Ghraib, 125
academic feminism, 22–26, 154–156
activism: feminist activism, 15–16, 22–24, 31; human rights activism, 7, 69; political activism, 138–139
activist beginnings, 183–185
actor-network theory (ANT), 35
Afghan Girl, 125
Afsar, H., 54
agency, concept of, 19–21
agential realism, 18–21
Agreiter, M., 221
Ahmed, Sara, 110, 111
Aikau, H. K., 16
Akrich, Madeleine, 35
Allen, D., 192
Allmendinger, J., 168
Alnebratt, K., 158
Alsop, Rachel, 98–99
alternative imagery, 119
alternative narratives, 82
analytical gaze, 49–50
analytically productive concept, 46–59
Andermahr, S., 139, 141, 142
'Angel of History', 74–76, 79, 84
Anzaldua, G., 145
Appadurai, A., 66
'Archival Methods', 96
Armstrong, I., 107
art criticism, 122
art history, 120–125
arts and humanities: focus on, 2–3; research methods in, 5–6, 91–104; research skills in, 95–96

Arts and Humanities Research Board (AHRB/AHRC), 93, 94
Asdal, Kristin, 30
ATHENA (Advanced Thematic Network in European Women's Studies), 1, 2, 148, 156, 204
Austen, Jane, 76, 95
authentic evidence, 5
autonomous gender studies, 184–186, 195
Azoulay, A., 124, 125, 126

B

baby boomers, 16, 25
Bacon, Francis, 32
Baer, Susanne, 7, 140–142, 152, 165, 170, 174–175, 177, 201, 215, 217, 273
Bakhtin, M. M., 234
Bal, M., 123, 127
Balsamo, A., 30, 33
Barad, Karen, 3, 7, 17–21, 37, 48, 146–148
Barrett, Michèlle, 113
Barthes, Roland, 106, 126, 262–264
Bartmann, Sarah, 248, 251
Bataille, Georges, 262, 263
Baudrillard, J., 126
Becher, T., 171
Becker-Schmidt, R., 216
Behar, Ruth, 62, 65
Beloved, 82
Belsey, Catherine, 99, 107
Benjamin, Walter, 84, 233, 241
Benoit, C., 192
Benstock, Shari, 107
Berendt, E., 220
Berg, Anne-Jorunn, 34
Berger, John, 121

Bergman, S., 183, 184
Bergqvist, C., 184
Bessin, M., 26
biomedicine, 29–38
biopower, 34
biosociality, 34
biotechnical phenomena, 35
Birke, L., 30
Birriel Salcedo, M., 198
Bock, U., 218
Boddington, P., 34
bodies: female body, 121–124, 129; identity and, 69; nudity/nakedness, 121–124, 129; studies of, 33, 38
Bohr, Niels, 17, 18, 19, 37, 146
Bologna Process, 8, 9, 93, 153, 191, 198, 202, 207–210, 213, 226
Boltanski, L., 126
Borderias, C., 155
boundaries, of sociocultural categories, 52–53
boundary-crossing, 6, 19, 138, 143, 152
Bourdieu, Pierre, 54
Boxer, M., 153
Braaten, E. S., 157
Brah, A., 46, 252
Braidotti, Rosi, 2, 38, 47, 145, 155, 269
Braun, K., 218
Braun, V., 32
Braverman, Harry, 34
Brenna, Brita, 30
Bronfen, E., 127
Brontë, Charlotte, 6, 82, 95, 105, 111–116
Brooks, A., 172
Broom, D., 32
Broude, N., 123
Brouns, M., 217
Brown, Dan, 78
Bruner, J., 46
Bryld, M., 50
Bryson, N., 123
Buikema, Rosemarie, 1, 2, 6, 97, 115, 119, 253, 273
Bulhof, I. N., 252
Burrage, M., 192
business: equal opportunities in, 45–46, 55, 200–202, 209–210, 213–214; sociocultural categories in, 46–48
Bußmann, H., 167

Butler, Judith, 38, 49, 60, 65, 145, 146, 216

C
Callibrations, 106
Calvert, M., 31
Carbin, M., 48, 50
Carby, H. V., 80
career paths (German universities), 216f, 218–221
career stages (German academy), 215f
Cartesian cuts, 19–20, 146–147
Cartwright, L., 32, 119
Casado Aparicio, Elena, 198, 200
Case, Sue-Ellen, 140, 141, 143
Castañeda, Claudia, 37–38
Cerwonka, Allaine, 4, 60, 61, 67, 97, 273–274
'Child Is Being Beaten, A', 246
Chun, W. H. K., 233
Clark, David L., 236
Clarke, A., 30
Clash of Civilizations and the Remaking of World Order, 78
close reading: contextuality of, 106; feminist approaches to, 107–111; feminist perspectives on, 6, 105–118; historicity of, 106; rereadings, 105–107; uses of, 116–117
Close Reading: The Reader, 106
coaching management styles, 45–46
Colebrook, Claire, 84
Collins, J. L., 125
Collins, Patricia Hill, 46, 52, 66
Collinson, D. L., 54
complex identities, 47
complicated relationships, 74–76
computer-aided discourse analysis, 98
Connell, R. W., 55
consciousness raising, 60–62
constructionist/constructivist, xvi
constructivism, 18–21
contemporary feminism, 16–17, 26
contextuality, 106, 109–110, 129
Cook, Jon, 93, 100
corporate masculinity, 45–46, 53–55
corporate world: equal opportunities in, 45–46, 55, 200–202, 209–210, 213–214; sociocultural categories in, 46–48
creative work methods, 100
Crenshaw, Kimberlé, 46, 50, 52
critical discourse analysis, 98

critical race research, 60, 61
Crompton, R., 192
'crossroads' metaphor, 50–51
Culler, Jonathan, 262, 264
cultural narratives, 97
'cyborg', 36–37
'Cyborg Manifesto', 37

D

Da Vinci Code, The, 78
Dad's Army, 97
Davies, B., 49
Davies, C., 192
Davies, K., 155
Davis, K., 32
de Beauvoir, Simone, 25, 32, 78
de Lauretis, Teresa, 122, 248
de los Reyes, P., 47, 48
de Man, Paul, 106, 241
de Saussure, Ferdinand, 21
Death of a Discipline, 234, 236
deconstruction, 21, 26, 106–109, 114
deconstructionism, 106
Deegan, Marilyn, 94, 98, 101
Deemer, D. K., 97
degree, attaining, 10, 261, 265
Deleuze, Gilles, 10, 21, 236, 238, 261–272
Derrida, Jacques, 236, 262, 263
Descartes, René, 245
desires of writing, 10, 259–272
Deuber-Mankowsky, A., 174
'Dialogue of Self and Soul: Plain Jane's Progress', 113
diaries as history, 81
Die Aufgabe des Übersetzers, 241
differentiation categories, 45–46
disciplinary apparatus, 17–22. *See also* neodisciplinary apparatus
disciplinary boundary-crossing, 6, 19, 138, 143, 152
disciplinary enhancement, 167–168
disciplinisation: autonomy and, 184–186; in Nordic gender studies, 185–189, 189t, 193–195; professionalisation and, 8, 17
dis-identification, 25
dissertation developments, 84
dissertation photo album, 9, 233–244
dissertation writing, 233–244
diversity: in feminist studies, 45–51, 141, 148, 172, 176–177, 204t, 205t, 215–216; political support for, 184; sociopsychological exploration of, 45–51

Diversity, Gender and Top Management, 45
Doane, Mary Ann, 122
Domanska, Ewa, 82
dominance and power, 7, 51–54
Dominelli, L., 184
Dorlin, E., 26
Dreyfus, H., 255
dualism, 17–18, 25
DuBois, Andrew, 106, 110
Duden, B., 32
Duganne, E., 126

E

Eagleton, M., 107
Easlea, Brian, 31
Eco, Umberto, 78
Edwards, H., 126
effectuation, 20
Einarsdóttir, T., 220
Ellestrom, L., 125
empiricist epistemologies, 143–146
Employment and Women's Studies (EWSI), 183–184, 193, 213
Employment and Women's Studies: The Impact of Women's Studies Training on Women's Employment in Europe, 8
employment opportunities: equality in, 45–46, 55, 200–202, 209–210, 213–214; impact on, 220f
End of History and the Last Man, The, 78
England, Lynndie, 125
Enloe, Cynthia, 162
epistemological aspect, 23
epistemological issues, 17–19, 21, 71, 147
equality: in business, 45–46, 55, 200–202, 209–210, 213–214; between sexes, 15–17, 31
equality feminism, 15, 23–24
Espinosa, Adelina Sánchez, 6, 95, 105, 276
essentialism, 20, 129
Esseveld, J., 155
ethnographic research methods, 98–99
ethnography, 60, 62
Everything Is Illuminated, 9, 234, 238–242
Evetts, J., 192
'Experience,' 65
experience: feminist research and, 60–73; methodological use of,

60–73; relational approach to, 67–70; in twenty-first century research, 60–73

F

faculty-based gender studies, 185–186
'false opposites', 17
Fanon, Frantz, 253
Fantone, L., 26
Faulkner, Wendy, 34
Fausto-Sterling, A., 30, 33
Favell, A., 140
Feigenbaum, A., 26
Felski, R., 78
female body, 121–124, 129
female masculinity, 10
feminism, and postfeminism, 16–17, 25–26
feminism, and postmodernism, 5, 110, 143–146
feminism, and poststructuralism, 5, 55–56, 106, 146
feminist activism, 15–16, 22–24, 31
feminist empiricist epistemologies, 143–146
feminist film theory, 122
feminist historians, 5, 31, 76–84
Feminist Methodology: Challenges and Choices, 2
feminist movement, 15, 24
feminist perspectives, on close reading, 6, 105–118
feminist perspectives, on visual cultures, 6–7, 119–134
feminist postconstructionist epistemologies, 143–146
feminist postmodern epistemologies, 143–146
feminist race theory, 46
feminist research: experience and, 60–73; histories in, 5, 74–87; identity and, 60–73; memories in, 5, 74–87; renouncing power in, 61–67; twenty-first century research, 4–5, 60–73
feminist researchers: in German women's studies, 9, 213–229, 215f, 216f; in Nordic women's studies, 8, 183–197, 189t, 192t, 194t; in Spanish women's studies, 8, 198–212, 204t, 205t, 208t
feminist science and technology studies (FSTS), 4, 29–42
feminist science fiction, 32

feminist standpoint epistemologies, 143–146
feminist studies: diversity in, 45–51, 141, 148, 172, 176–177, 204t, 205t, 215–216; institutionalisation of, 78, 137–138; interdisciplinarity in, 138–143; multidisciplinarity in, 6–7, 138–143; postdisciplinarity in, 6–7, 137–150; professionalisation in, 181–229; transdisciplinarity in, 138–143. *See also* women's/gender studies and women's/gender/feminist studies
Feminist Studies: A Guide to Intersectional Theory, Methodology and Writing, 2
Feminist Stylistics, 107–108
feminist theories, 3, 13–42
'feminist waves', 3, 15–28
Ferri, B. A., 53
Ferriss, Suzanne, 107
fiction, and history, 81–82
film theory, 122
first-wave feminism, 15
Fishman, J., 32
Foer, Jonathan Safran, 9, 234, 238
Forster, Margaret, 96
Foucauldian concept, 17, 53, 255
Foucault, Michel, 18, 34, 52, 65, 66, 98, 245, 255
Frankenberg, R., 54
Frankenstein, 114
Franklin, S., 32
Fraser, S., 32
Freidson, E., 192
Fresco, Nadine, 234
Freud, Sigmund, 245, 246, 251
Friedman, S. S., 137
Fuchs, S., 168
Fukuyama, Francis, 78
Fuss, Diane, 68

G

Gallop, Jane, 106, 116
Garrard, M. D., 123
gaze, concept of, 121–124
gender, and sexuality, 10, 245–257
gender bias, 144, 168, 208
gender equality: in business, 45–46, 55, 200–202, 209–210, 213–214; between sexes, 15–17, 31
gender studies: in Europe, 7, 151–164; in Germany, 213–229; meth-

odologies used in, 4, 43–87; in Nordic countries, 183–197; in Spain, 198–212; transdisciplinarity in, 6–7, 165–179. *See also* women's/gender studies and women's gender/feminist studies
Gender Trouble, 216
General News, 125
Generation X, 16
Genette, Gérard, 241
Gergen, K. J., 97
Gergen, M. M., 97
Gerhard, U., 219, 221
German gender studies: career paths in, 216f, 218–221; career planning, 223–225; funding for research in, 213–214; gender competence, 222–223; institutionalisation of, 217–218; networking, 225–226; postmaterialistic values, 221; professionalisation indicators, 9, 213–229, 215f, 216f; prospects for, 226; transdisciplinarity in, 165–176; university structures for, 213–217, 215f, 216f
Gernand, D., 220
Gibbon, S., 32
Gibbons, M., 139
Gilbert, Sandra M., 83, 106, 112, 113
Gillis, S., 26
Gilman, Sander L., 123–124, 251, 253, 254
Glossary of Feminist Theory, A, 139
Go-Between, The, 77
Göransson, A., 155
Gordon, D., 62
Goya, 123
Green, T., 153, 155, 157, 158, 160
Gremillion, H., 32
Grever, M., 77, 80, 253
Grewal, I., 67
Griffin, Gabriele, 1–2, 5, 8, 78, 91, 153, 155, 157–158, 160, 183–185, 190, 193, 198, 201, 209, 219, 274
Grosz, Elizabeth, 17, 21, 23, 24, 155, 267, 269
Grzinic, M., 26
Guattari, Félix, 236, 238, 262, 266–267
Gubar, Susan, 83, 106
Guillemin, M., 32

H
Haavio-Mannila, E., 184

Hagemann-White, C., 216, 218
Handbook of Literary Feminisms, A, 107
Hanmer, J., 193
Haraway, Donna, 18, 22, 30–32, 36–38, 47, 49, 145–147
Harding, Sandra, 23, 31, 36–37, 143–144
Hariman, R., 127
Hark, S., 154, 167
Harris, L. C., 50
Hartley, L. P., 77
Hartsock, Nancy, 64, 66
health movement, 32–34
Heaney, Seamus, 100
Hearn, Alison, 152
Hearn, J., 54
Heath, D., 32, 34
Helduser, U., 172
Hemmings, Clare, 5, 16, 23, 26, 84, 154–155
Henneron, Liane, 25–26
Henriksson, L., 192
Henry, Astrid, 25, 26
Henwood, F., 32
Herman, C., 31
Heywood, L. L., 15
Hidden Lives, 96
Hird, M., 30, 31
Hirsch, Marianne, 9, 24, 234, 241
Historical Angels, 74–76, 79, 83
historical narratives: alternative narratives, 82; feminist research and, 5, 74–87; types of, 80–82
historical perspectives, 78–82
historicity, 106
histories: challenging practices in, 76–80; crime fiction and, 84–85; diaries, 81; feminist research and, 5, 74–87; fiction, 81–82; historical perspectives of, 78–82; oral histories, 60, 80–81; in unexpected places, 80–82; writing about, 76–80
Hitchcock, Alfred, 122
Hitler, Adolf, 239
Hjelde, I., 157
Hobsbawn, Eric, 78
Hof, R., 167
Højgaard, L., 48
Holland, J., 2
Hollway, W., 97
Holm, U. M., 152, 153, 157, 158
hooks, bell, 63, 65

Horakova, Dana, 235
Hornscheidt, Antje Lann, 7, 140–142,
    152, 165, 170, 172, 174, 177,
    201, 215, 217, 274
'Hottentot nymphae', 245, 250–256
Hudson, Pat, 99
human rights activism, 7, 69
human-computer interaction, 94
humanities: focus on, 2–3; research
    methods in, 5–6, 91–104;
    research skills in, 95–96
Humm, M., 107
Huntington, Samuel P., 78

I
'ICT as a Research Method', 101
identity: feminist research and, 60–73;
    relational approach to, 67–70
identity politics, 47, 52, 57, 62–65,
    140–142, 145
identity theory, 46–47, 71–72
imagery, 49–50, 119
individualist ideologies, 5
individualistic methodologies, 15
institutionalisation: disciplines and,
    166; in Nordic gender studies,
    189–194; professionalisation
    and, 8; of women's studies, 7,
    78, 137–138, 192t, 217–218
interdisciplinarity: academic feminism
    and, 154–156; case studies in,
    158–161; in feminist studies, 6–7,
    138–143; gender studies and, 7,
    151–164; reaching, 157–158;
    women's studies and, 137–150
interdisciplinary dialogues, 2
interdisciplinary perspectives, 168–170
interdisciplinary research, 7, 158–161
intersectionality: as analytically produc-
    tive concept, 46–59; classical
    concept of, 51–52, 55–56; cor-
    porate masculinity and, 45–46,
    53–55; dominance in, 51–54;
    emergence and, 52–53; in femi-
    nist theory, 4–5, 9–10, 245–257;
    limitations of, 56–57; majority
    and minority in, 51–52, 54; met-
    aphors for, 49–51; oppression
    and, 51–52, 54; poststructuralist
    social psychology and, 55–56;
    power in, 51–54; racialisation
    and, 54; social categories and,
    45–51; theoretical adjustment
    and, 45–59

interviewing methods, 100
intimate truths, 9–10, 245–257
Irigaray, Luce, 21
IVF clinics, 33, 38

J
Jacobus, Mary, 32, 113
Jahr, V., 221
Jane Eyre, 6, 82, 95, 105, 111–113
'*Jane Eyre* and the Secrets of Furious
    Lovemaking,' 113
Jarausch, K., 192
Jefferson, T., 97
Jónasdóttir, A., 184
Jonsdottir, G., 184
Jordanova, L., 30, 32
Jordheim Larsen, C., 193
Jørgensen, M., 97
Just, Edyta, 10, 261, 274

K
Kahlert, H., 167
Kaloski-Naylor, A., 5, 154
Kamuf, Peggy, 107–109
Kaplan, Cora, 67, 113
Keller, Evelyn Fox, 24, 30–32
Kerber, L. K., 84
Keskinen, S., 153, 158, 185
Kirby, V., 21
Kirsch-Auwärter, E., 218
Klein, J. T., 138, 152
Klinger, C., 217
Knapp, G. A., 47, 217
'Knowing Your Place: A Marxist Femi-
    nist Stylistic Analysis', 107
Kofoed, J., 47
Koonz, C., 84
Kozyra, Katarzyna, 120–124, 121f
Krebs, R., 185
Kreutzner, G., 172
Krimmer, H., 214
Kristeva, J., 124, 127
Kvinnovetenskaplig tidskrift, 187

L
Lacan, Jacques, 10, 236, 261–272
Laclau, E., 145
Lambda Nordica, 187
Lamoureux, D., 26
Landström, C., 34
Laplanche, J., 250
Latour, Bruno, 94, 153
Le Feuvre, N., 155, 157
lectureships, 190

Lentricchia, Frank, 106
Letters of a Portuguese Nun, The, 108
Lettres Portugaises, Les, 108
Leviathan and the Air Pump, 36
Levine, L. W., 80
Lie, Merete, 34
Liinason, Mia, 7, 141, 151–153,
   157–158, 274
Literature of Their Own, A, 111
Lock, M., 32
Lorey, I., 177
Lovell, T., 139, 141, 142
Lucaites, J. N., 127
Lukić, Jasmina, 6, 95, 105, 275
Lutz, C. A., 125
Lutz, H., 217
Lykke, Nina, 1, 2, 6, 17, 19, 30, 46–47,
   50, 137, 141–146, 152–155,
   184–188, 217, 275

M
Mackinnon, A., 172
Madonna of warfare, 124–127
Madwoman in the Attic, The, 113
Magnusson, E., 184
Maihofer, A., 167, 171
majoritising movements, 51–52, 54
Mak, Geertje, 77, 82
Malkki, Liisa, 61, 68
Mamo, L., 32
Manet, Edouard, 120, 123
Mansfield Park, 95
Martin, E., 30, 32, 67
Martin, Karin, 255
Marxist theories, 34, 64
masculinity: corporate masculinity,
   45–46, 53–55; studies of, 34,
   246–247, 254
masculinity complex, 246–247, 254
masquerade, 122–124
materialisation, 26
'material-semiotic actor', 36–37
May, V. M., 53
Maynard, M., 54
Mazari, S., 218
McClintock, A., 255
McNeil, Maureen, 4, 19, 29, 30, 32, 275
measurement, act of, 19, 21
Medhurst, P., 153, 155, 157, 158, 160
medicine, 29–38
Meeting the Universe Halfway, 37
memorialisation, 78
memories, and research, 5, 74–87, 97.
   See also histories

Mención de Calidad, 203, 204
Merchant, Carolyn, 31, 32
metaphors for, 49–51
methodologies in gender studies, 4, 43–87
Metso, M., 155, 157
Meulenbelt, Anja, 16
Meyer, Susan, 115
Michael, M., 35
Migrant Mother, 125
Millett, Kate, 16
Mills, Sara, 107–108
Minh-ha, T. T., 47
minoritising movements, 51–52, 54
Mitchell, W. J. T., 119, 129
modernism, 83
'modest witness', 36–37
Modleski, Tanya, 108
Mohanty, Chandra Talpade, 66, 128
Moi, T., 107
Monroe, Marilyn, 127
Moore, Henrietta L., 10, 124, 245–247,
   249–251, 275
Moore, J., 107
Mørck, Y., 47
Morrison, Toni, 82
Moser, Ingunn, 30, 35, 47
'Mothers in the Fatherland', 84
Mouffe, C., 145
Mulinari, D., 47, 48
Müller, U., 218
multidisciplinarity, 6–7, 138–143. *See*
   also interdisciplinarity; postdisci-
   plinarity; transdisciplinarity
Mulvey, Laura, 121–122

N
Naistutkimus/Kvinnoforskning, 187
Name of the Rose, The, 78
Napalm Girl, 125
Naples, Nancy, 66
narcissism, 16–17, 123
nationalism, 2, 10, 83, 140
natural sciences, 31–39
Nazism, 238–240
Nduka-Agwu, Adibeli, 172, 274
Nead, L., 123
Nederlands Tijdschrift voor
   Geneeskunde, 246
Nederveen Pieterse, J., 254
Nelson, Cary, 139
Nelson, Diane, 68–69
Nelson, L. H., 17
neodisciplinary apparatus: reposition-
   ing, 15–28; wave model as, 3,

22–24. *See also* disciplinary
apparatus
neodisciplinary perspective, 152
neoliberal ideologies, 5, 153–154
neoliberalism, 5, 153–154, 222
New Criticism, 105–107
New Historicism, 106
Noble, D., 31
Nochlin, Linda, 119
nonexhaustive dichotomies, 17–18
nonhistorical projects, 82–84
NORA, 93, 187
Nordic gender studies: disciplinisa-
    tion indicators, 185–189, 189t,
    193–195; institutionalisation
    indicators, 189–194, 192t;
    lectureships in, 190; PhD pro-
    grammes in, 188; postgraduate
    programmes in, 191; profession-
    alisation indicators, 8, 183–197,
    194t; professorships in, 187–188
Nordic Institute for Women's Studies
    and Gender Research (NIKK),
    184–186, 195
Norma, 187
Northanger Abbey, 76
nostalgia, 16–17, 61, 235
*Not My Mother's Sister: Generational
    Conflict and Third-Wave Femi-
    nism*, 25
novels, and history, 81–82
Nowotny, H., 139
Nude Maja, The, 123
nudity/nakedness, 121–124, 129

O

O'Dowd, M., 80, 85
Olimpia, 120–124, 121f
ontoepistemological framework, 7,
    17–19, 148
ontoepistemology, 24, 147–148
'ontological choreography', 38
ontology, 18–21, 24, 105
oppression: intersectionality and,
    51–52, 54; violence and, 82
oral histories, 60, 80–81
Orr, J., 32
Other, the, 53–55
Oudshoorn, Nelly, 34, 49
Outram, D., 31

P

Palm, K., 174
Parker, R., 119

'partial knowledge', 36, 49, 146–147
Passerini, L., 81
'passport', 10, 261, 265
pasts, and feminism, 74–76. *See also*
    historical narratives
pasts, writing about, 76–80. *See also*
    histories
Pasveer, Bernike, 35
Pedregal, A., 206
Peräkylä, A., 97
Pérez Sedeño, Eulalia, 207
performativity, 20, 54
'personal is political,' 15
personal memory, 97
Petö, Andrea, 5, 61, 74, 77, 80, 81, 97,
    237, 275–276
Pfirman, S., 172
phallocentrism, 64, 109, 129, 236
Phillips, L., 97
Phoenix, A., 46
'photo snapshots', 9, 233–244
photograph, analyzing, 124–129
Pinch, T., 34
Pisan, Christine de, 24
Plows, A., 34
pluralism, 7, 171
political activism, 138–139
Politics of Friendship, 237
Politics of Translation, The, 241
Pollock, G., 119
Pomata, G., 80
Poovey, Mary, 82
popular culture, 15
populist methodologies, 15
Porciani, I., 80, 85
positivism, 18, 60–61, 146
postcolonial criticism, 106
postcolonial perspectives, 9–10, 47, 60,
    95, 107, 115, 119, 245–257
postcolonial research, 60
postconstructionist epistemologies, 7,
    143–146
postdisciplinarity, 6–7, 17, 137–150
postfeminism, 16–17, 25–26
Postgraduate Review, 92, 93
*Postgraduate Training in Research
    Methods: Current Practice and
    Future Needs in English*, 93
posthumanist performativity, 20
postmemory, 9, 234, 240
postmodern epistemologies, 143–146
postmodernism: end of, 18; feminism
    and, 5, 110, 143–146; feminist
    studies and, 146

poststructuralism, 5, 55–56, 106, 146
power: disciplines and, 166; dominance and, 7, 51–54; in intersectionality, 51–54; renouncing, 61–67
professionalisation: disciplinisation and, 8, 17; in feminist studies, 1, 7–8, 181–229; of German feminist researchers, 9, 213–229, 215f, 216f; institutionalisation and, 8; of Nordic feminist researchers, 8, 183–197, 189t, 192t, 194t; of Spanish feminist researchers, 8–9, 198–212, 204t, 205t, 208t
'Professions for Women', 74
progress narrative, 15–17
Promise Keepers, 160
Pryse, Marjorie, 137, 150, 157
psychoanalysis, 21, 67, 247–251
psychoanalytic feminist theory, 9–10, 121, 245–257
Puig de la Bellacasa, M., 153

Q

quantum physics, 146–147
Quayson, Ato, 105–107
queer theory, 34, 47

R

Rabinow, Paul, 34, 255
racialisation: intersectionality and, 54; process of, 10, 245–257; psychoanalysis and, 247–251
Ramazanoglu, C., 2
Rapp, R., 32, 34
Reading in Detail, 109
realism: agential realism, 18–21; constructivism and, 18–21
'reductive iconoclasm', 119
reflexivity, 51–52, 97
Reinhardt, M., 126
Reitsamer, R., 26
relativism, 146
'Re-Placing Race in (White) Psychoanalytic Discourse: Founding Narratives of Feminism', 254
representational codification, 21, 26
representationalism, 18–21
'Republican mothers', 84
research methods: in arts and humanities, 5–6, 91–104; in women's studies, 5, 89–134; writing about, 5–6, 91–104
research questions, 9, 231–257
research with 'waves', 15–28

'researching differently', 1–11
Rhoten, D., 172
Rhys, Jean, 114
Riboud, Marc, 127
Rich, Adrienne, 112
right to vote, 15
Riley, Denise, 100
Riviere, Joan, 122
Rivkin, Julie, 108
Roberts, Celia, 4, 19, 29, 30, 32, 34, 276
'robot visions', 38
Rönnblom, M., 184
Room of One's Own, A, 237
Rooney, Ellen, 109
Rose, Gillian, 97, 98, 123
Rosenbeck, B., 184
Ross, Alison, 269
Rossiter, M. W., 31
Russett, C. E., 30

S

Said, Edward, 10, 77, 252
Salter, Liora, 152
Samerski, S., 32
Santemases, M. J., 207
Sayer, Andrew, 140
Schaffer, Simon, 36
Schelhowe, H., 172
Scheurich, J. J., 47
Schiebinger, Londa, 30, 31, 33, 248
Schmidbaur, Marianne, 9, 192, 213, 219, 221, 223, 276
Schor, Naomi, 109, 110
Schorer, Mark, 100
Schrijvers, K., 77
science and technology studies (STS), 29–42
science fiction, 32
Scientific Revolution, 32
scopophilic practices, 121–124
Scott, Joan W., 65, 66, 76
Scott, P., 139
second-wave feminism, 15–17
semiotic sign, 121
semiotics, 18–21, 36–37, 120–123, 129
sensory imagery, 49–50
sequential negation, 15–16
sexuality: gender and, 10, 245–257; *Jane Eyre* and, 113–114; truths about, 9–10, 245–257
Shakespeare, William, 237, 238
Shapin, Steven, 36
Shelley, Mary, 114

Shohat, Ella, 67, 119
Short, Harold, 94, 98, 101
Showalter, Elaine, 111
Shuttleworth, S., 32
Sicher, E., 240
Silius, Harriet, 8, 153, 158, 183–185,
    190, 192–193, 209, 221,
    276–277
Silverman, Kaja, 122
Silverstone, Robert, 34
Singh, I., 32
Singleton, Vicky, 35
'situated knowledges', 36–37, 49, 146
Sliggers, B., 253
Smelik, A., 2
Smith, Dorothy, 61, 62, 63, 66, 76, 77
Smith, J. K., 97
Smith, Mark J., 140
Snow, C. P., 21, 166
social categories, 4, 45–51, 67, 216–217
social constructionism, xvi, 67
social constructivism, 18–19, 67
social science research, 61
sociocultural categories, 46–48, 52–53
sociocultural identification, 45–46
sociopsychological research, 45–57
Søndergaard, Dorte Marie, 4, 45,
    47–49, 55–56, 65, 79, 217, 277
Sontag, S., 126
Spanier, B. B., 30, 32
Spanish women's studies: in 2010, 202–
    207; academic professionalisa-
    tion in, 207–208; development
    of, 199–201; MA programmes
    in, 202–204, 209–210; non-
    academic professionalisation
    in, 209; PhD programmes in,
    202–205, 205t, 210; postgradu-
    ate programmes in, 202–205,
    204t, 210; professionalisation
    indicators, 8, 198–212, 208t;
    prospects for, 210
Spitzer, Leo, 108–109
Spivak, Gayatri Chakravorty, 114, 115,
    234, 236, 237, 241
Stacey, Jackie, 32, 122
Stallmann, F., 214
Stam, R., 119
standpoint epistemologies, 5, 143–146
standpoint theory, 46–47, 60–65, 71–72
Stanley, L., 83
Stanton, D. C., 15
Staunæs, Dorthe, 4, 45, 47, 52–56, 65,
    79, 217, 277

Steedman, Carolyn, 96
Stefan, Verena, 16
Stegemann, T., 235, 236
Stephan, I., 167
Stephan, Nancy, 31
Stoff, Heiko, 240
Stoler, A. L., 253, 254, 255
Strout, C., 85
study of scientific knowledge (SSK),
    30
Sturken, M., 119
Suárez, Isabel Carrera, 157, 158, 198,
    209, 273
Suárez, L. Viñuela, 157, 158, 198, 209
subjectivity truths, 9–10, 245–257
Suchman, Lucy, 35, 37–38
Summerfield, Penny, 97
Svensson, L., 153
Symbolic order, 262–271

T
Tamm, Peter, 235
Tarquin and Lucretia, 99
Task of the Translator, The, 241
Taussig, K., 32, 34
Tawney, R. H., 78
technology studies, 4, 29–42
Teichler, U., 220
'teleopoiesis', 237–238, 242
Terry, Jennifer, 30, 31, 33, 250
textual analysis, 95, 99–101, 120, 158
Tham, Mr., 188
theoretical adjustment, 4, 45–59
theory, writing about, 84
thesis writing, 10
Thinking Differently, 2
third-wave feminism, 15, 24–26
'Third-World Woman', 237
Thompson, Charis, 32–33, 38
Throsby, K., 32
Tidskrift för genusvetenskap, 187
*Time Travels: Feminism, Nature,
    Power*, 21
Titian, 99, 123
Títulos propios, 198, 202, 203
Tornhill, S., 48, 50
Torstendahl, R., 192
Towler, P. R., 171
traditional disciplines, 7, 120, 137–144,
    173–174, 184–191, 217–218
'trans-Atlantic dis-connection', 15
transdisciplinarity: challenges in, 6–7,
    165–179; in feminist studies,
    138–143; outlook on, 176–177

transformative dynamics, 72, 110, 120, 140, 154, 158, 201
transformatory practice, 7
transgressive identities, 47
transgressive methodology, 53, 56, 79, 254
transnational discourses, 1–2, 10, 68, 140, 156–157, 204, 237
trope, challenging, 124–129
truths about sexuality, 9–10, 245–257
Tuori, S., 183, 193, 221

U
underprivileged, 51–54

V
van der Tuin, Iris, 2, 3, 15, 18, 26, 80, 84, 143, 152, 277–278
van Ophuijsen, J. H. W., 10, 246–248, 252, 255
Vasconcelos, Luiz, 125, 126f, 127
Vehvilainen, Marja, 34
Venus of Urbino, 123
Venus pudica, 123
Vertigo, 122
violence, and oppression, 82
Visible Human Project, 34
visual analysis, 120–130
visual cultures, 6–7, 119–134
visual literacy, 119–120, 128
visual signs, 97–98
visual studies, 120–130
Visweswaran, K., 68
von Alemann, H., 220
von Braun, C., 167
von der Fehr, D., 184
von Stebut, J., 168
voting rights, 15
Vulnerable Observer, The, 62

W
Waaldijk, Berteke, 5, 61, 74, 77, 80, 97, 237, 253, 278
Wajcman, Judy, 34
Wakeford, N. 31
Waldby, Catherine, 34
Walton, Jean, 253, 254, 255, 256
warfare, Madonna of, 124–127
Warhol, Robyn, 107
Warner, M., 127
'waves', 3, 15–28
Ways of Seeing, 121
Webster, J., 31
Wekker, Gloria D., 10, 124, 245, 253, 278

Wenk, S., 185
West, Candace, 52, 53
Westman-Berg, K., 155
Wetherell, M., 53
Wetterer, A., 217
White, H., 83
Wide Sargasso Sea, 114
Widerberg, K., 157, 193
Wiegman, R., 137
Wiese, Doro, 9, 233, 265, 270, 278
Williams, R., 66
Williams, Sadie, 92–93, 95
Wilson, E. A., 30, 31
Wischermann, Ulla, 9, 213, 217, 221, 278–279
Witz, A., 192, 193
Wolkowitz, C., 139, 141, 142
Wollstonecraft, Mary, 24
Women Writing Culture, 62
women's/gender studies: disciplinisation of, 189t; employment opportunities and, 220f; in Europe, 7, 151–164; in Germany, 213–229; history of, 23; institutionalisation of, 7, 192t; as interdisciplinary field, 137–150; methodologies used in, 4, 43–87; in Nordic countries, 183–197; as postdiscipline, 137–150; research methods in, 5, 89–134; in Spain, 198–212; transdisciplinarity in, 7, 165–179. *See also* feminist studies
women's/gender/feminist studies, xv
Wood, J., 55
Woods, Susanne, 107
Woolf, Virginia, 23–24, 74, 79, 84, 237, 238, 242
Wrede, S., 192
Wright, E., 265
writing: about pasts, 76–80; desires of, 10, 259–272; as discovery, 100–101; dissertation writing, 233–244; linguistics of, 264; process of, 10; purpose of, 263–264; research methods, 5–6, 91–104; theory writing, 84; thesis writing, 10
'writing snapshots', 9, 233–244

Y
Yuval-Davis, N., 47, 50

Z
Zacharias, G., 220

Zapatero, Rodríguez, 206
Zarzycka, Marta, 6, 97, 119, 126, 279
Zemon Davis, N., 80
Zimmer, A., 214

Zimmerman, Don, 52, 53
Zimmermann, B., 137
Zinn, J., 220
Zizek, Slavoj, 265

Printed in Great Britain
by Amazon